The Adventures of Dan and Tina

Enduring and Recovering from Narcissistic Abuse

By
Dan McGrath

DanMcGrath.net
DanandTina.net

The Adventures of Dan and Tina
Copyright © 2021 Dan McGrath

This book relates a true story, but some names and locations have been changed.

FIRST EDITION

Published by Dan McGrath
DanMcGrath.net

Cover Art by Dan McGrath

ISBN: 9798463553010

Lies Hurt!

This is an entirely true story about enduring and recovering from narcissistic abuse. Compulsive lying, infidelity, gaslighting. triangulation and crazy-making are some of the hallmarks of narcissists and the damage they inflict on unsuspecting victims can be debilitating.

This book explores the manic ups and devastating downs of being in a romantic relationship with a Cluster B disordered person and how to heal when it's over.

Some names and places have been changed.

Contents

For all the other survivors of narcissistic abuse.
Life goes on.

With thanks to Debe.

Introduction: Lies Hurt – Narcissism and Lying

Being in a relationship with a cluster B personality disordered person can leave you feeling lost, broken, confused, humiliated and even hopeless. What may have seemed like magic in the beginning might have turned into a debilitating curse.

Fortunately, recovery is entirely achievable and there are some things you can start doing right now to speed that recovery along.

This book explores the manic ups and devastating downs of a real relationship with a "covert" or vulnerable narcissist and how I went about restoring myself into a happy and functional person when it was finally over.

When I first thought to write about the adventures of Dan and Tina, I had something more fun in mind, with anecdotes from the often strange and amusing experiences we'd shared. In fact, Tina and I often talked about it, saying "that's going in the book," when something especially funny or memorable occurred.

There remain humorous memories to relate and some of them even made it into the book, but it became more of a therapeutic outlet. It's a way to order and understand my thoughts, share my story, to heal and hopefully help others understand and heal from their own abuse at the hands of personality disordered people who were allowed too close to them.

I was, for a long while, embarrassed and ashamed that I allowed myself to be subjected to an emotionally and psychologically abusive, often humiliating relationship.

There are stories I've written here that I'd never previously told anyone, because I knew how my friends, family and therapists would react. I knew what they would say and I didn't want to hear it. I was also deeply ashamed of myself for sacrificing my self-respect on the altar of love for a compulsive lying, promiscuous, dangerously impulsive alcoholic and drug addict. I didn't want anyone to know. I couldn't face it, myself.

I prided myself as a reasonably intelligent and logical man, but I lost confidence in my ability to reason and the veracity of my own memory. I allowed a mentally ill woman to induce strife in my other relationships. A lot of them were destroyed during the course of my relationship with Tina. Nearly everyone who knew us warned me away from her. I threw sense and caution to the wind and dashed myself repeatedly into the rocks trying to hang on to the illusion of a beautiful, intense, seemingly almost supernatural love.

For a long time, I felt like a deluded sap and a fool and ultimately, responsible for my own misery and misfortune. Since I had essentially married my "high school sweetheart," and then met Tina mere months after my divorce, I'd never had the dating experience most of my friends did. I'd never been much exposed to women who live by deceit. My brain rebelled at obvious red flags, because what I sometimes thought I was observing simply could not have been reality in the world I was familiar with. It would be too outrageous for me to wrap my naive mind around.

I couldn't or wouldn't see the forest for the trees. I looked at everything as isolated incidents and refused to acknowledge the overall pattern of behavior. Compartmentalizing, denial and rationalizing are maladaptive defense mechanisms that allow narcissistic abuse to continue.

Ultimately, it was a single incident that became the key to open all the locked compartments and let me start putting together the pieces of Tina's narcissistic puzzle.

I'd never previously understood how and why battered women stay with their abusive husbands. My experiences provided me new insight. I don't fully understand all the psychological mechanisms at play, but I can sympathize with it. I can't judge too harshly anyone who stays in an abusive or toxic relationship. Love and denial are powerful forces that trick and cloud a rational mind in unexpected ways.

Through it all, as much as I came to hate Tina for warping my sense of reality, for humiliating me, for emotionally crippling me, a part of me still loved her and I hated myself for that.

Therapists and other knowledgeable people often suggest writing as part of the recovery from emotional abuse. It's definitely been important for my healing. With considerable time spent studying narcissistic abuse, I found that writing about it is nearly universal with victims, as though it is an instinctive healing behavior.

It's important to acknowledge the truth of your own memories. Reasserting objective reality and injecting it into the world is re-empowering. My perception matters. My experience and truth matters.

Tina's behavior could be so outrageous as to be nearly unbelievable. Sometimes, I'd stop and think, "It can't be what it looks like. Nobody would do that!" But, Tina would and did do that! Writing out the details was in a way necessary to avoid glossing over just how bad things were. Setting the story down in an ordered manner helped lift the mental fog that Tina brought about with her constant deception.

The diagnostic manuals don't specifically allude to lying as a symptom of Narcissistic Personality Disorder (NPD), but anyone who's dealt with narcissists knows that narcissism and lying go hand in hand.

Narcissistic Abuse is no small matter and generally speaking, it isn't a "time heals all wounds" kind of injury. I believe recovering from narcissistic abuse requires conscious effort and may require some level of professional help, such as anti-anxiety medication or talk therapy.

Amidst the grand finale breakup with my narcissistic ex, Tina, I said, "every lie you told me was like a tiny cut on my brain and after a while, my brain was bleeding so much that it couldn't focus on other important tasks like work. Every iota of mental energy was devoted to unraveling the hundreds and hundreds of lies and healing all of those little cuts."

One or two lies might not add up to much, but in a relationship with a narcissist who's entire reality is built on an ever-growing web of dishonesty and invention, the lies become overwhelming. Gaslighting is one term used to describe a kind of prolonged deception that's aimed at making you doubt your own senses and sanity.

Add to that a cruel and manipulative psychological game designed to keep you off balance, but hooked on your abuser and you have the makings of measurable, physical brain damage. The impact of a constant flow of stress hormones mixing with other exaggerated responses of brain chemistry shouldn't be underestimated.

Fortunately, it appears that at least a large part of the damage caused by narcissistic abuse can be repaired with effort and patience. This book explores healing from the physical harm as well as the psychological and emotional trauma.

My story began with an unlikely romance that seemed to transcend the known world, but devolved into a Hell on Earth I couldn't escape. I was utterly convinced, through all the tribulations, Tina and I were cosmically linked and "meant to be." Laboring under such delusion opened me up to accepting the most outrageous abuses that I denied, rationalized, compartmentalized and even blocked from memory.

With some help from stumbling upon a story written by another victim of narcissistic abuse, the scales began to fall from my eyes. Learning about Cluster B personality disorders and then reading the oh-so-familiar stories of others who'd tangled with them set me on a new road to recovery.

I also found that writing everything out has the added benefit of depersonalizing the story. It decoupled or at least diminished the emotions connected to the memories, like I could step outside of myself.

I hope telling my my story can help heal myself and others.

My aim is to shed some light on narcissistic abuse – what it looks like, how it works, what it does to a person and how to go about recovering from it.

I'm not a mental health professional and I'm not peddling cures, simply my own experiences and observations. I hope it's helpful, because I know the desperate agony caused by narcissistic abuse and feel compelled to help alleviate it for others.

What follows is my crazy, true story, woven-through with insights and observations gleaned through research, much hindsight and introspection. You will see how a romantic relationship with a narcissist unfolds and hopefully also understand why. Finally, I share my strategies for healing when it's over.

The Beginning

I was two-months divorced and fresh back from an amazing trip to Ireland, the night I met Tina.

I'd gone to Farmington to visit one of my oldest friends and regale him with tales of my adventures, have a few drinks and laughs.

It was a warm June evening and the sun was just setting.

I met Donovan at the ancient former farm house that he was renting for his family at the time.

Donovan mentioned that there was a street festival called Dew Days going on just up the road. That sounded like a rare diversion for the area, so we took to our feet and went to check it out.

After securing some wrist bands that indicated we were old enough to drink, we procured a couple beers and wandered around the fair-like environs.

There was a bandstand set up and some local "talent" was performing some loud, but not particularly well executed hard rock music. We lost interest pretty fast.

After a bit more wandering and eating some cheese curds, Donovan suggested a place to hang out, get a drink other than the beer available from the street vendors and smoke a few cigarettes. "Let's check out Pizza Man," he said.

Didn't sound like a very exciting hangout to me, but he insisted it was cool.

We started in that direction and ran into some old acquaintances who were there for a classic car parade. We'd missed the event, but a lot of the old hot rods were still parked around, so we ogled them a bit and got back on our way to this vaunted pizza joint.

The place was pretty packed and a DJ was keeping a group of young women dancing in the front. Squeezing up to the crowded bar, Donovan ordered us a couple mixed drinks. Whiskey-Coke for me and Rum and Coke for himself.

It was busy, so it took a while. The music was loud — modern pop-ish dance music sprinkled with some dirty country and assembly line hip hop. The crowd swirled, the girls shouted raucous remarks as they got their funky white girl groove on.

Drinks eventually in hand, Donovan led me to the back of the pizza restaurant-turned nightclub and pushed through the back door.

We emerged onto a spacious fenced-in patio replete with several open tables, ashtrays, unused outdoor heaters and speakers, so we could continue to enjoy the urbane beats the DJ inside was spinning at a volume more conducive to conversation.

We sat at a wire mesh table in a corner, lit our smokes and sipped our drinks, catching up with each other's lives. We hadn't seen one other for a while. No doubt, I dominated the conversation, so enthused was I about the trip I had recently returned from.

We ascertained, after a while that a bunch of the younger ladies at the pizza joint-turned-party spot were together for a birthday party. One of the revelers was a very intoxicated young woman in a wheel chair being pushed around by a long-haired blonde girl. She had a cast on her leg, so we had to ask.

"Skiing accident?" I teased.

It turned out that she had simply stepped off a stair too hard and broke her ankle. I imagined that she was probably less sober than at the moment I was observing her. Her name was Shayna and she was quite a boisterous character. A tiny little impish brunette.

"Can I sign your cast?" I asked, after a bit of chit-chat.

"Yeah!" she slurred enthusiastically. I made my mark, large and bold and was amused, since I didn't know the girl at all (yet).

My friend Donovan also made a more modest "Get well soon" signature on Shayna's pinkish cast.

There was a twenty-something young man making his rounds on the patio, hitting on everything with two legs and lumps under their tops. My forty-something friend and I observed bemusedly, almost taking pity on the poor soul. Almost, but not quite. He was striking out left and right. Probably a problem with his technique, I thought, which was very much confirmed just moments later.

The blonde who'd been pushing her chair-bound party mate around needed a break and spied safe harbor with Donovan and I. Donovan, who like myself is a bit of a sci-fi and fantasy nerd was wearing a rather loud Dragonball Z shirt. Myself, in a wool flat cap I'd just obtained from Ireland, with a conservative, but colorful button down shirt and slim-fitting jeans. I suppose we looked approachable.

"Is this seat taken?" She asked us.

"Nope. Have a seat," Donovan replied.

She lit a cigarette.

Paying her little mind, I continued on with telling Donovan a story from the Emerald Isle.

"So we're wandering down this sleepy lane for a good half-hour, and hadn't seen a car at all, taking in the sights on our way to the Irish Sea," I said.

"Uh huh."

"Rich and Thea were on the right. I was on the left looking over a wall with a high hedge row at some pastures below. All of the sudden, from a blind curve behind us, a car came roaring in doing at least 60 miles an hour. Being an American, I was startled, because it's on the 'wrong' side of the road and coming right at me with no signs of intending to stop.

"There was only a walk path on the right, so I had nowhere to go. I pulled a Spiderman leap up on to the top of the hedge row. I was saved, but bleeding. The damn hedges were full of thorns! The car never even slowed down."

"Oh my god," Donovan exclaimed.

"After the car had gone by, I peered over and got some perspective on the drop. It was easily 40 feet to the ground on the other side of the hedge. If I'd missed the hedge, I was dead. If I hadn't made the leap up, I was dead. I was bleeding from a dozen little cuts, but alive."

"Holy crap," responded Donovan.

"Wow. You got really lucky," the blonde at our table interjected, taking a drag off her cigarette.

"I gingerly climbed back down off the hedge, over the wall and onto the street. Rich and Thea were smirking at me from across the street and then, the best part... An elderly couple was walking along the designated pedestrian path on the right. The Irish gentleman doffed his flat cap towards me and said, 'Very elegant, sir.'"

Donovan and our blonde interloper howled with laughter. I did too. I almost died, but it was pretty fucking funny.

"Do you travel a lot?" The blonde asked me.

Almost noticing her for the first time, I turned towards her. "Not as much as I'd like, but I've been around."

"I bet you have."

We snickered.

"Not at all like that," I said. "I just got divorced a couple months ago, from, essentially, my high school sweetheart. Ireland was my first trip overseas, but I've been pretty much everywhere west, not too far east, except DC in the states. What about you?"

She thought a moment. "I just got back from Florida and I've been to Guatemala," the young blonde informed me. "I've been to Alaska, too. I'd like to go back there someday."

We talked about the seemingly endless days and nights, the Aurora Borealis and other things Alaska is known for.

"I bet that was really cool up there. I've seen the Northern Lights from my family's cabin once or twice, but it was very faint. No colors. I'd like to see it from Alaska."

We went on like this. Our conversation began to escalate in intensity. The world grew smaller.

"My dad works for an airline, so I've been able to travel some," she explained.

"Awesome. I've mostly done road trips, until I went to Ireland, but I've flown to Los Angeles a few times, Houston and DC."

By this point, Donovan ceased to exist. He noticed a growing connection between this blonde wheelchair pusher and myself, and left us to it, turning his attention to a woman closer to our own forty-something age whom I later learned was suffering a plethora of cancer-related problems. She was out on the town, though, having a good time.

"So, tell me more about Ireland," the blonde said, lighting up another Camel 100 and absently flicking her foot over a crossed leg. "Do you have family there?"

"Kind of," I replied. "Hey. I just realized I don't even know your name yet. I'm Dan." I extended my hand.

"Tina," she replied, taking my hand in hers. It was warm and soft and something else.

For some reason, I got a bit of a tingly rush from the contact, but I dismissed it as quickly as our hands separated. She was just a random smoking buddy at a bar who I'd never see again. I wasn't even from around Farmington, after all.

I told her the tale of Fungie the lone dolphin that likes to race tourist boats in Dingle Harbor on an eastern peninsula of the Irish Republic. Apparently, he doesn't get along with other dolphins, but he loves humans and likes to show off his swimming skills when the engines challenge him.

I showed her video of Fungie keeping pace with the high-powered boat we were riding to the Great Blasket Island and talked a bit about the history I'd learned there.

She seemed enthralled when I told her my fear that Fungie wouldn't be around much longer, but he had become a big tourist attraction for the little cliff town of Dingle.

"How long to Dolphins live?" she asked.

"About 50 years," I said. "And Fungie is estimated to be about 30. I guess he used to be a lot more playful, leaping out of the water and stuff, but he still likes to race and he can keep up with the big boats."

Sadly, Fungie disappeared from Dingle Harbor about five years later, in October of 2020 and is presumed to have passed on. I counted myself fortunate to have been one of the humans aboard a boat he raced with.

I couldn't honestly say how long Tina and I conversed. It might have been 20 minutes or a couple hours. Time was losing meaning. We talked about music, books and life in general. Our conversation was growing intimate. I felt like I'd known Tina a long time. We were old friends, already.

I thought she spoke like a writer. "You're a very literary person, aren't you? I like the way your mind works," I said.

We got on to enthusiastically talking about our mutual hobby of reading.

"Are you from around here?" Tina asked, snuffing out her cigarette in the ashtray on the black mesh table.

"Not really. I live in Minneapolis. I just came to town to visit my friend over there." I inclined my head towards Donovan who was presently engaged in conversation with Linda, the out and about cancer patient.

"Yeah. I saw you guys a few times tonight. I like his shirt," Tina told me.

"It's noticeable, isn't it?"

We chuckled.

"See that guy over there?" She made a subtle gesture to the hapless dick in the dark, still trying hopelessly to strike pay dirt.

"He grabbed my ass earlier — both cheeks! I would have elbowed him in the face, but I thought it was just one of my girlfriends fooling around," she told me. "That's kinda why I wanted to sit by you guys. You look like decent men and I can't be intimidated by a Dragonball Z shirt."

I laughed.

His ears must have been burning, because the hapless and ineffective "flirt" approached our table. "Hey. One of you guys have a light?" He swayed a bit as he spoke. Rocking back and forth, right to left.

I offered up my recently obtained Guinness Zippo, but kept a grip on it and lit his cigarette for him.

"I'm Andy," he said, more to Tina than the man who offered him fire.

"Tina, and this is Dan," she replied for us.

He tried in vain to engage us in conversation, but we were quickly bored with Andy and fell back into our own talks.

"So, Minneapolis, huh? I've heard that's kinda scary."

"What?!" I was floored. Farmington is only about 35 miles from my home city, so I couldn't imagine that perception. "No. That's silly."

"Lots of gang violence, shootings…" She suggested.

"No. No. No. It's not like that. It's really nice," I said. "Sure, there are places, people and circumstances to avoid, but if you know where to go, it's no problem and it's really great. All the best stuff is in Minneapolis."

It was silent for a few beats, then she fixed her eyes on mine and asked, "So are you offering to show me around?"

I had to reevaluate everything at that moment. I'd considered her no further than a random smoking conversation as will happen at bars. I looked her up and down (subtly). I reflected on my time in Wales when my friend Thea was almost beating too-young Welsh girls away from me with a shoe — apparently the American accent is an aphrodisiac for young Welsh women.

She was simply dressed. Jeans and a well-fitted camo shirt. Long, wavy blonde hair cascaded over her shoulders. She was by no means fat, but not a twig, either. She was pretty, but simple. Next to no makeup. She wasn't trying to look like anything other than she was.

I thought back on Thea's strong disapproval of my occasional, mild philandering with younger women while we were in Ireland and Wales. "How old are you?" I asked. Even in party-mode, I could see that she was younger than me, but I figured her around 30, not so much for her looks, but her intellect.

Now, to be honest, I was a bit tipsy myself by this point and math was becoming a challenge.

She gave me a number.

I'm not really sure what number she gave me that night, but I remember thinking, *that's close enough to thirty*. Thea couldn't object.

I honestly don't know why that was important, but Thea had taken to watching me like a hawk whilst we were overseas together.

"OK. Sure. Why not?" My final answer.

"Cool. Should we exchange numbers?"

"Are you on Facebook?" I asked, pulling out my phone.

"No. I don't use that," she said, pulling out her rather antiquated 'dumb' phone.

I flipped through the screens and got to my contacts app. "Here. Put your name and number in here. I'll call you."

Tina took my phone, scrunched her brow and began typing on my touch screen. She handed the phone back to me. "How's that?"

I glanced at the contact profile she'd created – first and last name, phone number, saved.

"Perfect," I proclaimed. I noticed her last name was distinctly Polish. "Ah. A Pollock, huh? My Grandma was Polish."

"I've never done that before."

"Never done what?"

"Well, I'm not used to smart phones and I've never just given my number to a guy at a bar before," she replied. "I'm surprised I was able to do it."

I smiled at her. "I'll call you tomorrow and set something up."

"I prefer texts."

"OK. I can do that."

Sensing that things were winding down, and number in pocket, I turned my attention back to Donovan and Tina rejoined her party.

Donovan was about ready to walk Linda home and they'd been chatting it up as long as Tina and I had been. I didn't quite know what I was jumping into when I sat at their table. I learned more than I wanted to know about cancer treatments, but we all hit it off.

When Linda was ready to go, Donovan insisted on walking her back home.

Donovan walked Linda back to her apartment and once they were inside, I sat on the grass, leaned back on a handy fence and waited.

He was out shortly, ready to head home.

Back at Donovan's, we had a couple more beers and discussed the night. I crashed on his couch in the wee hours.

When I woke, I was still feeling the effect of the prior night's revelry, but the blonde I'd met at Pizza Man was my first thought. I scanned the contacts in my phone, but realized her name escaped me.

"What was that girl's name I was talking with last night, again?" I asked Donovan.

"Tina," he said.

"Of course it is," I said as I located the entry. Tina Dziewkaski. The smart, cute polish girl who liked to read. Secure in the knowledge that I had both name and number, I decided to wait a couple days before contacting her. Text too soon: Desperate. Wait too long: Forgotten.

I sent her a text on Sunday night.

I'd been lazing in bed, reflecting on my life and feeling lonely. I had been divorced for about three months, but the marriage had been over considerably longer than that..

"It was fun meeting you on Friday night. When would you like me to show you around Minneapolis?" I texted.

There was no reply. I poked around on a dating app for a while before falling asleep. I had a couple dates set up, but I was still hoping to hear back from Tina.

Days went by and I didn't hear back from her. I figured she wasn't really all that interested, and wrote her off as I carried on with my daily life. I set up a date with an attractive lady named Carrie.

Then, I was laying in bed, getting ready for sleep on a Monday night, checking email on my phone in the dark, when it buzzed in my hands. A text message arrived.

"It's 11 O'clock on a Monday night, 8 days after we met... I've been thinking about you since that handshake, and I really would like to meet up with you sometime (if, of course, you're still interested). After the 4th sometime?"

I was surprised and delighted. I hadn't expected to hear back from Tina by that point.

"Nope. You ignored me... Bored now," I replied.

I didn't want to push that jest to hard, though and I immediately followed up with "Ahh... I'm kidding of course. You were too fun to ignore."

"Anyone bored wouldn't respond so quickly," she quipped moments later.

"It would probably have to be after July 13th," I wrote, considering my social obligations. Even though we were divorced, I was planning a birthday party for

Jessica the weekend of the 10th. My Mom's birthday was the day after. "But, I'd feel privileged to show you a good time on the town, my style."

"Besides, I've been told I'm kinda cute. After the 13th sounds good. Your style? Hmmm…"

Probably given that she'd taken a week, I felt like I had to justify my quick response. "It just so happened that the phone was on hand, but I wouldn't argue with anyone who said you're kinda cute. 'Kinda' cute might be an insult actually." I conjured a fuzzy memory of her appearance in my mind. "I'd argue you're very cute."

Her reply was rapid. "You're not exactly hard on the eyes, either. Bedtime for me. Sleep sweet!"

I was pretty excited and feeling flattered. It feels pretty damn good to have an attractive young lady compliment your looks. I went to sleep feeling quite contented after mapping out a few ideas in my mind of what sights to show Tina.

There were some false starts and canceled dates and then another week had gone by without any contact, so I'd given up on seeing Tina again by the end of July, but on a Friday at the end of the month I was going to Farmington to visit Donovan and I figured since I'd be in the area, I'd give her one last shot. I texted, "Hey Tina. I'm probably going to be in Farmington tonight, in case you'd like to meet up for a drink or a chat somewhere."

I was actually surprised that she replied. Our entire, amazing and terrible history was nearly averted – if only she hadn't answered that last text.

"I would love to" came back instantly.

I arrived early to scout the location, find a good seat and make a generally good, gentlemanly impression. The bar Tina suggested, Celts was pretty quiet when I arrived. I ordered a Guinness and took a seat on the patio where I could surveil the parking lot. At about 8:00, I got a text from Tina saying she was on her way and it wasn't long until I saw a silver Saturn coupe with two blondes pull into the parking lot. They exchanged a parting kiss before Tina got out from the passenger seat. The other woman drove away. It had been over a month since I'd met her so I wasn't even sure I'd recognize her, but I did, right away. She was, however, taller than I remembered. She was wearing a white dress and she looked beautiful. I greeted her at the entrance to the bar with a tentative hug and bought her a drink. It was a gorgeous summer day, so we sat on the patio and chatted. I learned that Tina's driver was her mother and that Tina didn't actually live in Farmington. Actually, I was a little confused by her living situation. She said she was moving and she was displaced.

Celt's had a sleepy vibe that evening, so we decided to wander. Tina believed she remembered the location of a bowling alley in walking distance. I left my van in the big parking lot and Tina led us on a merry stroll to Farmington Lanes. We were connecting better on the move than we had been at the pub.

After we got a lane and bowling shoes, picked out and joked about some orange 8-pound balls, I got us drinks. She was indecisive about what she wanted so I ordered whiskey-sours for both of us. I brought them back to the little table at our lane, sat down and as I tried to resume conversation, I made a sweeping gesture and spilled my full drink all over the table, the floor and us. I knew I wasn't drunk, but it probably looked like it.

How suave, I thought. *She's going to think I can't handle my liquor.*

I hopped to my feet and could feel the hot blood rushing to my face. "I am so sorry! Let me go get a towel. I'm sure they have one at the bar. So embarrassing!"

"At least it wasn't me, this time," Tina said.

I gave her a puzzled look.

"It's usually me," she said and that eased my jangled nerves a little.

I went to the bar to replace my drink and get a towel. The one bartender there was overworked and (it felt like) it took an inordinate time for me to return to my date.

By the time I got back, the towel in my hand was superfluous, but at least I'd refreshed my lost drink. Somehow Tina had managed to get the table cleaned in my absence.

I am not a good bowler. It's not a given that the bumpers should be inflated for me, but my ball usually gets acquainted with the gutter. I advised Tina that for me to break 80 bowling would be a miracle. She claimed equal incompetence, so it was pretty amazing that in three games, we both scored well over 100. To my astonishment, I bowled a strike my first frame and so did she. Tina was on fire and won two out of three, finishing the last game with a turkey (three strikes in a row). We had a great time cheering each other on in our unlikely hot streaks.

We were bowled out, sitting at the table with fresh drinks. I was contemplating the rest of the night. Was this the end of the date? I looked into her hazel eyes, trying to gauge her attitude when she suddenly cast her gaze to the floor, cheeks turning red. She slowly shook her cocked head. It was probably the cutest thing I'd ever seen.

"What?" I kept my gaze up.

She glanced up and immediately shot her eyes back down. "Something about the way you're looking at me," she said coyly.

"Oh? I'm sorry."

"No. It's making me feel all…" She shook her head again.

I smiled. "I was just trying to gauge your interest in staying out with me after this."

"I was going to ask you the same thing," she said. "You want to go somewhere else?"

"I'm easy."

"So am…." She broke off, embarrassed. "No. I didn't mean… I mean…"

I nodded, smiling at the gaffe. We cracked up laughing and she pushed my shoulder.

"Let's turn these bowling shoes in," I said. "I don't know Farmington. Do you know how far it is to that bar we met at?"

"Not exactly, but I think I can find it. Not too far. A few blocks? I don't know Farmington very well, either."

We wandered around industrial and residential Farmington roads for probably an hour. We crossed railroad tracks, wandered down a lane with a high chain link fence topped with barbed wire. I was trying to get a GPS signal on my phone. We were lost, but I was enjoying every minute of our extended moonlight walk. We seemed to share a sense of humor that flowed easily between intellectual and childish. We walked arm in arm for a while, not caring that much about our destination, but we did eventually find the main drag.

"I think I've seen more of Farmington tonight than I have in my whole life," Tina commented.

Gossips was the first bar we came upon. We'd first met at Pizza Man, but neither of us was exactly sure where that was from there.

"Wanna try here?" Tina suggested.

"Sure. You know me. I'm easy."

She laughed and gave me a gentle push. I opened the door for her.

Gossips was a completely different atmosphere than the sleepy pub we'd started our date at.

I remembered that Pizza Man had a nice patio out back and it was a beautiful summer night, so I was keen to be outside. Tina and I got drinks and found a bench to sit on out front. We were in and out of the bar, but mostly out.

"Can I kiss you?" she said. It didn't sound like a question.

"Of course."

I felt something stir. For a first kiss, there was nothing at all awkward. It was so natural, like we'd been kissing each other for years and before we drew apart, she left an impression by gently biting my lower lip, drawing it out between her teeth. I could feel her kiss for a long time after and it's all I could think about. We kissed quite a lot at that bar, that night.

Later, we met a pretty intoxicated man and learned that he was living off of some kind of trust fund. He seemed to be a druggie and dilettante. At first, I thought he was hitting on Tina, offering to buy her a drink, but actually, he was offering to buy us both a drink, if we'd come inside and sit at the bar with him. He wanted us to try his favorite, expensive bourbon. We didn't turn him down.

While we were waiting for the bartender, he started talking about his stash of drugs back at home and how crazy his life was. Then he had a notion that he wanted someone to write "because drugs" on his forehead. He started asking staff and patrons for an ink pen.

Tina fished a sharpie out of her purse and held it up with a flourish.

His eyes lit up. "Yeah. Perfect!" He closed his eyes and Tina held back his bangs while she scrawled "Becuz Drugz" in black indelible ink on his brow.

"How does it look?"

We regarded him thoughtfully and gave our approval. We drank bourbon with him and he soon departed, I'm guessing to get back to his stash.

We sat inside at an out of the way corner table for a while and got to discussing movies. We decided we each had a film we absolutely had to share with the other. A double feature of Idiocracy and Requiem for a Dream was settled on for a future date.

Tina and I went back outside to have a cigarette. I had to slip in another kiss before I lit mine. We sat close on that bench enjoying the evening and each other's touch. A small elfin-looking woman approached from the sidewalk. It was Shayna, the girl Tina had been pushing around in a wheelchair the night we met.

"Is this your date?" Shayna asked her.

"Yes. This is Dan."

"Hello, again, Shayna," I said. I don't think she remembered me, even though I had signed her cast.

Shayna lurched towards me and Tina reacted swiftly, swinging her legs over my lap. "No, Shayna! Mine!" She chastised.

It made me feel warm inside. She was already being possessive. I liked it.

Almost right after Shayna crashed our date, I spied my friend Donovan coming down the sidewalk towards us. Since I'd put off hanging out with him to take Tina out, he'd gotten bored waiting on me at home and decided to go out for a drink, not expecting to find us there. It was like a Dew Days reunion.

When it was just about last call, Tina pointed out Shayna who was across the bar in the company of an older couple. "Do you think you could give her a ride home when we leave?" she asked.

"Sure," I said. "She lives around here, I take it?"

"Yeah. I think those two are trying to take her home with them and I'm getting a bad vibe from them," Tina explained.

"Well, she's an adult…"

"I know but I'm going to talk to her. You'll give her a ride?"

"Yes."

"Thank you, Dan. Can you go and get your van while I talk to her?"

I agreed. I had my bearings, now and it was just a couple blocks to the pub I'd left my van at.

"Have van. Coming back for you, now," I texted. I drove back to Gossips and found a parking spot right in front of the door.

It didn't seem like Tina was having much luck convincing Shayna to come with us. "We'll give her a ride," the older man said.

"We'll take care of her," his female companion said.

Tina wasn't having it. She kept urging Shayna to get into the van. Donovan had also asked for a ride back and was waiting with me outside the van.

Eventually, Donovan just picked Shayna up and threw her into the back seat of my van. It could have looked like a kidnapping to outside observers.

Tina and Shayna sat in the back and Donovan rode shotgun. I pulled away from the bar and onto the main road through town. I opened Google Maps on my phone and asked Shayna for her address.

She didn't know it. She said she'd just moved and couldn't remember the address. She said she'd give me directions.

I followed her directions until we were driving past miles of corn fields and she seemed lost. She was also out of control. She was thrashing into my seat while I was driving, trying to climb over my center console into the front of the van, trying to kiss Donovan, trying to open the sliding back door while the van was moving and generally being intolerable. I desperately wanted her out of the van. It was two in the morning on a Friday night and I didn't want to attract any police attention. I just wanted to drop Tina off, get a goodnight kiss, a commitment for another date and be on my way.

Eventually, Shayna's directions led us down a dead end street in farm country. She and Donovan went into the fields to relieve their bladders while Tina was trying to formulate another plan. She apologized repeatedly for all the trouble and insisted that Shayna wasn't really her "friend," more of an acquaintance and she desperately hoped Shayna's behavior wouldn't reflect on her.

Tina was calling and texting contacts, ostensibly to try to find someone who knew where Shayna lived. Eventually she reached someone named Keith who said he'd put Shayna up at his place for the night, since we couldn't find her home.

I was willing to drop Shayna off anywhere. I just wanted the squirming, shouting, thrashing, drunk little imp out of my van and I was getting the impression I was being jerked around.

Tina gave me Keith's address and we got there pretty quickly. Everyone got out and Tina went up to knock on the door. Keith came out and lit a cigarette while Tina coaxed Shayna into his house.

Keith was older than Tina but younger than me, I estimated. He approached Donovan and I. "You got any weed?" was his greeting.

Now, I was getting some bad vibes, myself.

"Sorry. No."

Tina and Shayna were in the house for quite some time and when Tina did finally appear at the door, she called out to say she'd be staying there tonight, too, "to look after Shayna."

My unease was rising.

I'd just wanted to drop her off at "home," get that kiss goodnight and confirm our second date, like a successful first date should end. After a really wonderful time, I was dismayed by this very disturbing ending.

Like she read my mind, Tina decided to come out from the doorway. She came out barefoot, gave me a quick kiss and said, "Thank you for everything" before dashing back into Keith's house.

Donovan and I got back into my van and drove back to his place. I was perplexed.

It was about 3 AM and I shot Tina a text. "Sketchy ending, but a great night, overall. Sweet dreams… Looking forward to that second date!"

I spent the night at Donovan's. When I woke up the next morning, finding out what had happened with Tina and Shayna was my first thought. Tina still hadn't replied to my last text. I sent another. "I'm hoping the rest of the night went better for you and you have a wonderful Sunday. I spent the night at Donovan's and I'm still in Farmington in case you could use a ride home or anything."

After noon, she still hadn't replied and I was concerned. I hadn't delivered Tina safely home and I felt my responsibility to her was incomplete. Shayna, less so. "Please call or text when you get a chance. I'd just like to know you guys are safe and sound," I texted.

This time she replied right away.

"I am safe, so is she. I was able to make it back 'home' and sleep in my own bed; Shayna finally got to her place as well. I had a really great time with you. Sorry for the way the night ended – THANK YOU and Donovan!!! I've never seen her that messed up… Scary. She took me down twice after you left. Gonna have some new bruises."

Dating and Love Bombing

After that first date, we began a flurry of text messages that became quickly familiar. It was like we were in a relationship already, after one date that very nearly didn't happen. Her messages were peppered with flattery and affection.

We told each other about our days and whatever reservations I had after the way our first date ended were washed away by a steady stream of warm fuzzies and reports of Tina's wholesome-sounding activities. I felt like I'd known her a long time, even though I'd only seen her twice!

I arranged a second date with Tina pretty quickly. She was still at her mom's boyfriend Scott's, so I picked her up at his house in Farmington. Tina had told me that Scott was a man who cared more about her than her own biological father and that he wanted to meet me. That sounded wonderfully traditional and I was happy to present myself, but to Tina's disappointment, he apparently wasn't in the mood to meet me that night.

I'd brought Tina to a pub in my neighborhood called Merlin's Rest for Wednesday pub trivia hosted by the incomparably witty Bill Watkins.

Merlin's was long a favorite haunt of mine, especially in my heavy drinking days. It was a British Isles pub that featured a tremendous selection of whiskeys (and whiskys for those who enjoy a peaty scotch). I'd become acquainted with a number of regulars there over the years. We arrived early enough to have dinner before trivia started. I had fish and chips and Tina ordered a Reuben, which she raved about.

My friend Jeff showed up to make our team three and he seemed set on pushing the bounds of propriety with my new dating interest, talking about vinyl "gimp suits" with zipper masks and gag balls. Tina took it in stride, though and found it quite entertaining.

After trivia was concluded and Jeff had departed, we moved to the bar side. I introduced Tina to Hellcat Maggie Irish Whiskey and a few regulars. One such was an east-African man named Abraham. He was a union organizer at the airport. He was quiet guy who spent more time looking at news video from home on his phone than socializing, but I thought he was a decent sort. I made it a point to introduce

Tina to the pub's cultural ambassador, Bill, but the intent was to get to know each other better, so we didn't linger long at the regulars' corner.

Tina and I sat at a high table near the window. Alone, the subject matter turned personal. Tina told me some very personal details of her past – some disturbing. Then she asked me if I thought that made her "damaged goods."

I was aghast at the term. "Absolutely not!" I was adamant. I objected to that term being applied to a human being.

Tina beamed at my reaction. Next, she asked me what I thought about the debate over medical marijuana that was going on in the state legislature at the time. I told her I that I was basically a libertarian and wasn't inclined to oppose it. Again, she was pleased with my response.

"I'm so glad you said that," she exclaimed and went on to explain that she had a plethora of internal ailments and used marijuana to control her chronic acid reflux and nausea.

As a libertarian, I didn't think the government had much justification in banning recreational use of marijuana, either. It wasn't for me, I explained, but I knew people who used it and I considered it mostly harmless at the time (my opinions on that have been an evolution, however).

"OK. What do you think about prostitution?" she asked.

"Do I think it should be legal?" I asked to clarify.

"Yeah."

"Tricky," I said.

We snickered at the pun.

"I mean if it's consenting adults and not like child sex-trafficking," Tina added for my consideration.

"I don't know," I said. I felt like it was a morally wrong and spiritually destructive practice, but I also knew there had always been a market for it, always would be and some legal sexual arrangements ran pretty close to prostitution. I could tell that Tina fell on the side of legalizing prostitution, seemingly on feminist and libertarian grounds. I hemmed and hawed, but agreed that it wasn't government's job to regulate consensual sex.

All of that seemed like unusual second date conversation, but even though Tina had just been probing on marijuana to let me know that she used it, I took our discussion on prostitution as hypothetical and Tina seemed satisfied with my positions, which appeared to lend to the success of our second date.

At the table next to ours, two women were leaned in towards each other engaged in conversation. Tina was a people-watcher, I was learning. Her attention was neatly divided between her date with me and the lesbian first date she deduced was going on behind me. Astrology came up and one of the women said she was a Scorpio. Tina interjected. "Scorpios are highly sexual people."

I'm sure my eyes widened. I hadn't expected to be meddling in lesbian romance.

The women turned their attention to Tina. They looked intrigued. "What else do you know about Scorpios?" One of them asked.

Though she was the cause of the moment, she suddenly turned red, embarrassed. "Um. I think it's time for us to go," she said to me. We made a hasty departure and left the ladies to carry on their date in peace.

Merlin's became a fairly regular stop-off for us as our relationship progressed and Tina swiftly developed an affinity for Abraham. The two of them would chat at length. Something about their later conversations was making me uneasy, though. On one occasion, I was standing off to the side waiting on our drinks order. I couldn't hear what they were discussing, but I saw Abraham make a "call me" gesture. I wondered if Tina had obtained his phone number at some point and if so, for what? She had taken an interest in his country of origin and I saw her reading up on Eritrea on her computer one night. That night, she commented to me on the drive home, "he's very handsome."

The next time I was at Merlin's alone, I tried to engage Abraham in conversation and he seemed nervous and disinclined to chat with me. On my way out of the bar that night, I clapped Abraham on the shoulder when I said goodbye and he flinched.

I never really thought too much of all this, except that something was making me feel uneasy when I saw them together.

There were occasional moments when some oddity like that gave me pause, but it would be swiftly forgotten. Tina would kiss me or lock her arm in the crook of mine as we walked, and all was right.

After that second date at Merlin's Rest, I drove Tina back to Scott's house in Farmington. We sat in the driveway chatting a little and I moved in to kiss her good night. It got really heated really fast and I was kissing her neck, inhaling and becoming dizzied by her aroma. With effort, we broke away from each other and Tina retrieved her leftovers box from the back seat and I watched as she let herself into Scott's house.

My head was in the clouds on my long drive home. At one point, I had a cigarette dangling from my lips and two more were burning in the ashtray. That parting kiss overwhelmed my thoughts and body. I probably should have pulled over for a while, but despite being so distracted as to have three lit cigarettes going at once, I made it home safely. I was a little concerned that I'd been too forward, but Tina gave nothing but positive feedback.

Tina texted late the next day to thank me. She wrote that I was "living proof that chivalry isn't dead." She went on to say "After you dropped me off, I slept like a baby for the first time in several days. I fell asleep with a smile on my face and woke up still wearing it!"

I felt all warm inside reading her message and then another one followed it up.

"I used this morning to recharge my batteries, then started a new book that's sucked me in like quicksand... Two hours passed in 20 minutes. I've spent most of my day trying to think of all things not Dan – quite an effort. Exhausting, almost. I'm looking forward to seeing you again. So, smile and happy thoughts without words. Wish I had a goodnight kiss before bed tonight."

It felt like my insides turned to liquid. I was melting.

Tina and her mom were changing apartments at the Buffalo Hotel, moving from a way-undersized efficiency into the "penthouse" of the historic building and she invited me to come out to the new place once they were situated.

I was doing some moving as well – collecting my belongings from my former house and putting them into a storage locker.

Tina and I kept in touch daily and her love-bombing continued. We'd decided on mini-golf for our next meeting, but the date hadn't yet been determined with the chaos we both had going on.

"Let's try to make it sooner, rather than later, though, OK?" I texted.

"Well think of the poor Scorpio, LOL." She replied. That was an obvious reference to our last date when she told the lesbians that Scorpio's are highly sexual people. I assumed, anyway, that she was a Scorpio, herself. "The sooner, the better," she agreed. "Being away from you is, uh, unpleasant."

A couple days later, after things had settled down a bit, I shot Tina a text. "So, I'm trying to get some work done, but this one cute, sweet girl keeps interrupting me, popping into my head unannounced. What's a hard-working fella to do?"

"A good, handsome, hard-workin', whiskey-drinkin' fella should come to Buffalo this weekend... I bought a bottle of Hellcat Maggie (and I'll be here all alone and lonely)."

Yes! My ex-wife had been increasingly hypercritical of my drinking habits and had been sleeping in a separate bedroom for the last year of my doomed marriage. Tina's invitation sounded like an oasis.

"Well, we can't have you all lonely. That's just unacceptable," I replied.

"Friday would be best," she said, "but bad news: for the life of me, I can't hook up this TV."

"Awesome. Sooner rather than later!"

Even though Tina professed discomfort with talking on the phone, she called me a couple minutes later and we wound up talking for five straight hours. I was chain smoking cigarettes in my van having the time of my life. We laughed a lot and even cried together as we shared some traumatic experiences with each other. It was amazing how we clicked on absolutely everything. Unprecedented.

Tina made me make a promise that night. "Promise me that we'll always be completely honest with each other, no matter what – even if it's bad," she insisted. Her tone was deadly serious and I was in delighted with the sentiment. I readily agreed to total honesty even if it was bad.

We moved up the date to Thursday, since it turned out I had both Thursday and Friday off from work and we were impatient.

She texted the next day. "Hi! I think you set the record for my longest phone call ever. You deserve a trophy or a plaque or framed certificate of some sort. I can't wait to see you again. I drew myself a bath, poured some Hellcat Maggie in a wine glass… Still not relaxed yet."

"Did I do that?"

"I haven't been able to read, have to remind myself to eat… Can't stop thinking of you," she wrote.

"Wow. You're killing me with kindness." I felt my insides melting, again.

"Just being honest," she replied.

"That's the deal," I wrote. "Do men swoon? I think that's what I'm experiencing right now, but I'm not familiar with the sensation."

"I do not think that swooning is typically considered manly, but I'm way past the swoon, so I'm just glad you feel the same!"

The love bombing was intense and it was working. I felt like we were being swept along by inexorable waves of pure fate.

Fined for Smoking

Thursday, August 6th, 2015 arrived and I was practically shaking with excitement.

Tina had asked me to bring something we could watch her newly acquired South Park DVDs on, so I readied my work bag with my laptop – I'd also tucked fresh socks, underwear and a T-shirt in there. I wasn't 100% certain I'd be spending the night – more like 95% but I didn't want to seem presumptuous, so the briefcase served well.

It was a 50 minute drive out to Buffalo, so I had a lot of time to think and anticipate. I'd researched the area and located an entertainment center with mini-golf, bowling and some other attractions. It was a warm sunny day, which I thought would be perfect for an outdoor date.

Getting to the Buffalo Hotel proved a bit challenging. GPS did not know how to navigate around all the roads closed for construction. When I finally found the old brick building, both parking and even getting across the missing sidewalk to the front door were challenges.

Tina had told me she was in #19 on the top floor, but the front door may or may not be locked. It wasn't on this occasion. I entered the lobby and was disquieted. The space had a forbidding, abandoned look. The only light came through the plate glass windows. A well-worn couch sat unused next to an inoperable Pepsi machine. It was like stepping back in time or into a frontier ghost town. There was a dingy hotel desk with the old-fashioned message slots and key hooks on the wall behind it. Some boxes were stacked in a shadowy corner. All was still and I felt like a trespasser for some reason. I found the stairway. The once ornate banister's carvings were obscured by a hundred layers of paint. Its present color was black. The treads were well-worn, I noticed as I climbed the stairs. The building was once beautiful, I could see, but it had been repurposed with cheap construction materials and methods in piecemeal fashion over the decades. Mostly in the 70s and 80s, by the look of it.

I made my way to the 3rd and final floor and found #19 halfway down the hall, on the left. The door was newer and didn't match the other doors in the building. I knocked.

Tina greeted me with quick hug and kiss. I set my satchel down on the kitchen counter. She gave me the nickel tour. The living area was separated from the kitchen by a breakfast bar. There was one bedroom with a wide door-less closet and there was a tiny bathroom with blue plastic tiles.

Tina introduced me to Candace – her name for the futon that took up most of the living space, and showed me her view of the army in yellow conducting construction on the main road. Buffalo Lake was also visible from the 3rd floor window.

We didn't linger long. We had a third date to get through. Fun outdoor activities awaited. Bison Creek Mini Golf wasn't apparent from the road, but we eventually found it and got a round going.

I thought it was a gorgeous day. The sun was warm and bright, the breeze mild. Tina was full of smiles and jokes and seemed to be really enjoying herself for the first few holes, but she started looking ill by the 4th and we had to stop before moving to the 5th. She had gone from bubbly to looking like she was on death's door frighteningly fast. She said she was sensitive to the sun and it was making her feel ill. We moved inside to get a seat and rest. I bought her a bottle of water and a frozen cherry slushie to try to cool her down and hydrate her.

Her face was flushed, she started sweating and shaking. She complained of nausea and headache. It was alarming. I suggested taking her to the emergency room, but she refused that option. After we had sat in the air conditioned lounge for about a half-hour, Tina finished her slushie and said she was feeling somewhat better but didn't think she could finish our game. She just wanted me to take her home, which I did. She was unsteady going up the numerous flights of creaky wooden steps and had to stop a couple times on the way up, but we made it into the apartment. She suggested that I pour us each a drink and disappeared into the bathroom for a while. I found a half-full bottle of Hellcat Maggie and poured two short glasses. I finished mine and had poured another when Tina emerged, looking somewhat fresher, from the restroom.

"Were you saying something?" she asked.

"No."

"I thought I heard a voice, but it's like a jet engine in there," she said, referring to the over-loud exhaust fan. She sat and suggested we watch South Park for a bit while she reconstituted herself.

She sipped her whiskey, complained about the jetliner in the bathroom and told me how the apartment might be haunted while I set up my laptop and speakers to watch her DVDs. I had gotten her TV working while Tina was in the bathroom, but for DVDs, my computer remained the only option available to us at the time.

"The knobs in the shower will just turn on their own," she said, "and it'll go from ice cold to scalding hot."

"I think shower temperature changes are pretty common in apartments, but you mean you actually see the knobs physically turn?"

She nodded. "My mom's seen it too."

I wasn't dismissive. I've seen things I couldn't explain.

We got comfortable on the futon and had some laughs. South Park was a favorite of both of ours, as it happened. Lines from the show soon became a kind of shorthand for many of our inside jokes. After a couple whiskeys, Tina was feeling tip-top again and she was feeling something else. We started kissing and passions rose rapidly. Tina's shirt was half-unbuttoned when her phone interrupted us. It was a text from Maura, her mother and contrary to what we'd expected, she was on her way back to the apartment. That put a damper on things.

Tina suggested we move to the bedroom. "I can put a scrunchie on the doorknob. She'll know what that means," she said.

I didn't really want to meet her mother under those circumstances. In fact, I refused, but an alternate plan came to mind. "How about I get us a hotel room for the night?"

Tina tried again to reassure me that it would be no big deal for us to be having sex with her mom in the tiny apartment, but I wasn't having it. It was a small place with hollow doors. I briefly imagined coming out from the bedroom to be introduced to her mom after she'd been listening to us having sex. "No fucking way, Tina," I insisted. It's no big deal to get a hotel room either and then maybe I can meet your mom under more dignified circumstances tomorrow or some other time."

She agreed. "I just didn't want to you to have to spend the money and my mom really wouldn't care, but a hotel sounds fun."

"We can go out for dinner and drinks, if you're feeling up for it and pick up where we left off here in our room," I said.

"Oh, I'm feeling up for it," she assured.

Tina sat by the window and lit a cigarette while I fished my phone out of my pocket. I unlocked the screen, closed my GPS app and almost had a heart attack. I had forgotten what the very last thing I'd seen on my phone before I left home was, it was still there waiting for this moment. A friend had messaged me a picture of a topless woman just when I was heading to Buffalo. I didn't close it – just opened other apps on top of it.

That really really really didn't look good. I closed the messenger app fast as lightning and hoped Tina hadn't noticed and nervously began Googling hotels in the area. I was really afraid that gaffe spelled the end of our adventures together.

"Finding anything?" Tina asked after a minute.

"There are a couple nearby," I said.

"I saw that, you know."

"Oh. I'd hoped you missed that."

"Kinda hard to miss. Damn. I hope that wasn't your ex."

"No." I was feeling hot again, but not in a good way. "It's just a picture a friend sent – not a picture of the friend. I mean it's a guy friend… who sent the picture… of a stranger. Just some model or something… Nobody I know."

"Oh, good," Tina said, "because she looked way hotter than me."

I was at a loss. I think I opened my mouth, but words didn't come out.

"Go on," she said. "book us that room."

My rather unsteady hands managed to complete an online reservation at the Country Inn and Suites by Carlson. There's a reason I still recalled the entire name of this particular hotel so clearly, years later. More than one reason, I suppose.

Tina very quickly packed an overnight bag and we were ready to roll. We stopped by a liquor store for some Mickeys beer and checked into the room, only to put our things in there. I'd noticed a Mexican bar and restaurant next door to the hotel. We went there for dinner and, since we wouldn't need to be driving anywhere, several shots of tequila.

When we got back to the room, we were revved up and ready to go. Kissing our way through the doorway, we kicked off our shoes and were both immediately treated to the delightless sensation of soaked socks. Someone had left the refrigerator defrosting and leaking water into the carpet.

For most of my life, I've been self-conscious about taking my socks off, because I'd had a childhood accident that smashed one of my toes beyond salvage and it had to be amputated. It had to be addressed at some point.

I showed Tina. "Oh. It's cute," she said.

Cute! I doubted that, but as long as it wasn't repellent.

Once we had our wet socks off, other clothes soon followed. We fell into each other on the bed with ardor.

As the clothes were coming off, I paused for a responsibility break and inquired about STDs and condom use. Tina assured me that she was disease-free and I could confidently make the same claim. She pulled a little zipper pouch out of her bag. "I have condoms and lube, but I don't think we'll need that." She produced a condom. "We can use this if you want, but I'm OK if you don't want to. I don't think I'm very fertile and I trust you're clean," she said.

I'd always hated condoms. I was a little drunk and a lot aroused. The condom was tossed aside and we got back into it with no loss of passion for the intermission.

"Just so you know, I like it a little rough and I don't mind anal," Tina said very matter-of-factly just as I was sliding her panties down her thighs.

I missed a few beats while I processed that. It sounded practiced or routine – like she was reciting the day's specials. I wasn't in to anal and I wasn't sure what she meant by rough, but I was ready to feel my way through. I figured the butt stuff probably wasn't a first-time priority and left that off the menu.

Once we were well into it, she whispered, "Oh, you were worth the wait."

That also landed weird. Three dates over two weeks didn't seem like much of a "wait," but we were mid-coitus and that got filed for later analysis. We went at it all night. Between the booze, the sex, the love-bombing, the laughs and overall good times together, I was in an incredible state of ecstasy.

We decided to have one more beer and a cigarette before going to sleep, but we were undressed and Tina didn't want to put clothes back on to go outside. She convinced me to smoke in the non-smoking room. We opened the window and blew the smoke outside.

After, we had to fight our way into the bed sheets. Whoever made the bed had created some kind of origami puzzle with twisted, crisscrossed sheets. We got it partway solved, then just wrapped ourselves up with one another and fell into a blissful sleep.

Until about 8:00 in the morning. That's when Hell began to break loose with the crackerjack staff of the Buffalo Country Inn and Suites by Carlson.

First the very loud room phone rang. I answered groggily, unsure of the time. "Yeah?"

"This is the front desk. Apparently someone has been smoking on the second floor and we're trying to pinpoint it. Have you noticed any smoke odor?"

"What?"

"I'm asking if you can help me figure out what room the smoke odor is coming from."

"Nah. I'm sleeping," I said.

"OK. Well, if you notice anything, please call the front desk."

"Sure." I hung up and fell back asleep – briefly.

All of the sudden there was a knock on the door. There hadn't been a "do not disturb" sign to hang on the handle, but checkout wasn't until noon, so I didn't expected to be bothered. I did have an alarm set because I was going to see about keeping the room for another night. I looked at the clock. It was 8:05 AM.

"What?" I was groggy and getting grumpy.

"Housekeeping."

"No thanks," I said. "We're good."

I fell back asleep.

At 8:30 in the morning, three hotel employees burst into the room, waking Tina and I with quite a start. We were still naked in bed. That fact didn't seem to faze them. One of the women employees imperiously strode deeper into the room. "Yep, this is the one," she announced.

Tina clutched the tangled sheet to her bosom.

"You have ten minutes to get your belongings and get out," said the imperious one.

The overzealous staff at the Country Inn and Suites by Carlson had made a tremendous miscalculation. I contacted the Carlson Companies and my credit card's issuing bank and Tina and I spent the night there free of charge.

They were going to get two nights paid and if they'd tacked on the $250 cleaning fine the no smoking sign threatened, I would have paid that, too. Instead, after I'd explained what the staff did, the room charge was reversed and they got nothing.

For good measure, Tina stole their "No smoking" placard as a souvenir. Normally I wouldn't have approved. Those circumstances were far from normal.

We gathered our things and vacated, doing our perp walk past self-righteous eyes through the lobby.

We went back to the apartment, not feeling terribly lively. We lounged on the Futon for a while. I think we took a nap.

We were talking about our experience and I told Tina there was no way in hell I was going to pay for that room after that treatment. She was glad I was taking a stand and said she couldn't wait to see the letter I was going to write. From there, we got on to talking about sex. Our past relationships, preferences, precautions and the like. Thinking back on our pre-sex talk the night before, I mentioned that anal sex wasn't something that really did it for me. Tina brushed that off. "It's fine. We don't have to do that. I don't really like it either – just something I've tried."

I was game if it did it for her, but I was somewhat relieved to be off that hook.

"I don't know if I've ever really had that talk before sex," I said. "I feel so responsible."

"I'm glad we had that talk. I live in fear of STDs," Tina said.

That sounded a bit strong. Tina must have thought so, too. She started talking fast. "I mean – even if I haven't been with anybody – just the idea of them… I get checked… I mean I get checked at least once a year, even if I haven't been with anyone."

She seemed to be fumbling. I just nodded.

I revealed that before Tina I'd only been with three women. She said she'd been with or "tried" with 6 guys before me. She said she counted any time she'd intended to, even if it didn't go all the way. I didn't follow her reasoning, but didn't really need the details.

We were both feeling in need of a shower and decided to take one together.

It was very exciting. We'd already been naked together, but in dim light, in bed. Here, we were really seeing each other for the first time in all our natural glory. I liked what I saw. So did Mr. Happy. Tina made some comment about how big it was.

I was a little embarrassed. "It's adequate," I said.

"No. It's really big," she insisted. I like it.

"Not really, but I'm glad you like it. It's the only one I have," I said.

"Well, you probably haven't seen very many of them. Trust me. You're very well-endowed."

That was swelling both my heads, but it also kind of sounded like she was saying she'd been acquainted with a great many. Other more pressing thoughts drowned that one out. Like Tina's naked flesh pressing against mine.

We explored by lathering each other up and kissed under the spray until we couldn't stand it anymore and, still damp, we fell out of the bathroom, onto the futon in a slippery tangle. We'd established the precedent and forwent condom use.

"I don't see why you complain about your shower," I said after. "That was the best shower, ever."

We hadn't yet discovered the Buffalo Bar and Grill, so we drove a ways further up highway 55 that evening to get "Detroit Style" Pizza and shoot some pool at Norm's Wayside roadhouse. Neither of us had heard of "Detroit Style" pizza before and we agreed we'd been fortunate up to that point.

"Does 'Detroit Style' mean they top it with motor oil?" I wondered.

I spent that night out in Buffalo with Tina and we had sex again in the bedroom, but first I had to clear the room of an infestation of Asian beetles. Tina had two battery-powered bug vacuums. One looked like a pig, as I recall. I used them to clear the ceiling corners of a remarkable number of the invasive insects. They were less-spotted and paler, but otherwise identical to ladybugs.

We sat cross-legged for a while on the floor next to the open bedroom window and smoked cigarettes while we talked. Tina made me promise again to always be honest with her, "even if it's bad."

I readily agreed and then I told her that I was still kind of nervous and unsure about dating. I felt like I didn't know what I was doing, since I'd been married so long. Tina told me that she was terrified to start dating again. She said it had been over a year since she'd been with a man.

"That's why it took me so long to decide to meet up with you," she explained. "I haven't been with anyone for a long time and I knew from the moment you shook my hand that this was going to turn into something and it might be something wonderful or it might end in a fiery wreck. Either way it's really scary."

We agreed to be "scared together."

We went to bed curled up together and I woke to Tina's head on my shoulder.

Once our sexual relationship began, it was abundant and satisfying. Tina wasn't a very active lover, but her kisses and her scent were plenty enough to excite me and she almost never declined.

We spent most of Saturday together, too, and after a considerable amount of sleepy foreplay, we had sex again for good measure, but eventually it was time to get back to reality. Tina had a family reunion to get to on Sunday, otherwise, I might very well have spent another night. I asked to use the shower and Tina very politely brought me a fresh towel. This, I later noticed was her routine. Every time I took a shower at her home, she produced a fresh, clean towel for my exclusive use. She declined to join me that time, saying she needed to take a "business shower" which evidently required more focus and solitude.

I emerged from the steamy bathroom clean and mostly dressed.

Tina was on the futon tearing pages out of a fashion magazine.

"I really hate to be the one to have to tell you this," I got Tina's attention. "But I think there's something wrong with your shower."

"Oh no. Now what?" She was braced for disastrous news.

"I don't know," I said. "There's definitely something wrong. Somehow this shower just wasn't as satisfying as the last time I was in there."

"You brat!" she shoved me back a step and laughed. "I thought I was going to have to talk to Lord Buffalo." Then she hooked her arms around my neck and pulled me in for a kiss.

I was all smiles and in no mood to go anywhere, but the "sweet sorrow" of parting began as it must.

I had my own encounter with Lord Buffalo when I was getting into my van. Tina had directed me to park in her mom's designated parking spot, since she was away and building management, it seemed, was none too pleased.

"Lord Buffalo" was Tina's nickname for Jim, the Buffalo Hotel's semi-disabled live-in superintendent. He'd sent one of his minions to slip a notecard with a threatening, but misspelled message under my wiper blade. This parking spot was only for "tenets," it admonished. I could still feel Tina's parting kiss on my lips and it didn't damper my mood. It was better than getting towed! I laughed, lit a cigarette and was on my way down the road.

My own bed felt very empty back at home. I composed a late-night text. "I haven't slept. I smell you on my T-shirt and somehow, I can still taste and feel your last kiss on my lips. You make a lasting impression."

The next day, Tina texted back from her family gathering. "I tossed and turned all night. Didn't sleep at all. I can't wait to see you again. Every time I think about you, I have to look down at the floor so the family can't see the look in my eyes. Maura has informed everyone that I've been dating someone — add that to the stress of a family gathering! XOXO"

Quicksand Rescue

It was one of our early dates. I'd driven out to Buffalo to spend at least a day and a night with Tina. Her mom was staying with Scott down in Farmington so we had the apartment to ourselves for the night.

Tina didn't seem to have much explored her environs and wasn't sure where the nearest bars and restaurants might be. I'd previously identified a couple in the area, but they weren't in easy walking distance. Since the old Buffalo Hotel that served as Tina's home was in the historic downtown, I was pretty sure we were overlooking some nearby entertainment and I was determined to find it. We decided to go for a walk. It had rained recently and it was humid. The sidewalks still had a sheen of water. Central Avenue had been under seemingly perpetual construction and wasn't yet paved. Dump trucks had recently poured tons of leveling sand. I told Tina, who was weary of the project, that sand was a good sign. Concrete would soon follow, I assured her.

She wasn't convinced. "They already did this before. Then they tore it all up and started over."

Tina had boots on and I was wearing casual shoes, so we decided to directly cross the construction zone, but quickly realized our mistake when Tina took a step and sank to her knee in the damp, loose sand. Tina was stuck and as she struggled to free herself, she only became more mired. It was quicksand! By the time I was 44 years old, I was pretty well disabused of the notion that quicksand was ever going to be a potential hazard in my life, yet here it was.

I found a plank nearby and situated it behind Tina so I could stand on it and get firmer footing to pull Tina out of the morass without sinking into it myself. The rescue effort was successful and Tina threw her arms around me, proclaiming me her hero. I didn't realize the significance of the moment at the time.

We circumnavigated the treacherous main street and continued our adventure, exploring the town together. We found a place Called BJs to get sandwiches for lunch. We'd made an effort to brush the wet sand off, but apparently not enough of one. I was a bit embarrassed when we left the deli and I noticed a considerable amount of sand on the floor under the table we'd been sitting at.

Google maps seemed to indicate there was a bar right there, too, but it was well-hidden and we didn't discover the infamous dive that would become part of our mornings until some time later.

Tina showed me where the cinema was and we checked out a couple shops. Later that evening, we ended up driving up the highway to Norm's Roadhouse to shoot some pool and have some drinks.

When we returned to the apartment, Tina brought up the quicksand rescue again. "Have you ever seen the Princess Bride? Or read it?"

"I've never read the book, but it's one of my favorite movies," I told her. "Have fun storming the castle!" I quoted Billy Crystal from the film.

"I don't know if we have any rodents of unusual size in Buffalo, but I didn't know we had quicksand, either. You rescued me just like Westley rescued Princess Buttercup. You're my Westley," she declared.

In the earlier days of our relationship, sleeping together in the actual bed in the actual bedroom in Buffalo was still an option (before we became relegated to the futon, ostensibly due to perpetual clutter on the bed) and we smoked cigarettes and drank whiskey and made love in the dark little room. I believe that was the first time Tina told me she loved me. "I think I'm falling in love with you," she said.

Amazingly, I felt the same. I wanted to spend every possible minute with her. I thought she'd be put off if I'd admitted the depth of feelings I felt growing for her so very early on, but was able to reciprocate once she kicked that door open.

"Well, you know," I began, "I was thinking something along those lines, myself." I paused for the briefest consideration before plunging head-first. "Tina Mary Dziewkaski, I love you, too."

The euphoria in that room was off any chart, meter, scale or theoretical state.

Maura came back to the apartment the next day and Tina was enthused to tell her mom about how I'd rescued her from quicksand and pointed out the shelf I'd put up for her the day before. She was beaming with pride and adoration. It occurred to me later what a coincidence it was that she'd previously mentioned getting stuck in quicksand as a metaphor for becoming engrossed in a story.

From then on, Tina often referred to me as her Westley, which I just took to mean "true love," but I was missing something. Westley never denied his Buttercup anything. His response to even her most outrageous demands or abuses was always "as you wish."

Like Westley for his Buttercup, I indulged my Tina anything. That made me perfect supply for a narcissist, but I was blissfully unaware of the quicksand I was becoming entrapped in, myself. At that point, Tina was still in the early stages of idealizing and love-bombing me. I remember around that time, commenting on how much I was enjoying our time together and Tina shot back wistfully, "It's always great in the beginning." She went on to warn me about what a terrible person she was, which I found laughably absurd - she was delightful! "Just wait," she said. "You'll find out."

Even then, I think she knew exactly how our relationship was going to play out. She'd probably been through the cycle many times before she ever met me. Idealize-Devalue-Discard. She was probably in different points of that cycle with different sources of narcissistic supply (essentially, validation) even as she was building me up as her perfect savior and one true love, but on that weekend, I got to be the hero. I was loved and adored. That's all I could see at the moment.

Skinny Dipping

I had again driven out to Buffalo for what might have been our fourth or fifth "date." It was a warm summer evening and Tina and I went for a walk. She led me along some wooded paths and down some almost-hidden concrete stairs that eventually deposited us on the beach of Buffalo Lake.

We took a lazy stroll on the beach, her and I, the only people who mattered in the world. Our hands entwined and then fell away before she encircled my elbow and we continued on, arm in arm as the faintest hint of red began to tinge the western sky.

Delighted, Tina suddenly stooped over to pick up a red stone she'd somehow spotted with her notoriously faulty eyes. Holding it up for closer inspection, she verified an agate find.

I hugged her and congratulated her on the discovery, having already learned of her obsession with agates.

We came upon a rocky nook in a stand of trees at the edge of the beach, where Tina wanted to stop and sit for a while. We both plopped down on the stony sand and watched the waves gently lap the shore.

"Twitterpated." Tina said, "it's the word I think of when I think of you." She was aware of the word being used in Bambi, but thought of it as her own word to describe the flutters in her heart and stomach she associated with my presence. It was tremendously flattering and endearing.

I leaned back on my elbows and Tina snuggled close to me as we looked at the glinting lake.

"The water looks so cool and refreshing," Tina said, suddenly sitting upright, simultaneously loosening all the bits and pieces that covered and supported her bits and pieces. "Skinny dip?" she invited.

Her bosom exposed so suddenly and gloriously, it was hard to say no, but I did. We had a sense of being alone, but I was aware that we were on a public beach and there was plenty of daylight left. I was startled by her impulsiveness.

I gently persuaded her to cover up, promising to go skinny dipping with her when we were able to get up to her grandpa's cabin.

Tina pulled her top back on with some reluctance and within moments we heard voices coming from the vicinity of the stairs. Two women emerged onto the beach with three children just then and I breathed a sigh of relief.

"That was close," I said and we decided it was about time for us to vacate the beach. We could be all the naked we wanted back at the apartment.

Histrionics are associated with exhibitionist tendencies and people afflicted with narcissistic or histrionic personality disorders are often oblivious to consequences and act impulsively. I'd learn over time that Tina could be dangerously impulsive, particularly when she'd been drinking (which was always).

We passed by the family group and made our way back up the steps toward the Buffalo Hotel.

Tina led me over to the dumpsters before going in to the building to show me something she wanted retrieved. There was a silver-colored hard case atop the heap of garbage in one dumpster. It looked like the sort of case a traveling salesman might use and it appeared in pristine condition. She wanted to salvage it, but hadn't been able to reach it herself. Ever obliging, I hopped up, planting my belly on the rim and stretched out to grab the handle. I could just reach it and held it aloft triumphantly when I got my feet back on the ground.

We went through the narrow alley, where Tina pointed out a number of potted plants and flowers, on the ground and on window sills. She said the building manager, Jim had ordered the tenants responsible for them to get rid of them. He believed they attracted bugs. That sounded a bit crazy to me. There was a lot I still had to learn about the Buffalo Hotel.

When we entered the lobby of the old brown brick building, we encountered a small, older woman with dyed red hair coming down the stairs. She shared a name with my dear departed grandma: Irene. She stopped on her way out to tell Tina that Jim wanted to see both of us in his apartment.

"Oh, great," Tina said after Irene had left the lobby. "I wonder what I did this time."

"Both of us?" I'd heard a bit about Jim before. Tina referred to him as Lord Buffalo. I couldn't imagine why he'd want to see me, though, or even how he knew who I was or that I was in the building.

Jim lived on the second floor. Tina knew the way. Something told me to leave the hard case behind. I left it on the floor near the landing and followed Tina down the dim and narrow hall. The door to Jim's den was open. It wasn't an apartment as such. It appeared to be no more than one large bedroom with some sort of water closet. A double bed dominated the room and Lord Buffalo sat on it like a throne, eyeing Tina and I in obvious judgment.

Jim was an older man with unwashed, longish-thinning gray hair combed across his head. He was wearing only a dirty A-frame shirt, black socks and boxer shorts.

There were shelves on one side of the bed stacked with canned foods and shelf-stable microwave meals. He didn't appear to have a refrigerator. On the other side of the bed was a bank of security monitors. That seemed wildly out of place. I didn't understand what kind of place the Buffalo Hotel was.

"I'm glad you both came," Jim said. "I've been wanting to talk to you."

"Me?" I was stunned.

"Yes." Jim sat up straighter. "If you're moving in, there's going to have to be an adjustment to rent," he said.

"Moving in?" I chuckled nervously. "No. I live in Minneapolis. I'm just visiting." I was really puzzled. I'd spent a couple weekend nights there by then. That was all.

"And he's your… what?" he looked to Tina.

"He's my… This is Dan, my boyfriend."

"I see. Because there's extra water usage and things like that, so if you're going to move in, we'll have to renegotiate."

"I'm just visiting," I assured him. "I'm not moving in. I have my own place in Minneapolis."

"Uh-huh. The lady who used to have your apartment used to slip me twenty bucks when she'd have a man over," Jim said to Tina.

I was entering the Twilight Zone.

"I saw you two at the dumpster," Jim went on. "That's the main thing. Whatever you took out of there, if it's going in your car, that's one thing, but I don't want you bringing it in the building." He took a moment to look us each in the eye. "Bugs." He finished.

I felt relieved I'd left the case back at the landing.

"OK," Tina put in, "Don't worry. That went right into Dan's van and I for sure won't be bringing anything in from the dumpster. I promise," Tina said.

"How do you like the new apartment?" Jim asked.

"It's way better," Tina said. "So much better."

When I'd first begun dating Tina, she and her mom were in the process of moving from an even smaller efficiency unit down the hall into apartment 19.

"It's the best apartment in the building," Jim said with a hint of pride. "Used to be part of the ballroom, back when this was a hotel. Do you know? There are marble pillars inside some of these walls. Marble." he chuckled.

It was an odd juxtaposition to imagine, cheap plastic tiles were falling off the bathroom walls, but behind the sheet rock were marble fixtures from past glory days.

"There's a lot of history in this building – but your apartment – that one, we did up really nice. So you like it, huh?"

"Oh, yes." Tina said, mustering some enthusiasm. "We're really grateful that we were able to get that unit."

"I thought it would be good for you and your mom," Jim said with an air of satisfaction.

From there, we got a brief history lesson on the Buffalo Hotel. Jim knew quite a lot about the subject. In all, I'd guess we stood nervously in Jim's doorway for about 20 minutes before he finally gave us leave to go about our business.

Tina was relieved. "The last time I was summoned to Lord Buffalo's lair, I got stuck talking to him for an hour," Tina explained. "And at least this time he had a shirt on."

The Buffalo Hotel wasn't an ordinary apartment building. That's something I was just beginning to learn and it continued to baffle me as time went on. That historic frontier-style structure and the people who lived there could be the subjects of an entire book.

Back in the penthouse, Tina opened the pristine, but contraband dumpster case. Inside, were foam inserts with product cutouts, as I suspected, but no sign of any bugs. The case was in like-new condition and Tina was pretty happy with the score. She had an endless need for containers.

"What's with Jim's obsession with bugs?" I wondered aloud. "Besides, I assume this case was, until recently, somewhere in this building. If it had bugs, they would have come from inside here."

Tina picked up a clip board with one of her adult coloring pages on it and sat on the futon. "Could you pour us a couple drinks?" She asked as she rummaged in her box of colored pencils.

"Of course, my lady." I found the bottle and mixed a whiskey and Diet Coke for her and one with regular Coca-Cola for myself.

Tina was stressed by the visit with Jim. I'd learned that, similar to my ex-wife, her coloring hobby was one of her relaxation techniques. That, weed and alcohol. And sex. She made use of all of them that night.

I understood the coloring hobby, but Tina had another habit that was more puzzling to me. She was engaged in it the next morning while we watched South Park on my laptop and picked at a plate of crispy bacon I'd fried up for us. She went through fashion magazines and catalogs and tore out pages, setting them in piles. When she reached the end of a magazine, she'd throw what was left of the decimated book away. Nearly all of the pages she deemed worthy of sparing were outfits or clothing items she seemed to like. Sometimes, jewelry. It puzzled me, but for some reason I never asked her about it.

We didn't linger in the apartment long. I had a radio interview for work that afternoon at the State Fair and since I had to be there, I was bringing Tina along to make a fun day of it. Before we departed for the Fair, Tina gathered up the torn out magazine and catalog pages and put them in a manila envelope. She put that envelope in a magazine rack.

Then we were out the door and I didn't give it any further consideration until the next time I observed the odd ritual.

The Music Mirror

In the beginning, Tina made me feel like I could do no wrong. It was as if we had literally been created for one another. We fit together in every way. Despite our sizable age difference, we even shared tastes in music, film and other pop-culture – or so it seemed. It eventually occurred that it wasn't cosmic coincidence. She was mirroring me, but I only understood that long after it was too late.

Mirroring is one of the first things a narcissist does when hooking a new source of narcissistic supply. It's part of the love bombing stage.

I'd hazard a wager that one of the earliest "mirrors" in a budding relationship with a narcissist is a shared taste in music. Close runners-up would probably be liking the same kinds of movies and authors.

Early on, I was surprised that Tina seemed to share an appreciation for a wide range of older music with me. Being that she's from a younger generation, I didn't expect a huge amount of cross-over in that department. From old school hip-hop to 80's synth-pop, Tina thought my taste in music was exceptional.

I knew that couldn't be the whole story and I'd garnered enough bits and pieces to know Tina also liked some metal and grungy rock. I was prepared to give it a go, but she was oddly reticent about it.

Every once in a while, I tried to coax some of her other likes out of her. I didn't want to monopolize the radio, so to speak.

We were in our bubble out in the Buffalo penthouse listening to Pandora on amplified speakers connected to my laptop. Internet was streaming from my cell phone's hot spot. Entertainment options were pretty limited at Tina's apartment unless I brought my bag of electronics out with me - so I always did.

The usual mix of 80's funk and newer electronic dance music was pumping out of my speakers. Tina was singing and dancing along as we enjoyed a bottle of Hell Cat Maggie whiskey together. I tried again to open Tina up about her other musical tastes. Pandora was pretty much the only way I listened to music anymore and it was always on during our many long road trips together. So, I proposed creating two new Pandora stations. First, I'd create one based entirely on Tina's favorite songs and bands, then I'd merge my station with hers for what I expected would be a mutually enjoyable mix. We'd never be subjected too long to something we didn't like and we'd be exposed to each other's tastes, offering a chance to learn to appreciate them. I thought it was a damn good idea, but Tina was a still a little reluctant.

"It's like, when I'm with you, I like to listen to your music," she tried explaining. "When I'm with Amber, I like to listen to Amber's music, which is more the hard rock and metal kind of stuff."

"But what does Tina like for herself?"

The odd thing was, she didn't seem to have an answer to that.

I did eventually get a list of songs and bands out of her, though. Not a long list, but enough to start her customized station. KTIN, I called it. Mine was WDAN and the merged station that I created about a week later was dubbed KTND.

I figured the merged station (K-Tina-N-Dan) would become our road trip staple, but Tina would usually ask that I switch it back to WDAN, actually preferring to keep her music choices out of the mix of what we listened to together.

It's not so simple as to say that Tina simply pretended to like whatever I liked. She did have some background on some of the things we had in common. She could rap along with NWA, for example. The first movie we saw together was Straight Outta Compton, because of that genuine shared interest. It was sometimes simply pretending. Sometimes, it was a matter of emphasis or exaggeration. The point was to amplify perceived commonalities and sideline any differences. This probably takes place to some degree with any new relationship, but much more so with a narcissist.

It was a rare moment of honesty that provided some insight into Tina's chameleonic nature when she explained how her musical preferences varied to fit her current company.

Sometimes she'd say things that gave pause, but if she saw even subtle signs of my discomfort, she'd quickly backpedal and start spinning some word salad to confuse and disorient me and then swiftly change the subject while I was still trying to detangle a near-meaningless sting of words. She was really good at blowing past topics she didn't want to discuss. She'd leap three topics ahead so by the time I figured out how to respond to her latest statement, I'd generally forgotten what had caused me concern to begin with. For a while, anyhow. Those topics usually swam back to me when I was by myself, away from Tina.

During one of our early weekends together in the Buffalo penthouse, she told me how she used to have all of these psychological problems. She'd been through treatment for drug and alcohol abuse and used to engage in dangerous and self-destructive behaviors. She assured me that she was "so much better now. Yay for personal growth!" she said.

She told me about a time that she was going out one night to meet some man for a "blind date." She'd stopped at the liquor store for a bottle of whiskey and then drove off in the dark of night into some farmer's vast field to find this man she'd never met before. How this blind date got set up was never revealed. I was horrified by the incredibly careless way she'd put herself in danger, though and she assured me that she wasn't like that any more, then moved swiftly on through other topics and the story was dropped. I just said something like "We probably wouldn't have gotten along back then."

There were red flags. Warning signs were peeking out from the very beginning. Tina was sometimes flat out telling me what she was up to and what to expect, before backtracking and misdirecting. I had promised to listen to her, but ironically, the one thing she frequently said that I really should have paid heed to was the only thing I dismissed. "I'm not worthy of you," or some variation of that sentiment. "I'm not good enough for you." I should have listened.

A Chilly Reception at Scott's Farm

Wednesday, September 9th 2015 was the day I met Scott and his son Doug at their Farmington estate.

The day before, I'd tried a few times without success to reach Tina. That was a Tuesday. I hadn't noticed it yet, but there was a pattern with Tuesdays. Tina was never available on Tuesdays. I missed her and at the end of the night, I'd texted her a little rhyme.

"Lying in my lonely bed;
Upon my shoulder, Tina's head;
I'm missing;
Looking forward to next time's kissing!"

Tina finally responded to my messages around noon on Wednesday. She wrote that she was down in Farmington for a funeral for Scott's aunt. "I'm in a CATHOLIC CHURCH," she texted. "I even took communion. Sadly, no wine was served. I haven't burst into flames yet, but that might just be because my greatest temptation is currently in Minneapolis."

"Please try to avoid spontaneous combustion," I replied. "I'm out of prednisone and my back is making an effort to murder me. Not getting much done here in Minneapolis, today. Miss you!"

A few hours later, Tina texted again. "I wish you weren't dealing with a homicidal back. I wish I could kiss all the pain away. I'm still in Farmington and I miss you."

"How long are you going to be around there?" I asked.

"If you'd like to come here, you may. My mom will have to spend the night because she's been drinking, but we could go out to Buffalo," she replied.

That sounded perfect to me! "Do you need a rescue? Damsel in distress?"

"If that's what it takes to see you... Help me Obi Wan Kenobi. I need your help (almost?) Ha. No worries, but I miss you so much it kinda hurts."

She was pretty close with the Star Wars quote and I was impressed. Love bombing was still underway and made me feel good enough that I could overcome the knife between my vertebra. Tina reminded me of the address and gave instructions to drive to the back of the barn when I arrived.

I packed up an overnight bag, and put my computer and speakers in my briefcase to bring along.

It was getting close to dusk when I arrived. I drove around to the far side of the big barn as instructed. The main barn doors were wide open and a small party was going on inside. Tina spotted me right away and met me with an enthusiastic hug as I climbed out of the van. She offered me a beer and made a few quick introductions to Scott's two preteen daughters and a heavy-set guy named Mark. I said hi to Maura and then Tina led me out to find Scott and make that long-anticipated introduction.

We came upon both Scott and his son Doug by a large fire pit full of brush that they were just getting lit. Scott was about my age, about my height, with dark hair, very tan skin and a short beard. He shook my hand firmly as Tina made introductions.

"Nice to finally meet you," I said. "Tina speaks highly of you."

"I don't know about that," Scott replied.

"And this is Doug," Tina said.

I turned my attention to him. He was about my height and build with dark hair like his father and had a scruffy beard of fine whiskers. He looked to be about Tina's age. Maybe younger. I reached out my hand, but Doug with a beer in his right hand couldn't be bothered to uncross his arms to shake it. He twisted slightly to point his left hand, projecting slightly from under his right elbow, in my direction.

I briefly grasped half of four limp fingers. "Nice to meet you, Doug," I said.

A less than enthusiastic half-nod was his reply.

Neither Scott nor Doug seemed very interested in further conversation with me. I was surprised to be getting something of a cold shoulder, especially since Tina had told me several times how Scott wanted to meet me. Here was his chance and he had nothing much to say.

"Well, I guess we'll leave them to building this huge bonfire," Tina said and led me back toward the barn. "I slept with him once," Tina confided quietly as we made our way. "Doug, I mean."

"I figured," I said and then shuddered at the thought of her and her mother sharing a lover, when Tina raised the specter of the alternative by clarifying.

She gave me a quick tour. In the barn, there was a platform built with carpeting, upon which was a pool table. The other side of the barn was full of machinery and toys, like dirt bikes. Scott, Doug and Tina's brother Nick were dirt bike enthusiasts. Semi-pros, actually. Scott had created a big dirt bike track on the property for him and his son to practice racing and stunts. Evidently that track is what brought Tina's and Scott's families together. Maura had somehow spotted it years ago and asked if Nick could ride on it sometimes. That's the story as I was told it, anyhow.

I suspected there was something else that brought Scott and Maura together. Ultimately, they did have an affair and became something unspecified, but akin to friends with benefits. Tina told me with some annoyance that Scott wouldn't "claim" her mother, as she put it.

Tina and I finished the beers we had in hand, said goodbye to her mother and got on the road to Buffalo. It was going to be an hour and a half drive, but the road looked infinitely more appealing than spending any more time with Scott and Doug.

On the drive, Tina hinted that there might have been more to her relationship with Doug than she'd let on. First, I'd been told that they had just been family friends for years – almost like cousins. That night, I learned she'd had sex with him *once*. She told me he had a girlfriend named Olivia, but also told me with irritation, that she had to find out about her through facebook. Then she backpedaled and told me that although, she'd found it useful to learn about Olivia, she didn't use facebook herself.

"Why do you care if Doug has a girlfriend?" I asked.

"I don't," Tina said. "It's just that he's a player with all these girls and he always insisted to me he was single, but I found out his facebook says he's engaged! It doesn't matter. This was a while ago, anyhow. Never mind. I'm not making sense."

She wasn't, really, but her confused jumble of words raised some unease for me.

What Tina was doing, unbeknownst to me at the time was a favorite manipulation tactic of narcissists called triangulation. That's when a narcissist uses a third party to belittle or instill unease in their target. A lot of times, it's a jealousy play. At the same time she was triangulating Doug against me, she was simultaneously using me to triangulate Doug.

I think Tina could tell that I was growing more uneasy and she shuffled through a number of topics in rapid succession, having the effect of resetting the conversation.

"Have you ever been to a strip club?" She asked.

"Yeah. I've been to a couple," I said.

"Do you think it would be bad for your career if you were dating a stripper and people found out?"

"Uh. I don't know. Possibly," I said, hesitantly. I was the head of a conservative-leaning, political non-profit at the time. "Why?"

"Just making conversation. Although, I did think about it. Stripping. Scott's friends said 'I'd pay to see that.' I think I'm too fat now, though."

"Look, as your boyfriend, I'd very much prefer it if you didn't take your clothes off in front of other men, but you are in no way fat. You're incredibly sexy." I assured her.

Tina shuffled through a number of other topics and talk of Doug faded to distant memory. We joked around, laughed, sang along to Depeche Mode and generally enjoyed the rest of the drive out to Buffalo.

As usual, we had a great night alone in our bubble in the little efficiency penthouse atop the Buffalo Hotel.

The next day, we decided to take a walk around town. I was still certain there was a bar hidden in Buffalo's historic downtown and I was determined to find it. On the way out, Tina noticed she had mail. The lobby of the historic hotel-cum-flophouse still had a front desk and behind it, old-fashioned wooden mail slots with key hooks beneath, like you see in westerns. Not at all secure, but quaint.

We wandered into a gift shop where Tina fell in love with an antique jewelry box. Her birthday was about a month and a half away, so I made note of it. She ended up buying a couple wooden tiles with numbers engraved. A six and a nine. 69. Tina never got bored of that number combination.

My Kind of Crazy

After a considerable and revelatory walk around historic downtown Buffalo, we took the long way back towards the apartment. This brought us along a meandering path by the lake and into the back of the big parking lot, near the library. We crossed the lot and were cutting through the narrow alley between the Buffalo Hotel and the tax preparer's office when Tina said, "sometimes I worry that I'm crazy."

That seemed to come from nowhere. "I don't know about that," I replied after a moment, "But if you are, you're my kind of crazy."

The words sounded sweet and appropriate when I said them but I didn't give it much thought. Maybe they sprang from deep rooted instinct. Those words were far truer than I realized.

Certainly a big part of what made Tina and I fit together so well for a while was that we both suffered psychological problems born from childhood trauma.

I grew up with an alcoholic drug-using father. My parents were in an on-again, off-again relationship that was more than a little destabilizing to the home life.

Actually, I was so worried about not making the same mistakes as my father had that I didn't even think to keep an eye on avoiding my mother's pitfalls. She was codependent. And like my mother, I adapted to my uncertain surroundings by fawning, freezing, denial and other unhealthy codependent tendencies. My brain was already wired up with defense mechanisms, including a tendency to forget certain traumas and unpleasantness and right around that time in my relationship with Tina, those subconscious tricks and trapdoors started activating. I couldn't tell anything was amiss. If anything, my bond to Tina seemed stronger and more familiar because of it. It began to feel like somehow, I'd always known her and we were meant to be together.

Narcissists fit with codependents like a key in a lock. The initial stage of love bombing and mirroring was beginning to give way to trauma bonding, triangulation and periodic ghosting. Intermittent reinforcement and minor abuses were beginning, but I was blissfully overlooking them as I swallowed the hook ever deeper.

Back in the apartment, Tina opened her mail and was disheartened. There was a notice from the county that her recently obtained food stamp benefits were about to be revoked unless she either obtained part-time work or began participating in a job-readiness program.

Her mom worked and paid all the bills. She also bought Tina cigarettes, alcohol, medication, and an abundance of marijuana. Some help with groceries via Wright County Human Services and keeping the apartment reasonably clean was Tina's contribution to the household.

Tina had various reasons for being unemployed. Some seemed reasonable. She told me she had a genetic defect that compromised her immune system so she didn't want work that involved frequent contact with the general public (like cashiers, receptionists and bank tellers). She was a recent transplant to Buffalo, but simultaneously dwelt in Farmington and at her dad's house in Cold Spring. She was largely beholden to her mother for transportation and without me around to afford her some travel freedom was often compelled to tag along to wherever Maura felt like being. She didn't have a car of her own, but kept insisting that her dad was eventually going to give her one of his fleet of Saturn sedans he'd collected since the company stopped manufacturing them.

I hated to see Tina unhappy and I was a natural problem solver. I had a solution in mind almost immediately and it was brilliant in it's elegance.

I was the president of a non-profit political organization. It was fairly well known and had been well-funded until recently. I'd been falling behind on fundraising and needed help in that department..

One of the stipulations for Tina to keep getting her full (rather generous) food benefit from the county was that she work no more than 20 hours per week.

Fundraising for my outfit was a part time job we could easily keep under the limit and also avoid the need for the job-readiness program that Tina definitely didn't want to participate in.

Tina had been complaining that her laptop had stopped working. She had an outdated cell phone and there was no internet at the apartment unless I was there with my hot-spot-enabled smart phone.

I drafted a fundraising agreement and put together papers to register Tina with the state attorney general's office as a permitted fundraiser. I had a spare smart phone with a wi-fi hot spot capability that I could activate and give her, as well as a spare work laptop that she'd need to do the fundraising work from the corporation's donor database. I solved so many problems at once, I'll admit I was pretty damn proud of myself. It looked like it would be win-win-win for both of us.

I added the other smart phone to my own cell phone plan, unburdening Tom of the need to keep paying for Tina's phone (I thought), which finally hooked Tina up with internet.

I started training Tina by showing her the script I loosely followed for fundraising calls and Then I made a call to show her how I go about it, logging the results on my own computer. I was going to pay Tina on commission and from my first sample call, I garnered a $1,000 donation, which would have been $150 in Tina's pocket just like that, so I gave her that commission as encouragement. I'd gotten lucky. It usually takes more effort than one call to raise a thousand dollars, but I thought it was a good demonstration.

When I left for home that evening, I thought our future was looking bright.

Tina texted me later to let me know that I'd left my coat behind. The weather was nice so I hadn't thought of it when I packed up to leave. "Since your coat is hanging up here, Jim's going to count this as you moving in and raise my rent," she joked.

The Coincidental Donor

My next trip out to Tina's involved a bit of business. I got out to Buffalo much earlier in the day than usual. I brought Tina an internet hot-spot-enabled smart phone, a Windows laptop and documents to sign and mail to the attorney general, as well as Wright County. That was all to list her as a fundraiser for my organization and certify her part time employment with me so she could keep her food benefit going.

I had put together a spreadsheet for Tina's use in making fundraising calls and was showing her how to use it. Although there were thousands of entries, as we began to go through it, Tina immediately spotted a name she recognized. "Oh, wow. I know her," she said.

"Really?" I looked over the record. Becky was a mid-range repeat donor and the record showed that she also regularly participated in action items we sent out. She was a valuable member.

It turned out that Tina used to have a pretty close relationship with her and her husband, Ben. They lived down the road from Tina's dad's house up in Cold Spring and Tina used to spend time over at their place. Becky was an artist. Ben was a good friend of her dad's who, she said, and had been helpful to Tina when she'd gone through rehab for substance abuse (she was adamant that it wasn't a problem for her anymore).

I suggested that should be Tina's first call. I figured it would be a really easy way to get that ball rolling.

Tina didn't think it would be so easy. "She and I had a falling out," she explained. Evidently, Ben who had been sober for an indeterminate period of time had given a lot of his time to Tina when she was going through her efforts to stay sober, years back," but Becky, who was the supporter who needed to be called, didn't want anything to do with her.

Tina said she didn't know why, but Becky had turned on her, out of the blue, and didn't like her anymore.

We moved on from Becky's entry in the database and I discovered that the organization actually had a number of other supporters in the small town of Cold Spring.

I suggested a few starting points for Tina, went over the script with her and was ready to coach her through her first batch of calls, but ultimately, she declined to make any calls that day. She wasn't feeling up to it anymore, she said.

I was disappointed, of course, but just closed the laptop and suggested we go out for some lunch.

I spent the night out in Buffalo and Tina told me a few stories from her "wild days" that had led to rehab for her. Some of it was fairly disturbing. And I concluded that she and I probably would not have hit it off back then.

One incident in particular was pretty disturbing. She told me that she'd had a "blind date" set up one night (by whom or by what means was never expounded on) and she was meant to meet the man for the first time at his car which would be parked in a remote field. She'd gone to the liquor store and picked up a bottle of whiskey and set out to find this date. To say the circumstances she described were questionable would be a bit like calling the deeper beliefs of Scientology, "unlikely."

Probably fortunately for Tina, she was unable to locate her would-be date.

She followed the directions provided to her (by sources never revealed), but after searching fruitlessly for an hour or so, she gave up and went home.

I was trying not to react too strongly, but Tina definitely detected some amount of recoil. "I was pretty messed up back then," she went on. "I'm much much better now. I would never do something so stupid, now."

"I should hope not!"

"I was really out of control back then and I ended up having to to go rehab. Actually, after I got out, Becky's husband Ben was helpful to me. He'd quit drinking, too and he was the only one who really understood what I was going through."

At the time, I was without question a problem drinker and Tina drank even more than me and she smoked weed daily, but for some reason, I believed that she had gotten her substance issues under control. I guess it was comparative.

We drank plenty of whiskey and beer.

We had sex on the futon. Tina had told me our first time that she liked it a little rough and I usually tried (in probably what she'd consider a mild manner) to oblige her preferences, but took control in a very slow, gentle and loving way on this occasion. She didn't mind. "So that's what making love is," she commented after we were spent. I felt sorry that she'd been unaware prior.

We cuddled for a long, warm, fuzzy while atop a tangle of sheets and blankets, naked limbs entwined, before Tina finally got up to light a cigarette. "That's something I really like about sex with you," she started before taking a drag of her cigarette. "You stay in bed with me and cuddle. It really makes me feel close to you," she said. "And you look me in the eyes."

It never hurts the ego to be complimented on one's lovemaking prowess, unless it's followed by something along the lines of "Like the times me and Doug had sex... It was always just wham-bam-thank-you-ma'am and he'd get off and be gone," which was exactly what Tina said next.

She'd told me before that she'd slept with Doug 'once.' That didn't sound like once. That bounced around unpleasantly in my head for a few minutes, but Tina put her naked body back up against mine after her cigarette, caressed my skin, called me "incredible" and told me how she loved me more than agates and tofu. I settled back into more pleasant feelings.

I spent the rest of the weekend with Tina out in Buffalo. We went to Walmart to stock up on groceries, stopped at the liquor store for Mickey's beer and more Hellcat Maggie whiskey. We shot pool at the Buffalo Bar and Grill, got Bloody Marys at Jay's Down and Under, and had more sex. It was a fun weekend, as usual, but trying again the next day, I was again unable to get Tina started on her new job doing fundraising. Sunday, I left feeling a little frustrated by that, but I'd had a great weekend overall, so I could let it go pretty easily. I figured I'd try again next time.

Tina had opted to spend some idle time coloring some intricate drawings and tearing pages out of a magazine. Those, I noticed, went into a manila envelope, which she put into a magazine rack and they'd later disappear. It was an odd practice, but Tina had quirks and I never asked her about it.

When I got home, I realized I'd been forgetful again and texted Tina, "Oh crap... I moved in again.. Left my coat behind. I guess that's a good excuse to see you again, sooner, rather than later."

"Since You've decided to move in, I suppose I'll have to grease the palms of Lord Buffalo," Tina replied. "I'll have to find a new street corner to sell my wares; I'm waayy too classy for just a curb and a deserted dirt path. At least today is sunny and warm. A wool coat would cook a Dan faster than his oven on wheels. I miss you terribly. I keep looking for your van in the lot. *sigh*."

Cabin Confessions

I went to my old home, where my ex-wife and dog resided along with a considerable amount of my property that I hadn't yet moved out.

I was collecting mail, picking up a few odds and ends and visiting for a while. I sat on a reclining, rocking love seat that was called "the snuggler," by the manufacturer. It was slightly too big for a chair and slightly too small to be a typical love seat. It had been part of a large and exciting redecorating purchase Jessica and I had made about a year after buying the house.

Clyde, my cocker spaniel hopped up onto my lap and a short while later, Jessica sat down next to me. The nature of the chair put us very close. It felt very familiar. It felt like a typical day at home, almost like I'd never moved out, months back.

Jessica seemed likewise comfortable with the familiar and she kissed me. Nothing seemed immediately amiss as I reciprocated, but I snapped out of the moment as Tina flashed through my mind. I thought about her weekends at Scotts, about her murky relationship with Doug and thought with almost a mental shrug, "maybe it's going to be one of *those kind* of relationships."

At first, I relaxed and let things progress. Things heated up and before long, Jessica and I had made out way into the bedroom and clothes were starting to come off. Again, Tina crossed my mind, but more forcefully and distinctly. Her face, which I regarded as quite beautiful swam up into my mind's eye. I felt a tremendous sense of love. Not from my ex-wife who was pulling her bra off, but from my new lover. My love for Tina came rushing to the forefront. I'd told Tina I loved her but until that moment, I hadn't fully realized how much she'd come to mean to me. I put on the brakes.

Jessica was disappointed, but understanding when I said, "I'm sorry but I can't do this." I put myself back together and left the house with some haste.

There wasn't going to be anyone but Tina. There couldn't be.

I was ashamed. I'd probably caused Jessica some degree of hurt and embarrassment and I was being unfaithful to Tina. I'd allowed an all around bad situation to develop and I knew I was going to have to tell Tina about it, so I was filled with dread for the near future, too.

Tina and I had made a pact of sorts, a policy of total honesty, "even if it's bad." Tina had insisted on it, and I had wholeheartedly agreed. It had been easy enough to abide by up until that point, but now there was a cost and consequences, because I'd fucked up. I wasn't accustomed to being in such a position.

I was determined to tell Tina and I'd do it in person. It was the right and honorable thing and it was my only option.

Tina and I had made plans to head up to Cold Spring for a weekend getaway to her grandpa's lake cabin. That happened to be just down the road or across the bay from her dad's house. Time alone at the lake was our main purpose, but I was also going to be meeting Tina's dad, Tom for the first time. That caused a bit of anxiety alone, but something else was weighing on me as I approached Scott's driveway to pick Tina up for the trip.

I had to tell Tina about my inappropriate encounter with my ex-wife and I had to do it straight away. It'd be no good to tell her when we were 100 miles away, not knowing how it would resolve.

So, an abbreviated version of the story was among the first things said when Tina climbed into my van.

"So, remember how we agreed to tell each other everything, even if it's bad?"

Tina looked trepidatious. "Yeah..?"

After I'd summed up, I was surprised at how easily Tina dismissed and forgave my indiscretion.

"You didn't fuck her?"

"No."

"It's not going to happen again?"

"Definitely not."

"And you actually told me about it. If anything, that just makes me trust you more," Tina said. She kissed me.

I was frankly amazed. The topic quickly shifted to more pleasant matters and we were on the road to the cabin.

We had a wonderful weekend, just the two of us on the lake.

Tina brought her German shorthaired pointer, Jasper over from her dad's which was just across the bay. He and I became fast friends (I still miss that ridiculous beast and hope he fared well over the years that followed). I met Tom, Tina's dutiful and somewhat laconic father, but the encounter was brief. Most of the time was just Dan and Tina time and that was always the best time. Looking back, Tina often referred to that getaway as "magical," and I agreed.

We went skinny dipping as I'd promised her – secluded and under the moonlight, but while we had great sex, where we really connected connected was in conversation. It was emotionally charged, rolling from lows to highs, as we shared bad and good aspects of our pasts. Tina confided some lows that activated my protective instincts and all of it served to strengthen my bond to her. Together, we turned everything into a positive. It seemed truly meaningful at the time.

I was beginning to picture a future for us.

Free Love

It was a cool fall night. I think it was the first time we paid a visit to what would become our regular haunt in town. One of the first times, at any rate. We were out on the patio of the Buffalo Bar and Grill to have a smoke. We were talking about the music that was playing. Tina was schooling me on the difference between Aerosmith and the Rolling Stones when we were joined by a black guy who was new to the neighborhood. He introduced himself as Daryl, but had to clarify that it was pronounced Dare-Ell, not Darrel.

We learned that Daryl moved to the area for work and was staying at a motel a few miles down the road. "Y'all smoke weed?" he asked.

I didn't. Tina did, but I wasn't interested in socializing with Daryl on that level.

Tina pointed at a yellow peace sign pin on her bag and, making air quotes, answered, "free love."

That struck me as an odd response, but I could make the leap from weed to peace to hippies to free love as a bit of self-deprecating humor and rolled with it.

Daryl said he was looking for a more affordable place to stay, closer in to Buffalo and Tina suggested the Buffalo Hotel, where she and her mom were living. "Here. Let me give you my number and I can give you details, later."

I raised an eyebrow at that, but rolled with it and shrugged. "There's a sign in the window that says there are vacancies. It's just a mile up that way," I offered.

"There are always vacancies," Tina added.

"Yeah. Cool. Cool."

Tina declined to smoke weed with Daryl and after a little more friendly conversation, he announced that he had to be moving on and left Tina and I to our evening.

About a week went by and I was planning to spend another weekend with Tina out in Buffalo. Before I left Minneapolis, she texted, "can you bring your drill?"

She had another task for me. I never minded doing the little repairs and improvements for her. She made it like foreplay. She'd act like she was turned on by me doing man's work, but it might have been more of a transactional thing. Sometimes she'd be explicit about that, like when we walked to the liquor store in downtown Buffalo and I bought her a big bottle of Windsor Canadian to keep her stocked. "Thank you, Dan. I'll make it worth your while," she'd said. "I'm going to thank the shit out of you later."

I felt uncomfortable with the idea of trading favors or whiskey for sex. There was no obligation in my mind. I did things for Tina because I cared about her and thought we made love because we both wanted to make love. Maybe I'm a sappy romantic, but still, I wasn't complaining.

I was certain that my drill was still in the back of my van from my last trip out to Tina's. I packed a small overnight bag and grabbed my briefcase, in case my computer was needed and got on the road. It was about a 50-minute drive to Buffalo and just as I was crossing the city limits, I realized that I'd used my drill to help my dad earlier in the week and left it behind.

Letting Tina down was about the worst thing I could imagine, so I drove to the local Ace hardware store and bought another drill before proceeding to the Buffalo Hotel. I texted to let her know I'd arrived. Since the front door to the building was locked, she came down to let me in and helped me carry everything up. I helped hang an antenna and some art for Tina and we settled in to drink whiskey and watch South Park.

Tina's phone bleeped and we both glanced it at. There was a text from Daryl. I noticed that his entry in Tina's phone had a last name. It was an Irish surname. "What's good?" read the message.

That looked more like fishing for a booty call than inquiring about an apartment for rent, to me.

She ignored the message that night and I don't think anything was said about it, but another week or two later, Tina brought it up, just to let me know that she'd never answered Daryl's message. That struck me as odd, but I took her at her word and didn't think about it again, until a similar message came through from someone else.

Looking back over the years, I realized that there was a repeated pattern in the way Tina would randomly bring up past oddities and re-frame them with new explanations or clarifications. It was like after some thought, she was editing history. For the most part, it worked on me, but my subconscious was still noting all of the inconsistencies and my body started telling me something was wrong. I'd get a sensation like anxiety when my perception of reality was being manipulated.

After observing her over and over again and coming to understand what was really going on with Tina, it's not hard to imagine that Tina responded "free love" to an inquiry about smoking weed to signal she was "down to fuck," providing there was weed to be smoked. Helping Daryl find an apartment was just a pretense to give her number to another guy right in front of her boyfriend. That's just the kind of thing she did, but it was beyond my comprehension at the time. I just couldn't imagine a person could be that shitty and Tina offered more innocent and preferable revisions to history so I didn't immediately see the obvious. Once time could be a harmless fluke. Twice? Isolated incidents. Over time, it became a pattern, but I was compartmentalizing.

Another pattern in Tina's behavior I learned too late was that when she used superlatives or absolutes, whatever her statement, the opposite was true. For example, when she was putting her number in my phone at the bar the night we met and told me "I *never* do this," the truth was she *always* did it. It's like it was pathological. Actually, it was part of the narcissistic pathology. Narcissists are always on the prowl for potential new sources of supply, either secondary or potential replacements for their primary supply.

The psychology books ascribe unstable relationships to borderline personality disorder, but I'd wager it's a common feature of all cluster B disorders, even though the diagnostic manual doesn't include it for narcissists.

It's just that they expect to eventually suffer some losses as they are discovered. It's a lifelong repeated cycle, so replacements would have to be perpetually cultivated, tested and groomed.

Crocodile Tears – Do Narcissists Cry?

As a recovering codependent, it seems, I'm inclined to be a rescuer. I'm empathetic and when I sense someone else's suffering, I feel compelled to intervene with whatever resources I have at my disposal. No doubt, that makes a tasty snack for a narcissist who tends to feel like a victim entitled to compensation.

I enjoyed helping people, but with Tina it was a devotion. I never minded helping her with any of her minor troubles, or even the big ones. As connected as I perceived us to be, helping her felt pretty much the same as helping myself, only more urgent.

Not everything I did was to meet physical needs. It wasn't always about money or possessions. In fact, most of the rescuing I attempted with Tina had to do with her unstable moods. Those were situations where I knew I couldn't necessarily "fix" anything, but I could lend a sympathetic ear. Listening was one of the skills Tina most valued in me, or so she said.

Next to listening, was reassurance. Convincing Tina that things were going to be OK and that she was OK was generally what was called for. She needed external validation. That's the essence of "narcissistic supply." Sometimes, when she was upset about some conflict with another person, I might have felt she could have been in the wrong, but it was my job to be on her team and put as positive a spin on it as I could.

It was more difficult when random tears would appear and Tina had no explanation to offer for her sometimes sudden sadness.

It was one of those days. We'd been carrying on pleasantly in the Buffalo penthouse as we so often did when the waterworks turned suddenly on.

Sitting side by side on the futon, we were casually conversing. I don't recall the subject except that it was innocuous. Tina was coloring some kind of intricate drawing when, unheralded, a sadness shook her body with sobs. Tears streamed down her face.

"Oh, no," I said, "Sweetie, what's wrong?" I put my hand on her shoulder briefly, then thought to get her a box of tissues, which she accepted gratefully and began dabbing her eyes. "What's the matter?" I reiterated.

She shook her head and took some time before trying to answer.

"I don't know," she eventually said.

It wasn't the first or last time I'd encountered this enigma. In the past, I'd tried jogging her subconscious to see if we could bring the unseen reasons for her sadness to the surface, but that had rarely worked. Sometimes, she'd offer an explanation after some time had passed, so I figured that was the best thing, to give her the space to work it out, but let her know I was ready to listen, whatever it was.

Then, I set out to cheer her up by reminding her how much I loved her and reassuring her that I'd do anything for her. Whatever I could do, all she need do is ask.

One of the ways a covert or vulnerable narcissist gets the special attention his or her ego needs is by playing the victim. It definitely always worked to make me sit up and take notice, ready to spring into action. Tears brought compassion and comforting gestures. Once the crying would stop, I was primed to acquiesce to any request Tina might make.

If she wanted to go out to the bar, I'd take her out. Choice of dinners? Her decision. If she needed beads or wire to make some earrings, I was eagerly up for Walmart trip #4,407. Then, she'd put her smile back on and the world was made right.

Tears without a reason might have been a lazy manipulation tactic. Maybe she wasn't aware the theatrics weren't really necessary. Maybe she just liked to keep in practice, but, I'd do these things anyway. There's a chance that sometimes her tears were coming from a genuine sense of grief and she just couldn't or wouldn't share the reasons with me, but I know Tina was quite aware how crying activated my rescuing instincts

Do Narcissists cry? Yes.

I know some people think that narcissists are devoid of emotions and thus only ever shed tears of the crocodile variety, but I'm certain that's not true. Probably all narcissists, but particularly, the covert or vulnerable variety do have feelings that can be hurt and they might even cry. What they lack is instinctive empathy for other people's feelings and as a consequence, they tend to overlook or dismiss them. After all, no one else's feelings could ever be as deep or meaningful as the narcissist's own.

Narcissists are generally skilled manipulators, with feigned emotions among their favorite tools, but sometimes their tears come from genuine sorrow. A vexing thing about dealing with people who lie compulsively is that it can be very difficult to tell when they're being sincere. But, that's probably by design.

It was months before I realized that Tina's coy routine when I'd fix her with an either loving or lustful gaze was a practiced act. It was cute, endearing, convincing and like many of her emotional expressions, completely contrived.

Bruised and Broken

As my relationship with Tina was rapidly progressing, my ex-wife Jessica was asking me to get my remaining possessions out of the house that had once been "ours."

I had been staying with my mother, and I wasn't keen on moving a large volume of my possessions into her home, even if there had been space to spare – and there wasn't, so I'd been planning to lease a storage locker, rent a moving truck and recruit a few friends to help me move everything, but with everyone's busy lives, that just got difficult. I felt hurried and against my better judgment, I arrived at the house one day to begin loading things into my van by myself.

Years prior, I had severely injured my back from repetitive lifting, bending and twisting at work. I had managed to herniate two lumbar discs and completely blow another one open. I was in daily pain and couldn't stand up straight for months. It wasn't something I wanted to repeat.

I was healed and feeling perfectly normal by the time I was divorced, but I knew to be cautious with my back. I threw that caution to the wind on that occasion and I suffered mightily for it.

In the course of moving a lot of heavy boxes and objects by myself, I re-injured my back and the debilitation and agony that ensued was even worse than the first time.

For a while, the pain would come and go, but then, I was out of commission for weeks straight. Some days I couldn't walk more than a few steps before I'd collapse. I had taken to sleeping on the floor, because my soft bed created instant agony, any way I positioned myself on it. On good days, I could only drive short distances and could only tolerate that by covering the seat cushion with a wooden board to sit on.

Maura had even acquired a hard metal folding chair for me to use when I visited. My "uncomfy" chair, we called it. It was good for my ailing back, though.

These circumstances were not ideal for my new relationship. Tina's apartment in Buffalo was a 50-minute drive. When she was at Scott's down in Farmington, that was a 40-minute drive. Either way, it was too far for me to manage most days. I had to break plans with Tina a couple times and was reluctant to make new ones. She seemed very patient and understanding. We kept in contact almost daily but I was desperate to get back to her presence.

I felt especially bad when Tina took the initiative to plan an event for us and I had to bow out. She'd surprised me and obtained tickets to Oktoberfest then sold them to her brother when I couldn't go.

Her mom had taken Tina down to Scott's the following week and I'd made tentative plans to pick her up from there on a Friday night, but when I'd tried to drive to the corner store that day, I found it unbearable and with tremendous regret, had to cancel again. Tina seemed completely forgiving and understanding. "We'll get together soon, when you're feeling better," she assured me with all her love.

Tina invited me out bowling with everyone down in Farmington on Saturday. I tried some pain pills, hopeful I'd be able to get off the floor, but eventually told Tina I wasn't sure if I was going to be able to make it.

"As much as it pains me to say it, don't come," she told me. "Take some more pain pills and some whiskey if it will help. It pains me to know you're in pain."

Later that night, she sent such a sweet text. "I miss you more than stars miss the night sky when daylight dawns… You are my new day. I love you."

Sunday, I was still not in driving condition. Tina texted, "Love you more than bats love the night-bugs. Can't wait to wrap myself around you."

I suggested that maybe her mom could swing her by to see me in Minneapolis on their way home to Buffalo, but Tina replied, "My mother invited her parents over tonight, so I'll be in Farmington for another night. Miss you. Need to kiss you… My phone is outta juice."

The next time I heard from her was late Monday night. Near midnight, she sent me a text message with a picture of her bare thighs. Each was marred with several dark, mostly oval-shaped bruises from mid-thigh right up to the hem of her bikini-style animal-print panties.

"I can't call you tonight. I can't leave," her message began, "I can't talk with or disown my mother, but I think it's finally time for the two of us to separate. I don't want you to be in pain in order to get to me, but once I get to you I don't want to leave. I know I'm totally fucked-up and 'tarded, but I know I'm better than this… I'm sorry for the way I am. I would do anything to be better for you."

I was still awake, trying to lie on my bed with moderate pain when the message came through. I sat upright. The pain was forgotten, replaced by alarm, and nothing in the text exchange that ensued did anything to relieve my anxiety.

"What happened? Why can't you leave? Are you OK?" I wrote back immediately.

"I'm fine. Just peachy. More emotionally bruised than anything… If only I had my own set of wheels, I'd be better as of yesterday. Stuck. Stuck and sad. I can't hurt myself, though. That's a real good thing! I tried – can't. Yay for personal growth. I also can't just get 'wasted,' unfortunately. Just crying myself to sleep again."

I couldn't make much sense of all that, but all of the words in that salad seemed dire. "Where did those bruises from from? Why are you 'stuck?' Do you need me to come and get you? I can. I will." With adrenaline now coursing, my back didn't feel like an obstacle.

"Keep all of this between you and me. I want you to come and get me, but it can't be until they both go to work tomorrow morning. I'll explain it when I see you… Is your Doctor appointment today or tomorrow? No way I'll interfere with that!"

"My appointment is Wednesday. I'm very worried. You're an adult. Unless you are being kept against your will, you can leave."

"I have a bed to sleep in and a mother to NOT worry… I am not in danger, just poked to the limit. If you can get me tomorrow, I'd be so grateful. I just want to get back to Buffalo. I'm done with this shit."

"Of course I will, if that's what you want and you're absolutely certain about waiting until tomorrow."

"I'll call you when I 'wake up,' probably around 8:00. Love you even more than I'm sorry, which is a LOT."

I was missing a lot of information. Sorry for what? I was struggling not to jump to conclusions. I don't think I slept. Barely, if I did. Tina texted again at 7:30 in the morning to tell me her mom took the day off work and was going to drive her home, so I needn't pick her up at Scott's.

I was worried about Tina's physical and mental state and had a head full of questions with a body abuzz with anxiety. I determined that I needed to see her as soon as possible. I asked if I could meet her out at the apartment and she agreed.

I gave Tina and her mom plenty time to travel and get settled back in Buffalo and drove out to meet them that afternoon. With the plank under me, I managed fairly well on the almost hour-long drive. I had to stop a couple times to get out of the car and stretch, when the sciatic pain in my right leg got too severe, but I made it there and then somehow managed to shuffle up the stairs to the third floor of the Buffalo Hotel.

Tina let me in to the small apartment, but didn't greet me with her usual kiss. Her mom was sitting on the futon. We all exchanged pleasantries and chatted a bit. The conversation was shallow and Tina looked uncomfortable when I tried to steer it to the events of the night before and to the explanations Tina had promised me. I suggested she and I take a walk so we could talk privately.

"If it's not going to be too hard with your back," Tina said.

"Don't worry. walking feels good right now. Sometimes it's helpful," I assured her.

It was sunny, but the fall chill was in the air as we walked down the block from the Buffalo Hotel. We turned towards the lake. Tina chattered idly. After a while, I said, "so, are you going to tell me what happened last night?"

Her eyes welled up and she shook her head.

I gently tried a couple other tacks, but the only answer Tina would provide beyond tears was "I don't want to talk about it right now."

This was interminably frustrating and heightened my unease. I'd expected she'd talk to me once we were away from her mother. We had a Total Honesty policy, after all, "even if it's bad."

Tina was full of other trivial subjects and petty complaints to discuss as we walked. Realizing I wasn't going to get anything of consequence from her and feeling chilled, I suggested we go back in.

We made our way back from the lake, coming up the opposite side of the Buffalo Hotel. Tina seemed in better spirits. "I'm just so glad you're here," she said, looping her arm in mine.

We went back into the apartment, where Maura was watching TV and the three of us ended up relaxing on the futon, watching a movie. No one was talking much, but at one point, I heard Maura say, quietly to Tina, "Well it got him here, didn't it?"

Tina responded with a scowl and a brief shake of her head.

My weary brain started work on computing the meaning of all that. It had been an exhausting and confusing day already.

Tina had a wobbly ottoman next to the window that served as the smoking section. She moved over there to have a cigarette, but didn't finish it. Half-way through, she stamped it out in the ashtray, closed the window, stood abruptly, unbuckled her belt and yanked her pants off. She faced Maura and I in her underwear, revealing the dark marks that peppered her upper thighs.

"Mom, you have to talk to Scott about this," she said. "You have to tell him to leave me alone!"

Maura seemed only a little surprised by the sudden theatrics. I was stunned and all my computational power was immediately redirected.

"Okay," Maura said slowly, seeming to wait for more information or comprehension to come.

"We were out in the barn," Tina began," and Scott said he was worried that he was losing his grip strength, so he wanted to test his grip strength and I was sitting there and all the sudden, he just grabbed both of my legs, and, uhhhh!" she acted out Scott leaning forward and squeezing with both hands.

"Okay…" Maura said, again.

"I need you to talk to him about this. This isn't OK," Tina said, emphatically. "Look what he did!" she swept her long arms in front of her bare and bruised thighs.

"OK, Tina," Maura said, calmly. "OK, Tina, I will."

"Thank you!" Tina concluded her presentation. She went to the bedroom and came back out wearing pajama pants.

Theatrics such as those are often associated with histrionic personality disorder, a close cousin to narcissism. That was the end of the show and we watched the TV together without much further conversation. The apartment only had one bedroom, plus Candace, the futon in the living room. Maura offered the bedroom to Tina and I while she spent the night with Candace.

Once we were alone in the bedroom, Some fresh triangulation began. Tina told me that she'd been observed talking in her sleep over the weekend. "No. Dan. I love Dan," Scott told her she had murmured. "'You don't love Dan,'" he added. "'I saw you flirting with Doug by the pool table last night.'"

I felt uncomfortable as Tina related this, but didn't really know what to think. Tina was weaving a web of confusion and nothing was clear.

Tina assured me that Scott had it wrong and she hadn't been flirting with Doug – just being 'silly' while they shot a game of 8-ball.

"I love you so much," she concluded. "Now that I have you back, I'm never letting you go again." She wrapped herself around me tightly.

I was more moved by the emotions Tina conveyed than by any of her confusing clusters of words.

We went from tender hugging and kissing to arousal, but when Tina's pants came off, I couldn't help but look closer at the marks on her thighs. They appeared even more pronounced and certainly looked more like bites or hickeys than fingerprints.

"Stop looking at my bruises," Tina admonished. She turned off the light.

We made love and Tina fell asleep, but sleep didn't come easily to me that night. I'd begun to drift off comfortably next to her, but my subconscious hadn't ever stopped it's computations and it suddenly began sounding alarms. My body physically jolted as the conclusion came. Tina was certainly lying. I had the very distinct feeling I'd had the wool pulled over my eyes. I kicked my leg involuntarily, then laid there stiffly, jaw clenched. It was all pretty obvious, but almost too appalling to believe. Tina had sex with another man and then had the gall to send me a picture of the marks he'd left.

I got up and went into the bathroom where I attempted to reproduce on myself, the bruising on Tina's thighs, by the means she described it. I dug my fingers into my pale flesh, squeezing as hard as I possibly could, I pulled and thrashed, for good measure. I squeezed and pressed and pinched and pulled, trying to match the position of the bruises with my fingers. For all my effort, I couldn't produce a mark that looked remotely like the dark ovals on Tina's upper thighs. Nor could I match the placement of marks by spreading my fingers. She'd have had to been manhandled pretty roughly for those to be caused by fingertips and a couple were in a decidedly "personal" zone.

I'd hoped to find Tina's explanation plausible, but could not.

Maura was asleep on the futon, right next to the bathroom door. I made my way out and around the apartment as quietly as I could, gathering my things. I didn't fully understand her game, but I was certain that everything I'd seen and heard that night had been a production meant to confuse and confound me – to pull the wool over my eyes. I felt insulted and indignant. After I had my bag packed, my wallet, keys and cell phone in my pockets, coat and shoes on, I hesitated. Something about slipping out, without a word, in the middle of the night, after making love, seemed wrong. I decided I owed Tina an explanation. I went into the dark bedroom and felt around until I found her shoulder and jostled her gently. "Tina. Tina. I'm leaving," I said as she roused.

She was groggy. At first she just said, "Um… OK," but as her consciousness returned, she stopped me. "Wait, what? Why?

"Because I don't feel like you've been honest with me," I replied.

Now, she was fully alert and she seemed terrified. She begged me not to leave."If you were anyone else, I'd have just said, OK, bye! But it's you. I love you so much, I don't ever want to lose you. Please take your coat off and stay. Don't go. Don't go. Please! Just come back to bed."

She began talking fast, stringing a series of emotionally loaded words together in an almost random fashion. Between her salad of charged words, assurances of her honesty, promises of later explanations for her odd behavior and repeated professions of profound and unprecedented love, she wore down my resolve and I stayed.

She was the victim here, a damsel in distress.

I didn't feel at ease, but Tina had planted doubt and left me unsure about what happened. I was snowed. She might have cheated – maybe she'd come clean and we'd work it out. Maybe something had happened against her will. Maybe it was even as she described it, as ludicrous as it seemed. What did that say about Scott?

All I could firmly latch on to in that moment was that Tina loved me and needed me. I must have already been half-hooked by her love bombing. She had been slathering the affection on really thick from the beginning and it soothed me everywhere I felt rough.

"Promise me you'll never leave me like that. No matter, what, tell me what's going on, OK? Don't ever just disappear. I don't know what I'd do."

I promised.

I undressed and crawled back under the covers with her, my arm draped over her warm body, our legs entwined, and slept.

I often considered that night a turning point. Besides tainting my view of Scott, his farm and his son, Doug, It colored the next three years of my on-again, off-again relationship with Tina.

It had been my best, most obvious chance to escape and failing to do so entangled me with Tina's illness in a way that will undoubtedly affect me to some degree for the rest of my life. It was a pivotal moment and I allowed myself to be sucked in to a mad, imaginary world. It's a decision I may regret forever. I could have been free.

It didn't help matters when, months later, Tina offered an alternate explanation out of the blue, saying that Scott had caused those bruises by repeatedly 'poking' her. By then, it was too late for me. I was in deep.

Seven Degrees of Something Bacon

I was invited to a party at the home of my friend Rich and his wife, Thea. It was a bacon-themed party and everyone was expected to bring something bacon-related. It was mostly food, but Kevin Bacon memorabilia was equally acceptable.

Tina and I were spending the weekend together in the little top-floor apartment of the Buffalo Hotel, so I asked her to come along with me.

We concocted a recipe for bacon-wrapped Parmesan and bacon meatballs and had a great time testing our cooperation in the small kitchen. We worked well together, joked around, kissed between steps and I was completely swept away by how perfect we were together. It was bliss.

We'd not been dating more than a month or two by that point, but I was fast falling in love.

Tina knew how close I was to Rich and Thea and had heard many tales of our adventures together in Ireland, but she had yet to meet them. She was nervous about it. She said she'd had a dream that my friends had thrown her into a river, which I guessed was influenced by Scott's initial warning to her about dating me. Upon learning I was from "dangerous" Minneapolis, he'd told her that if she went out with me she'd end up cut into pieces and dumped in the Mississippi. That seemed a bit extreme to me. In retrospect, I wonder if he just didn't like the idea of her dating anyone.

I assured her that everyone who would be over at Rich and Thea's was super-cool, friendly and absolutely no one was of the river-dumping sort.

I ran through a mental list of likely attendees and when Chris came to mind, I thought a disclaimer might be in order. I'd known Chris for years. I liked him and he was Rich's number-one pal. He was smart and often hilarious, but his choice of words, subjects of conversation and sense of humor were sometimes not well-taken by people new to his acquaintance. I called him "Crass Chris."

I wanted Tina to feel comfortable in my circles. I wanted her to have a good impression of them. I recognized that one's choice of friends can reflect on oneself (a principle I seemingly failed to apply when evaluating what little I saw of Tina's circle).

"There's this one guy, Chris who will probably be there. He's really fun and totally harmless, but his sense of humor can rub people the wrong way sometimes. Just don't take him too seriously. He's a good guy."

"Like what does he do?"

"He doesn't have a filter," I said. "He'll talk about gross, crazy stuff. Weird sex, injuries, disease, racist jokes, crude language... swears a lot. And if he wants to show you something on his phone, brace yourself."

She laughed. "I think I can handle him. I know plenty of people like that."

We put our first batch of meatballs into the oven, poured ourselves some drinks and chatted on.

The meatballs were absolutely delicious and we congratulated ourselves on our teamwork. Our first joint-venture in the kitchen was a tremendous success. High-fives and meatball kisses.

It was a bit of a drive from Buffalo to White Bear Lake and we were going to be drinking, so we were planning on spending the night. We also had an early obligation the next day. We packed up an overnight bag while the second batch was baking, then got ourselves out the door to head over to the party. It smelled so good in my van on the way that I wanted to tear the foil off the tin pans and start munching. "Forget the party – let's just keep all these meatballs to ourselves," I joked, my stomach rumbling.

After making the effort to issue a warning about Chris, I was a little disappointed that he didn't make it to the party so she could see what I was talking about for herself, but Tina was getting on well with everyone and we were having a good time. Someone brought some barbecue bacon-wrapped water chestnuts that we decided were even better than our meatballs, but our contribution went over well with the crowd, too.

As the night went on and people were getting tipsy, Tina pulled me aside and told me that someone had come on to her and it made her feel uncomfortable. "I told him I was with you and he was like, 'Dan? Who's Dan?'"

"What?" I was pretty surprised to hear that. "Who was it?"

She elaborated, "That blonde guy cornered me in the back hall and said he had something to show me down in the basement. 'C'mon – it'll only take a minute,' he said. I was like 'gross,' and if it only takes a minute, who would want to anyway?"

"Kevin?" Kevin was Jasmine's newish boyfriend. She was an old friend of Thea's and the ex-girlfriend of the guy who owned the recording studio I used to work at. She was really sweet and I got along with her well.

"Yeah. I think that was his name."

"Kevin is Jasmine's boyfriend," I told her, growing irate, "and he certainly knows who I am."

I was bringing Tina around this group of friends for the first time, wanting everything to go well. *This guy is rudely coming on to my new girlfriend, disrespecting me, disrespecting Jasmine, making my date uncomfortable*, I thought.

"I wasn't sure if I should tell you," Tina said. "I don't want to cause any trouble. He just really creeped me out."

I considered options. Kevin was completely smashed and since Jasmine was also drinking, would probably be spending the night, too. Tina's comfort was paramount and I was angry. I considered confronting Kevin, but decided not to make a scene at Rich and Thea's party. "Maybe it's time we head out," I said.

"You want to drive all the way back to Buffalo? Haven't you been drinking?"

"We don't have to go all the way back to Buffalo," I said. "How about I just get us a room at a hotel near here and we can take a taxi? We can come back for the van in the morning."

"OK," Tina said. "That sounds good. Thank you, Dan!" She put her arms around my neck and kissed me.

"I'm sorry he made you uncomfortable. Just stick close to me until we leave."

I found a room about a mile away and arranged a cab, which arrived about 20 minutes later. We said our goodbyes, thanked our hosts and went out the front door.

Kevin was sitting out on the stoop by himself, smoking a cigarette. We walked by without acknowledging him.

"Oh. You guys are together?" he asked. He seemed surprised.

"Yeah," I said darkly.

I opened the back door for Tina and she got seated in the cab, I realized I'd forgotten to grab our bottle of whiskey. I asked the driver to pop the trunk and ran back into the house to locate the liquor. It took a minute, because I'd forgotten I'd put it in the freezer downstairs. I retrieved it and went back out front. Kevin was still sitting on the front steps. Kicking the back of his head crossed my mind for a split-second.

"I thought you were with that other Jessica girl," Kevin said as I stepped around him.

"We're divorced." My blood was on the verge of boiling.

"Alright. Have a good one, man," he said.

"See you later, fucker," I said over my shoulder.

"What?!" Defensive anger rose in his voice instantly.

I stopped and looked back at him. He stood, swaying on his feet. "Have a good night, Kevin," I said and climbed into the cab with Tina.

Tina later gushed that no guy had ever shown protective instincts for her, before. I found that unlikely, but she seemed happy with me. She told me she didn't think she'd want to go back to Rich and Thea's because of Kevin, which was greatly upsetting to me. I counted those guys among my very closest friends. Something would have to be done to resolve this.

Over the following months, the situation with Kevin had caused a bit of a strain on my friendship with Rich and Thea. We mostly avoided having Tina and I at the same social events as Kevin, but he did show up unexpectedly for Halloween, dressed as Teen Wolf. I actually didn't recognize him until he was about to leave.

Chris and Tina had met on a couple of occasions and hit it off famously. Halloween might have been the first time. Tina seemed to have no trouble at all matching his dirty jokes and innuendo that night. That night, Tina and I had dressed as dirty hippies and Tina had selected my old painted B-Boy jean jacket from my high school days as part of her costume. She asked me to paint a graffiti jacket like it for her birthday, actually, but that was only 10 days away and I knew I'd have no time. I promised I'd paint one for her next birthday.

In the following months, Tina and I began joining Rich and Thea for Trivia nights at a bar in their neighborhood. Chris always came along, leaving his wife, Lisa at home with their kids. He and Tina continued to get along well, but I was just glad everyone was integrating and having a good time because Thea had expressed concerns. For a while, those concerns seemed allayed, but they would resurface before long.

For Christmas that year, I had bought Tina a modest gold and diamond "promise ring." Something about Chris' reaction when Tina showed it to him at Rich and Thea's New Year's party seemed out of place for him. It seemed too melodramatic. It was a stronger reaction than even her mom had displayed when we actually got engaged months later. After a lurching forward with a split-second wide-eyed gaze, he leapt in, gushing enthusiasm. "Oh my God! Congratulations, you guys! When's the date?"

Tina and I were both back pedaling. "It's a promise ring," we clarified.

"Oh." Chris' attitude did an instant and complete reversal into nonchalance. "Pffft..." He waved a dismissive hand at the modest symbol of my devotion on Tina's finger.

When you've known someone for a long time and their body language, words and tone aren't matching up, it's noticed, even if only subconsciously. My spidey senses were tingling. I felt suddenly uncomfortable but couldn't quite determine why.

Chris and I got to talking, later and he wanted to know what the drama had been between Kevin and I. He'd only picked up bits on the periphery. I told him the story and embellished my disapproval by adding "I just wanted to stomp right on the back of his neck when we were leaving – but of course, I'd never do something like that, unless I had no choice."

"Hey, man, just so you know – if you ever do get into a fight with Kevin over that and he starts getting the upper hand, I'll jump in and back you up. I don't like that guy, anyway," Chris told me.

"Thanks, but I wouldn't fight him unless it was self-defense or a more urgent need to defend Tina – like if he was getting physical."

"I know, but, just saying. I'd jump in and fuck him up."

Eventually, things did normalize with Kevin and we all put it past us, but Thea was perplexed and was growing wary of Tina. "She was acting all flirty with Kevin last time, throwing popcorn at him and stuff. I don't see how there was a problem," she'd said to me one night. "I'm still reserving judgment, but she might be trouble. I'm not sure I trust her. I mean, is she going to stir up some shit with Chris, next?"

The Proposals

Tina's dad, Tom was going out of town and had asked Tina to house sit and take care of the family dog. We had just gotten back to Tom's place on the lake from a farther "up north" ice fishing and snowmobiling trip. We were sitting in the living room, watching TV. Jasper, Tina's neurotic German shorthair pointer was sleeping between us, his head on my lap. Tina was crocheting a blanket that I didn't yet know she she was making as a gift for me.

It was a cozy night. It felt "domestic." I felt like we were a family. There were other things weighing on my mind, though. Tina and I had been dating for eight months and I was completely devoted. I wasn't sure about Tina's level of commitment, however. I'd observed and implied some disturbing behavior on her part over the past couple months. Besides the photo of her thighs all marked up with what looked like bite marks she'd sent from Scott's, I was ignoring other signs that she'd attempted, with varying degrees of success to seduce friends and acquaintances of mine. Where she'd find success, she'd also create a co-conspirator who was obligated to assist in gaslighting me. Tina's gaslighting campaign was fairly successful at managing my perception of reality and keeping me confused. With Tina, the past and future were nebulous and pliable. Her reality existed only in the moment. She kept my focus there. In hind sight, My drinking habits made it all the easier for her to massage my recollections, too.

I didn't at all understand the ways my perception and emotions were being manipulated at the time, but I had these moments, when my anxiety would rise. My body was telling me something was wrong and I'd try putting pieces together. The missing pieces were often things only Tina could provide, so I'd have to rely on her to fill in those blanks. When I'd ask her about what happened some night when something had raised my suspicions, she'd often respond that "nothing really happened" and "the night was all one continuous note." Whatever that meant.

By that point, Tina had pretty successfully positioned herself as the arbiter of reality. She wasn't a good liar, but she was unflinching. Between her veracity and my natural desire to believe her, she could turn my mind around pretty easily. My gut wasn't always convinced, but I trusted my brain more than any kind of intuition.

So, I was enjoying our time together and feeling familial. I think that was the first time I really contemplated the future with Tina. I imagined us living together, getting married, buying a house – maybe even having kids. Anything seemed possible. I wondered if Tina was as willing to commit to me as I was to her. I had these dark thoughts and suspicions intruding into my otherwise warm, loving feelings. I was wrestling with all of that sitting on the couch with Tina's dog on my lap and Tina eventually noticed my distance and snapped me out of my contemplation.

"Dan, is something wrong?"

"What?"

"Are you OK? You look disturbed," she said.

"No. I'm fine. I was just thinking about the weekend. There are some holes in my memory," I said. "I think I drank a bit too much."

"Nothing really happened in those holes," she said. "Everything was fine. I had a good time. It was all like one continuous note."

She'd said that before.

"Is that all? You look really deep in thought," she said. "It's making me worry something's wrong."

"Worry? Why worry?" I asked.

"What else are you thinking about?"

From there, everything happened at the speed of light. My thoughts formed in rapid succession and turned to action before any internal checks or audits could begin.

In one swift, fluid motion, I slipped out from under Jasper, took Tina's hand and swung myself around to face her on one knee.

I've forgotten what Tina's voice sounds like and what she smelled like, but I will never forget the look on her face that night. It's burned permanently into my memory. She instantly recognized what I was doing and watched it unfold in startled astonishment."

"Tina Mary Dziewkaski," I intoned solemnly, "will you marry me?"

She didn't hesitate. "Yes!"

"Then you've made me the happiest man in the world," I said. Jasper was perturbed by the sudden flurry of activity and slinked off the couch with a huff as I sidled up to Tina and kissed her. My eyes welled up a little.

As impulsive as my action seemed, it really did feel right. I also foolishly believed that engagement would somehow solidify Tina's commitment to a faithful relationship. Engagement would make me feel safe. All my concerns vanished.

After my divorce, I was never more sure of anything than vows I'd made to myself that I would never marry again. I surprised myself almost as much as Tina with the sudden proposal.

The barreling train of thought to action took less than a split-second, but went something like this:

Tina asked me a question. What am I thinking about?

Well, I'm thinking about a lot of things. I'm thinking about whether I can trust her – Can't say that. I'm thinking about where our relationship is going. I'm thinking that I could imagine a time in the future when I could see myself proposing to her. I can't say that, either. Too wishy-washy.

I agreed to a policy of total honesty, even if it's bad. I'm obligated to answer her honestly. I'd rather keep it positive. It would be bad form to say I might ask you to marry me one day. It'd be more proper to just go ahead and ask her to marry me on the spot. That's crazy! You can't do that! That would be an honest reflection of your thoughts and maybe resolve the deeper question of whether she's really committed to me or not, or at least spur a conversation about it. She's waiting for an answer… Take the shot. Here goes…

That succession of thoughts happened like sparks off a match.

The night had begun calmly, quietly, comfortably but now, we were abuzz with fresh excitement. We talked enthusiastically about our future for hours and had planned our wedding in some detail before the night was through.

"Are you about ready? Ready to pick our date?" She asked excitedly.

We'd already determined that we'd get married on the lake, so we were looking at a summer wedding. I had opened the calendar on my phone, navigating around any other significant dates and was zeroing in on what I thought might be a suitable Saturday in July.

Before I suggested the date, Tina said, "Can we make it this summer?"

"Uh… 5 months? I mean, I guess that could be possible. It's not a lot of time to get everything together. I was thinking we need some time to find our own place to live together and…"

"I'm just afraid if we don't do it right away, it won't happen," she said.

I thought that was a very strange sentiment. "Why wouldn't it? If we can't last a year, year and a half engaged, I don't see how we'll stay married, anyhow, right?"

She couldn't fault my reasoning. We settled on a year and a half long engagement. July 22nd, 2017 was the date.

"OK, so, now that we're engaged, that means you can't have sex with my mom," Tina proclaimed from some dimension beyond left field.

"I hadn't been planning on it," I said, expecting that she was joking around.

"Or my dad or my brother, for that matter," she went on.

"Um. OK. Yeah. I'd appreciate it if you would refrain from sex with members of my family, too," I said.

This began a back and forth of who was off limits for sexual activity. I was just playing along, but got bored with the exercise and tried to wrap it up by saying, "how about we just make it simple and say we don't cheat on each other with anyone at all?"

Without missing a beat, Tina came back with "Would you consider prostitution cheating?"

"Uh..." I was a little slow to come around to the new conversational tack and she was talking over me somewhat as I began answering as if she'd asked a philosophical question. "Uh... That depends..."

She started talking faster, adding. "A little extra money to help out with the household... Of course, we'd double-bag that thing – wrap it up tight. Don't want to bring anything home."

I wasn't keeping up with her. I assumed we were dealing in the hypothetical, but I wasn't entirely confident of that and it was a little concerning. Ultimately I concluded that she couldn't be seriously suggesting contributing to our household finances by fucking other guys. Still, I hedged with my answer while keeping it in the realm of libertarian philosophy instead of answering like it was a real proposal. "I guess whether it's cheating depends..."

"On whether you're the pimp?" There was an excited enthusiasm to her tone.

"No... What I was going to say was, that whether it was cheating would depend on whether it was known about and agreed upon ahead of time. Technically. Hypothetically."

Like a hyperactive child, Tina flashed through a number of other subjects, leaving the moral philosophizing about post-marital prostitution well in the dust. It was soon forgotten behind the flurry of other matters.

Tina got a notebook and was writing all kinds of details for a wedding plan. We were even starting a play list for the DJ. I Melt with You by Bad English topped the list for our first dance.

We drank, and caroused and dreamt up a future together.

I attempted to entice her into the bedroom. It seemed a perfect time to make love. I was rather astonished when Tina put a stop to my advances. We'd been having constant sex for eight months by then, but she chose that moment to insist that we begin using condoms, which, since we'd never used one before, I did not have handy. The nearest store was about a half-hour drive and would have been closed before I could get there.

I was mightily confused (and vexed) by Tina's newfound interest in safe sex.

The following morning, I was up early. I fed Jasper breakfast and let him out to relieve himself, after which, he went right back to bed with Tina. While they slept, I went outside to smoke a cigarette. It was a warm morning, for February. I wandered the property. I lit another cigarette, looking back at my tracks in the snow. An idea struck.

While I smoked, I tromped through the snow in the front yard. I made several passes, doing my best, without proper perspective, to create a giant heart shape. It was oriented to the living room picture window. Just a little surprise for Tina to see when she finally woke up.

Tina spotted the heart right away after she got up. It earned me a kiss. She was still excited and took delight in the novelty of calling me her fiance. She was bursting to tell her mom the news, but thought it should be in person, so she texted Maura to ask her to come up to the house to join us. She enticed her by intimating at big news without telling her exactly what it was. I'd bet Maura thought she was going to be a grandmother.

Tom would probably not have been thrilled about his ex-wife being in his house while he was away. I'd inferred that he still harbored some understandable resentment over Maura sneaking off to Scott's with Tina covering for her while Tom and Maura were still married. At any rate, that was their family business I didn't feel any place in and it was, in my estimation, a particularly special circumstance.

It would be several hours before Maura could join us. Tina wanted to make love and I said I would drive to the store. "What should I get, like two 24-packs? How do they even come? What's the biggest box?"

"What are you talking about?" She asked.

"Condoms," I said. I haven't really bought them, but I think we're going to need a lot of them. Like, three or four 48-packs, for starters," I joked.

"Oh. I don't care about that," she said and taking my hands, guided me back to the messy bed.

My longevity wasn't what we were accustomed to – maybe I was too excited after having been rebuffed the night before and it had already been a while.

"Sorry that was kind of brief," I said, looking down into her eyes when I'd recaptured my wind. "Let me get a drink and I'll be ready to go again."

"You should never apologize for having a good time," Tina shot back.

Something about the way she said that, in that moment struck me oddly. It felt like a rehearsed line. It definitely didn't feel genuine. I felt a rush of anxiety and suddenly didn't feel like that second round anymore.

We found a light breakfast in Tom's kitchen and ended up having a discussion about condoms and babies. Tina said she was thinking that she'd like to have a year married before having a kid, but was also worried that she might not be able to get pregnant without some medical intervention. She said she previously had conflicted feelings about having a child. She had a desire to become a mother, but she worried about passing on her "problems" to any offspring.

"But, you change everything," she said. "With you for a partner, I feel like we could handle any challenges. You're everything I never wanted."

Ultimately, we decided that we'd "roll the dice" on the low-odds of a natural pregnancy, which would be welcome, even if "early," precisely because it was unlikely. Then, if a year of marriage still didn't produce a pregnancy, we'd look into medical options. We were both of the mindset that we'd be happy together with or without having any children, though.

That slice of 'future-faking' was probably critical in cementing my bond to Tina. I'd given up on the notion of ever having children in my previous marriage, but suddenly, everything was possible. I imagined myself a father. A husband. Facing the world with my best friend and lover. Things would only get better for us.

Condoms were never discussed again, but Tina did occasionally express concern about how her child might turn out. "I'm afraid my baby will end up like me," she'd say.

I knew Tina took a plethora of medications, some for depression and anxiety, but when she said things like that, I always assumed she was referring to her physical ailments: Her digestive problems, the mystery illnesses she suffered as a child that led to organ extraction and numerous, repeated, seemingly fruitless medical tortures.

"It's possible that our child could inherit some of your problems, or maybe not. My genes play a role, too and if there are problems like you've suffered, you'd be uniquely qualified to guide doctors to the right cause, since you've already been there."

Tina mentioned that her seemingly abandoned interest in medicine had leaned towards pediatrics for that very reason – to be able to help prevent children suffering like she had.

Long after we'd broken up, I heard from other people that Tina had told them she never wanted kids. She said she was afraid they'd turn out like her, but their take was different than mine. They assumed she was talking about her disordered personality.

I was so wrapped up in being Tina's everything (primary narcissistic supply) that such a thing never (consciously) occurred to me. I was telling Tina that I thought she'd be an excellent mother, based on how I'd seen her interact with my niece and nephews and what I'd heard from her about helping out with Scott's preteen daughters. I thought she was a loving, caring woman. Maybe she was – when it suited her, but I learned she could never be that consistently.

When I was married to Jessica, we'd suffered the loss of two pregnancies due to miscarriage and that was all she would tolerate. She decided children weren't going to be in our future. I was ambivalent about it, but resigned to that reality. I enjoyed the freedom and reduced responsibility that came with being childless, but sometimes wondered how much I'd be missing out on. With Tina, no doors were closed. Our world was clay to be molded into any future we desired for ourselves.

The first chilly afternoon of our betrothal progressed and we were running low on crucial cigarettes, so we decided to make Jasper the happiest dog and take him for a ride into town after I took a quick shower.

I didn't see any sign of Tina or the dog when I emerged from the steamy bathroom. I guessed they were outside. I dressed, tugged on my hat and shoes and stepped out. They were out there on the snowy driveway, but I was surprised to see someone else, too. Tina was Hunched over by the window of a pickup truck I didn't recognize, talking to the driver, a balding man with a long gray beard who I didn't recognize. He didn't linger long and Tina didn't offer any introductions before the truck set off to ascend the steep driveway.

"That was Ben," Tina explained. "He's a friend of My dad's. He comes by to check on things when my dad's away."

"Oh. OK." I had a recollection that he was attached to the coincidental donor to the non-profit I ran: the woman, Becky, who didn't like Tina any more for no reason she could explain.

"You ready to go?"

I checked my coat pocket and produced my keys.

"OK!" Tina tromped over to my van and slid open the back door, calling her dog. "Jaspo! Car Ride!"

It wasn't his name that turned the ranging dog's head. It was the promise of a ride. His long legs bore him galloping towards my open vehicle.

Maura arrived a while after we returned to the house and was excited and happy for us when Tina broke the news of our engagement. She didn't seem especially surprised, but maybe she was let down that we weren't announcing a pregnancy. Looking out towards the lake, she saw my snow-tramped message to her daughter. "Oh my God, is that a heart?" she exclaimed.

Tina beamed. "That's my Dan," she said.

For a time Tina and I were swept up in the fresh excitement of our deeper commitment, a new future to imagine together and a fun wedding to plan. She showed me a book she'd bought. It was a really thick wedding planning manual with questionnaires and tips and tricks and lots of worksheets for. We agreed that 80% of it was bullshit that wasn't going to apply to our less conventional wedding, but it became the repository of every detail of the wedding plan. She usually kept it at the apartment in a magazine rack.

Sometimes there was a manila envelope in that magazine rack that contained pages of catalogs and magazines Tina had torn out. Sometimes there was no envelope there. I wondered if she was filing them somewhere.

Another week of our engagement bliss passed before trouble reappeared in paradise.

Trouble in Cold Spring

Two days after Tina accepted my proposal at her dad's house in Cold Spring, I headed back to Minneapolis. Tina stayed behind to watch the Dog, since her dad was out of town for a week. I had to work, but had plans to return on the following weekend, and ultimately drive Tina home when Tom got back from his trip.

That Friday afternoon, Tina called while I was in transit between jobs. I pulled into a convenience store parking lot and took her call in the car. Her purpose was to check on my estimated time of arrival back in Cold Spring.

"Are you coming back up today?" She asked. Even though it was she who called me, Tina seemed somewhat distracted.

"That's the plan," I said. "I might be a bit later, though. This day got busier than expected," I explained.

"That's OK," she said. "Could you give me a rough time, though? Doesn't have to be to the minute." It sounded like Tina was in a moving vehicle. The faint sound of a motor and wind came across with road noise.

I ran some calculations on how long it would take me to drive to different locations and complete certain tasks, pack a bag and drive another hour and a half up to Cold Spring. "Around seven if I'm lucky," I figured.

"Oh. OK. That's fine. Could you call me when you're on your way, though, so I can make sure I finish everything I want to get done before you arrive?"

"Sure," I said. I was about to ask where she was going, but she pressed an end to our call.

"OK. Talk to you later. Bye." She hung up without our customary "Love yous." It was a very quick conversation.

I went into the store to buy some iced tea. It was an old Tom Thumb that I hadn't been in for many years. I was shocked to find that half of it had been converted into a head shop, selling all sorts of pipes and bongs and other weed-smoking paraphernalia. Tom Thumb was a national chain, so I was pretty surprised to see all that inside. I took a couple pictures, because I thought Tina would find it of interest. I bought my refreshments and got back into the car and sent Tina a quick text with the pictures, then got back on with my work day.

It struck me odd that Tina would be calling me from a moving car. I was certain she would never make a call while driving. That made her a passenger. Now, I was wondering who she might be riding with. She didn't deign to respond to my text about the incongruous head shop inside the Tom Thumb.

I finished up one task and decided to stop home before going to the office for my next project. I had a quick lunch with my mom and decided to pack my overnight bag and take it with me to save some time when I was done working.

Something about Tina's call earlier wasn't sitting right with me. She had prior complained that the steep hill leading off her dad's property was too slick with packed snow and ice for her to make it up the driveway in the Saturn coupe she'd been delegated. She was stuck and lonely, with only Jasper for company, as she told it.

I'd learned earlier that calls Tina made from her dad's house showed up on my phone bill specifically as WiFi Calls instead of displaying the number. Cellular reception was terrible there, so I'd set WiFi Calling up for her. As I was packing, I popped open my laptop and pulled up T-Mobile and looked at Tina's call history. Her last call wasn't a WiFi call, so she hadn't called me from her dads.

I tried calling her to update my ETA, but she didn't answer. I decided to cut my work plans short and start making my way up north a bit earlier. I had a few pressing tasks that couldn't wait, though. That all took another hour, but I was already packed, so I was on the road for Cold Spring immediately after.

I tried calling Tina again. This time, she answered. It sounded like she was breathing heavy. I told her that I was going to be arriving a bit earlier than expected, but didn't specify a time.

She told me that she'd still not gone anywhere, but that she had tried. She said she'd been out spreading the last of her dad's dwindled supply of sand to make the driveway safer for my arrival. She also said she'd tried a few times, unsuccessfully to charge up the hill in the Saturn because she'd been going stir crazy alone at the house and wanted to get away. After getting stuck off to the side of the driveway on the steep hill, spinning her tires for a while, she said, she managed to get the car backed down the driveway again.

I asked her if she needed me to bring anything.

"Only you," she replied, sweetly.

I hung up to drive and put some music on. I had a long drive ahead of me and the wheels were turning in my head almost as fast as my rubber on the road. Something still didn't feel right. I had a strong sense that Tina was lying to me. Something had seemed amiss all day, actually, but I wasn't making sense of why, yet.

I called again. She answered, but before putting the phone to her head and saying hello to me, she said, distantly, "Um, OK." it had sounded very much like a response to an inquiry from someone else who was with her.

Then, at a normal volume, "Hello?"

"Hi," I said. "Who was that?"

"Who was what, now?"

"It sounded like you were talking to someone when you answered," I said.

"No," she said. "Maybe Jasper. I've probably been talking to myself, though. I am going a little crazy."

My suspicion level was jumping off the charts, now. I felt extremely nervous all of a sudden.

I had been doing something that's illegal, now, but to be clear, even if unwise, was permitted at the time. I was holding my phone to my head instead of using my van's bluetooth, because it was hard to hear me at freeway speed over the road noise on that microphone.

The phone slipped from my fingers and landed somewhere under the center console where I couldn't see or reach it.

I left it there for the nonce. I figured I'd retrieve it when I eventually stopped at a liquor store, which was something I was in the habit of pretty much always doing on my way to Tina.

It had grown dark by the time I was out of the Metro area and heading west on I-94. I decided to stop for gas and booze when I was in the vicinity of Buffalo (Monticello, probably). I dug my phone out from under my console and tried calling Tina back from the gas station. She didn't answer. I figured she thought I hung up on her, which is something I might have been considering. Actually, the more I thought about it, the more I was considering just turning around and heading back to Minneapolis.

I decided it would be better to deal with whatever was going on in person. Maybe proposing had been a mistake. Maybe it was time to break up. It was going to be a serious conversation, whichever way it went, when I arrived.

After gassing up and getting myself a Red Bull, I pulled into the parking lot of a liquor store I'd stopped at a time or two before. I tried to call Tina again, but I called her old cell number. She answered that phone.

"I'm about an hour out," I said. "I'm stopping at a liquor store. Do you have any requests?" It was actually more like 35 to 45 minutes from that point.

She gushed a sigh and spoke with a tone of relief. "Oh, good." She sounded like she'd just switched from crying to an elated emotional state. "I'm so happy you're coming," she said, her voice cracking a little. "I am alone. In the House. Nobody is coming back," she began.

"Nobody…" I started to question.

"Oh! Shit! Fuck!" Tina cried out, interrupting my inquiry.

"What's wrong?"

"I'm baking muffins," she said, "and I just burned the fucking shit out of my fingers on the oven rack."

That seemed too convenient a distraction. "Are you sure that's what's wrong? Maybe me coming up is what's wrong?"

"Noooo…" Tina intoned. "What's wrong is my fingers hurt like hell and I gotta find some burn cream and bandages."

"OK," I said. "You better do that, then. Did you want me to pick something up for you?"

"Just get whatever you want for yourself. I've just been craving Mickeys, but I'm going to try one more time to get up that driveway so I can say I got out of the house, today. I'll go into town and get that myself."

"Alright, then," I said with a sigh. After supposedly trying several times to get up the steep driveway without success when the sun was still up and it was warmer, she was going to try again at night with her notoriously poor night vision and when conditions were doubtlessly icier?

I wasn't buying it. What I did buy was a bottle of Windsor Canadian. I also picked up a 12-pack of Mickeys because I was pretty sure if Tina tried getting up that driveway again, she'd fail.

I continued on the road with a sort of grim determination. There was going to be a confrontation.

I started up KTND, the Pandora station that was supposed to represent the tastes of both Tina and I. Immediately, the bouncy, four-on-the-floor, dance song, "Cry for You" started playing. "You'll never see me again… so now who's going to cry for you? You'll never see me again… No matter what you do," sang Petra Marklund, September's Swedish vocalist.

The song was both sad and empowering to me. It became my anthem. It was the theme song of my journey.

When I finally turned down the dark, icy and winding lakeside road that led to Tom's house, I noted tire tracks in the fresh snow. There were two sets – probably one going in and one coming out. There were a few other houses and cabins that the road serviced, so they could have been anyone's, until I proceeded onto Tom's private drive and the tracks continued. I followed them down the steep and treacherous hill and onto the expansive parking area behind the house. Oddly, the tire tracks vanished abruptly at the bottom of the hill. The entire parking area was covered, end to end and end to end in boot prints. Not an inch of the fresh-fallen snow was left untrod. I parked my van next to the house and got out into the cool, but not biting night air. I looked around the driveway, puzzled. There was only one style of boot tread, but it was everywhere, as if it had been the intention to pack down every inch of the fresh snow on this roughly 25 by 40 yard driveway.

I noticed the Saturn Tom had left for Tina to use. It was backed into it's parking spot and had two or three feet of tire tracks between it and the trodden snow. There was only one set, though, as if it had been driven forward and then straight back without ever turning the wheel. If it had gone anywhere, it was with amazing skill and determination that it had been backed in to park precisely in the same tracks it made when it departed.

I wandered back over to the hill and turned on my phone's flashlight feature. The tire tracks, now partly covered by my own van's tracks went perfectly up and down the drive, without any apparent skids or slides and there was certainly no indication that any car had gone off the pavement as Tina said happened to her earlier.

What I was seeing didn't jibe with what Tina had been telling me.

I went back to my van, grabbed the bottle of whiskey and 12-pack of Mickeys then went to the door.

Tina's appearance – which was extraordinary – didn't immediately register, so intent was I on pressing for answers. I was bracing for an end to our relationship.

I swept past as I entered, bypassing her attempt to hug me.

"I had some fun playing dress up," Tina said, presenting herself with a flourish. I looked closer and her hair, makeup, earrings and lingerie (for lack of a more accurate term) made more of an impression, but still, I put that on the shelf to address later.

I got two glasses from the kitchen cabinet and poured a couple fingers of whiskey for each of us. "I have to talk to you about something serious," I said. "I think a strong drink may help." I pushed a glass of Windsor to Tina across the counter. "I picked up a 12-pack of Mickeys for you, too, since I didn't figure you'd make it out of the driveway." I noticed there was already an unopened 12-pack in the kitchen. It wasn't in the fridge, though. It was just sitting on the floor near the laundry room and way into the garage.

Tina picked up the glass. "OK. What's up?" She said casually.

"Well, it's not easy to say," I began. I took a big swallow of whiskey. "I think you've been with another man, today and I think you've been lying to me all day to try to hide your tracks."

Tina's laugh was silvery, mirthful and seemed wildly out of place. "That's funny," she said, smiling.

"I see you do already have a 12-pack of Mickeys," I said. "I guess extra doesn't hurt. When did you get that?"

"I already told you," she said, big hoop earrings dangling as she looked from the beer back to me. "I decided to try again to get up the hill and this time I made it. I bought it in Avon."

I frowned. The nearest liquor store was at least a 20-minute drive, each way – under ideal conditions. It had only been about 40 minutes since she told me over the phone that she was considering making the drive and at that time she was ostensibly burning her fingers, baking muffins, then hunting for burn cream and bandages.

"You know, if someone wrongly accused me of something, I don't think I'd be laughing," I said. "I'd probably be defensive. Maybe angry."

Tina's expression changed to match my expectations. "Oh, I am upset," she said.

I looked at Tina more closely. Her blondish-brown hair was done up big, with ringlets and probably a lot of styling product. Aside from more make up on her face than I knew she owned, she wasn't wearing much else. A lot of skin was showing. What little she did have on was a silky white something I didn't have a name for, but comedian Dave Chappelle might have described as a prostitute's uniform.

"How did you find the time to play dress-up so… elaborately and make your way up the hill and to the liquor store and back?"

"It didn't take long for this," Tina said. "A little hair and make up…"

"Uh huh. And baking muffins. It doesn't look to me like your car has been anywhere."

"I just drove it," Tina said.

"Really?" Forward about 3 feet and straight back again?"

"No… Up the hill and to the liquor store."

There is one set of tire tracks in front of the car. It's been backed in. If you had gone anywhere and came back, there's no way your tracks would line up that perfectly.

"I've backed into a spot and drove exactly over my old tracks before," Tina replied.

"The entire driveway has been tramped out, as if someone was obscuring some other tracks," I said. "Every inch of the driveway is covered in boot prints, except right in front of your car."

"Heh. 'Tramped out,'" she repeated. "That must be from all the men who were over for my services today." Tina chuckled.

"You sure make a lot of jokes about prostitution," I observed.

"Are you calling me a whore?" her voice went up half-an-octave and took on an almost English accent, like a kid's impression of an actor.

"No." I took a step back. "I would never…"

Tina moved towards the short hall that led to the bathroom and upstairs bedrooms. "I was going to do you so good," she said. "Now, I don't think so." She turned around with a disgruntled flourish that reminded me a bit of Miss Piggy scorned and went into the bathroom.

She was gone for a while. I finished my drink and poured another. I touched the bottles in the 12-pack on the floor. They felt room-temperature. I put the other, colder 12-pack I'd brought in the fridge. I noticed a pan of muffins on the counter was covered in Saran wrap.

Tina eventually came back out, but she'd traded her work clothes for sweats and had washed her face. We sat together on the couch. She didn't seem upset by my questioning. She said she could see how I thought something was amiss with what she'd been telling me, but she continued to insist that she'd been completely honest. "It was just a strange set of circumstances," she said. She told me that when she'd said nobody would be coming back, she had just meant she didn't expect her dad or brother. It was well established and shared knowledge that they'd both be away. "Nobody's been here today," she said. "Well, nobody but Ben," she added as an afterthought.

I assumed she meant he'd driven by to check on the house as Tina had told me before he made a custom of doing when Tina's dad was away.

Her dog, Jasper started tugging on a band-aid I hadn't previously noticed on Tina's index finger. "No, Jaspo," she said with a hint of humor in her voice. "I need that." she held the band-aid in place with her other hand and pulled away from the curious dog.

I had the oddest feeling that Jasper was actually trying to show me something. I supposed the bandage was there to cover the sudden oven burn she'd suffered when mentioning that nobody was coming back.

There was one more question bothering me. "But you must have gone somewhere, earlier," I said. "whenever you call from your dad's, it shows up as a wi-fi call, but your call from this afternoon wasn't a wi-fi call."

Tina thought about it for a moment. "I told you earlier about how I was having trouble with the wi-fi," she said. I had to reset the router a few times. "That's probably why it came up on the cellular network, instead."

I thought about it. I had no recollection of Tina mentioning any connectivity problems and I considered that I had set up wi-fi calling specifically because there was zero signal on her T-Mobile phone at her dad's house. My brain was getting a bit fuzzy, though and Tina went on about something else and I let it all go. It was ultimately just easier to go along with Tina's version of events.

We sat and talked and drank and somehow, by the end of the night, I was apologizing to Tina for questioning her. She readily forgave me, wanted to put it behind us and we went to the bedroom together. On the dresser, a row of objects caught my notice: An empty Mickeys bottle; a blackened spoon; Tina's vibrator, half-wrapped in a paper towel; and a pack of sanitary wet-wipes. I was a bit drunk by then and only pondered those items for a moment before Tina turned off the lights, but I later realized that empty had to have come from an as-yet unaccounted for additional 12-pack of Mickey's.

Neither of us was in the mood for sex just then, but we cuddled up under the blankets and then Jasper hopped up and plopped himself in the crook of my knees, pressing his heavy body against me.

In the morning, we did end up having pretty energetic sex. Tina made breakfast for us and everything seemed normal between us. We went outside for a cigarette and I noticed that the sun had been melting all of the curious evidence out in the driveway. The tire tracks and boot prints were gone. I was mildly disappointed, because I'd been thinking a closer look in the daylight might be more revealing, but then I thought, *It's for the better. No sense dwelling on that, now.*

Tina showed me that she only had one cigarette left in her pack. Eventually, we ended up smoking the same blue boxed American Spirits that I favored, but at the Time, she preferred the Gold Marlboro 100s. I offered to drive to the store to get her a pack, but she declined.

"I haven't been smoking as much," she explained, "and we'll be leaving soon, anyhow, so I'd rather wait until we're on the way back."

Made sense to me. "As you wish."

Tina had a number of bedrooms. Each seemed to be fairly well stocked with clothes, books and shoes. There was one at the Buffalo Hotel, of course. By then, Tina maintained a nearly full wardrobe, with a supply of makeup and other lady essentials in my bedroom. She kept a fair amount of property at Scott's and there was her teen den in her dad's basement. That room still looked almost occupied by a younger Tina, but was overstuffed with a picked-through array of clothes, books and curios strewn throughout. The bed was invisible beneath half-sorted piles of clothes and sundries.

Tina set to work packing various things from among the mess that she wanted to take back to buffalo with her. She told me she needed an hour to work on that and then she wanted to leave.

I left her to it and turned on the TV. Jasper hopped up on the couch and put his head in my lap.

No more than five minutes elapsed before Tina came up the stairs and told me she'd changed her mind about cigarettes, but only for Jasper's benefit.

"Jasper's going to hate it when we leave and I feel bad about that, so could you give him one last ride to the store before we go?"

"It'll take like an hour to go to the store and back," I reminded her.

"That's perfect," she said. "I should be ready to go by then."

It was snowy and icy out there and I didn't relish the idea of an extra hour of driving in it, especially since Tina had just let me off that hook minutes earlier.

"Please? Please, Dan? Do it for Jaspo?" She stuck her jaw out, showing her bottom teeth and tilted her head in an imitation of an often befuddled Jasper. "I will love you forever."

"You already do."

"Jasper will too." She gave me puppy dog eyes and I acquiesced.

I Pulled on my shoes, coat and stocking cap and called to Jasper with his favorite words, "car ride."

About an hour later, I was turning back onto the hilly, winding back road that led down to Tom's house on Big Watab Lake. There were odd, narrow little turn offs here and there down side roads and private drives. I wasn't very familiar with the area just yet and had a moment of confusion at a fork in the road.

Left or right?

I started turning to the right, but something caught my eye that told me that was wrong and I quickly corrected my steering back to the left. The van didn't agree, however, and rather than follow my inputs to the left, it kept sliding to the right. To my horror, I noticed my new unstoppable trajectory was towards an obscenely steep downward slope into a private driveway.

Despite my valiant and heroic efforts and my canine copilot's unwavering calm, my minivan didn't come to a stop until we reached the bottom of the drive.

For half-an-hour, I made several attempts to charge my Kia back up the incline, but, though I could get tantalizingly close to the top, the van always lost traction and began to slide backwards, fishtailing against full power just before cresting the hill. After nearly making my situation even worse, I decided to call it quits and let Jasper out so we could walk the rest of the way back to Tom's. Jasper didn't mind at all.

After carefully making my way down Tom's own steep driveway, I went into the house and called for Tina. She came up the stairs.

"Well, there's good news and bad news," I began. I fished into my pockets and produced two packs of cigarettes. "Mission accomplished on the smokes," I said.

"And Jasper got his journey," Tina added.

"Yes. The bad news is I had to leave my van about a quarter mile back and it's not going anywhere without some help."

I explained what had happened and Tina began to cry. I wasn't prepared for that reaction. "It's not the end of the world," I said. "Worst case, I call a tow truck and winch it out."

Tina was not mollified. Sobs wracked her body and tears were flowing like a loved one had suddenly died.

"Your dad's supposed to be home today. Maybe he could tow me out. If I have to spend money on a wrecker, that's fine, too. It's all going to be OK. It's just an inconvenience."

For some reason beyond me, it was much more than an inconvenience in Tina's mind.

When she was composed enough to speak, she said, "Don't call a tow truck, whatever you do. Around here, it'll be at least two-hundred bucks."

I sighed. "If that's what it takes."

"No. Don't do it." She was adamant.

"Here," I said, holding up the freshly procured tobacco. "Let's go out and have a smoke and we can consider our options."

Tina nodded and we went outside. I handed Tina a cigarette and lit one of my own. Tina didn't light hers, though. She set it in the ashtray on the side of the grill, said, "I'll be right back." and disappeared quickly back into the house.

That seemed odd. After I smoked about half my cigarette alone, I snuffed it out and went to look for Tina. I heard her voice, quietly, from the bathroom, mixed with stifled sobs. She was on the phone with someone and crying. The floor creaked as I stepped close to the bathroom door and suddenly, it was silent. Tina stopped crying, stopped speaking. I was mightily puzzled.

This little trick with the cigarette, by the way, was something I'd eventually see Tina pull again. That's when I finally realized I'd been snookered on this occasion as well. Getting me smoking was a way to keep me outside for a while.

Tina eventually emerged from the bathroom, seeming calm and composed. She tried reaching her dad on the phone, hoping to find out when he was expecting to be back – if it would be before dark or not. He didn't answer. Eventually, Tina resigned, with an apparent great deal of reluctance, to ask the neighbor, Ben for help.

Tina said he had heavy equipment that could handle just about any situation.

I didn't understand Tina's reluctance, then. It sounded like a fine solution and from what Tina had told me, this long-time family friend had been willingly charged with checking in on Tina and the Property when Tom was away. He lived quite close, as well.

Tina sent Ben a text message and it wasn't long before she informed me that he was on his way over. "So, we should head over to your van meet him," Tina suggested. "Just let me do all the talking."

That struck me odd, but I just nodded as we pulled our winter coats on and headed out into the bright winter day. Tina took the pan of muffins that had apparently burned her finger the night before.

We arrived at the hill my van had slid down just as Ben was slowly pulling up in a high-set pickup truck. Tina held a hand back to gesture for me to "stay," as she approached the driver side window. Out of earshot, she spoke with the bearded man for a while. Eventually, he got out of the truck and assessed the situation. My van was stuck in a snowbank, halfway down the hill from my final, aborted attempt to charge up the icy incline. Ben produced a long tow rope, but found it wasn't quite long enough to connect our vehicles without moving his truck down the hill as well.

The slope proved too much for his 4-wheel drive, too and before long, Ben's truck was as stuck as my van, half-way down the drive.

At that point, I finally deigned to speak with him. I didn't see any harm in offering a suggestion.

"My van is only two-wheel drive and I made it this far back up the hill by going all the way down to the garage, there and getting a running start. I bet your truck has a better chance of making it than I did."

Ben nodded and backed up all the way to the bottom, where there was a level driveway before the house and garage. With a charging start, he rescued his own truck after two skidding attempts, barely cresting the hill back to the relative safety of the road. "I'm going to go back home and get a bigger truck," he announced.

Tina and I waited by the van for Ben to return with some of the heavier equipment Tina mentioned. I was pretty surprised when he showed up with it.

The vehicle Ben drove looked like it belonged to the military, with huge, studded tires and a forward winch arm that looked like a battering ram.

"I don't know why he didn't bring this one to begin with," Tina muttered. This time, there was sufficient tow cable and Ben's mechanical beast pulled my van up the hill effortlessly.

Apparently as a token of gratitude, Tina gave Ben the pan of muffins she'd baked the night before while I was on my way up. She exchanged a few words with him, out of earshot while I warmed up the van, but I shouted a final "thank you" out the window before he drove away. I'd seen Ben leaving as I was arriving at Tom's a couple times in the years Tina and I were together, but those were the most words I'd ever spoken with him.

I'd had the impression that Tina had some kind of plans she'd been in a hurry to get home for, but after the long ordeal with the stuck van, whatever she was hoping to do had blown over, so when I drove her back to the Buffalo apartment, I stayed there with her and Tina's mysterious behavior at her dad's was forgotten for the nonce.

Tina later explained that since Ben had stopped drinking, he'd taken to sweets, so she'd baked those muffins for him. "Becky tries to keep him on a diet," she said, so now he hides donuts like he used to hide liquor bottles. We used to spend a lot of time together, but Becky put a stop to that."

"Why's that?" I asked.

"I don't know. She just didn't like me anymore."

Taking out the Trash

It was a new year, I had a new fiance, new plans and dreams and was feeling pretty good about life. Tina and I were almost inseparable. I was working on setting up a job for her at my organization. The future was looking bright for us. Come February, in a moment of spontaneity fueled by the "total honesty" policy Tina and I had agreed to, I found myself on one knee in front of Tina in her dad's living room.

I'll never forget the profound look of surprise on her face, but she didn't hesitate. "Yes!" She]d exclaimed.

I was so full of love and happiness, as sappy as it sounds, it felt like my heart might burst from joy. Since it was spontaneous, I didn't have a ring yet to replace the $100 promise ring, but we were both enamored with the interlocking hearts design and figured it would serve for the time being.

After my divorce, I'd sworn to never walk down that aisle again, but here, just 8 months into my relationship with Tina, I was throwing caution to the wind. I just knew it was right. She was my light and joy. I never wanted to be without her. When we were alone together, it felt perfect.

Her Mom came up the next day and Tina told her the news. There was a lot of rejoicing. Maura looked out the front window at the snowy yard and frozen lake.

"Oh my God, is that a heart?" She exclaimed.

That morning, while Tina was sleeping in, I'd gone out to smoke and spent a half-hour or so tromping through the snow to create a giant, fairly symmetrical heart shape for Tina to wake up to. It took up the whole yard.

As cloyingly romantic as all of that may sound, Tina and I didn't really do anything special on Valentines Day that year. We had more of a Valentine's week. I had some time off from work and I think we actually spent around 12 days together, boozing and sexing it up. We didn't have any responsibilities at the time. It was fantastic. Maura had been staying at Scott's, leaving us the Buffalo Hotel "penthouse" to ourselves. We were in our bubble up there, in our private love nest. I don't know if I've ever been happier.

One of those lazy, fun, sexy, buzzed-up February days, I was making dinner for us while Tina was rummaging for something or other in the bedroom. I heard her phone go off and glanced over to it sitting on the counter. There was a message on the screen from a number I didn't know. It just said, "'Sup, Nucka?" None of that meant anything to me and I just got back to what I was doing.

When Tina came back into the kitchen and patted my butt while I stirred the skillet, I told her, "Someone's trying to reach you," and nodded towards her phone.

She picked it up, bit her lip and said, "I told him not to text me like that."

That piqued my interest. Who?

"What? Oh. Nobody. Nothing." She dismissed the question, put her phone away, and in a way that she was well-practiced, changed the subject.

We watched South Park, drank whiskey, had sex on the futon, took turns sitting in my uncomfy chair by the window to smoke cigarettes and Tina fired up her pipe. I almost never toked with her, because I didn't really like the stuff, but Tina smoked weed about daily. Alcohol was my drug of choice – well, my second choice. My fiance was my real drug – the one I felt like I couldn't live without.

As the night went on and Tina was increasingly drunk and high, the conversation took a weird turn. She brought up Chris and we ended up talking about him for at least half-an-hour. She didn't think his wife was a good match for him. "I just don't see how those two got together, "she said.

"They were high school sweethearts," I answered. "Further back than that, I think."

"He's so funny. I like him, she said. I think it's funny that you felt like you had to warn me about him."

"I wanted to make a good impression with my friends."

"How long have you known him?"

"Oh, I don't know. 15 years? Rich started bringing him around for game nights ages ago."

She went on talking and asking questions about him and I remember tiring of the conversation and wanting to wrap it up and move on to another topic. "Yeah, he's a good guy, I said. The kind of friend you'd want in your corner, like a friend will help you move – a good friend will help you move... a body. He was just telling me that if I got into a fight with Kevin and started losing, he'd jump in and help me kick his ass."

"So if you killed me, you'd call Chris to help bury me?"

"Don't be silly."

"I mean, I know you'd never hurt me, but hypothetically. Say there was an accident and you'd go to prison or something..."

"Sure, I said. He might be on my list to call if dirty work was required. If something awful happened and I had to dispose of your body or die, I think he might help me out."

"But only if I was already dead, right? I mean, maybe he'd help you move my body, but he wouldn't help you *make* me a body. He wouldn't kill me just because you asked him to..."

"Oh, I'm sure of that. Especially you," I said. I was kidding, of course.

"No he wouldn't!"

"Oh, yeah. I think if you became a problem that needed to be eliminated, he'd be happy to help." I was smiling. I was not serious. I was just teasing her on this ridiculous conversation, but she became histrionic.

"No, he would not! Chris would not hurt me." She was getting louder.

I pressed on. "Sure he would – especially if I slipped him some cash. Like I said, he's a good friend to have in your corner. I think he'd help me make the body and then move it."

"I'm going to ask him next time," she said with a determined air of defiance. She picked up a spiral notebook and scrawled in big letters, taking up a whole sheet of paper, 'Would Chris kill me, just because Dan asked?'

"There," she said, showing me the page.

It was getting really weird. Tina had met Chris on approximately two occasions and I'd known him for a decade or more. I was kidding around, but she was quite adamant that in the crazy hypothetical scenarios she was concocting, this guy she barely knew (as far as I was aware) would be incapable of harming her. She was behaving like she thought she had some kind of special relationship with him, presuming to know him better than myself. By no means do I believe Chris to be a killer, but if you went with the premise that he would help me carry out a murder, why would Tina think she'd be off-limits?

"OK... Anyway..." I was still looking for a way out of this bizarre conversation.

"If it was anyone else, sure, she said. Do you know he showed me his guns? He has so many freaking guns! Have you ever seen his guns? He said he never shows anyone, but he showed me." She beamed. "Well, he showed me pictures," she added.

"Yeah," I said. I shrugged. I knew Chris had a sizable collection. I'd seen and handled a couple and I guess I was special, because I'd even seen some pictures of his rifles and shotguns, too. I tried again to change the subject and finally succeeded by segueing into guns. "You know, there's a shooting range near here. I've been thinking about picking up a handgun. I have a line on a Sig nine millimeter, but I was thinking about looking at revolvers."

"Will you take me shooting?"

"Of course."

The next day, Tina and I got groggily back to the land of the living and had some breakfast. As was becoming our routine, we stayed up very late and drank way too much. I had some work thing to do the next day, so I was planning on finally departing the love bubble after staying over a week, but I was in no hurry to get going. I found a movie for us to watch and we reclined cozily amid a pile of pillows and comforters on the futon.

Something in the movie put me on to thinking about the weird conversation about Chris from the night before and I was struck with some amount of anxiety. I'm thinking it's not surprising that something wasn't sitting well with me about that recollection. I connected the text message with her sudden interest in Chris and when she went to the bathroom, I stole a look at her phone. The only recent message was "'Sup nucka?" When I looked at the actual message, I saw it was from someone named Chris. It seemed pretty likely that "'Sup Nucka" was from my move-a-body buddy. I made note of the number and texted Rich to ask for Chris' cell phone number, then waited for confirmation.

We got to binge-watching episodes of Shameless, but Tina wasn't paying much attention to the show. She was busily tapping away on the slide-out keyboard on her phone for quite a while. She looked happy or amused. It was uncharacteristic. Tina often ignored her phone and tended to the terse side with texts.

"Are you writing a book?"

"What? Oh. I'm just texting my dad," she said, setting the phone down for a moment.

That was even more unusual. Tom was the king of brevity.

"That's a lot of texts for you and your dad," I observed, but I knew her relationship with him had been strained, Maura didn't think they talked enough and I was glad that she was communicating with him.

"I'm not really writing that much. I just keep deleting and starting over."

"OK..."

A little later, Tina told me she'd got a text from her mother, who'd been staying at Scott's down in Farmington. "She's coming back to the apartment after work," she told me. There was some strife between her and Scott and she had a headache so she didn't want to see him that night.

After a bit, Tina was back to texting while the Shameless marathon rolled on. Maura came in around 5 PM and settled on the futon with us and we chatted for a few minutes, but things quickly turned from there.

"When do you have to get going?" Tina interjected.

"I have to get up in the morning, so I can't be up too late, I said. I figure I'll head home after this last episode." I gestured to the screen.

"Oh. OK."

We all sat together and watched the show for a few minutes, but Tina was seeming agitated. She went to the kitchen and started cinching up trash bags. She asked if I could take out the garbage. I said I definitely would on my way out. The apartment was on the third floor of the old Buffalo Hotel so it was a minor chore but I was happy to do the man's work.

"Do you want some help carrying your bags out to the van so you don't have to make another trip up?"

I had the pretty distinct impression that I was getting the bum's rush. I was confused, hurt and I didn't like it. I dug in my heels. My curiosity was piqued. I deliberately dragged out my pending departure, feigning ignorance. My suspicion was on high-alert and I became determined to gather as much information as possible before I left.

"Nah, you don't have to do that, I said. I'll take care of it all by myself."

Tina was struggling to maintain a semblance of normalcy, but I could see that she was becoming frantic and manic. She started gathering my things from around the apartment.

"C'mon, Tina said, Let's take care of this while my mom's still up so she can help bring everything down." She turned off the program.

Maura had gone into the kitchen and at one point, was bent over, elbows resting on the stove, fingers on her temples, cradling her head. She looked... frightened? She seemed to me like a person powerlessly resigned to pending disaster.

"I really don't need any help..."

Tina, still wearing pajamas, was putting her boots on. She was moving swiftly, packing my suitcase, gathering the garbage by the door. I moved slowly but began making progress towards leaving. I took my time tying my shoes, triple-checked that I wasn't forgetting anything I'd need, paused to re-verify some details of our pending plans, but eventually, the three of us were going down the stairs with my work bag, my suitcase and a few bags of garbage.

As we trudged across the snowy parking lot, Maura looked over at me and said, "You look like a kicked puppy."

"That's about right," I muttered. I don't think I was heard.

Van loaded, Tina gave me a quick peck and said she'd call me later. I was a bit stunned. I started the van, but just sat there for a minute, letting everything sift through my mind. I lit a cigarette and put the van in reverse. I slowly rolled out of the parking lot and started towards the highway. I was reasonably certain someone was coming over. Someone I wasn't meant to see. After a few blocks, a notion struck. *Maybe I should see.*

I turned the van around.

I parked in a public lot that was kitty-corner from the Buffalo Hotel, at an angle that allowed me to easily see the front door of the building, but where it was unlikely I'd be noticed. I looked at my phone and noticed I'd missed a text message from Rich. He'd sent me Chris' phone number, as requested. I didn't need to cross-check. I recognized it. It was the same number that Tina had received the message from earlier.

I watched the street in front of the Buffalo Hotel for over an hour, but finally decided it was a silly exercise. I'd been sitting there wasting gas to keep the van warm and I was behaving like a stalker. It was getting late. Time to go home. I stepped on the brake and put the gear selector into reverse.

The front door to the Buffalo Hotel opened and I paused to refocus my attention there.

A woman stepped out into the cold, wearing a long, tan-colored wool coat. She had a scarf wrapped around her head and was wearing big sunglasses. She looked like a Hollywood starlet of yesteryear trying to avoid the paparazzi, but she also looked to be Tina's height and build.

I couldn't see her hair or make out her face, but I recognized that coat. It looked like one that Tina had worn once before. She told me that it used to belong to her grandmother.

She turned to her left, and walked towards the back of the building on the street-side, which surprised me. Tina and I never walked that way. It would lead to the building's small parking lot and dumpsters, but as visitors weren't welcome to park there, I always parked in a public lot more directly accessible from the other side of the building.

I backed up the van and tried to quickly get around the block and over to the side of the Buffalo Hotel. There was no one in sight when I got to the small back lot, but I caught sight of vehicle exhaust coming from the other side of the library, just next door. I drove over there, and discovered that several unoccupied vehicles were idling outside the library. I guessed that the staff must have been warming up their cars before the library closed and backtracked. I drove through the public lot I usually parked in and saw no people or running vehicles. I'd missed out on seeing where Tina actually ended up, but I assumed she got into someone's car in the public lot and drove off in the other direction.

I struggled with what I'd seen. It was possible that I was mistaken. Someone else in the building could have owned a similar coat. I hadn't been able to make out the woman's face.

I drove home and tried texting Tina to let her know I'd made it back and just say goodnight, but she didn't respond until late afternoon, the next day.

"I just woke up," she texted. "Me and my mom both fell asleep on the futon right after you left and just got up now."

"You've been sleeping for 21 hours?" I wrote back incredulously.

"Yes. Well, I might have woken up once or twice, but my mom was sleeping on the outside of the futon, so I was trapped. And couldn't get up."

A moment later, she added, "I did get up to use the bathroom, though."

None of that made sense to me. I'd known Tina to stay in bed for extended spans, up to 12 hours, maybe, but there's no way I believed that Maura had slept for 21 hours.

How did she use the bathroom if Maura had her trapped? She said she was unable to get out of bed.

I didn't say anything about my sleuthing the evening before and eventually I simply accepted Tina's unlikely story – until I finally understood her nature, that is. This was one of many memories I had to revisit and reevaluate after our tumultuous relationship finally ended.

Do I get to fuck your Girlfriend?

In my life, I'd observed on occasion, a witless or uncouth man come on to my date, but never with the frequency or astonishing level of disrespect I experienced when in public with Tina.

We'd gone to our frequent watering hole, the Buffalo Bar and Grill and as was our routine, we were shooting pool and drinking whiskey. We struck up a doubles game with a couple men. One older, one younger. It was a typically good time, but Tina was disappearing for extended periods, ostensibly to the restroom. I assumed she was having some digestive trouble. She and the younger shooter had been gone for quite a while, so the older guy and I shot a game one on one while waiting for them to return. The game and conversation was going pleasantly enough when the older man turned to me and said, "so if I win this game, do I get to fuck your girlfriend?"

"Excuse me?" Words had vibrated my eardrums, but that could not possibly have been a string of cohesive English.

"If I win this game, does that mean I get to fuck your girlfriend?" Unabashed, he restated his proposition.

I was overwhelmed – not initially with anger, but astonishment. I felt like I'd slipped into the Twilight Zone and though I now heard, registered and comprehended his words, I couldn't fathom the situation. It was so completely alien. I had to clarify what exactly he expected to accomplish by speaking to me about the love of my life like this. "What the hell is wrong with you? Are you trying to pick a fight with me?" Up until this point, everything had been friendly and nothing seemed amiss.

He grinned a gray-bearded, drunken grin and shrugged. "Yeah," he said. "Then do I get to fuck her?"

"That's it, fucker!" I snatched up my pool cue and gripped it like a bat, tip down, fully intent on cracking it over his head and then jamming whatever was left in my hand right through his eye, but when I drew my arm back, it did not strike. The younger man we'd been playing with had returned, unnoticed (by me, anyhow). From behind he'd caught my wrist in his meaty grip. He was taller than I and probably about double my weight. He grappled. I struggled, but he quickly had both my arms pinned. I felt impotent. I could not break free of him and he disarmed me of the pool cue. "I'm going to need that," I said, suddenly calm and no longer struggling, but still intent on carrying out my initial plan to jam that cue into the old man's eye.

"I can't let you hurt him." he said.

"Did you hear what this mother fucker said?" I was righteously indignant.

The young man seemed embarrassed. "Yeah, but he's my dad."

I understood his dilemma.

"Look, he's trashed. I'm going to take him home."

I was mollified – I didn't have much choice but to be quelled. The son released me and urged his drunken father away.

All this went on while Tina was away. I refilled our drinks while I waited alone by the pool tables. Some time later, the vulgar old man – now in a Vikings jacket – approached me again with his son. I sprang to my feet.

"I thought you were getting him the fuck out of here," I demanded.

"He wanted to come over and apologize."

"Yeah," said the old man. "I'm sorry. I'm pretty drunk." I nodded, prepared to accept his apology and move on with my night, but then he added, "but I still want to fuck your girlfriend."

That time, I leapt straight to rage. I yelled "Mother fucker!" or something appropriate to the situation as the son lunged to interpose himself between his dad and I.

"I'm sorry. I didn't know he was going to say that," the son said as he pulled his dad away, towards the exit.

"Get him out of here," I said. "If I see him again, somebody's going to have to call the cops."

"C'mon, Dad. Let's find Mom and I'll get you home."

His wife was at the bar with him! I shook my head in amazement. Tina finally returned, having (apparently) missed all of the excitement and I related the highlights.

"I would have handled that old man, myself," Tina said. "You don't have to get yourself arrested defending my honor."

I explained "fighting words." A man talking about another man's lady like she's trash is a provocation that can't go ignored. To me, crazy talk like that is the same as a direct threat. Someone who'd say things like that is dangerous and capable of anything. Even taking the insult to honor out of the equation, self-defense becomes an immediate probability.

We went out into the cold to get our nicotine fix. Sitting at a table on the patio, we watched the man in the vikings jacket being guided to a car by his son. A woman a step behind was repeatedly hitting the man with her purse, all the way across the parking lot.

We laughed.

It was one for the book.

Looking back through the lens of experience with Tina, I can't help but guess there was more to the story than I was aware of. The old man probably knew about something going on that I didn't. That both his son and Tina had been absent for quite some time was worth considering.

These kind of things that were pretty much new to my experience just tended to happen with Tina around and things usually happen for reasons.

Crack and Crime in Farmington

I was excited to discover a pool hall in Farmington. Scott's was still Tina's home away from home, so it was a convenient spot for an occasional date. It was a dive as pool halls go, but we'd gone there together once or twice and found the staff and patrons to be agreeable. It was cheap, too.

Even though we were out in Buffalo, one weekend, I arranged for Tina and I to get together with Donovan to shoot pool at Farmington Billiards. It's about an hour and a half drive between the two small towns. Farmington and Buffalo were at opposite ends of the Twin Cities Metro Area. It was a drive I had to make on occasion for Tina's sake, ostensibly to deliver her to her mother at Scott's. I generally didn't mind the drive. Though many of my stories are about strange and unpleasant events, I absolutely adored Tina's company (particularly when we were alone) and our conversations made the travel time go by pleasantly. This time, taking her to Scott's wasn't the purpose, though.

Tina was excited to learn that we were going to see Donovan. A little too excited, I felt. It turned out that Tina had a shirt she'd been waiting for the chance to wear and seeing Donovan again was the occasion. She pranced off into the bedroom to fetch it and emerged in a new, form-fitting, pale-blue Superman T-shirt.

Donovan often wore Superman-branded clothes and Tina credited him with super-heroism for picking up Shayna and throwing her into my van, kicking off the disastrous end to our first date.

I frowned. It was the first time I noticed Tina's way of mirroring a person she was interested in. She was triangulating me with my friend. I didn't know the psychological terms or manipulative reasons at the time, but it didn't make me feel good.

I set aside my jealous pangs. It's just a T-shirt. Maybe she just wants to fit in, I thought.

But it wasn't just a T-Shirt. There were little comments here and there too, like "the night we met at Dew Days, it was Donovan who first caught my eye." Normal people don't tell don't tell a significant other that they were the second choice, but that's part of the way narcissists manipulate and control their prey.

While bombing me with love and affection, she was also loaded with poisonous little darts like that to inject here and there. If I ever questioned them or expressed displeasure, they were just "jokes," "no big deal," I was being "too sensitive," or she'd just deny having said it.

We arrived in Farmington around 8 PM and met up with Donovan, his daughter and her boyfriend. That night was one of those infrequent, but occasional times when I was made to notice the age gap between Tina and I. Tina was closer in age to Donovan's daughter than to me, but she still seemed more a peer of Donovan and I (to me).

Tina showed off her shirt for Donovan, but whatever her message, it didn't seem to land on him.

We were having a good time shooting pool, but after a while, Tina disengaged. She seemed distant. Eventually, she nodded across the hall toward a boisterous corner of apparent regulars. "See that guy over there? The one with the beard?"

I glanced over and nodded.

"He keeps staring at me and it's starting to creep me out," she said.

I looked back. He didn't seem to be paying her any attention at the moment. "Do you know him? Maybe he's trying to figure out where he recognizes you from. Then again, you are very pretty." I smiled and gave her a quick kiss.

"I don't know," she said, thoughtfully. She seemed unduly concerned.

"Don't worry. I'll protect you." Perhaps I was a tad glib, but I didn't think the grizzled old drunk looked like much of a threat. Maybe I just didn't recognize what *kind* of threat he posed.

Tina looked like she'd rather be anywhere else at that point. "I'm not feeling well. I think I need to eat something. Can we go get dinner pretty soon?"

"Sure," I said. We were playing on two tables. Our game was finished, but Donovan's daughter and her beau were still in the middle of one. "How about we go after those two finish up?"

"OK. Come have a smoke with me?"

"Sure."

On the way out, I stopped and quickly related our plan to leave with our companions. It was agreed all around.

Out front, I lit Tina's cigarette and then my own. We were only alone for a few moments before the thing Tina seemed to want to avoid happened. The older guy with the scraggly white beard who'd been eying her stumbled outside to join us.

He was plainly very intoxicated, slurring a bit and swaying on his feet. "Hey," he said, looking right at Tina, seeming not to see me. I moved closer to her, protectively.

Tina blinked at him, seeming unsure of what to say.

"Hey. You wanna know what?" he slurred.

"What?" Tina took a drag off her cigarette.

"Hey, what are you doing tonight? You wanna smoke some crack?"

I moved closer to Tina so that we were shoulder to shoulder.

"No, thank you," said Tina.

He took a step back, seemed to notice me for the first time. He grinned an odd grin and shook his head. Then, he took a step towards us again and I moved forward half a step to interpose myself, but keeping in contact with Tina.

I was flabbergasted by what happened next. This is the kind of thing that could only happen with Tina. When she and I were out in public together, people behaved in ways I'd never seen before in my life.

First, he made kind of a chopping motion with his hand, as if he was cutting Tina and I apart from one another. Then, he stuck his cigarette between his lips to hold it and free his other hand. He put both hands together like a wedge and physically forced that wedge between our persons, trying to separate us by moving his hands apart. Tina pressed in firmer against me and I put an arm out in front of Tina. He withdrew his very unwelcome touch and backed off a step.

I threw my cigarette down and balled my fists, keeping between Tina and the increasingly creepy old drunk.

"Hey, You don't wanna come to my place and smoke some crack?" he said to Tina.

"No. I'm good," she replied.

"You wanna go into Farmington and do some crime?"

"We're in Farmington," she replied.

"We're not interested," I interjected.

"Oh." He waved his finger back and forth between us. "You two… OK…" he trailed off.

"Let's see if they're ready to leave," I suggested, nodding to the door.

Tina snuffed her cigarette and led the way back into the pool hall.

"OK. Have a good night," said the drunk.

I went up to the counter to settle the bill and mentioned the creepy drunk bothering Tina to the attendant.

"Oh, that's just Bob. He's had too much to drink. He's harmless," I was told.

"Maybe someone should call him a cab," I suggested a bit darkly.

I paid our bill and we got everyone out of there in short order. We went down the road a few blocks to Carbone's Pizza, hoping to get dinner, but the place was empty except for a skeleton staff and we were informed the kitchen was closed. Just the bar was open. We weren't told that until after we'd been seated, ordered drinks and examined the menus we'd been provided. Further, the signage indicated 2-for-1 appetizer specials until midnight. It was about 10:30 when we arrived. That was Farmington!

After that night, Tina would often put on a dolt's voice and repeat, "Wanna go into Farmington and do some crime?" I didn't think much of it – it was just a weird occurrence to joke about later, but after knowing Tina for years, I realized there was more to it. She often repeated sentences or sentence fragments that had really bothered her. Sometimes, out of the blue, with no context but a sneer or sarcastic tone, she'd quote something someone had said to offend her, or something she wanted to re-frame.

At the time, I assumed that the old drunk was just a crazy stranger trying to hit on Tina, but the whole story makes a lot more sense by changing that assumption. If he'd met her before and had reason to expect a more receptive response, his behavior would have been more understandable. Looking back through the filter of what I now know about her double and triple lives puts that memory in a different context.

When I first told Tina about having discovered Farmington Billiards, she said she'd not been aware of it, but I wonder. A year or so later, Tina and I ran into Sean at the Cardinal in Minneapolis. He was an old friend of mine who was a master pool player. We got to talking about Farmington Billiards and it turned out that Sean knew Bob, the old drunk who'd wanted to smoke crack and do crimes with Tina. He was one of the owners of the pool hall, as it turned out, and it was a further revelation to discover that Tina seemed to know him by name when she talked about him with Sean. I had no recollection of him ever giving his name during our encounter.

The night Bob accosted us was the first time I'd seen him. Tina and I had been to Farmington Billiards a couple times prior, but it stands to reason that he was there a fair bit if he owned the place and it's exactly the kind of place Tina would have wanted to hang out at, just a mile down the main road from her home away from Home at Scott's.

Narcissists tend to lead double (and triple and quadruple) lives. Tina didn't have a car back then, so her territory was pretty small, increasing the odds that her separate worlds would collide.

Whether Tina had smoked crack with Bob sometime in the past, I could never say for sure, but, if nothing else, she was a constant magnet for trouble and the downright bizarre.

The Bachelor Party Guys

As I recall and write my stories (and there are so so many of them), I'm forced to confront the biggest burning question, "what the fuck is wrong with me?" There was no one holding a gun to my head forcing me to stay in the humiliating, abusive relationship I was in with Tina. There were many times when it would have been obvious to any outside observer that I should have ran fast and far. So why didn't I?

I felt an emotional connection to Tina that was unlike anything I'd ever experienced in my life. It was powerful.

When Tina wasn't being a complete asshole, she was smart, witty, charming and complimentary. She flattered me. She stroked my ego. We never ran short of compelling conversation. She was an intellectual match. I loved her. When we were alone together, it seemed like impossible magic. Introducing other people into our world brought out a different Tina, or Tinas. She changed her personality like a chameleon changes colors around some company. Now I wonder if I ever really knew her or if I was just enamored of the chameleonic reflection of myself I saw in her as she adapted to my "colors."

It wasn't more than a month after she'd accepted my first marriage proposal and the two of us were spending some time alone in the top-floor apartment of the Buffalo Hotel. Newly engaged and excitedly planning our wedding, we drank copious amounts of whiskey, smoked a lot of cigarettes and had a lot of great sex. It was a blissful, care-free time. It was winter and we'd been spending a lot of time in the small apartment. We were quite happy, but decided to brave the cold and get out for a while.

I drove her to the Buffalo Bar and Grill, where we were becoming known as regulars. There are a few pool tables there and another of Tina's favorites: A claw machine game. To my amazement, had I won her a stuffed animal on my first try on our first visit to that bar. I found some cosmic significance in that. It was meant to be.

We got our usual order to start the night: Two Nordeaster beers and two double shots of Windsor. The bartender was always really friendly to us and poured rather too generously, but we weren't complaining! I always tipped really well.

After we shot a game or two of pool and tried our luck at the Claw machine, we went out for a smoke in the chilly night air. When we got back inside, there were a couple guys shooting pool at the table adjacent ours. We struck up a conversation with them and wound up taking them on in doubles eight-ball. They were very personable and decent players. Tina and I admired the custom-made cues they'd brought to shoot with.

At some point in the night, it came up that Brendon and Sam were only visiting the area for a friend's bachelor party that was coming up.

Tina took a tremendous interest in the bachelor party, pressing them on what they had lined up for entertainment. It became apparent that it wasn't going to be the cliched strippers and hos kind of bachelor party and the guys didn't seem very interested in discussing that any further but when drunk, as Tina was, she lost any ability to read social cues and pressed on. Insisting that they had to at least have a stripper if they were going to show their buddy a good time before he tied the knot. She said she could hook them up with a dancer.

"You know a stripper?" I asked, a little surprised. I remembered her talking before about thinking about trying it out herself. Some of Scott's friends had told her, "I'd pay to see that."

Tina just nodded, barely acknowledging that I was even there anymore, so wrapped up in the bachelor party discussion that she wouldn't let drop.

We'd bet a round of drinks on the outcome of our last game with Sam and Brendon and we'd lost. I excused myself to the restroom and stopped by the bar to order a round of beers. I went back to the pool tables to tap Tina for help carrying all the drinks back and saw her doing the thing she "never does," for at least the third time since I'd started dating her. She was exchanging cell phones with Brendon. It appeared that they'd each just finished adding their contact information and they were just then swapping phones back.

I was a bit drunk myself at this point and it didn't fully register it at the time, but recalling this night on the following St. Patrick's Day led to a pretty big blow-out between Tina and I on the subject of obtaining other guy's phone numbers.

We'd gone to Rich and Thea's to have corned beef and cabbage and go out bar-hopping in White Bear Lake. It was a pretty small group. Chris was with. His wife stayed home with the kids. Richard's kids were out around town, too, but we didn't really see much of them.

I was probably fairly drunk by the time the argument started. I started asking questions about why Chris and Tina were texting each other. I think that night, her excuse was getting weed from him, but later she told me it was about arranging for all of us to go shooting together (something he later vehemently denied when I casually brought it up).

Chris, hearing all this as we walked between bars admitted to texting her. "Yeah, I texted her, but I would never…"

"Fine. You wanted to buy weed – even though you're well stocked and I thought your mom bought all your weed for you, but whatever. What was your business with those other guys at the Buffalo Bar I saw you exchanging numbers with, then?"

She usually had explanations, but she didn't have a ready response. She did remember their names, though. "Oh, you mean Brendon and Sam?" She said their names with a certain fondness, a sly smile curling her lips.

Rich, who'd been walking ahead of us suddenly turned and hollered, "shut the fuck up, Dan!"

Rich was very slow to anger. He'd never raised his voice to me in the decades I'd known him. I respected and trusted him. That stopped me in my tracks, stunned. If Rich turned on me in anger, I must be way out of line, I concluded. I clammed up, shamed. I must have been wrong about all of that.

Tina looked approvingly at her new defender and we continued on our way to the next bar. More whiskey will solve all this!

Why didn't I leave her then and there? There were many times that question should have been seriously considered. I always gave her the benefit of the doubt. I preferred to assume there were innocent explanations. She often had excuses or scapegoats. I tended to believe her, but never entirely, I suppose. I drank away memories of embarrassing moments. She reassured me of her devotion with sex and flattery (yes, disappointingly, it appears that I am that stupid). Our relationship carried on, but I've actually lost track of how many times we "broke up" over incidents like this, always to reunite. We didn't immediately call it quits after that night in Buffalo, but when it came up on St. Patrick's Day and we argued, we were separated for a couple weeks afterwards and then it was me, doing all the apologizing.

Life with Tina was confusing, disorienting and confounding. It could seem like there were two Tinas or that she was in a kind-of Shrodinger's quantum reality where she could exist in two contradictory states at once. She loved me and at the same time, she didn't. There were time I wondered if she might have covertly despised me. She was somehow simultaneously faithful and disloyal. It was mind-bending, trying to reconcile the idea that these two (or more) distinct individuals could occupy the same space in one body. Keeping me off balance was part of the manipulation that led to forming a trauma bond.

It was destabilizing to me and challenging to imagine the chaos going on behind her bright hazel eyes. The webs and pathways holding her tenuous, contradictory reality together must have been a tangled complexity. I imagined only someone with Tina's intelligence could manage a semblance of normalcy, which she often did, but as I continued to get closer, the cracks were showing. She maintained different worlds and sowed discord between to prevent them colliding. When they did occasionally, inevitably brush together, things got messy and complicated and Tina struggled. Gaslighting or ghosting, and ultimately both inevitably ensued.

Trying to reconcile Tina's seemingly diametrical personalities into one was like trying to force the same pole of two magnets together. Ultimately, I had to realize that, of course, there were not two Tinas. There was no quantum mystery box. There was just the one damaged, destructive, emotionally stunted girl and she did all the shitty things. That same person also did all the nice things. She hid the love notes in my briefcase before I left her apartment. She flattered me, took my arm or hand when we walked, gave occasional gifts and made delicious chicken noodle soup.

The "good" side of the one Tina was not necessarily genuine, however. Or, at least, it wasn't reflective of her greater nature. The woman who'd collect other guys' phone numbers and accept the drinks they offered in bars was Tina in her natural form. The young woman who liked my old 80's synth pop and gushed about how incalculably much she loved me several times a day was a mere facade, of no real substance. That was a mask, easily changed out for other company. It's purpose was to keep me captive and providing what she needed: validation for her own existence, also known as narcissistic supply. She wanted me to love her, but probably never believed that she could be loved as she was. Perhaps I could have, but she would never have taken that chance. Instead, she adapted a persona to what she thought I would love, to create for both of us, an illusion of love.

There was just the one Tina all along: a cunning, wounded monster with many faces but only a single, blackened and insatiably empty heart; an incomplete person to whom other humans were disposable objects, kept and valued only so long as they served, without suspicion or reservation, to pour their souls into her bottomless void. A narcissist.

Waxing Poetic

While we were out of contact after St. Patrick's Day, Tina was on my mind all the time, but I could not access her. I began writing some of our experiences as a precursor to a very different planned version of this very book as a way to maintain a sense of connection and on a very low level, satisfy my cravings for her company (the ultimate purpose of writing the book as it came to be was quite the opposite). I also wrote a poem and had a notion for a romantic gesture that could recapture Tina's attention.

I obtained a huge piece of reflective copper poster board, trimmed the corners and carefully inscribed my ode to Tina with a black paint marker on the shiny, 2 foot by 3 foot sheet.

Tina, fair of hair
I'd go with her anywhere;
I've traveled 'cross the state
With my best friend and lover
Every moment's great
And I could place no one above her

To her loving hazel eyes
I hate to say goodbye;
I long for her, I pine for her
Whenever we're apart;
Filled with constant wonder
How ever did this magic start?
From Farmington to Buffalo

To Brainerd, White Bear Lake
Cold Spring, Minneapolis
The journey started with a handshake

Every time I see her
The Earth below is moved
Growing ever nearer;
Closer, our souls, fused

I sense her from a distance
Feel her emotions from afar;
Spooky Action, for instance
Or it's magic from the stars

She takes my breath away;
Her love is pure and sweet
So I know she'd never stray
But however did we meet?

The stars aligned and she designed
To make our love complete

Once thoroughly dry, I rolled up the giant poem, boxed it up with a letter and sent it to Tina's apartment without any identifying return address.

My gesture had the desired effect. I'm told it arrived just as her dad was picking Tina up to go back to Cold Spring. Tina said that after seeing it, she told her father that she loved me too much to stay away. Tom reportedly wasn't happy with her decision to contact me again, but she did get in touch a couple days later and we swiftly resumed our chaotic romance.

Feeling that everything was made right and no longer feeling depressed, I also resumed drinking. When things subsequently would go wrong, I'd often blame myself because I thought I wasn't communicating well enough due to being under the influence. I began to get the idea that most of the troubles that arose between Tina and I were because of my failure to express my thoughts and feelings just right.

Although I'm now sure Tina understood me quite well, when she'd act as though she didn't understand where I was coming from, that naturally reinforced my (erroneous) notion. In essence, I was being gaslighted and blaming myself for miscommunication, but as long as Tina was still by my side, life was good enough and I was confident we'd conquer all obstacles to our fated blissful future.

Two Dicks at a Bar

I witnessed and experienced things when in Tina's company I'd never come up against in any prior relationship. It got bizarre in some cases and I wondered how it was that Tina attracted such trouble. Some of it was just happenstance and perhaps she and I went to some questionable establishments on occasion, but some things were so strange and outrageous, I sometimes suspected that she was bringing them about by subtle signals or just by way of being a magnet for trouble.

She and I had gone to a local bar that had changed hands a few times in my life and with each new owner, the establishment, now called the Howe, became more gentrified.

Sitting on the back patio to sip our drinks with cigarettes in hand, we engaged in friendly chatter with some fellow patrons. One was a platinum blonde woman who made a comment here and there but mostly looked at her phone. Another was an obese, twenty-something man overflowing his black metal chair, legs posed in a way some silly radicals might call 'manspreading.'

After some time, which I say so as not to give the impression that it was the first thing my eyes were drawn to, I noticed that not only was his fly open, but his bits were plainly visible in the yawning opening. Maybe it was laundry day or maybe he had a grudge against undergarments. Maybe he was simply deranged.

I've never seen a penis exposed at a bar or anywhere in public before, so I denied I'd seen it at first and had to look again. Yup. his little beige dick was plainly visible.

Tina was chatting with a girl off to her side and I wanted to subtly share this unusual experience, so I texted her, "OMG. Dick out!!!"

After she read it, she glanced around and her eyes settled on the thing. She nudged me and stifled a giggle, mischievous eyes twinkling. Tina absolutely delighted in any form of naughtiness. After a few moments of consideration, she decided to dive right in. "Excuse me, but your fly is open," she said.

The man glanced down, but probably couldn't see his crotch over his belly. He shrugged.

"Um. We can see your uh, package," she said.

Unperturbed, he shrugged again, saying, "OK. No big deal," and he took a swig of his beer.

"Aren't you going to…"

"Nah. I don't care."

Tina and I looked at each other, wordlessly acknowledging that this was another moment destined for our pending great memoir of strange and funny anecdotes.

The overweight exhibitionist excused himself to the restroom, shuffling back inside the bar. Tina followed after him, excusing herself to the restroom shortly after. She was gone for quite some time. I was beginning to notice she frequently disappeared into restrooms for excessive spans when we were out drinking.

After a while, Tina came back to the table and lit a cigarette. We were shortly joined at the table by a man with longish wavy two-toned hair. He seemed to be acquainted with the platinum blonde girl Tina had been talking with and joined our little conversation. We learned that he was a partner in a new recording studio that had opened up the road. Since I was trained and experienced as an audio engineer, we pleasantly talked about the changes in recording tech over the years, with Tina chiming in about instruments.

Rather abruptly, and to my great surprise, the man turned his face to Tina and asked, "Can I buy you a drink?"

This is going to be interesting, I thought for less than half a second.

Without the slightest hesitation, she just replied, "sure."

The man stood up, gestured for her to follow and the two disappeared into the bar before I could even wrap my head around what was happening, let alone speak.

I flashed for a moment on our first date in Farmington, where a drunk and drug-addled dilettante with a trust fund offered to buy both Tina and I a shot of "good brandy" if we'd drink it with him and write "because drugs." on his forehead in Sharpie. This was not that.

I sat there, stunned, looking at the empty table in front of me. I guessed that they must be soon returning, so I lit another cigarette while I waited alone on the patio and pondered the situation.

After finishing my smoke and not seeing my fiance or her new benefactor, I went in to the bar. I noticed the two of them sitting together at the corner of the bar, backs to me, leaned in to talk to each other, fresh drinks before them.

I went to the restroom to relieve my bladder and to take a pause. When I came back out, they were still seated at the bar. I was apparently just forgotten about and abandoned. The flash of wounded ego was fast replaced by indignation and anger. I glared from across the room, arms crossed, considering how to comport myself. The recording studio guy glanced over at me and Tina followed suit. She saw me icily posed, staring daggers, but just turned back to her new company without even so much as a wave in my direction.

I'd thought up a few rejoinders to address the situation, like "are you going to buy a drink for her fiance, too," or "Thanks for your generosity, but I can afford to buy the drinks for my date," but seeing Tina's non-reaction to me turned everything red and my impulse was to turn around, walk out of the bar and drive home, leaving her behind with her new friend. Maybe he'd drive her back to Buffalo when he was finished with her, I thought.

I stalked up behind and leaned in between them. "I'm leaving," I seethed. "Now."

Tina wrapped a small hand around the tumbler in front of her. "At least let me finish my drink first," she replied glibly.

"Bye." I turned around and made for the parking lot. She didn't make any immediate move to stop me or follow. I climbed into my van, started it up and lit a cigarette, the lighter trembling in my hand.

I'd dated a sketchy girl or two in my youth, but no one had ever treated me this poorly. I'd never felt so insulted. Ever. I felt humiliated, disposable and rejected. My world was crashing in on me. If any other woman on Earth had done something like this on a date, I'd never have seen her again. But here was the love of my life, my bride-to-be. She'd earlier that very night professed her profound and unshakable love for me, now displaying dismissive disdain. I was still in shock from the audacity of her rude behavior when she stepped up to my open window.

She looked at me wordlessly for a moment.

"I'm leaving right now. If you want me to give you a ride home, get in." I put my foot on the brake and set the van in reverse. Tina glanced back toward the bar, seemed about to say something, but thought better of it and came around to the passenger door.

"I thought we were staying at your place tonight. What's the problem?" She fastened her seat belt as I slowly backed out.

My head was spinning. I couldn't answer her right away.

Once on the road and down the block, words came to me. "What the fuck, Tina?"

"What, that guy buying me a drink? What's the big deal? It's free alcohol."

I stammered incoherently, unable to formulate a response to such glib inanity. Finally, "You don't realize the kind of signals you're sending when you accept a drink from a guy at a bar? To him and to me and everyone else?"

"What?"

"I can't believe I'm explaining this. That's how guys come on to girls in bars and you showed him and me that you were receptive."

"It's just a drink. It's free alcohol. You should be happy I saved you some money."

"I can afford to buy our drinks, Tina. I've never been so insulted in my life. You just fucking left me sitting there like an asshole while you ran off to flirt with another guy. I was so shocked I couldn't even comprehend what I was seeing. It actually took a while to register..."

"He said I shouldn't be with you," she interrupted.

"What?"

"When he saw you staring at us, he said, 'who is that guy?' and I told him, 'oh, that's my fiance.' 'You shouldn't be with that guy' is what he told me."

This was an example of "triangulation," but I didn't know about that narcissistic tactic yet.

Head spinning. Wordless spluttering. Then, "Why should either one of us care what some stranger who's hitting on you in a bar thinks about our relationship? Are you serious?"

"Jeremy," she said.

My head jerked incredulously. "I don't give a fuck what his name is."

"I'm sorry. I didn't think it was any big deal. It's not like I was going home with him."

You very nearly had to, I thought. I also wondered if she'd exchanged numbers with Jeremy before running out to the parking lot to secure her only sure transportation back to Buffalo.

The next day, we were back to normal. In fact, I actually felt good about our relationship and had an errand in mind to enshrine a particular symbol of it.

Maura had taken a couple photos of Tina and I walking together on the frozen shore of Buffalo Lake. One of them, a close up photo of Tina and I looking into each other's eyes was sublime. It was legendary. If anyone had any question or doubt about my relationship with Tina, that photo answered all. It captured a part of our relationship that seemed genuine and exuded love.

Maura had observed on a couple occasions, "As long as you two keep looking at each other like that, you'll have no problems."

I had a 3×4 copy of the picture and I had a mind to frame it. Tina suggested that we find a frame for it at Savers. Critics of our age difference sometimes assumed Tina to be a gold digger, but she enjoyed thrift shopping. Between that and her propensity for the Dollar Store, I thought her frugal and thereby, somehow, wholesome. If she ever asked me to buy her something (with a couple rare exceptions), it was from Walmart rather than Macy's.

We'd been out at the bar the night before, so we weren't up early, but after we had some breakfast, we made our way to Savers. The thrift store, which was associated with a couple non-profits, had daily deals on items tagged with a certain color and various themed discount days. That day, yellow tags were 50% off and Senior Citizens enjoyed an additional 20% off all purchases.

We browsed around the store and found a suitable frame Priced $2.00, but with its yellow tag, it was only going to cost a buck. It looked new and it was a quality frame of solid oak.

"See? That would have been like twenty dollars at Target," Tina proclaimed. "A dollar!"

I never disagreed.

We shopped around some more, browsing randomly and I came across a pair of black leather dress shoes that appeared unused. It wasn't a yellow tag, but the pair was priced $6.99 and it was my size. I needed a new pair for work, so I picked them up.

"You know how my wallet keeps leaking things out of it?" Tina began.

I didn't, really, but nodded.

"Yeah. I think I'm going to see if I can find one, here," she said.

"OK."

We went to the wall of purses, bags and billfolds and Tina touched a couple, rather disinterestedly. "Hey, why don't you get a new belt to go with those shoes? There are some right over there." Tina pointed. "Why don't you go look for one while I look at these?"

I sensed something. Something was off with Tina. I shrugged, turned and walked a little way to the belts that were displayed on the same wall.

I could immediately see there was nothing that suited me and I started back towards Tina. I could see she was just opening a small ladies wallet with a strap, like a billfold-purse hybrid. As I approached, she held up a crisp twenty-dollar bill.

"Hey!" She exclaimed, "Look what I found in this wallet!" She closed it and hung it back on a peg. "Well, I'm good to go," she said, suddenly.

"Don't you want to look at some more wallets?" I asked, surprised. "Lots of other options," I gestured. She had only examined one of the dozens that were on display. "Maybe you'll find more money."

"No. I'm good," she answered. "Let's go check out. Hey, your stuff is on me."

"I guess it's a profitable trip to Savers. You're still leaving with more than you came in with after buying this stuff." As far as I knew, Tina had zero dollars when we walked in.

I put the shoes and picture frame on the counter and stood behind Tina as we waited for the customer before us to finish up. Tina snapped her fresh twenty a few times.

The Cashier, a young woman with dark hair and a hoop through her septum like a bull greeted Tina and started ringing up the items. She paused and looked over to me. "Oh, is she using your senior discount?"

I almost fell over. My jaw dropped open. Witty rejoinders started forming, but quickly fled my brain.

"Just ring her, up," I said. Tina was smiling widely, thoroughly amused.

"I am, but if she's using your senior discount, it's 20% off," Bull Nose insisted.

I should have just accepted the discount, but I was offended. Tina was my fiance, not my granddaughter! Just how old did I look?

It reminded me of the time Tina told me I reminded her of her grandfather. When I objected, she said, "No, it's a good thing. A compliment. You'll understand when you meet him. He's an amazing man and so are you! I wasn't saying you're old."

Tina and I joked frequently about Savers and senior discounts after that. It was another story for the book. I was always a bit suspicious about the chance discovery of that twenty, though. I had the distinct feeling I'd been manipulated, as if Tina needed an excuse to show me why she had money. She didn't. Though I was under the impression she was penniless at the time, if she'd produced a twenty from her own wallet, I wouldn't have had any questions about it.

The Voicemail from Hell

With time and increased wisdom, my perspective changed dramatically on this, but for quite a long time, I believed my two biggest mistakes (like, ever) had been getting carried away in that near-miss with my ex-wife and misinterpreting a "pocket dial" voice mail I'd received from Tina in February of 2016, but didn't hear until many months later.

I had been clearing old messages out and came across one that had gone unheard from my dear love, Tina. She hardly ever left voice mail. Maybe twice in out entire relationship, so this seemed like a rare treat.

I started playback, but quickly realized it was an accidental pocket dial. That explained why the message was over 10 minutes long! The sound was distant and muffled and ordinarily, I'd have simply deleted such a message, but for two things. First, I distinctly heard the word "condom" cut through the muffled noise and second, part of my brain was apparently desperately trying to cut through the thick fog of denial I'd been breathing for months.

Tina's inadvertently broadcasting phone had captured at least two people talking, I realized. Tina and a man whose voice I didn't recognize.

To say I obsessed over that message would be an understatement. I copied it to my computer to use some audio engineering tools and tricks to enhance the sound and listened to it repeatedly to try to piece together the conversation. Much of it was unintelligible, no matter what enhancements I tried, but what I did glean was concerning. Talk of putting on a condom, for example was particularly concerning.

I eventually confronted Tina with the recording, leading to a month or more of strife between us. She was adamant that she didn't recall any such conversation and guessed that it must have been me she was conversing with when she redialed me by accident. I reminded her that we had never once used a condom in the course of our relationship, which had her flummoxed.

Well.

It turned out that it *was* me in the recording. I eventually pieced enough of it together to shake loose a memory of the conversation. It had been the night I proposed to Tina. We had discussed condoms that night.

When that revelation came to me, I became physically sick. Tina left me and though I'd lost count of all of our breakups, that was one I fully understood and took responsibility for. There was no mystery to it. I'd caused it and that brought an overabundance of caution on my part, later.

Tina and I did reconcile and the incident was a speed bump in the rear view mirror until the next incident. I no longer trusted my own eyes and ears and there was no way I was ever going to question her after that. All red flags got buried.

I'd already had a tendency to give Tina the benefit of any doubts, but now she was infallible. My mistakes were Tina's armor and she made use of it.

Sickness & Revelations

Tina and I had been on a several-day drinking binge in our love bubble at the Buffalo Hotel and I had just discovered my new superpower. I didn't get hangovers anymore. We'd been down to Jay's Down and Under, the most divey of all the dive bars I've ever seen and wandered around town on nice days, but mostly, we were holed up by ourselves in the penthouse. We were drunk and fucking and talking and laughing for days and It was glorious, until the sickness struck.

Tina fell ill first and within a day or two, I felt like I was at death's door, myself. For the first couple days, I was Tina's diligent nurse. But then the nursing role flipped and flopped between us as the mystery ailment grabbed hold of me, too. Somehow, it worked out that our energies ebbed and flowed in a way that when one of us was at a low, the other was rallying for just long enough to take care of things for us. That's how it was at first, anyhow. After a while, Tina began to overtly resent doing anything to care for me.

I've never been as sick in my life. It was nearly a three-week ordeal and on more than one night, I privately considered my odds of survival less than 50%.

It ended up being the most consecutive days we'd spent together to that point. I commented to Tina that I wished the circumstances were better, but I was glad to have her with me.

Maura stayed away from the mystery illness, opting to shelter at Scott's while Tina and I convalesced in the apartment. After the first week of illness, not only was there no sign of recovery, but our condition worsened and within a span of nine days, between the two of us, we'd visited the emergency room 5 times.

Doctors were unable to provide a specific diagnosis. They said we had a viral infection with a likely secondary bacterial infection at once. Tina was in agony from pressure in her ears and I was choking on my own uvula, which had swollen enough to interfere with my breathing and was making me gag and vomit.

The vomiting was probably the worst symptom. For each of us, it was incessant. Nothing would stay down. The bile we were spitting out was a bright green and after days of it, our throats were raw from all the acid.

That led to an end to the drinking binge. If the slightest amount of alcohol touched my throat, I would immediately retch without any delay. Tina was similarly afflicted, but not to the same extreme. She was smoking a lot of weed, though.

My first day trying to cope with the illness sober, Tina tried to encourage me to leave, but I still didn't feel in any shape to make the drive home. I could barely walk. I was vomiting hourly or more. She said she was afraid that we were never going to recover, because we might just be passing the same germs back and forth.

I told her I was very confident that immunology didn't work that way and she eventually came around and accepted that I was going to be stuck there for a while longer, but I had a strong impression that, despite the illness, she had something she wanted to do without me around.

Later that day, I was looking out the window and observed a big, black pickup truck out in the parking lot. I could hear it's engine revving loudly, as if to get someone's attention. A while later, the black pickup was joined by a black limousine that parked along side. I observed people moving back and forth between the vehicles, a couple guys from the limo climbed into the pickup, then three people from the pickup got into the limo. They were parked out there, moving back and forth, occasionally revving the pickup's engine for a good half-hour or so.

I mentioned this odd parking lot behavior to Tina, but she just shrugged and showed no interest in looking out for herself. Years later, though, she brought it up out of the blue. She said she'd cracked the code on the strange behavior out in the Buffalo Hotel's back lot and it had been meth dealers meeting with clients. She said she'd seen it many times while she lived there. I thought it was strange that she revisited that oddity so long after the fact. It was one of those moments that felt like Tina was revising history, but besides the odd way she brought such an obscure memory up out of the blue, I had no reason to question her.

The black vehicles eventually departed and the illness ravaged on.

The next afternoon, while I was languishing on the futon, I heard a piano playing in the distance. It seemed to be coming through the window from somewhere across the parking lot behind the building. There were some businesses back there, but I couldn't find a logical source for it. It seemed like someone was practicing, because I'd hear the same parts of old traditional songs like She'll be Coming 'Round the Mountain repeated. Tina complimented my hearing when I mentioned it, because she heard no piano.

Later that day, I heard Irene's voice coming from next door or down the hall. It sounded like she was talking about me and I worried that the Buffalo Hotel management had taken offense to the number of consecutive days I'd spent there. I was expecting her to come to the door and give us a hard time. I arranged all the pill bottles we'd acquired from the hospital on the counter to be visible from the doorway, in case she did and Tina called her mom to ask her to let management know I still hadn't "moved in," but was too ill to make my way home.

Of the five trips we'd taken to the Emergency room, I'd driven for four of them and it was challenging. On the fifth, while I was choking on my own uvula, Tina refused to drive me. After a lot of desperate pleading, she did eventually get Linda, the downstairs neighbor who slept on cedar chips instead of a bed to drive us. It was a challenge, even to walk. I was dizzy, weak and disoriented.

Ultimately, management didn't come around to make a big fuss and I've since concluded that neither Irene's overheard conversation about me nor the repetitive piano music actually existed.

That night, lying beside slumbering Tina on the futon-turned-sickbed, I heard something I could not explain at all. It was the Hines and Berglund morning show from the top-40 radio station, WLOL.

"Get me up, (in the morning), W-L-O-L," the jingle went. John Hines played the fool to Bob Berglund's straight man. They played Madonna's "Material Girl."

Knowing that 99-and-a-half FM WLOL, with their silly morning disc jockeys had gone off the air over twenty years prior, I was mightily perplexed. It was not a memory. It was not imagination. The sound had a source. It came from a specific direction. It seemed to emanate from the kitchen window, where the air conditioner was humming away.

I drifted off to sleep for a while as I was trying to solve the mystery of what I was hearing. I don't think I slept long before I awoke in a panic. I was sweating profusely, but freezing cold. There was a tremor in my legs and a flutter in my chest. It felt like there was pressure on my stomach, too, but nothing touched it but the weight of my T-Shirt.

I felt nauseous and waves of tingles like mild electric shocks flowed up and down my arms. My hair was wet. My breathing felt strained. I wondered if I was having a heart attack or if my fever had reached a dangerous new high – or both. Something was definitely very wrong. Everything was wrong. I'd been more miserably sick than ever up until that point and somehow, it just got exponentially worse. I very seriously believed death was likely near and, with Tina slumbering next to me, I began to pray.

I prayed for forgiveness, mostly. For my sins and my mistakes and regrets. I wanted my conscious clean to meet death. I wanted to leave all of that behind in this mortal world.

I didn't really expect an answer, but instead of dying, I received a visit.

I sensed a presence other than my sleeping fiance in the dark apartment. Whispering voices from no source I could see began speaking to me. They sounded female. There were at least three of them and they wanted me to leave. Immediately.

From the windows facing the parking lot, I could hear a crowd urging me to heed what the voices inside the apartment were telling me. They erupted in encouraging songs that varied in volume and sometimes became distant and indistinct.

I had the impression that these were agents of God. Angels, perhaps, but they had a dangerous and threatening edge to them.

"We aren't what you think," one of the voices told me. There was a sense of menace.

What I was experiencing was no dream and it wasn't imagination. I was fully awake and there was a spacial source for the voices, in the room. Just as the chorus of encouraging songs came distinctly from the windows.

At one point, I took a call from some otherworldly source on my cell phone. The man's voice was distant and fading, but he told me to "put down the cup," which I took to mean booze in general and "go home to your true family."

I objected that I was in no condition to drive. I was experiencing dizziness and I was unsteady on my feet. I was still dreadfully ill and I felt I was still affected by alcohol, but I didn't understand exactly how. I didn't have a clear sense of how long ago my last drink had been.

"You must have faith," the man told me. I had the impression that he was driving as he spoke to me. I could hear wind, like he had the top down in a convertible but it was no ordinary cell phone he was calling from. It was something unearthly. He changed tacks.

"I'm going to be at the Buffalo hospital in the morning," he said. "I could pick you up from there and take you back with me." I understood that my body wouldn't be going on that trip, wherever he was going to be taking me. The hospital was being foretold as my place of death.

Like the other voices, the one on the other end of the call washed in and out like waves lapping the shore. I found that I had to hold the phone tightly to one ear while covering the other, or the voice disappeared.

"Think about it, but you don't have much time. Call me back if you're ready to get picked up." He gave me a six-digit number. I was scrambling to find a pen in the kitchen. Then, in red ink, I scrawled the numbers hastily on a magnetic notepad on the side of the fridge. It was challenging, holding the phone, blocking my other ear with my shoulder while I wrote.

He gave me another number to call if I had questions. That one only had five digits. I wrote them down and the apparent would-be soul collector ended the call, saying, "Good luck and be smart."

After thinking a while, I dialed the five-digit number. I was pretty surprised to be connected to an automated recording. Phones, cars and voicemail systems weren't how I expected the mechanisms of the spirit world to work.

The recording provided a menu of 4-digit extensions, with letters corresponding to the numbers. "Dial TIME, 8463 for more time," was one of the options. Another was apparently a connection to the voicemail box of God, himself. "2636 or AMEN." There were several others and while I was frantically scrawling numbers on the notepad, an operator came on the line.

A woman's voice addressed me as Daniel and told me I was fortunate because my name meant I'd already been "on the books," and that I was doubly blessed. "I like you, Daniel," she said with a southern drawl. I couldn't see her, of course, but I had a sense from her voice that she was black. "I'm going to tell you, there's going to be a judgement, but you've already been judged, in a way. Ooh. You have a very dirty mind."

I had the idea that she was either probing my memories or, perhaps pulling up records of my life experiences on a computer screen. Either seemed equally plausible at that point.

"That's OK, sweetie," she went on. "What matters now is you gotta put down that cup. Do you still want to live, Daniel? Because there are still people outside who can take you now if you want to go with them, but they're leaving, soon. I'm going to let you go, now. back to the menu, but I'll be keeping an eye on you, Daniel."

I was disconnected and the recording resumed listing off alpha-numeric extensions I could dial. I didn't recognize the screen on my phone. It was like a different operating system had taken over. I tapped 8463 and instantly, a far-away, yet powerful voice said, "Time," and I felt it. Just like that, I'd been given more time! I didn't know how much, precisely, but I felt it was more substantial than a few days or weeks. Years, maybe.

That seemed like a good ending to my midnight odyssey. I put the phone down, and made my way back to the futon. Several cajoling voices again attempted to persuade me to leave Tina, but after a while, I dismissed all of that and slipped under a blanket to cuddle my love. I was willing to defy God to stay with her.

Once spurned, the voices inside the apartment were no longer friendly. I felt one of the females hovering above me menacingly. There was pressure on my chest. The others inside the apartment began to chant, "you're going to break your neck," in a singsong, teasing sort of way that stretched 'neh-eck' into two syllables. I could hear them plotting my death from across the apartment.

"Why don't we just harvest him the old fashioned way," one suggested murderously.

They made another attempt to lure me up and out of the apartment, promising to reveal themselves to me if I'd follow their voices.

Curiosity got the better of me. I agreed and got back up but the voices I was following out into the hall were disappointed that I took Tina's keys with me so I could let myself back into the building. The chorus from the parking lot groaned their collective dismay that I wasn't charging headlong into the destiny they desired for me. I preserved the option to turn back.

I stepped out into the dimly lit hall and the voices urged me to come closer as they moved away and toward the stairs. "All will be revealed, just come a little closer," one said. When I reached the landing, I could hear a different voice. A human voice. One that I knew. It was Jim, the building manager conversing with someone I perceived to be a younger person. "I'm not saying it's all because of the booze, but I know I wouldn't have ended up this crippled up if I'd stopped drinking when I was younger," he was saying. He went on about a number of dire health problems he suffered now for youthful indiscretions.

I got the idea that I'd been led to that point to hear Jim's testimony. I listened to the conversation for a while, until Jim and his companion parted ways, presumably back to their own apartments or sleeping rooms.

The otherworldly voices continued and I followed them down the stairs, but I kept a firm grip on the rail and moved slowly down each step, one at a time, cognizant that these beings had threatened a broken neck. I wasn't completely steady on my feet, either.

Once outside in the still night air, I followed whispers that became less and less distinct. I was having a harder time pinpointing their direction. I crossed the deserted Central Avenue and the whispers seemed to get louder, but I couldn't clearly make out what they were saying. It sometimes seemed like another language. As I followed, I noticed I was nearing a dark and foreboding looking cellar stair. The sort one could fall into and break one's neck. I backed away.

I was somewhat spooked and the voices had failed to reveal their visages. As completely vivid as the surreal experience had been, I wasn't entirely convinced it was genuine and I grew tired of chasing after phantoms. They seemed to be losing interest in me and fading, anyway. I went back inside. Once more, I returned to the futon, and somewhat defiantly, snuggled close to Tina. I wouldn't leave her.

I did start giving consideration to cutting back on my alcohol consumption, but I didn't realize how important that was. I had never experienced alcohol withdrawals before, nor did I yet realize that was likely at least part of the cause of the incredibly realistic audio hallucinations I experienced.

Sometime later, I realized that the sounds I was hearing came from such discernible directions, because my brain was reinterpreting and modulating the frequencies of real sounds into music and voices. The inconsistent hum of the refrigerator and air conditioner compressors coming on and off, Tina's noisy oscillating fan grinding away, turning back and forth. Those were the sources.

Despite the later realization that I may have been experiencing dangerous hallucinations from alcohol withdrawals (alcoholic hallucinosis) and fever, I was profoundly affected. I still consider it a metaphysical event.

Maybe God's servants were using my near-death state to get a message through or maybe I was merely accessing a suppressed part of my subconscious that had been desperately trying to warn me off all along. As weird as the whole experience was, what it boiled down to was simple advice: "Quit drinking and get away from Tina (or you'll die)."

Whenever it was that consciousness returned to me the next day, there were some milder lingering auditory hallucinations, but only when I went into the bathroom, with the jet engine exhaust fan running.

The worst symptoms and super-high fever abated after a couple days and the hallucinations went with them, but the illness persisted for some time.

In all, Tina and I were ill for over three weeks. It was by a mile, the longest I'd ever been sick, but eventually, our immune systems prevailed. We could eat without vomiting and our strength returned. we recovered well enough for normal activity just in time for the 4th of July and we had plans to go up to the lake for the occasion.

Out in Puffs of Smoke

Ghosting, the act of abruptly disappearing from someone's life without explanation can be painful even after a first date, but after months or years in a relationship it can be completely devastating. The psychological wound opened defies closure and festers in rumination.

In my case, I was planning a future. We were engaged. We had just endured a dark and horrible illness together, but the sun was finally shining again. I thought.

Ghosting or silent treatment by a narcissist is something all victims of narcissistic abuse have probably experienced. Likely more than once.

The first time Tina vanished without a word for an extended period (of more than a few days) was right after my mom's birthday, July 2016. It was confusing, disorienting, life-changing and above all, agonizing.

Tina and I had what I thought was a pretty minor tiff. We never really argued (not over anything of consequence – we argued for sport over trivialities sometimes – that was more like debating). Usually, even if I disagreed with Tina, I'd acquiesce to her way of thinking, or at least humor it. On this occasion, I felt a sense of righteous indignation and let Tina know how I felt. It never even remotely occurred to me that it could lead to a breakup, but now I know about narcissistic injury and I'd inadvertently caused one.

Tina and I had finally recovered from the Double Death illness, just about in time for Independence Day and we took a trip up to her dad's place in Cold Spring for the occasion. It was a good time. Tom took us out on his double-decker pontoon with Tina's brother, his fiance and Jasper, the "stink dog" (Tina gave the German shorthair that nickname for his perceived attitude, not any odor). We went swimming. Tom grilled chicken, burgers and brats for everyone.

Tina and I stayed a few extra days at her Grandpa's cabin across the bay. We were still enjoying ourselves, but it came time to get back to the cities because both of our mothers had birthdays in the coming week. My mom's was on July 10th. Maura's, the 14th.

We stayed a couple days at my mom's and I was getting back to work, so I'd left Tina at the house with my mom for part of a day. When I got back, I was happy to learn that they had apparently got on well.

At the time, Tina and I were in serious discussions on cohabitation. We had been considering taking over the lease in Buffalo, as her mother was considering moving in with Scott. It was going to be a bit of a drive for me to work, but the rent out there was so cheap that it seemed a viable option, at least for a while. The bonus was that we wouldn't have to move much in that case. That idea seemed to be falling apart as Maura and Scott had a sudden falling out, so we were looking at other options. Or, rather, I was. I discovered, as we were discussing it after my mom's birthday party that Tina considered it entirely my responsibility to find and decide on our housing options.

It had been an odd day. A sizable contingent of family had come over for my mom's birthday and I was grilling for everyone at the party. Tina, however had been reluctant to come out of my bedroom and join the festivities. It was becoming conspicuous. Aunts and uncles were asking after her. "Is Tina feeling OK?" and the like.

I went up to the room to check on her every hour or so that she eschewed making an appearance. She wasn't ill and she assured me she'd be out soon. To try to make her more comfortable and sociable, I started having a drink with her every time I popped into the room. After a while, it seems, my sudden intoxication was noticed by some of my family. Around that time, Tina finally decided she was ready to join everyone in the back yard.

After the party had wound down and we were alone back in my little room upstairs was when the dispute began. We had both been drinking, but that was nothing unusual. I had to go to work the next day, so I asked Tina if she could use my computer to look online for houses or townhouses for us to rent around the metro area while I was at work.

"That's your job," Tina responded, with a noticeable hint of ice in her tone.

Finally free of a near-month-long illness, I had a lot of work to catch up on. Affairs at the non-profit I was in charge of had fallen into a pretty shabby state, due mostly to neglect of my duties. I was also doing side work with my dad in his contracting business, renovating an old duplex. Tina had no responsibilities to speak of, so I was irked that she flat out refused to participate in the hunt for our future home. It was surprising to me.

I made a brief attempt to persuade her, but she was immovable on that point. If I wanted us to have a home together, it was entirely up to me to make that happen.

"You aren't doing enough," she told me. She wanted nothing to do with the hunt or even the decision making. I was wounded and that should have been a pretty significant warning, but I let the matter drop for the night.

The next day, before I went to work, Tina informed me that she wanted to get together with her mom and wanted me to drop her off at Maura's place of work at the end of her shift. I had expected that we'd all do something for her birthday together, but Tina wanted to get a jump start on that and she hadn't seen her mother in quite some time by that point.

I left the duplex job around 4 and I picked Tina up to drive her out to her mom's place of work in Maple Grove. It was closer than bringing her all the way back to Buffalo, at least.

Tina always over-packed for trips, but on this occasion, she brought a relatively small load with: one bag for some of her clothes and another that contained her latest crocheting project.

The drive started out pleasant enough. We were both in good spirits, but that changed when I brought up the housing situation again. When she persisted with the notion that it was all my problem to deal with, I was offended. I'd expected some teamwork from my partner and I had a lot on my plate just then. I told her as much and my irritation drove me to criticism.

"I'm working two jobs right now and I've got a lot of catching up to do. We need to figure out this housing situation soon and you have the time. I mean, while I'm at work, you're at home smoking weed, coloring pictures, crocheting and watching TV," I blurted. "I think you should be able to find a little time in the day to look for our future home, and frankly, I'm offended that yesterday, you suggested *I* wasn't doing enough."

Tears instantly welled up in Tina's eyes and I felt like a jackass. There was actually nothing at all wrong with what I'd said, but I never wanted to hurt Tina and here, I'd made her cry.

I began to apologize and backtrack. I assured her that I'd take care of the housing situation. "Don't worry about that," I said. "I'll take care of it and I'll do it quickly so we don't have to worry about it anymore." I reminded her how much I loved her, apologized some more and eventually, the tears stopped rolling down her cheeks.

We were pretty close to Maura's work by then and Tina said, "I just wish we could have parted on good terms."

I apologized some more, offered more reassurances and pledged eternal love. Eventually, she was nodding, smiling and it seemed we were OK.

When I parked in the lot, Maura was already in her car, ready to go. I carried Tina's bags over to the silver Saturn and said hello to Maura as I put them in the back seat. Tina and I embraced and she kissed me goodbye.

"I'll call you later," I said.

"OK. I Love you," Tina said.

"I love you too. Everything will be alright," I said. And she was gone.

Tina didn't answer my call that night, or any day or night to follow. My text messages seemed to disappear into a black hole.

With no reasonable cause I could discern at the time, Tina ghosted right out of my life.

The world stopped.

With each passing day, my mental state deteriorated, my brain spinning and spinning trying to decode what had happened. July of 2016 became the darkest month of my entire life. I had already developed very bad drinking habits with Tina, but now, I plunged into the bottle, swimming deeper and closer to the bottom every day.

I used to say that Tina was my best friend and lover, but she had become closer to my everything by that point. No one and nothing else really mattered. With every decision I made, I considered it's impact on our future. My entire life was being built around that false future.

Trying to figure out why Tina left me without any explanation was driving me completely insane. It was all consuming. All I could think about was solving hundreds of unsolvable theories, because only Tina knew for certain and she wasn't saying. I didn't know if this was permanent. I didn't know where she was. I didn't even know if she was alive and well.

My mind was too preoccupied for the complex mental work I needed to do for my foundering non-profit, but I attempted to work for my dad. It was hard to keep moving with even simple tasks, like patching plaster or painting a ceiling line. I was sneaking nips off a fifth of vodka that was stashed in my van on smoke breaks.

My uncle was working at the duplex with me one day while I'd been drinking a little to get through my tedious day of painting. He took control of the radio and tuned in a country station. By the end of my work day, my head was so full of thoughts of cheating hearts, lost loves, dead dogs and all the other awful things country singers wail on about. It took me down even lower. I had never known such despair.

I decided I needed some company and went out to see my friend Donovan down in Farmington. It was a little disturbing, because I drove right past Scott's on the way there and had a pretty strong feeling that Tina was there. To be so near, yet so tremendously far from her tore at me.

Tina was all I could think about and no doubt, my friends were sick of hearing my frantic musings and unanswerable questions. Donovan was a compassionate ear as we proceeded to get completely bombed together, however.

Eventually, he said something that was a cold hard slap in the face. "Dan, she doesn't love you."

I couldn't find fault with his assumption, given the way I was discarded, but it didn't line up with the previously constant barrage of Tina's professions of love for me.

Donovan and I passed out early early in the morning, but I only managed to sleep a couple hours before my inner torment woke me. I went out to my van to grab a fresh pack of smokes. The sun was barely up, but shining brightly in a clear blue sky. I stayed outside for a while, lit a cigarette and stared down the road in the direction of Scott's house.

I decided to try texting Tina for the thirtieth time since she'd vanished. I was beginning to weep while I composed the message, knowing it wouldn't be answered. I went back into the dark house. All the curtains were closed. It might have been night time. Time lost meaning as I sank further and further into my own darkness. What had begun with weepy tears evolved into uncontrollable sobbing as I scrolled back through loving text messages from before Tina's abrupt disappearance. An unending stream of tears were splashing on my phone's screen like raindrops.

Weeks had passed and instead of getting stronger and moving on, my condition only worsened. Still extremely drunk and in a new unfathomably low depression, my body convulsing for what seemed like hours awake alone in the dark, I concluded that I would be this miserable or worse for the rest of my life. Every new day was darker than the one before. There was only one solution.

I went back out into the bright morning, squinting against the sun and pretty quickly formulated a plan. I located Donovan's garden hose. I figured I could just open my passenger side window on my van just a crack and put one end of the hose in. The other end, into my tail pipe. The hose was only half the diameter of the tailpipe, but I figured a bit of duck tape would solve that disparity. I grabbed a pint of tequila from the kitchen, hopped into the driver seat and started the van. I felt a sense of peace come over me, as I considered the idea. I could just drift back off to sleep and I'd never feel that kind of agony again.

I put on some music, drank a couple swigs of the Tequila and lit a cigarette. Then, I put my seat all the way back and down, so I could lie comfortably, pretty much flat and also unseen. I was comfortable. The music was soothing. I felt like I'd hit upon the best and only answer, but some part of me resisted. Obviously, I didn't die that day. I'm not sure why, but I called my dad, instead of seeing my simple plan through.

It was the darkest, lowest point in my life and when I sobered up, I started to seek some help to begin to put my shattered mind and soul back in some recognizable shape. I began to see a counselor.

Dissecting the On-Again, Off-Again Relationship

Unstable relationships are a hallmark of Cluster B disorders, like borderline and narcissistic personality disorders. On-again, off-again relationships can be terribly damaging and often, they can be the result of a prolonged, repeated pattern of narcissistic abuse.

Narcissists tend to target very empathetic and conscientious people, because they can mistreat them longer, with less chance of them leaving. By sporadically giving them hope, they can string several people along at once. Of course, a large harem requires maintenance and can present scheduling problems.

I believe this is part of why narcissists are so unreliable. Aside from the fact that their impaired empathy prevents them from really caring about anyone else's feelings, they need to make time, often in secret, for the various harem members they've been stringing along. This necessitates last-minute cancellations, changes of plans and occasional no-shows. Insidiously, this erratic behavior helps to cement the trauma bond between victim and narcissist.

I wasn't aware of it, but I was part of Tina's harem. She cleared her schedule for me in the beginning love-bombing stage and a lot of the time, I was her main source of supply, but periodically, I was rotated out. I can see now that this generally followed some kind of narcissistic injury. Unintentional slights or minor disagreements that would roll off the backs of most could be grievous blows to a narcissist. Criticism was intolerable. That kind of injury demanded retribution.

Ghosting is one of the narcissist's favorite weapons. It certainly was one of Tina's. Disappearing without explanation for days or even weeks and sometimes months was a psychologically and emotionally torturous punishment and also allowed time to maintain relationships with the secondary sources in her harem.

Ghosting creates a wound that only the narcissist can soothe, because without the narcissist to explain why she left, there is no way to close the case on that

132

mystery. The mind will spin itself into a frenzy trying to figure it out, but only the narcissist could solve the puzzle.

With one relationship on hold, twisting uncertainly in the wind, a secondary supply source would have been eager to prove their worth to the narcissist, would lend a sympathetic ear and commiserate over perceived, exaggerated injuries. The most important job of secondary supply was to reassure the narcissist of her own faultlessness.

Of course, eventually, everyone lets a narcissist down and they move from idealizing and love-bombing into devaluation when they realize their target is not perfect and then to discard, when they rotate to another (former or new) source of narcissistic supply. They lose some along the way, so a narcissist is constantly on the hunt for potential new sources. Everywhere I took Tina, she was shopping for my temporary or possibly permanent replacements. Sometimes she'd collect numbers or accept drinks from other men right in front of me. That was a power play called triangulation.

Put simply, triangulation is using a third person to belittle or create insecurity in a narcissist's victim. This psychological manipulation tactic is used to secure control. A crafty narcissist could even be accuser and defender at once, like when Tina told me "all my friends are against us being together, but I told them that you're the love of my life and no one has ever made me happier."

Since I'd had almost no interaction with Tina's friends, the only way they could have formed a negative opinion of me would have been based on what Tina told them, so who was she defending me against? During the devaluation stage, narcissists smear their victims with friends, family and even mutual acquaintances, then get their support for inevitable discard. That didn't occur to me at the time, though, because I was put on defensive and felt I had to redouble my efforts to prove my worthiness. The immediate threat took precedence over any deeper examination. Besides, Tina was telling me that she talked me up and "defended me" to her friends!

After a variable time apart, with me struggling in vain to figure out what had gone wrong, Tina always came back in what's known in psychology circles as a "hoover." She'd suck me back in. She'd heal the self-esteem wound she caused by vanishing without a word and commence with a new period of idealization and love-bombing.

Each time this cycle repeated, the trauma bond became stronger. Each discard was more devastating and painful than the last.

A trauma bond is, essentially, a powerful, chemical/physiological addiction to one's abuser.

When I questioned Tina's behavior, she'd either ghost again (which I was always walking on eggshells to avoid because the withdrawals that ensued were increasingly unbearable agony) or engage in gaslighting to get my inquiring mind under control.

She often made little suggestions to make me question my mental health. I'd ask about something that seemed out of place with her words or behavior and she'd in turn suggest that I could benefit from anti-depressants, for example. More often, though, she'd make me doubt the veracity of my own memory.

For the first two years, we drank together, a lot. Somehow she always had crystal clear recollection of every incident and conversation on those drinking nights and she could get me to doubt my own memories, because I'd been drinking. It got to a point where I'd think I must have dreamed or imagined her bad behavior, because she'd so-often call my memory into question. I began thinking of it as my "half-heimers." It even worked on me after I'd stopped drinking. The funny thing was, once free of Tina's direct influence, my recall seemed to improve miraculously.

Gaslighting is a way of concealing the truth by causing the victim to question his own eyes, ears, recollection or sanity. It eventually warps one's entire perception of reality and destroys self-confidence. This is where conscientiousness plays a role in victim selection. A more conscientious person is more willing to entertain suggestions of their own shortcomings in memory and mental health. Conscientious and empathetic people expect that those close to them have sincere and well-meaning intentions, give the benefit of the doubt and consider how they might, themselves be wrong.

Tina's ability to successfully gaslight me had another force at play in my mind. It's a revelation that only came after being years-separated from the manipulation. On an almost subconscious level, it was preferable to accept the gaslighting, no matter how ludicrous it became, than to face a reality that would necessitate separating. The stronger the trauma bond became, the more I feared the horrific agony I'd suffer from the inevitable withdrawals if we broke up.

There can be other reasons for on-again, off-again relationships. Relationships between addicts and co-dependents can often result in a lifetime of separations and reunions. That dynamic also happened to apply to Tina and I, but the on-again, off-again relationship dynamic perfectly matches the narcissistic abuse pattern of idealize, devalue, discard, hoover.

Trauma Bonding

Narcissists (and other emotional abusers) rely on manipulation of primal emotions, love and fear to hook their victims.

A rudimentary study of psychology introduces us to the concepts of positive and negative reinforcement, which narcissistic manipulators employ, but the most powerful, dangerous and damaging psychological reinforcement is random and intermittent. Not being able to predict what actions bring rewards and which bring punishment put a victim in a continual confused, excited state. That's the doorway to trauma bonding. Expected rewards are not as impactful as surprises and likewise, punishments out of the blue are more fearsome.

In not much time, the more intense chemical reactions to intermittent reinforcement begin to create an addiction.

The narcissistic abuse cycle begins with "love bombing," where the abuser begins to hook a victim with sometimes over-the-top, premature professions of love and admiration. During this phase, the narcissist learns about the victim's strengths and weaknesses, likes and dislikes and fears. The narcissist mirrors his or her victim, sharing tastes and interests to become a near perfect companion. It may seem like a match made in heaven, but it's an entirely artificial manipulation tactic.

The narcissist may say things like "I never believed in it before, but I think we're soul mates" to make the victim feel special and imply a supernatural bond outside the normal bounds of reason.

Love bombing causes feel-good chemical responses, like release of dopamine and oxytocin into the brain. Dopamine is a neurotransmitter associated with pleasurable feelings and oxytocin is associated with love and bonding.

To gain a victim's trust, a narcissist may reveal "secrets" about themselves very early on in a relationship. This encourages the victim to become more open and vulnerable in return which creates the illusion of a more intimate connection and fosters both trust and sympathy. That also makes the victim more susceptible to suggestion and manipulation. By this point, the groundwork for gaslighting has already been laid and the narcissist is already gaining control of his or her adoring and protective victim. A malignant narcissist will also use any secrets learned against his or her victim.

Next, a campaign of devaluation begins. This occurs directly between the narcissist and victim and with outside friends of the narcissist the victim may not be very familiar with. The narcissist begins finding faults with the once idealized victim. Vacillation of positive and negative reinforcement begins and over time, the negative, fear-based manipulation is employed more often than the love-based encouraging behavior. Ongoing negative and intermittent reinforcement creates a chain of minor and major emotional traumas, inducing a near-constant state of anxiety. This is the root of complex trauma.

As the positive reinforcement becomes more scarce, it also becomes the main thing the victim seeks, because he or she is addicted to the early chemical highs brought about by love bombing and will now do nearly anything to get those feelings back! This is sometimes called "breadcrumbing." Random and intermittent reinforcement like drips or crumbs keep the confused victim hopeful and chasing (and working harder to please the narcissist). That's what really sets the hook.

The narcissistic abuser will use either subtle or overt negative reinforcement to make their victim fear losing him or her, often triangulating with other people by introducing a romantic rival ("Joe keeps hitting on me") or by suggesting that someone else is being critical of the victim. "I was talking to my brother and he said he doesn't think you're any good for me," for example.

Then comes the gaslighting. "I never said my brother thinks you're not good for me. You must have misunderstood what I said. Have you ever seen a therapist for that paranoia?"

The abuser can even be antagonist and savior at the same time. "My friends say you're no good, but I told them how much I love you and you're perfect for me."

This makes it seem like a case of "you and me against the world," and even though the narcissist is causing the injuries, it seems like only the narcissist can heal the wounds.

A narcissist's reality isn't objective. It's only consistent with what they feel, so it's always in flux and they are always manipulating, massaging, stretching, exaggerating, bending and outright breaking the truth.

Over time, reality seems fuzzy and only the narcissist can be the arbiter of what is real. The victim loses faith in his or her own observations and judgment.

After the devaluation period, there usually comes an abrupt discard. The narcissist may just up and vanish like a ghost with no explanation. "Ghosting" is another horrendously psychologically damaging tactic and it's one that leaves the victim dependent on the abuser for answers. No one else can explain, "why." This creates an open wound that defies healing, or "closure."

During the discard phase, the narcissist is usually spending time love-bombing a new or secondary source of narcissistic supply. He or she may be absent for days, weeks or even months before reappearing to "hoover" back the confused and traumatized victim. A new period of love bombing seems to heal all wounds and makes the victim ever more dependent on the abuser for a sense of well-being. The cycle repeats – each time inflicting more cumulative trauma and also strengthening the bond. Gaslighting may also instill in the victim a sense that his or her neuroticism was to blame for the discard or whatever strife (real, manufactured or imagined) led up to it.

For myself, I found that each time I was devalued and discarded, it was progressively more painful than the last and that became something to be avoided at almost any cost.

This abusive manipulation keeps a victim in a constant state of excitation and prolonged, continuous exposure to stress hormones like cortisol causes physical changes to the brain that make it easier to trigger anxiety and even panic. At the same time, those stress hormones attack and weaken regions of the brain responsible for forming new memories and logical thinking. The changes to the size and functionality of the amygdala and hippocampus in particular help cement the trauma bond to a narcissistic abuser.

Created by inducing confusing and contradictory but intense emotions through a push-pull dynamic with intermittent (or unpredictable) reinforcement, a trauma bond could be compared to the "Stockholm Syndrome," observed after hostages developed a bond with their captors in a 1973 robbery of a Swedish bank. The hostages "fell in love" and sympathized with the very robbers who were using them as human shields.

While terrified and treated poorly, any kindness would bring intense relief and an overblown pleasure response from dopamine and other feel-good chemicals.

After being ill for an extended period, just getting well and feeling normal can seem ecstatic! Those intense chemical reactions are addictive. A trauma bond is essentially a very powerful addiction to one's abuser and the fallout could also be compared to what some used to refer to as "battered wife syndrome."

Various sources have compared breaking the trauma bond to breaking alcohol or even heroin addictions. Like any other addiction, denial, secrecy, excuses and horrendously skewed priorities naturally follow.

Trying Again and Triangulation

At some point during what remained of my summer of despair, I realized that alcohol was only making the depression I suffered after Tina's abrupt disappearance worse and, for the most part, I stopped drinking. That alone was not enough. It helped, but I still thought about my wayward love daily and wistfully.

I was also seeing a therapist to cope with the depression and anxiety that accompanied my still unexplained separation from Tina. I think it's entirely appropriate to describe those symptoms as withdrawals.

A psychologist I met with around that time had somewhat disinterestedly administered a routine questionnaire and barely looked at me when I provided my answers. His head was down as he tapped away at the computer keyboard in his office, until one of his last questions.

"What's your drug of choice?"

"Tina," I responded without thought or hesitation.

On that, he turned, looked squarely at me and touched his glasses.

I hadn't considered that "Tina" is also slang for crystal meth.

"No no no no," I clarified. "Tina's my ex future ex wife."

We both laughed.

The addiction comparison was more apt than I realized at the time. The trauma bond formed to one's narcissistic abuser is very much a chemical dependency. It's a matter of brain chemistry, between stress hormones and pleasure inducing dopamine and endorphins. A narcissist's mind games are powerful manipulators of those chemical responses and they're the same kinds of responses produced by illicit drugs, both stimulants like meth and opioids like heroin.

Narcissistic triangulation is one of the more common ways a covert narcissist abuses and manipulates a victim. They're always playing people off each other to create drama or to prevent certain people communicating with each other. Driving wedges between people can be just as important to their strategy as sowing conflict to watch the sparks. Using triangulation to make a victim feel threatened or insecure is also a way of cementing a trauma bond and exerting psychological control.

Of course, I didn't understand any of that at the time and reconnecting with Tina was among my top priorities. It was probably my primary objective. She met with me once in August to restart a dialogue and after that, it was about a month of intermittent contact until we seemed to be firmly "us" again.

I was often back out out to her apartment in Buffalo on weekends, but, not every weekend. To my dismay, she was spending more time at Scott's down in Farmington, again, which tended to preclude us seeing each other.

It was also around then that I noticed the odd pattern of her unavailability on Tuesdays. She didn't work or have any obligations besides keeping the Buffalo apartment in livable condition and she never mentioned any Tuesday activities. She'd sometimes make commitments to me, either to see each other or talk on the phone on Tuesdays, but those were always broken. She basically ghosted every Tuesday. She wouldn't answer calls or texts.

Aside from those inconveniences, I thought things were going well with us. We were jovial and I'd say blissful when were alone in our bubble out in Buffalo.

We'd made plans to go to the Renaissance Festival that September, In Minnesota, that's a major occasion. We were going to accompany Rich and Thea. I was expecting a grand time.

I'd spent Friday night with Tina in Buffalo, so we could depart early on Saturday to meet my friends at the Festival. Tina really wanted to wear a sword for the event and I had a couple, so I fashioned a scabbard for her (I already had one for my heavier sword), and we were both armed with steel on our hips. We were also semi-costumed, as is common for dedicated patrons of the annual event.

We took a shuttle from a Radisson Hotel to avoid the long parking lines that backed up the freeway for miles during the festival. I decided it'd be nice to spend the night there, since we'd be drinking at the festival and it was a really long drive from Shakopee back to Buffalo. Unfortunately, the hotel only had top-tier suites left, so it cost around $500.

Chris had accompanied Rich and Thea, I learned when we arrived. His wife had stayed home. We five wandered the grounds, enjoying the sights, food, beer and mead. Chris, I noticed, had gotten really drunk, really fast and he was making a point out of aggressively flirting with every attractive woman who'd cross our paths. Some of it was witty and amusing to observe. Some of the banter was just sad and ugly, though. More fell in the latter camp as he got more drunk. I didn't think much of it at the time, but later, it occurred to me to wonder if Chris had been trying to triangulate with Tina and make her jealous, since he had to mind his manners while I was with her.

Tina fell in love with a heavy, Celtic-inspired sterling silver necklace on offer by one of the artisans selling their wares, so I happily shelled out $200 for what I thought would be a memento that would always remind her of me. It was a joy to make Tina happy.

Tina told me she hadn't enjoyed the Renaissance Festival when she'd been there before, but going with me changed her perception of the place. She said I made it fun. I'm sure I beamed.

The next big event on our calendar was my friend Jeff's 80s-themed birthday party. That event was destined for disaster. Tina got us off to a bad start.

Initially, Tina had told me that although her mom was trying to entice her over to Scott's that weekend, she had no intention of going. She'd shared with me some texts she had exchanged with her mom about it. In those messages, Maura had made a point to let Tina know that Doug would be there, and that his fiance would not be. It was a long exchange, with Maura trying to convince Tina to come to Farmington and Tina giving her details about her plans with me.

The exchange ended with Maura writing, "Doug will be here. No Olivia."

Only after I read the messages, did Tina re-read them herself and think to address that last bit. "And I don't know why I should care if Doug is over there or has Olivia with him or not, but I'm not going over there, so it doesn't matter. I don't really ever want to go over there again," she'd said.

Something had happened to upset Tina on her last visit, but she'd never elaborated on what it was.

Although she had repeatedly insisted she didn't want to, she did end up going to spend that weekend with her mom's at Scott's. With Doug. No Olivia.

She didn't tell me she'd changed her mind about going to Farmington until she was already there, but it least it was in the neighborhood of the party. Then, after I'd already driven all the way to Farmington, she called to say she was behind schedule and wasn't going to be ready at the predetermined 7:00 time for me to pick her up at Scott's, where she'd been staying with her mom, to my chagrin.

I wasn't welcome there, so when Tina called, last-minute to tell me she needed another hour, I had to circle, as it were. I went to wash my van and did some shopping around Farmington, waiting for 8:00 to roll around.

We had extensive plans following the birthday party. Tina had a doctor's appointment coming up in St. Cloud and I had oral surgery scheduled to remove some troublesome wisdom teeth, so we were going to drive each other for those appointments, with the Buffalo Hotel being our central base of operations.

I had intended to avoid alcohol at Jeff's party so I could drive us straight from there to Buffalo. We'd planned on making it an early night. Tina could drink as she wished and I'd be the sober ride.

At 8:00 I arrived at Scott's and waited at the end of the driveway. Things changed again as soon as Tina climbed into my van. She had a big lion's mane of hair, too much blue eye shadow and elbow-length lace gloves. She looked ready to set the controls on the Wayback Machine to 1984.

I had on a bright Polo shirt with collar turned up, tapered, acid-washed jeans and I wore my sunglasses at night.

I started down the road and then Tina dropped the bomb, saying she needed to be back to Scott's by 10:00.

"What? That's like two hours! besides, we're supposed to be going to Buffalo tonight."

"That's the thing. I wanted to ask you if you can come back and pick me up at Scott's tomorrow, instead. There's someone coming over I want to see and Scott won't let me come back in the house if I'm out past ten."

I was floored. There was a whole lot wrong with what Tina was saying. She had a ten o'clock curfew like she was a teenager – at her mom's boyfriend's house. She was changing plans without giving me any notice and just expected that I'd happily do all the extra driving from Minneapolis to Farmington, back to Minneapolis, back to Farmington and then all the way out to Buffalo. Then, of course, I was going to follow that up with driving her out to St. Cloud.

When I pointed that out, she offered to give me money for gas.

"That's not the point. This is a big extra inconvenience for me, with all the extra driving and you're springing this on me at the last minute. I might have thought differently about picking you up tonight or going to Jeff's party if I'd known about all this before I got down here."

I had a bag packed for staying in Buffalo and the rest of our planned trip in the back of my van.

"Please, Dan, will you just take me back to Scott's tonight and come back to get me tomorrow afternoon?"

"It's the weekend," I observed. "Scott's always up until at least 3 in the morning, drinking in the barn. There are going to be people partying in there all night. Why should he care if you come back after 10?"

"I don't know," Tina said. "His house. His rules. I guess he doesn't want me to wake up his daughters."

That wasn't making any sense to me. Scott and Maura were just as likely to wake them up coming in from the barn party at 3 AM as Tina was coming in from hers.

"Will you just do this for me, Dan? There's someone I haven't seen for a while that I really want to see."

"Who?"

"Just an old friend from Farmington," she said vaguely.

I hoped she wasn't talking about Doug, but I didn't ask. I think I instinctively knew she'd just lie if it was and I wasn't prepared to wrestle with that, just then.

"Fine," I eventually said. "I really don't want to, but I will. For you." That was pretty much as close as I'd ever come to saying "no" to her.

141

We arrived at the party, where Jeff's girlfriend had really gone all out setting the stage for 1980s nostalgia. We sang 80s pop songs on the karaoke machine, played with Rubik's Cubes and dazzled our tongues with Pop Rocks.

Everyone had brilliant costumes, each with their own take on different aspects of 80's culture, from headbangers to B-Boys to preppies. It was a fun party and after an hour or so, Tina, who had been drinking quite a bit, announced to me that she didn't want to go back to Scott's after all. She didn't want to go to Buffalo yet, either. She decided she'd rather be at this party.

At first, I figured that saved me a headache. I checked with our hosts to see if there might be a spare bed for Tina and I if we decided to spend the night and they could accommodate us, so I decided I might as well have a few cocktails myself.

It wasn't long after that when the trouble resumed. First Tina clarified that although she didn't want to go back to Scott's that night, she did want to stay there for a while the next day. So, in the morning, I was still going to be expected to drop her off in Farmington, drive back north to Minneapolis, then return south to Farmington to pick her up later to drive us back out to Buffalo, which was (roughly) an hour north of Minneapolis.

Tina was adamant. Again, I wondered who it was that was so important for her to see. Again, I didn't press that question and again, I gave Tina my strongest, refusal: "I don't like it but I'll do it. For you."

She and I went out on the back deck to smoke cigarettes. I think we were the only two who smoked at the party at the time. We were alone back there with our smokes and drinks.

Out of nowhere, Tina said, "Never cross Scott."

"I beg your pardon?"

"He'll kill you. Never cross him."

"What are you talking about?"

"Never cross Scott," Tina repeated. "He'll kill you."

I was vexed and perplexed. "I'm not welcome over there, anyway, so I wouldn't worry about it. I don't expect to ever see Scott again."

"No. You don't understand. He'll kill you. He wouldn't throw the first punch, though. He'd try to provoke you into hitting him first and then he'd kill you."

"Don't worry about it, Tina. I'm not intending to 'cross Scott.'" I was more annoyed and ready to move on to another topic, but bizarrely, Tina wouldn't let it go. It was like Scott was threatening me by proxy through Tina, but now I'm pretty sure it was a matter of narcissistic triangulation.

"He's a scrapper," Tina said. "He's been in a lot of fights and no offense, I don't think you have the fighting experience he does. Don't cross him. I'm telling you."

"Look, I don't know where this is coming from, but if I perceive Scott to be a threat to me, you or us, I'll take him out before he gets a chance to throw a punch.

You're right. I'm not a fighter, but I wouldn't be interested in a fair fight. I'd go right after his bum knee with a fucking tire iron. If I'm in a situation like that, it's destroy my assailant by any means necessary, not a boxing match."

"You can't do that!" Tina was aghast. "his knee is already bad enough and how would he go to work?"

"Who's side are you on, here, Tina? If Scott threatens me or you or us, I'll take him out before he even sees me. And if he does lay a finger or a nose on me, I'll for sure have him charged with assault and that would go really well for his custody hearing, wouldn't it? So, let's hope Scott keeps his hands to himself."

"No! You can't do that, either. You don't know how terrible their mother is and Scott needs his girls!" Tina was visibly upset.

"So, Scott's going to kill me and you don't want me to do anything at all in my defense, is that it?"

"You don't understand."

That crazy conversation went on in circles for half an hour or so and had me very upset by the time Tina finally dropped it. Tina evidently wanted me to feel threatened by Scott and essentially demanded that I do nothing at all to defend myself should Scott decide to kill me. Some loyalty I was getting from my fiance, the supposed love of my life!

We went back inside and separated to mingle with other guests. I poured myself a much stronger drink after that. In hindsight, that might not have been the greatest idea I'd ever had, but I'm certain it didn't ultimately alter any long-term outcomes.

The party sashayed along entertainingly until I realized I hadn't seen Tina in quite some time. I wondered where she'd gotten off to and wanted to reconnect, hoping she'd moved on from pushing the Scott button. I made a circuit through the house, but didn't see her.

I went out onto the deck in back, which was the designated smoking area. She wasn't out there, either. Since I was out there, I smoked a cigarette before I went back in to resume the search. I made my rounds through the rooms of the house again and still didn't find Tina.

I decided to look around in front of the house and check my van, parked on the street. Jeff stopped me before I pulled the front door open.

"Dan. Where you going?"

"Oh. I'm not leaving. I was just looking for Tina. I can't find her anywhere. She seems to have disappeared on me. Again." It wasn't the first time I found myself at a loss to explain what had become of my date.

"Hmm. I haven't seen her for a while, I don't think," Jeff said. "I doubt she'd have gone that way. Did you look out back? She's probably smoking."

"Yeah. She's not." I said. I pulled the door open walked out to my van. It was empty. I went down the street to the corner and peered around. No one was in sight. I went back in, feeling anxious and looked around. I started asking the other party-goers, but no one knew where Tina might have gotten off to.

She did eventually reappear, but I'd gotten pretty drunk by then and as the party was winding down anyway, so I figured it was about time for bed. Kim and Jeff showed us to what would be our room for the night and we both crawled under the covers.

When I awoke the next day, I found that Kim had laid out some quick and easy breakfast foods – fruit and muffins, orange juice and such. I had a glass of juice and chatted with Jeff and Kim for a while before Tina peered around the corner into the kitchen, looking tired. She accepted some of the breakfast Kim offered and we talked about our plans for the day. I was going to drive home and hang out for a few hours and pick Tina up at Scott's a few hours later. Tina said she'd call with a more specific time, later.

After breakfast, we said thank you to our hosts and I drove Tina back over to Scott's farm.

I had just gotten home and was going up the steps to the front porch when my phone alerted me to a text message. It was from Tina. "Dan – This is not working. Please arrange another ride tomorrow. I need to be done. Thank you for everything. Don't pick me up tonight."

I nearly fell over. Instead of going inside, I took a seat on one of the chairs on the porch. I re-read the message and then replayed the morning. Nothing had seemed amiss when I dropped her off.

"Really? Holy fucking shit. What the fuck? What happened? Why?" I wrote back.

There was no reply.

To say I was distraught would be a colossal understatement. It wasn't long before I made my way to the liquor store to buy some coping fluid. It stopped me shaking, but did nothing to improve my state of mind. Over the next few hours, I sent Tina a string of text messages that vacillated between desperate questioning, anger, expressions of love and a few plain old "fuck yous." None of those angles elicited a response.

I was baffled but primarily, devastated. We'd only just reunited a month or so back. This was a moment of discovery. I realized that each time we'd broken up had been more painful than the time before it. Instead of getting easier as many things do with repetition, it became unbearable.

It was some time before answers started coming. None from Tina. She had gone radio-silent. Tiny slivers of memories swam into my mind from the night before. When we'd gone to bed, we didn't go immediately to sleep, I now recalled. There was a conversation. I couldn't remember it, but I had a sense it had turned to an argument.

I sent Jeff a text. "Did Tina and I have some kind of fight last night?"

"I thought I heard raised voices coming from your bedroom at one point," Jeff replied, "but I have no idea what was said."

I'd blacked it out. It wasn't a true drunken kind of blackout, though, because bits and pieces of the conversation-turned-argument kept coming back to me over time.

I really only ever questioned Tina's behavior when there was sufficient alcohol in my system and even then, I usually locked those kind of thoughts away. On that occasion, though, my dam had burst and I ended up questioning her more pointedly about who was so important for her to see and her threatening insistence that I understand Scott would kill me.

I remembered telling her I thought she had 'daddy issues' and that our engagement was just a fantasy she was living without any intention of following though. Somehow, I had developed a notion of "future faking," though I'd not yet heard the term.

I went on about her spending weekends with "former" sex partner, Doug, then turned even more accusatory. I remembered asking her point blank if she was some kind of escort or stripper. Tina had a lot of questions about that and I gave her a slew of reasons for me to wonder about it

Later, looking back on it all, I had a strong impression that I'd often been used as Tina's transportation to her next trysts.

At least, the unexpected break up by text message made sense after recalling some of that thrilling bedtime chat. It was probably a year before I could confidently recall most of the details from that conversation, but I realized enough of it within a few days.

After a week went by with no response from Tina, I concluded that this was probably our final breakup. I had a piece of unfinished business I intended to wrap up, though.

At Tina's request from a year prior, I had been painting the back of a jean jacket as a gift for her upcoming birthday. That was still a month away, but, sitting in my room, looking at the nearly-complete work of art, I felt it needed to wind up with it's intended recipient. It was, in my estimation, one of my better graffiti-inspired paintings. It was worthless to anyone else and I didn't want it hanging around, but I could hardly throw away a piece of art I'd toiled over and put a piece of myself into.

Over the next couple weeks, I sank into alcoholism, spending much of my time sequestered in my room, not working, not socializing – just drinking and thinking. I sporadically worked on the jacket until it was close enough to my final vision that I was comfortable abandoning further effort and calling it done.

I packed it up in an oversized cardboard box that I'd spattered paint all over to make it colorful and attention-grabbing. I included a bunch of pencil sharpeners, since she was always struggling to find one that worked well for her colored pencils, a couple other sentimental trinkets and a pack of orange (for Halloween) Kit Kats that she said were her favorites.

Finally, I blew up a bunch of balloons, and painted messages on them and overstuffed the box with them, hoping that they would pop up and spill out somewhat once the box was opened.

I mailed Tina's birthday present to the Buffalo Hotel a few weeks early. I wanted it out of my sight.

Another week passed by and I considered Tina's jacket a parting gift. It was over.

Permanently.

For a time, it felt liberating to believe that.

The Wilderness

Between October of 2016 and February of 2017 was the longest span Tina and I were separated during the roughly three and a half years of our tumultuous, on-again-off-again relationship.

A lot happened in those 5 months. It felt like years. For one thing, I started a new relationship during that time that carried on for 3 months.

I was unaccustomed to being treated respectfully and like I was a priority. She drank too much, like I did, but she was also pretty responsible, a homeowner with a good job and she was a mother to a teenaged daughter. She was good to me, but I still hadn't learned to break the trauma bond I'd developed with Tina, or even that it was a trauma bond, for that matter.

I couldn't get Tina out of my mind. I still ruminated and obsessed over unraveling the tangled mysteries Tina had woven around me and that was not fair to my new girlfriend, who was saying she loved me. I broke it off with her in February. My timing was not great, since it was just before Valentine's Day when I made up my mind to do it. I still feel bad about that, but there's really no good time for such things. I felt the important thing was to be honest and face it head-on. She was a really wonderful person but I was too broken to accept genuine love and kindness.

As if by cosmic design, after a long silence, Tina contacted me just a couple days later. Narcissists, I'm told by other victims of their attention, have uncanny timing. Tina said she missed me. She said she always loved me, never stopped loving me. She told me that as the new year had come, her "only, lonely kiss" had been reserved for me. She invited me to come down to her new apartment in Farmington and I obliged.

I was excited but very nervous and I made the mistake of taking an anti-anxiety pill before I got on my way. I found myself pretty drowsy and fell asleep early that night, but that started a period of occasional contact with Tina. We weren't exactly together, but we weren't entirely apart. We had a couple dates over the next couple months and had sex a couple times, but it was all entirely on Tina's time.

She'd started a new job working with her mom scheduling medical appointments and was training in Minneapolis, so I picked her up when she finished early one day one day and took her out for lunch. That led to shooting pool and eventually, sex back at her apartment. I was proud of her for landing a good job, even if her mother had arranged it for her. Sometime later, Tina had insisted on treating me for a change, since she was getting a paycheck. She paid for our dinner at Pizza Man, the place we'd met.

I began to think we were moving towards reestablishing a "proper" relationship and I mentioned it to Thea on St. Patrick's Day. Her and Rich were hosting a party and served up Corned Beef and Cabbage and I drank considerably more than I should have.

Thea wasn't pleased to hear my news and initially tried talking me out of getting back together with Tina. "She's bad news, Dan. She's trouble," Thea insisted.

When I wouldn't back down, Thea snapped, "Well, she's not coming over here."

That was distressing. Rich and Thea were my best friends, but Tina was my best friend and lover. It was going to complicate seeing Rich and Thea if I couldn't bring Tina along, because I was planning to be spending a lot of time, especially on the weekends with the woman I considered the love of my life.

We argued in the kitchen, but I thought it was good-natured – not an angry, yelling argument – not at first, anyway. That much I remember. It gets really fuzzy, really fast from that point. I believe I was channeling Monica from Friends when I pushed Thea back, probably harder than I intended and she spilled her drink on herself. I believe, without specifically recalling, that the argument got heated from there, and Richard and Chris joined in.

The next thing I remember clearly was kneeling on the floor, first stunned and then trying to find my phone to summon an ambulance. I'd been knocked silly by multiple blows to the head and to my alarm, my jaw wasn't working right. It was my understanding that it was Rich who delivered the blows, but I don't remember. Rich is about twice my size and worked a very physical job. I was far too drunk to fight back, if I'd even been inclined to. Some damage was done.

I remember Chris kneeling by me, his face uncomfortably close to mine, trying to convince me not to call for an ambulance, but I did eventually get my two-thousand-dollar ride to the hospital.

After an examination and x-rays, the doctor concluded that I had a strain or sprain around my temporal jaw joint, but not a broken jaw bone as I had feared. The doctor said the severity of any ligament tears would be apparent within a couple days and that it would likely heal on it's own, but could require surgery if it didn't.

I took a taxi back to Rich and Thea's. It was early morning and the birds were chirping by then. I laid down in my van for a while, and eventually drove home.

Over the next few days, my injury worsened. The side of my head swelled up like there was a tennis ball in there and I couldn't eat solid foods for over a month, because chewing caused unbearable agony.

My memory clouded by trauma and booze, I didn't understand the sequence of events that had transpired. These were my best friends, so I figured I must have deserved what I got, the problem was I didn't know exactly what I'd done to earn it. I tried reaching out to Thea in hopes that she could fill in the blanks for me, but she refused to speak with me.

Richard was vague and elusive. I sent Thea an apology card, but that was pretty much the end of that friendship. I might have put more effort into restoring it, but, after what I learned later, I realized their ongoing friendship with Chris would make it impossible for me.

After all that trouble over Tina, she, herself became distant and unresponsive. She ghosted on me for a couple weeks and I thought perhaps I'd argued with Thea needlessly. Maybe Tina wasn't going to be back in my life, after all.

The hoover did eventually come again, though. Tina sent me a really nice and funny card for my birthday. It arrived in the mail, perfectly on my birthday and I was elated. I tried calling to thank her, but she didn't answer.

That weekend, Donovan and I went out to celebrate our birthdays (his being the day before mine, we had a long-standing tradition of celebrating together). We went back and forth between the two main street bars in Farmington: Gossips, where Tina and I had our first kiss and Pizza Man, where Tina and I first met. Needless to say, Tina was on my mind. She had moved into an apartment just 2 blocks away.

Donovan and I had a good time, but eventually, the pull was too strong and I excused myself to have a wander over to Tina's place. I told Donovan I wouldn't be gone long. I lit a cigarette and walked over there, a bit nervous. When I got to the drive way, I could see the glowing ember of a cigarette in the shadows around the stoop. I approached and found Tina sitting on the concrete step smoking.

"Hey!" she said. She was surprised, but sounded really happy to see me, which was a relief. Even though she'd sent a nice card, I wasn't sure where we stood at that point.

I thanked her for the card. She told me sweetly that she'd been too keenly aware of my birthday approaching and felt compelled to send the card.

We talked for a few minutes, but I told her Donovan was back at the bar waiting for me to return. I asked if she'd want to visit after I dropped him back off at home and she invited me to come back after I did.

I practically sprinted back to the bar where I told Donovan what had transpired and cut the night a bit shorter than it otherwise might have been.

Tina and I had a good visit and had sex twice – once in the back of my van and once in her bed, where I spent the night.

I told Tina about the falling out I'd had with Rich and Thea, my hospital visit and subsequent weight loss by involuntary liquid diet. She seemed oddly disinterested – as if she'd heard the story already.

In the morning, when I was ready to head for home, Tina made a strange request of me. She wanted me to exit via her bedroom window.

She explained at the time that she didn't want her mom to know that I'd been over and spent the night. She told her mom about it later that same day, so that didn't make a lot of sense. Something else might have, though. I didn't know about him quite yet, but Cassidy had just moved in upstairs at the beginning of the month and their two apartments shared a common entrance on the driveway side. Slipping out the side window would make it less likely that he'd see me leaving.

I was in the area again a couple weeks later to go out for drinks with Donovan and thought since it had worked out so well dropping in on Tina the last time, I'd try it again. It was earlier in the evening when I excused myself to walk over to Tina's. Again, I found her outside on the stoop, smoking a cigarette, but this time she wasn't alone. There were two men smoking with her.

Tina introduced me to Cassidy, her new upstairs neighbor and his friend, Brad. We exchanged brief pleasantries and then Tina took me inside to speak with me alone.

"Those two are really cool, she" said, when we were downstairs. "I smoke weed with them almost every night."

That felt uncomfortable.

"Look, I'm happy to see you, but I'm not going to be around tonight," she went on. She had some kind of plans with her mother that I don't recall, or so she said.

I was disappointed, of course. "With your new job and my erratic schedule, it's going to be difficult to find times to see each other," I noted.

"Nah," Tina responded. "My new job is in scheduling, remember? We'll be able to make time."

"How about next weekend?"

"If it's convenient for me," Tina said rather flippantly.

That stung. "How about we figure out when exactly is convenient," I suggested.

We went into her room so she could consult her planner. She found a pencil and I got my phone out of my pocket top open the calendar app.

After some back-and forth, it was determined that Tina had a completely free weekend. Disappointingly, it was a few weeks away, but she assured me, "I'll be all yours."

Tina wrote it in her planner and I put it down in the calendar, then I made my way back to the bar to rejoin Donovan. The night had seemed productive enough and I had a good time hanging out with my friend. From my perspective at the time, things were looking pretty good.

Although the fact that Tina was smoking weed nightly with some new guys raised some unease, I was completely unaware that I'd been shunted into the role of secondary supply. Once I'd been her primary supply, but I had become just another member of Tina's harem, or stable of narcissistic supply. She had me on a string.

Pssst and Other Lies

Tina and I used to tell each other "I love you" so often that people who spent too much time around us might have been at risk for diabetes. Over time, we developed our own secret shorthand for it. It began with Tina saying "pssst" to get my attention and when I responded, she just whispered "I love you." She did this often, randomly, when we were walking hand-in hand, riding in my van, or just sitting on the futon. I was always delighted to hear it and said it back. Over time, I would also get her attention with "psst" and we both knew what would follow, so we'd try to beat each other to saying it and eventually, "pssst" evolved to be all that needed saying. She'd just say "pssst" and I'd "psssssst" back (with the extra esses for emphasis).

The problem with adopting something so common as code for our love was that after it was all over, reminders were everywhere. "Pssst" is used pretty damn often in our culture. Oops.

There were other times when Tina would do or say something sweet and my response would be a meaningfully spoken "I love you," sans the "pssst." Her standard reply was "I love you more." That could turn into a competition, each of us (playfully) trying to one-up the other's love. Honestly, I was pretty certain I loved her more, but she always ended the debate when she'd say, "you don't even know."

I knew my feelings for Tina were profound and I figured if she felt even a quarter as strongly about me as I did for her, I was a lucky man. "I think I have some idea," I'd say, but let her have her way that she loved me more.

Love bombing is common to people with narcissistic personality disorders, but it isn't genuine in a way healthier people would understand love. It's part of the psychological trap that leads to addiction or trauma bonding. Though it's primarily a manipulation tactic, I do believe that on occasion, Tina meant it when she said she loved me, but her conception of love was very different than mine. Hers was probably an immature, transient joy she'd feel when I was providing something that made her happy in the moment. It wasn't a persistent, enduring, compassionate or emotionally mature love.

Sometimes the game was "I love you more than…" We'd name off our favorite things in another bid to one-up that Tina seemed determined to win.

"I love you more than giant agates and tofu soup," she said.

"I love you more than pizza and Star Wars," I answered.

Tina said she'd told her mom that I was the only man she could marry. "If it isn't Dan, it's no one," she said. She told me that she didn't care if we had to live in a cardboard box as long as we could be together.

"I think we can manage a bit better than a cardboard box," I told her, but I appreciated the sentiment.

Tina said before meeting me, she'd resigned herself to single life. She gave up ideas of commitment, marriage and family long ago. "You're everything I never wanted," she said. She meant it as a compliment since I'd ostensibly changed her mind.

There were times that the love talk took strange turns. Often, while we were making love, she'd say things like "I'm yours," which would have been a romantic thing to say, but then she'd follow it up with something I thought went without saying, like, "I'm *only* yours," and something about the way she said it seemed like she'd only just decided in that moment even though it was a refrain. Then, there was the time she said, "How do you do it? Are you trying to fuck the Doug out of me?" but that's a whole other story.

I often told Tina she was beautiful. When I'd catch a certain look in her eye, notice the way she was looking at me, see her in an alluring state of undress or see the outfit she was wearing to go out with me. She usually responded the same way. "I believe it when you say it."

Who else was saying it (well, Doug, for one, I learned) and why didn't she believe them?

She certainly should have believed me because I meant it. To me, at the time, she was the most beautiful woman in creation. She actually gave meaning to Sinatra singing "I only have eyes for you." While I could still objectively tell other women might be attractive, I experienced no attraction to anyone but Tina.

Tina mostly said things I wanted to hear. She mostly knew what to say to be convincing, but sometimes, she left me scratching my head in confusion or worse, with cognitive dissonance. Sometimes I imagine, she just slipped up, since she wasn't really speaking from the heart and was only guessing at the "right" things to say – the things healthy, sincere people might say. Other times, she might have been deliberately triangulating to keep me uneasy.

Tina made it clear early and often that she didn't like surrogate pronouns like babe and baby in particular and I was in total agreement with her. "Those are things people who can't remember each others' names call each other," I commented.

"Exactly," she assented.

She didn't care for honey, darling or sweetheart, either, but I had taken to calling her sweetheart or sweetie (never in bed), because I genuinely thought she was a sweet person. She permitted that. "I don't mind it when you say it," she said.

Who else is saying it?

I never asked, but while she was pledging love and fidelity, it turned out that she was more like Rocko's girlfriend from the Boondock Saints: "I can't buy a pack of smokes without running into nine guys you fucked!"

The Spiral to Rock Bottom

My relationship with Tina was nebulous and intermittent at the time, but I felt like we were making progress. Tina had made my whole birthday and we had plans to spend a weekend together coming up that I was looking forward to.

For some reason, Tina was never interested in going out for dinner with me after she finished work and was generally only interested in seeing me on weekends, but I was working with my dad in her neighborhood in early May and figured there'd be no harm in stopping by to say "hi" on my way home.

The day had been warm and sunny, but it was cooling as evening set in.

Again, I found Tina already outside, sitting on the stoop and smoking a cigarette when I pulled into her driveway.

"Your timing," she said, smiling. "You have a way of showing up at just the right moment."

"Magic from the stars," I suggested. I thought she meant catching her outside. Maybe that wasn't it.

Tina scooted over and offered me a cold seat on the concrete. I sat down and lit a cigarette. I asked about her work and we chatted pleasantly a bit.

"I'm not looking to stick around long," I mentioned. "I was just in the area and thought I'd drop by to say hello. I'm looking forward to our weekend coming up, though."

"Are you sure?" Tina threw herself over my lap and looked into my eyes saying, Take me now. Right here."

I blinked back at her and was about to suggest we move downstairs to her bedroom. I had time, but she quickly added, "Just kidding," and sat back up.

"I can wait until next weekend," I said. "It won't be easy, but I can," I was half-joking.

She was nearer now, and put her hand on my thigh. "Say, you're a man…"

"Last I checked," I replied.

"Let me ask your opinion on something."

"Sure."

"I have this friend at work who was talking to me about this guy she likes. She was like a Jehovah's Witness or something like that but left whatever church and started having sex. This guy she's been seeing had sex with her one time, he didn't have any of that — like no religious hangups and he's single, but she can't get him back into bed."

"Maybe he's not attracted to her. What's she look like?"

"She's pretty good looking," said Tina.

"And they're in a relationship?"

"Kind of, Tina said. They live together."

"They already live together and they've only had sex once?"

"It's not exactly like that. It's kind of like a duplex, I guess. He lives upstairs from her."

"Oh. Maybe she's not being obvious enough with her signals. Guys can be kinda dense about that sometimes."

"No. She said she was pretty overt, but, as a man, what do you think she could to to get him back in her bed?"

"Maybe he's gay," I suggested.

"No. That's not it..." Tina seemed lost in thought for a moment and the familiar way she said that made me wonder if she was really talking about a friend.

"Perhaps he's seeing someone else."

"I don't think so..." Tina was distant again, then snapped out of it. "Oh, never mind."

Dusk was setting in and I was hungry. I didn't figure Tina would want to go to dinner with me, based on her recent answers to weeknight date offers.

"I should get going and let you get on with your night," I said, pulling away from her warm body.

"Yeah. I still have a lot to do before I go to bed early," she said.

We both stood. we hugged and kissed briefly and said our good nights.

I was momentarily uneasy that night, but later, fully realized the truth of that conversation. Tina was the 'friend' in her tale and the reluctant man was Cassidy, the new neighbor who'd just moved in upstairs from her. I guess I was the "church" for purposes of Tina's story.

Tina, knowing how much I loved her and planning our next weekend together had the sheer nerve to ask my advice on how she could get another man into her bed. I was later able to verify that was exactly the sick game she was up to that night.

These are the sort of triangulation and humiliation games covert narcissists love to play and they have zero remorse for the destruction they cause. Tina always said she loved me, but what she really loved was to be able to covertly degrade me.

When I first met Tina, I was a fairly successful non-profit executive. I made a decent living, was generally well-regarded in my field (I believe), had a healthy bank account and excellent credit. In two years, I was broke, my credit in shambles, drinking almost daily and barely clinging to employment as a cashier in a downtown gas station.

Before I met Tina, I was already on a somewhat slippery path with alcohol use, however. I had been drinking more frequently as my marriage was deteriorating. The night I met her, I'd just gotten back to the United States from a trip to Ireland and Wales, during which I consumed some amount of alcohol on 12 of the 15 days I was overseas. It was largely an epic pub crawl, with visits to castle ruins sprinkled in. Still, I was pretty stable, considering I'd just gotten divorced and forced to retreat back to living at Mom's house.

That said, things spiraled rapidly after getting wrapped up in Tina's particular brand of narcissistic madness and as it follows, I was working at that gas station on a Friday night when a text message from Tina triggered an avalanche-like downward slide to a deeper layer of the abyss.

Tina and I had been intermittently seeing each other, after being apart for several months. I'd attempted to move on with another relationship during that time, but as great as the new girlfriend treated me, I wasn't psychologically or emotionally ready to be in a real relationship. It might have even felt a little strange to be treated well. The trauma bond with Tina remained. I didn't know that's what it was, of course, but it was a powerful force that kept me thinking about her and it wasn't fair to Lalla, so I'd broken it off.

Not long after, Tina and I resumed some sparse communication. Eventually, my thoughts turned to reconciliation and reuniting. I'd believed we were making progress towards that.

She was training for a new job at a facility in Minneapolis and called me to arrange a lunch date, which went very well and we ended up back at her place. From there, we had a couple more brief, but pleasant encounters and decided to spend a weekend together and see how it went for us.

I was proud of Tina for landing that job, but it created new scheduling challenges for us. I was working 2nd shift and occasionally helping out with my dad's business on weekends and I'd never known Tina to have a job before, so it was new territory that required a bit more advance planning to get together.

After considerable consultation with and juggling of our calendars, we arranged the big weekend together weeks ahead of time and I'd planned on either getting us a hotel room or a little cabin for our getaway.

The week before our scheduled weekend, Tina called and talked me out of spending money on a getaway. She said she'd arranged for her mom to be out of town that weekend and she just wanted us to spend the weekend together at her newish apartment down in Farmington. Sounded fine to me. I just wanted to spend time with her and hopefully reestablish a "regular" relationship. I was also aware that the Anniversary of our first meeting was a month away and I had an idea for that, if the weekend went well. I was going to rent a cabin by Lake Superior so Tina and I could go hunting for some famous Superior Agates. She was an obsessive agate hound, so I figured she'd really enjoy that.

First, we needed that big weekend alone together and there were obstacles. The scheduling gods hadn't been kind and I ended up having to trade work days with one co-worker and pay another to cover another shift to free up the weekend. I also had to work until 11 PM that Friday night, which was much later than I wanted to get started, so I greased another palm for the chance to leave work a little early that night.

Thursday night, the day before the big weekend, Tina had called me after work and we talked for an hour or so, which was unusual for phone-phobic Tina. I had the impression that she was looking forward to the weekend as much as I.

That Friday, before work, I'd gone to rent a DVD of a sci-fi romantic comedy that had reminded me of Tina and I and picked up a bottle of premium 10-year aged Bushmills Single Malt whiskey. I packed those things into my overnight bag and had that in the back of my van, so I could go straight from work to Tina's and begin our much-anticipated weekend. I was excited for days beforehand. I'd conquered all obstacles. I was prepared. I only had a couple hours more to work before I could slip out early and start the drive down to Farmington. I'd been practically dancing my way through the work day.

My phone bleeped and buzzed in my pocket. I glanced and saw it was a text from Tina, so I after I dealt with the line of customers, I popped out back for a smoke break and gave it a read.

"Dan. Don't come tonight. It's just too late and I need to stay on track."

The cigarette fell out of my mouth and dropped to the earth at the same speed as my heart. I was shaken. More than that. I was disoriented. I literally stumbled back into the store. A coworker looked at me with grave concern. "Dan are you Okay?"

I was told I looked ashen and I was shaking. The store was busy and I was needed. The job wasn't very complicated and I was able to get back to work like an automaton for a while as my fog-filled brain distantly wrestled with understanding what I'd read.

Eventually, between customers, I pulled my phone out of my pocket, quickly texted back, "What? Bullshit."

A minute later, my phone started ringing. I knew it was Tina. I really shouldn't have stepped away, just then, but it was beyond decisions of the rational mind. I just went. I threw up a "Next Register Please" sign and trotted outside to take the call. "What?" I answered, icily as I pushed through the door.

"Dan. Dan. Dan. It's not you. It's not you. OK? It's… I had a friend I haven't seen for a long time come down to have lunch and her husband had just gotten married or I mean, her ex-husband and she never drinks, but she was so drunk before she even got to me."

"Uh-huh," I prompted as I lit a cigarette. I was going to need to keep the call short. The shift manager would be freaking out because it was crazy-busy inside.

"Anyway, I couldn't have her driving in that condition, so I invited her back to my place and she's in there, sleeping on my bed right now and I'm just so exhausted from taking care of her, I'm just going to go lie down on my mom's bed and go to sleep, OK?"

"I see. Well, how about we just get together tomorrow, then," I suggested, some degree of warmth and spirit briefly returning to the icy-feeling void that had formed in my chest.

Tina blasted that away. "I'm going to be with Nate and Amber," she replied.

Nate's was a name I'd only heard for the first time on the phone the night before. All I knew was that he was Amber's roommate.

"I arranged for the whole weekend off, I said. What about Sunday?"

"I'm spending the weekend with them," she replied. "I promised them and I have to be up super early on Monday."

"I see. Alright then," I began. I was numb. My voice, monotone.

Tina could sense that I was terminating the call.

"Dan. Dan. Wait. Dan…"

"Bye."

If the story about the drunk friend was true, which I doubted, that could be considered beyond her control, but ignoring long-laid plans with me to promise her time to Nate and Amber was a clear choice and it was a blow to the gut.

I walked over to my van, opened my suitcase, fished out the bottle of 10-Year Bushmills and took a long pull off the bottle. I replaced the cork, put the bottle back, got out and locked the van.

Then, I turned around, unlocked the door, got back in the van and took another big swig of whiskey before actually going back into the store.

I worked a bit longer, not really feeling anything. I may have been in shock. When things slowed down a bit, I went out for another smoke break, but it was also a whiskey break.

An hour later, it was my arranged early clock-out time, but I was too drunk and distraught by then to even count my till. I had a co-worker finish that up for me and went out to sit in my van. Now with ample time, I tried calling Tina back. It had only been an hour since we spoke, but she wasn't answering. I took another swig of the Bushmills I'd been looking forward to sharing with Tina.

The next thing I remember, a police officer was rapping on my window. I'd passed out there in the parking lot. I explained the reason for my state to the officer, promised that I wasn't driving and wasn't a danger to anyone, told him that I worked there and just needed to sleep a while and amazingly, the cop left me alone to sleep it off, but he told me it was a co-worker who had called the police to check on me. Maybe they didn't know who I was. I don't know. I slept a while longer, then drove home, probably still not in the best condition to be doing so.

Back in my room in the small hours, I continued to drink as I ruminated on Tina's blindsiding blow-off. I tried calling her again, then sent a couple texts asking for a better explanation, but there was no reply. I only slept an hour or two. My brain was spun up and not keen on letting me sleep it off. I checked my phone there was still no response from Tina. I drank some more and by the time the 750 ml bottle of 10-year aged Irish whiskey was empty, irritation and despair had blossomed into rage.

Unremarkably, it gets fuzzy, here. I knew in my bones Tina wasn't being straight with me and I know I sent a number of increasingly desperate and angry text messages. I do not know precisely what they said. I passed out sometime after and recall, upon waking again and checking my phone, being horrified by some of what I'd written to the love of my life. I recall composing and sending a lengthy apology for my unkind words and then deleting some indeterminate number of the nasty-grams I'd sent, because I couldn't even bear to read them myself.

I recalled, fuzzily, that for my own protection, my drunken intent was to make damn sure Tina would never talk to me again because by that point, I knew I lacked the will to stay away from her, no matter how terribly she treated me.

A week went by before I heard from Tina again. It was a week I'd spent pretty much continually drunk and I'd given up the gas station job I was sure to be fired from, anyhow. The message I'd received from Tina, as she was departing on a trip to Fort Meyers Florida had been loving and renewed hope for me that we could still work things out.

I was determined to try again, but now, effectively unemployed and drinking daily, I began to evaluate where I'd wound up. I realized I was going to have to get sober. I was hitting rock bottom with a narcissist. I still didn't realize that, but I did wake up to the danger of using alcohol to cope, so something positive began to emerge.

Feeling Bad About Reactive Abuse

I generally only felt emboldened to call Tina out for lying or disrespectful behavior when I was drinking. I thought that maybe if I approached those issues in just the right way, stated my displeasure with just the right words, soberly, that Tina would understand my point of view and we could have a constructive discussion that would lead to positive changes.

I was wrong! I didn't understand the nature of personalty disorders, but I began to believe that if only I'd sober up, I'd not spout off impulsively in reaction to Tina's abusive behavior. If I could phrase things just right, with patience and compassion, maybe we could get back to a blissful relationship like we'd had in the beginning. I suppose the next month or so that I worked to get a grip on sobriety was, in my mind, as much for Tina as it was for my own health and well-being.

I ultimately ended up blaming myself for my imperfect reactions to Tina's behavior rather than holding Tina responsible for the abuse that prompted them. I ended up apologizing, but adjusting my approach wouldn't have changed anything. Tina was going to Tina no matter what. For example, years after that Friday when Tina abruptly canceled our long-laid plans, I learned the truth of that night. She had actually been partying with and screwing Cassidy, the new neighbor who had just moved in upstairs a month or so prior. The very guy she'd asked my advice about hooking back up with. My sense that Tina was lying to me, again, had been completely correct. In fact, after Tina and I were through, I eventually chatted with Cassidy. She'd been lying to both of us all along and it sounded like she was fooling around with one of *his* buddies, too!

Some takeaways about narcissists:

Narcissists will drag you down.
Narcissists will jump at novelty over love.
Narcissists enjoy, like a game, getting away with tricks and deceptions.
Narcissists aren't dependable with plans or promises.
Narcissists Lie. A lot. Almost constantly.
Narcissists aren't worth the trouble.

A Cold Rejection

Just before Tina took off for Florida, she'd sent me a couple pleasant and even loving text messages, so I was still hopeful, even after the ruined weekend and the series of ruinous texts that I sent Tina in the wake of that.

I knew she was coming back on a Thursday, so I left a note by her door on Wednesday that just said I was sorry for my angry tirade and that I forgave her for the last-minute cancellation of our big weekend.

I determined to give her a couple days to settle back in and drop by for a visit on the following Saturday. That was one week before the anniversary of our first meeting, which I was still holding up as something special. I was hoping we could still manage a weekend together for that occasion.

I had sent Tina a text inquiring about that weekend while she was in Florida, but she hadn't replied.

Saturday evening, I parked around the corner and approached Tina's driveway, wondering if I'd chance upon her outside smoking as I had on a few recent and serendipitous occasions.

As it happened, she was outside, sitting on the concrete stoop, smoking a cigarette.

"Hello," I said, making my way up the driveway.

She looked at me but didn't initially reply.

"How was your trip?"

"Just fine," she said. She took a drag off her cigarette.

I was taken back a bit by her cool reception. I hadn't been sure what state Tina would be in but I expected something other than cool indifference.

The door behind her opened and two men, Cassidy and Brad came out. Wordlessly, they lit cigarettes and stood behind Tina, arms crossed and looking deliberately imposing.

"I just wanted to talk," I pressed on.

Tina's face changed. The way she looked at me, I didn't recognize her. "There's nothing to talk about. You're always accusing me of things I didn't do," she said.

"You forgive me?" her tone was ice. "I never did anything wrong to be forgiven for," she said.

I was stunned. When I accidentally bump into someone or step on toes, I apologize. Even if she hadn't intended to hurt me, by her actions, she certainly had.

I was struggling to formulate an adequate reply. With Tina and her new henchmen staring at me, I felt small and despised.

I realized I wasn't going to get anywhere with that dynamic and took a step back.

"Just go," Tina prodded.

In case Tina hadn't been home, I'd brought another note and a small gift to commemorate our upcoming anniversary. It was an agate carved and polished into the shape of a heart. The note read:

Tina,

This is my heart.
You already own it.
I gave it to you or you stole it.
Treat it well and it's your forever.

Your Dan

2 years and eternal love.

The note and agate were in a large ziplock baggie that was in my back pocket.

I retreated down the driveway, somewhat dazed. When I rounded the corner on the way back to my van, I passed the egress window for Tina's bedroom. I dropped my small but earnest gift into the window well.

I had arrived at Tina's sober and intended to stay that way, but I went straight to the liquor store after that nerve-rattling encounter. There would be a few false starts before I finally found surer footing on my road to sobriety a couple weeks later.

That encounter had been part of the equation. If Tina, the one who called me the love of her life could dismiss me so harshly, clearly, I had done something terribly wrong, I reasoned. Sobriety, I was sure, would prevent any such future missteps or falling out. I was ridiculously wrong, but a group I joined actually further reinforced that notion, after hearing all the stories my peers would tell me about their colossal fuck-ups while drunk. Making amends is always a part of 12-

step groups and it's emphasized in a way that may not always be helpful. Sometimes, even when you're drunk, you aren't wrong!

Sobriety & Reunion

June 17th, 2017 was the beginning of my journey into a sober life. By that day, I'd been drinking so consistently, that I ended up suffering over a week with terrible withdrawals once I stopped. It was sheer force of will that kept me from reaching for the bottle to relieve the misery. I was shaking, secreting a viscous, oily substance from my sweat glands and flashing between teeth-chattering chills and feverish hot flashes. Walking or standing for any more than a minute or two brought about vertigo and a sensation of electricity crawling under my skin. It also induced nausea and vomiting and frequent dry heaves.

Anxiety and panic attacks began after a couple days and I found it impossible to keep any solid food down. I was back to a liquid diet, mostly relying on protein shakes for sustenance.

I had a good treatment facility lined up and I was expecting to be admitted in a matter of days, but an insurance glitch caused me to miss the opportunity by one day. I had to sweat it out solo for a while. I'll admit it was a struggle, but I managed it on my own.

I think it was made more manageable by the experience I'd had with other, more powerful withdrawals. Those caused by separation from Tina. A trauma bond, an attachment to one's abuser is far far harder to break than any mere substance addiction. Kicking alcohol was no walk in the park, but after what I'd endured already, I knew I could do it.

After white-knuckling my way through 30 days of sobriety without any support except my mother, I got in to some counseling and a peer group. Freshly sober, the gas station job had taken me back and a political outfit I had long ties with decided to hire me on as a consultant at the same time.

When I had something to share in my peer group, it was more often about Tina than about alcohol use. Tina remained my true addiction.

In that group, I was subjected to tales beyond counting of the terrible things my peers had done while under the influence of various substances. Taking responsibility for our actions and making amends where practical was a big part of the recovery philosophy and I was increasingly taking guilt and blame on board. I

165

became more convinced than ever that all of the problems between Tina and I must have been my fault – because of drinking.

One of my peers had been telling stories about his ex girlfriend that were remarkably similar to some of my experiences with Tina. Stories of lies and infidelity and irrational, crazy and crazy-making behavior. Then after hearing me talk about Tina, he said to me, "You're dangerously naive. You're so naive that you're a danger to yourself."

I didn't think so, but those words rang in my head for months afterwards. He was right. I didn't understand what I was dealing with at all when it came to Tina.

After a couple months of successful sobriety and gainful employment, I began to strategize on getting back in contact with Tina. I was dead certain my sobriety was the key to making it work with her. Never mind that she was drinking a gallon of whiskey a week and smoking weed daily on top of whatever else she could get into!

I determined that I needed to make amends to Tina. I wrote her a letter to that end, but, receiving no reply, I didn't know if she'd even seen it. Her mom had a tendency to make letters from me disappear, or so Tina would have me believe.

Over that summer, I'd been maintaining the barest connection to Tina by messaging her pictures I thought she'd find funny that I happened upon surfing the internet. She'd provide a brief, amused reply once in a while, so I used that channel to try to arrange a meeting in person to make my amends. I was determined to try to reestablish a relationship as well, but even if that failed, I felt like I'd be better off on my road to sobriety if I'd at least left things on better terms with Tina.

After exchanging a fair number of vague and non-committal text messages, she did eventually agree to meet with me. She seemed intrigued by my sobriety.

We arranged a date, but she pushed it off. We arranged another date and she pushed it off again.

It was September 10th. Donovan and I went to shoot pool at a billiards hall called Shooters. It was a place Tina and I had frequented when we were together and naturally, I thought of her. I stepped outside to have a cigarette and sent Tina a selfie of myself in front of the illuminated sign.

To my surprise, Tina texted back right away. "I haven't been there since you and I were last there," she wrote. "I haven't been there without you, ever."

I was glad to have a reply and suggested meeting up. "I could drop by for a few, when I leave here," I suggested, hopefully.

"Tonight's not good. I'm about to hop into the shower, then it's straight to bed. I have a busy morning."

"I bet you'd have time to have a cigarette with me before bed," I suggested. She didn't reply to that one.

Donovan and I finished our last game of pool and I drove Donovan back to Farmington, putting me back in Tina's neighborhood.

I parked around the corner from her apartment and texted her again. "I'm just around the corner in case you want to come out and have that cigarette with me before bed."

This time, she replied, right away. "LOL!"

That seemed like a pretty strange response.

"I'll be right up," she added a minute later.

So, I walked over to her driveway and she came out the door just as I was approaching. She didn't look like she'd just been in the shower, but she greeted me pleasantly. Then, she apologized for putting me off before and assured me that she wanted to meet with me to talk very soon. "I don't have time to talk tonight though," she finished.

"Ok. Sure. I'll head out after this cigarette." Tina had one in her hand and I lit mine.

"No. I don't even have time for that." She looked around furtively. "I have a friend coming over," she said with an air of reluctant resignation.

"Oh."

"So... go." She said, sweeping her hand towards the street.

She'd lied to me about her shower and early morning. Maybe she had been truthful about getting into bed, but she didn't owe me any explanations.

"Alright, but call me, OK?" I was backing away, down the driveway.

"I will. I promise. We'll talk soon."

I sauntered down the block toward my van parked just around the corner and I saw headlights approaching. I paused at the corner and watched as a white SUV with one mismatched black fender pulled into Tina's driveway. There was a man driving, a cigarette dangling from his scruffy face. He looked right back at me as he parked. I recognized him. It was Cassidy.

I turned around, got into my van and made for home.

The next morning, surprisingly early, Tina texted to say she wanted to meet me that afternoon, if I was available.

I replied that I was and suggested that I take her for coffee somewhere. She agreed and said I should pick her up at her place at 1:00.

A couple hours later, she texted again to cancel. She said she wasn't feeling well and was too tired.

An hour after that, she texted again. "Never mind" she wrote, "I'll just have a triple espresso shot, but let's make it 2:00, if that's OK?"

"I'll see you at 2:00," I replied.

I more than half expected her to cancel again, but I got on my way and arrived at Tina's apartment on time, as planned.

My main purpose was to make amends, but I had a second motive. It was a long shot, but one I was going to take. Since I had convinced myself that everything wrong had been my fault because of drinking too much alcohol, I brought along a piece of collateral (or two) to guarantee my "good behavior," if Tina would consider my secondary intention.

I was nervous when Tina came out. Besides the New York minute the prior night, I hadn't seen her for so long, I wondered what kind of connection we'd still have, if any at all.

After an awkward few minutes, we were talking like best friends again. Tina directed me to a coffee shop called Blue Nose, a short way up Highway 3.

The place was hopping – far too busy for the one harried woman who was staffing the inside counter and the drive through by herself. Our order took quite a while, but we were entertained enough by each other's company as we explored the decor of the seating area and small library (Tina always loved bookshelves).

Finally, mochas in hand, we adjourned to the sunny patio, which we had to ourselves. It was ideal for a private conversation.

Tina was getting some pep from our chat and the caffeine boost and she brought up a fond memory that had involved drinking too much coffee before a road trip we took with her mom. We were all singing along at the top of our lungs to 80s music on the road in my van to visit some of Maura's friends in Wisconsin.

"It's a good thing I had my seat belt on or I would have bounced myself right out of your van," she gushed with a broad smile, bouncing in the metal patio chair, green-brown eyes twinkling.

We reminisced, laughed a bit, caught up and then Tina turned more serious. "I've kind of been seeing someone," she said.

"I kind of gathered," I said, remembering the mismatched black and white SUV from the prior night. "Is it serious?"

Tina's tone was airy and flippant. "No. Not serious."

That sounded like an opening for my secondary purpose.

"So, What was it you wanted to talk to me about?" Tina cued.

"Well, first, of all, did you receive my letter?" I'd sent Tina a letter taking responsibility for everything that had gone wrong and accepting all of her tall tales as true. That was my codependent sort of way of making amends.

"No. I never saw a letter from you," she said.

"It's a good thing I happen to have a copy," I said, producing a folded piece of paper from my back pocket.

"You want me to read this now?"

"It's good background for the rest of what I have to discuss," I prompted.

Tina unfolded the letter and began to read. Within a minute, her tears were spattering on the paper.

The letter read:

Dearest Tina,

Besides being a "step" in my ongoing recovery, making amends to you for my past harms to you is very important to me.

To begin, let me address something you brought up at least a few times in trying to understand my sometimes erratic behavior: Projection.

At the time, this notion, as I understood it didn't make sense to me. If I were questioning your fidelity, for example and it was because I was projecting my issues onto you, it would mean that I was unfaithful and therefore projected that misdeed onto you. Since (excepting one very very wrong close call) I was never unfaithful, how could I project that character flaw onto you?

I've learned more about projection, however and it begins to make sense.

What's projected can be an emotional state. It can be a transference of feelings about one person onto another person. It can even be feelings about events or situations or personal problems that are irrationally projected onto a person.

In my case, it was a fear of abandonment that I was projecting onto you. I never took time to come to grips with the circumstances of my divorce. It did psychological damage to me. Never in my life did I imagine myself a divorcee and after we parted, my ex started dating my old friend and former roommate, whom she'd been spending considerable time with before the divorce.

I was and am so in love with you, to have your love and adoration in return was sheer bliss. I've never been so in love and so happy in my life. Your love is more precious than anything imaginable. Believe me, I'd do anything to protect our love, but I saw threats everywhere. Between my increasingly excessive drinking inducing paranoia and never having come fully to grips with what happened in my last relationship, I became hyper-vigilant.

Any circumstance that I judged out of the ordinary or inexplicable could quickly rise to suspicion in my mind. I was trying to fit puzzle pieces together that didn't fit. It was a defense mechanism, I suppose, but misguided and unfairly misdirected at you.

We discussed the self-fulfilling prophecy before. It certainly applies. My biggest fear was losing you and lo and behold, I drove you off with my irrational paranoia.

I've apologized numerous times, of course, but repeated the behavior.

Through therapy and sobriety, I finally see and understand what I was doing and why. In your mind, it may be too late a revelation, but it's real and profound to me.

I fully admit that I was wrong. I struggled a bit with whether I should list out all of my misdeeds, since the last thing I want is to call all those bad memories to your mind but if I'm going to try to atone for my sins, I decided I should be clear and specific. I was often drunk so I may miss some things, but I need to apologize for being so drunk that I'd forget, as well.

I'm sorry I hurt and offended you. I'm sorry that I didn't trust you. I'm sorry that I unfairly projected emotions and characteristics onto you that belonged elsewhere.

I'm sorry for:

Questioning your love, intentions, motivations, actions and meanings;

Irrational paranoia;

St. Patrick's Day, Chris;

Angry Driving;

The goddamnable pocket dial voicemail that I obsessed over, but turned out to be a recording of us discussing wedding plans (ugh!);

Freaking out over a canceled weekend;

Worrying about Doug;

Worrying about Scott's intentions/motives;

Threatening to leave you;

Being overly protective and jealous at bars and parties;

Questioning your mirror-selfie;

Playing Columbo at your dad's and spoiling the evening when you were so happy to see me;

Drinking too much;

Concealing how much I was actually drinking from you;

Snooping;

Making out with my ex while we were dating;

Misunderstanding the discussion about open relationships and "hall passes;"

Fighting with you at Jeff's birthday party;

For the existence of Mr. Hyde;

WRONG!

If I've forgotten or omitted anything, please point it out to me. Seriously. Let me have it.

Your diagnosis was right when you suggested projection. I just didn't understand how it applied to me at the time. I surely do now. I see it so clearly. I regret it so deeply. I broke my rule: Listen to the Tina. I was a drunken fool. There's little more maddening than the arrogance of one who is wrong.

I love you with all my heart, soul and body. If you'll have me, I am entirely yours and will be faithful and loving to you forever. I will not project my past pains onto you. What's us is us. Our future is ours. What's past is gone. It's dust.

I want us to try again. No – "try" is the wrong word. I want us to be whole again. I want us to fill the Dan and Tina sized holes in our respective hearts and BE together.

I understand that you have trepidation about this proposal. I can't blame you for not trusting me with your heart again. I understand why you've raised your shields to maximum power. I'll do anything to prove my worth and capability to you, however. I don't want to live out my days in a state of regret, feeling like I've lost the best part of my life by my own actions, wondering how great it could have been instead and missing you forever.

Come back to my embrace, Tina. Let me kiss you and love you and show you the best Dan you've ever seen. Give us the chance to be happy together. Remember the man you fell in love with and imagine none of the things I've had to apologize for could happen again. They won't. I can't promise perfection, of course. I'm human and I'll surely make some mistakes, but not those.

I am so confident that I have defeated my paranoid affliction of projection that I want you to take possession of something and ownership of another. This is a gesture to demonstrate my sincerity, confidence and seriousness.

I texted you a couple pictures – the two most valued things I own. Leo the Lion, which sat on the mantle at Grandma's cabin and my flat cap. Leo is a rare, antique stuffed lion made by Steiff in Germany after the First World War. Just financially, the vintage plush toy is easily worth hundreds of dollars, but that's not where its value resides. Leo is important to my entire extended family. It has extraordinary sentimental value. I want you to hang on to it for me for a while. I will insist on this.

My flat cap is only worth about $50 USD, but as you know, I obtained it on my trip to Ireland from the ancestral home of the Clan McGrath. To me, it is irreplaceable and of immeasurable value. It's the cap I was wearing the night I met you. It's my lucky cap.

I want us to leave past hurts and mistrust behind. I want you to come back to me. I want you to take custody of Leo for one year. If I should break faith with you and hurt you by words or deed with unfounded suspicion, accusation or infidelity during that year, Leo is yours to do with as you please. Let Jasper go to town on it, sell it, keep it for yourself, burn it or whatever you wish. It will become your property in that event. After one year, I should think I'd have proven myself worthy of your love and trust and I'd ask you to return Leo to me, since it's a family heirloom of sorts and I'd think you wouldn't need to hold any security any longer. Of course, if you should happen to leave me for reasons other than my breaking faith, Leo will remain my property and I'll expect him returned.

As of now, the flat cap is your property. I'm assigning ownership of it to you in writing. As far as I'm concerned, it now belongs to you and you may take possession of it by demand at any time. I'd appreciate it if you let me borrow it and retain possession of it for now, since I like wearing it when I show up to see you, but that's up to you. If we reestablish Us and I break faith as described above, leading to a breakup, I'd naturally return the flat cap to you, along with anything else I may have borrowed from you since it is your property. That would only be right.

I'm so serious about this, Tina. Let me prove myself. You won't regret it and if you do, well, you can sell Leo and buy something nice to distract yourself or gain catharsis by doing something awful to it. You can wear your cap as a badge of courage or light it on fire.

I'm willing to risk it. I know absolutely that it will not come to that. I'll gladly and confidently put up this "collateral" to prove it.

This apology and promise is only the beginning of my attempt to make amends.

I love you. I love you. I love you.

Always,
Your Dan

Tears still in her eyes, Tina looked up from the letter and said "Yes. OK."

I was surprised and overjoyed by that simple reaction.

"We need to start over," Tina said. "From the beginning. Like it's a new relationship and friends first."

"OK." I wasn't entirely sure what she intended by that, but it looked like a wide open door and I stepped through eagerly.

"So, you're really sober now?"

"Haven't had a drink in three months."

"That's so great. Maybe you can help me with that."

"If that's something you want. No pressure from my end. Can I kiss you?" I said.

"Not right now," Tina replied, seemingly lost in thought. "I'm going to have a lot to take care of," she said. "Can you take me home, now?" She was still wiping tears from her eyes.

"Of course." I thought her refusal to kiss me was because she didn't feel right about it until she'd broken off her "not serious" relationship with Cassidy, so, while it stung, I ultimately took it as a positive.

When we got back to her apartment, I fished Leo out of a bag and handed it to Tina. She took the old lion into her arms and was quick to retreat into her apartment. "Now, I have to take care of all my shit," she said. "I'll be in touch."

I drove home feeling very optimistic. The meeting had gone almost better than I'd hoped.

I got a text from Tina later that day that changed my perspective. "So happy I can call you my friend, buddy."

I recognized the South Park reference, but it worried me. It sounded like I'd been "friend-zoned."

I tried calling her to clarify her intentions, but she didn't answer. I texted, "I'm not your buddy, pal," then followed with "I need to talk to you."

I didn't hear from Tina for days after that and it was a couple weeks before I actually saw her again.

Tina invited me over, surprisingly early in the day, but it was another instance of her hemming and hawing, going back and forth on time and whether I should come over at all. She finally settled on a time and I drove down to Farmington. She had texted to just let myself into the apartment when I arrived, so I went down the stairs and found her in the living room, seeming happy to see me, but she said, a bit sheepishly, "I'm sorry. I got nervous about seeing you, so I drank."

She didn't seem especially hammered or anything like that. "No big deal," I said. I wanted it to be clear that just because I'd decided not to drink anymore didn't mean she couldn't. For some reason, I hadn't considered Tina's (in retrospect really heavy) drinking a problem at the time. Only my own.

We chatted for a while and Tina said she was a bit hungry, so we decided to go to Perkins. It was about a 10 mile drive and Tina seemed like her usual bubbly self on the drive, but once we entered the restaurant, she took a turn. She looked suddenly ashen and she said she wasn't feeling well.

"Will food help, or should we just forget it and go back to the apartment?"

"No. I think food would make it worse. I'm sorry. Can we just go back? I can find you something at the apartment if you're hungry," she said.

"Of course, sweetheart. I hope you don't mind me calling you sweetheart. It's not a 'friend' kind of thing to say."

"That's fine," she said. "I like it when you say it."

We got back in the van and started back towards Farmington.

We were chatting along the way and suddenly, I heard what I thought was a loud sneeze and I felt something wet on my right arm.

"Oh my god," Tina said, "Oh my god. I'm so sorry."

When I looked over, I saw that it wasn't a sneeze. She'd vomited rather explosively all over herself, my dashboard, my seat, the carpet and on myself.

"Oh my god, I'm mortified," she said.

I tried to reassure her that it was OK. "Don't worry about it. It'll clean up. No big deal," I told her.

"I will wash your entire van," Tina said.

"Don't worry about it, sweetheart. Really. We'll just get you home and cleaned up so you can lie down for a while. I'll take care of this."

And I took care of Tina and then I took care of my van.

We were exchanging texts every couple days or so, but It was another few weeks before I saw Tina again. She called me out of the blue and invited me over to her Aunt's ranch-like property where she was watching after the house and horses with her mother while her Aunt was out of town.

It was out in Independence, near Buffalo. A long drive, but I'd made that drive a hundred times for Tina before.

We had a nice time together. Tina was staying in her cousin's room downstairs. It had it's own bathroom and the shower had a stone bench in it. Tina was oddly insistent that we had to have sex on that bench in the shower and we did, of course. Or rather, we attempted it. It didn't work out quite how Tina had imagined it.

It was after that night that we reestablished the romantic relationship I recognized. We were seeing and talking to each other regularly, going out on dates and spending nights together when we could. Starting over or being "friends first" was done – though I *always* called Tina my best friend back then. During our frequent breakups, it was our conversations that I missed the most. Sex and romance had just been a bonus.

Jesus Didn't Leave Those Footprints

I initially guessed the footprints that appeared on my van windows must have been a prank by Maura on her way to work in the morning.

"Cute, Maura. Weirdo. That was baffling at first," I texted Maura when I discovered them. I was getting ready for work myself and had stepped outside to have a cigarette in the morning sun. My van was parked next to the stoop.

Someone's bare foot prints were on the mid-row windows on both sides of the minivan. I was up early that morning, but Maura had gotten up much earlier. She was usually already well into her work day by the time Tina and I would roll out of bed.

"What was baffling?" Maura texted back after a couple minutes.

"Uh-huh." I was convinced that she was just playing dumb. Tina was still sleeping in bed.

"I'm confused," she wrote back.

"Footprints on my windows."

"I didn't do that. On the outside? Barefoot or with shoes?"

I looked closer. "Inside. Barefoot. Both sides. You really telling me you didn't do that?"

"I didn't. Did Tina do it?"

"I'm pretty sure she never got up before me... Maybe, though."

"WTF?" She wrote back. I was satisfied that it wasn't a prank of Maura's.

"Tina must have gotten up at some point without me noticing," I concluded.

It was late October, just a month and a half after Tina and I got back together. I'd only arrived at the apartment around midnight, allowing barely enough time for sex and sleep before my morning appointment. I shrugged off the mystery for the time and got on my way to the meeting that was the reason for rising so early.

At some point during the day, Maura asked Tina about the footprints and Tina denied any knowledge or connection. When I got back to the apartment, she told me about the discussion she'd had with her mom and reiterated to me that she had no idea how those footprints got on my van windows.

It was a mystery, but seemed initially like an unusual but harmless prank and after wiping my windows down, I forgot about it – until Tina brought it up again a couple days later.

"I know how those footprints got on your windows," she said, rather sheepishly.

"Oh, really?"

"Yeah. I just didn't want to say anything at first."

"What? Why?"

"Because I thought you'd think I was crazy," she said.

"I doubt it. Why?"

"Well, you remember when we had sex in your van?"

I did.

"Well, that's when it must have happened."

I shook my head. "Tina, that was like a year ago."

"That's why I didn't want to say," she reiterated.

"So, you're saying those were your footprints, and they've been there for a year and they just showed up now?"

"Yeah."

There were a bunch of problems with Tina's thesis. If the footprints had been there a year, they'd have been noticed long ago. I was a smoker, so the inside of my van windows required occasional washing, or they got hazy. Year-old prints would have been washed off by then. On the chilly, early-morning that we'd had sex in the van, both of my back seats were out and we were on a blanket on the floor of the van, I remembered. There was no way her feet would have reached the windows the way the prints were positioned. That would have required lying on the middle row seat. Tina's explanation did give the footprints a different implication I hadn't even considered, though. I didn't initially attribute them to sex.

Like so many puzzling memories, I had to think through this one again after discovering what Tina was really capable of. I theorized that Tina got off on debasing me.

It was almost unthinkable that Tina would have snuck out in the middle of the night to have sex with someone else in my van while I slept downstairs in her bed. Almost.

As a failed, covert narcissist, I figured the way she got her sense of power and control was by degrading her betters. She would even go so far as to build them up, first. She did with me, anyhow. She'd often tell me that she felt unworthy of my love and sometimes felt intimidated by me because I was "already so accomplished."

I was somewhat known in the public arena of Minnesota politics and had some successes but I never considered myself all that accomplished. I felt that I still had a long way to go on accomplishing my goals.

Tina played on that to build me up. It was, at first, I assume, part love-bombing, but later it was a prelude to her sick game of debasing me. She had to build me up to get maximum satisfaction from tearing me down. Later, if she was feeling low, she could look at "accomplished" me and think, "If you only knew I just fucked your friend... and I even did it in your van while you were sleeping just 20 feet away." That was how she felt powerful. She could put one over on me, defile my property, abuse my trust and I'd still come home to her, kiss her, tell her she's fantastic, tell her I love her and buy her another bottle of whiskey to boot. My love became the butt of her jokes.

I imagine in situations like this, she also got a thrill out of the danger of being caught and a big boost of dark narcissistic supply when she'd "get away with it." She was probably as addicted to that feeling as to the drugs and alcohol that kept her going every day.

I couldn't say with any certainty who she was with that night when she planted her bare feet on my van windows, except that it wasn't me.

I heard from the old upstairs neighbors in Farmington after I first made this story public on my blog. If I'd had any lingering doubt about my conclusions, it was dispelled by the husband upstairs.

He texted, "Wait, so it wasn't you fucking Tina when the windows were fogged up and we were flashing a really bright light in the van window?"

I definitely had no recollection of anyone ever shining a light on us under any circumstances. "Did that actually happen?" I wrote back.

"Yes."

"I never had sex with Tina in my van while you were living there – and never in the driveway, for that matter," I told him.

"We were in our bedroom and I kept hearing a sound like a hand on glass kind-of thud so I went and looked out the window. Your van was totally fogged up, hardcore. My wife saw it, too. I could see hands and feet back and forth on the glass. So, I got my cop flashlight out and pointed it into the van window. All movement stopped. I couldn't see what was up through the fog so after about 5 minutes, I shut the light off. But. yeah. The van was moving and then when the light went on, it stopped."

This was, in part how Tina was able to gaslight me. She had me questioning the veracity of my own recollection. Faulty memory, a prank or some other explanation seemed more likely than what it looked like – to think that she'd have sex with me, wait until I fall asleep and sneak out to do another guy right in my van was too outrageous to believe. The thought seems crazy and Tina often reinforced the idea that I was crazy. That's a major part of the gaslighting strategy.

What untold trauma compelled her to heap this kind of abuse and humiliation on a good-hearted, generous and gentle man like myself?

Cars

During the first year we were together, Tina told me that nobody had ever really done anything special for her birthday, so I was determined to make up for that. I bought Tina an antique jewelry box and took her out for a night on the town at some of the best, most expensive places I know in Minneapolis for her birthday.

The next year, I spent a month painting a jean jacket for her in old-school graffiti style. The third year, I bought her a car.

Tina had told me she was very anxious about where she was going to live and where she was going to work at the time, since her mom kept changing her mind about where she wanted to be and Tina was dependent on her for transportation.

Maura had floated the idea of staying at her dad's cabin for at least a summer. Tina felt like she didn't have any control and told me she didn't want to start a job in the area if she was just going to have to move and have no way to get there.

I'd always been concerned about how isolated and dependent on her mother and others she was to get around and before we'd broken up the last time around, I had been planning to get her a car. We'd only been back together for a couple months, but it seemed like a car was what she really needed most just then, so, for her 28th birthday, I gave her a used Kia Optima. It was in great shape with low miles and I got it for a song because it didn't run. It only took about $700 to get it going but the repairs meant she wouldn't have it until a couple days after her birthday.

On her 28th birthday, I was working until 10:30 at night, but I was hoping and expecting to see Tina afterwards. She texted in the middle of my shift to let me know that Nate was going to take her out "for a little while" and that she'd keep me posted.

When I got done with work, I tried calling and texting, but Tina never answered. She didn't make any effort to "keep me posted" at all.

I went home to my lonely bed. Just before midnight, I shot her a Happy Birthday/Goodnight message and drifted off to sleep.

I was up before the sun and feeling anxious, for some reason. Maybe I was just upset that Tina ignored me on her birthday while she was out with Nate.

181

I tried texting her, not knowing if she'd be asleep, still up, or even where she was. There was no reply and I decided to drive over.

I guessed she'd be hung over, so I put together a care package of Gatorade, Monster Energy drinks and smokes and drove to her place while the grass was still dewy. There was an unfamiliar black Toyota parked in the driveway and I realized that Nate had spent the night and was still there.

I wasn't thrilled, but I gave her the benefit of the doubt. Maybe he just needed to crash out on the couch for a while.

I had some work to do, so I left without disturbing them and set to that for a few hours. After work, I stopped at Target and got a fancy gift box, freshened up Tina's care package with a new, cold Gatorade, added some snacks and went back to her place.

The black Toyota was gone. I knocked on the door. Maura let me in. Tina was sleeping in Maura's bed. I let myself into the dark bedroom, feeling my way onto the bed and found a lump of hungover Tina under the covers. She roused easily and gratefully swigged her Gatorade.

She was in terrible condition for the rest of the day so I didn't end up taking her out for her birthday. She didn't say anything about Nate spending the night, and neither did I, but I did gently chide her. "I thought you were going to keep me posted," I said, draping an arm over her.

She told me she'd gone to bed "as soon as Nate dropped her off."

After I delivered Tina's birthday gift, Scott and his daughters became the primary beneficiaries of the car that I kept fueled and insured. It turned out that I was mostly just paying for Scott's daughters to get to school and back because all Tina really ever used the car for was to transport those kids at her mothers' insistence.

When Mom Left

December 29th, 2017 was the day I lost my Mom. She'd hosted Christmas for our extended family just 4 days prior. Tina, claiming to be down with a migraine, had declined to accompany me. I was disappointed, but my mom commented, "maybe that's for the best," when I mentioned it.

I'd gone to Tina's family function on Christmas Eve.

My mom's sister Linda had been staying at the house for the week and my other Aunt Ileen, who lived in the neighborhood had been visiting frequently. The three sisters seemed to be having a grand time.

It was a Friday and I had been trying to reach Tina in hopes of spending some time together over the weekend, but she'd not bothered to take my call or answer my texts. I'd given up on her and decided to go visit some friends.

I took a shower and was just getting dressed when my aunts both began shouting my name up the stairs. It sounded urgent. I pulled on my shirt and dashed down to the living room, asking "what is it?"

My Aunt Ileen ushered me towards the dining room, where my mom was lying on her back on the floor. Her head was propped at a severe angle on a one-gallon paint can that had been left there for a project I was getting ready to do. She appeared to be unconscious.

I was struggling to comprehend the situation – it was far from what I'd expected. I thought maybe they'd seen a mouse or something like that.

"She's not breathing," Linda said.

"She's not breathing?" I repeated, trying to force that information into my brain.

"Do CPR!" Ileen said. "It's 2 breaths and 30 compressions, I think."

"They don't teach breaths anymore," I said, academically. "It's just chest compressions." I was scrambling to recall how to go about it, beginning to panic as realization of the dire situation finally started to penetrate. My mom was dying? I flashed on a memory from health class. I failed the CPR unit, having "killed" the Resusi-Anne Doll, the computer indicated, by breaking her ribs with too much pressure in my compressions.

"Call 911," I said as I began pressing on my mother's chest. After about 10 compressions, she noticeably exhaled, her breath fluttering her lips with a snoring kind of sound. I didn't know what a death rattle was at the time, but looking back, I believe that's what it was.

I stopped compressions for a moment to see if she was breathing on her own. She didn't seem to take another breath, so I resumed.

Once an operator was on the phone, my aunt held the phone to my head and I did my best to explain the situation. They started counting compressions for me, because I was going too slow at first. "One-two-three-four…" She counted rapidly to thirty and started again. Time ceased to have meaning, but firefighters and paramedics crowded into the house with big jackets and heavy boots to take over the lifesaving attempt. I think they arrived pretty fast. A matter of minutes.

"She was just standing, there, talking to us and suddenly fell over," my aunt said. When she fell, her head hit the paint can. It was gruesome. I wondered what additional damage that may have caused.

I sat on the couch, definitely in a state of shock and looked on as they cut my mom's shirt off and attached electrodes. They used a machine for respiration and compressions. There was a flurry of activity. It seemed like at least 6 people were working her. I'm not sure. It's hazy.

"Look away, Dan," one of my aunts said.

I had the presence of mind to begin informing people of mom's situation. I tried calling my brothers but neither answered, so I sent texts. I texted my ex wife while I was at it, and Tina.

"Mom collapsed," I wrote. "I think she's dead."

Tina replied to that message quickly and said she would rush to my side. I was grateful but didn't know where we'd be and told her to wait.

A paramedic came over to explain what they were observing. She said mom's heart wasn't pumping, more like it was twitching and they were going to transport her to the hospital.

Everyone converged on the Emergency Room. I drove my aunts and was reminded of the time a few years prior I'd driven my mom and these two aunts to the hospital when my grandmother had similarly collapsed.

Terrified, but hoping and praying, my brothers, my uncle and others began to arrive and fill up the family room we'd been assigned. Eventually, we were given the word that Mom was dead. She'd had a massive heart attack that killed her almost instantly. For all our efforts, she'd been gone for quite some time.

I went, alone into the dark room where she lay and spoke a quiet goodbye, apologizing that I couldn't save her, lamenting the hard life she'd lived, feeling guilty and hoping that I'd somehow prove myself worthy of all she'd done for me.

Once we were leaving the hospital, I texted Tina again to ask her to meet me back at Mom's house. She said nothing could keep her away and she'd be there as fast as humanly possible.

I was on the front porch having a cigarette in the cold when I saw Maura's silver Saturn pull up in front. I was surprised. Just a month prior, I'd given Tina a car for her birthday, so I expected she'd drive herself, but I soon understood. She was drunk and thanks to someone's wisdom, she'd gotten a ride from her mom.

My aunts offered to stay with me at the house, but I had my Tina and that was all I thought I needed. They went home for the night. My ex-wife, Jessica who had been very close to my mother was in shock, herself. At one point, I remember her picking up copious amounts of medical debris that was left strewn across the house and frantically scrubbing a blood stain that had been left on the floor where Mom had lain. I never knew for sure where the blood came from.

Once we were alone in the house, I found Tina a great comfort. We cuddled up in my bed and I was finally able to drift off to sleep. I remember feeling bad for Tina, because we'd missed any chance to close the rift between her and my mother before she left. Now, I'm sure Tina didn't care a bit, but at the time, I thought it would bother her.

Our newly-rejoined relationship had seemed spotty before Mom's death, but an intense new period of devotion and love bombing ensued after.

Tina stayed by my side or at the house for several weeks immediately following Mom's death and her mom came to stay for frequent overnight visits. That was my new family, for a time.

Just a couple days after my mom had died, I awoke at Tina's apartment to news that my van had been hit by the neighbor. Chaos and madness ensued. Police were called. Twice.

Tina and the upstairs neighbors didn't get along. I didn't understand the apparent hostility between them until after Tina and I broke up. I got the impression that Tina was always trying to "win" some unseen battle with them. She looked for ways to tear them down or somehow prove their inadequacy as neighbors and tenants.

The upstairs neighbors, a young married couple had replaced one of Tina's sex partners as tenants in the tri-plex in September, the same month Tina and I decided to take another shot at a relationship.

Tina, I was told, said she was lonely, had no friends or boyfriend and the new neighbors tried to be friends with her.

One night that fall, Tina was drinking heavily with them in their garage and out of the blue said to the young mother, "I respect marriage, but I want to blow your husband."

I guess that wasn't taken very seriously, because she went into the house to check on their kids while Tina polished off a bottle of whiskey. When she came back out, Tina was trying to give her husband a lap dance.

That spelled the end of that budding friendship. Learning that, I finally understood all the weirdness between Tina and the neighbors.

Tina and I had decided to give it another try on September 11th (perhaps I should have paid more mind of the date). The neighbors had moved in on September 2nd. They later told me they were always seeing Tina come home with different guys. One day, the husband asked her which one was her boyfriend.

"I don't have a boyfriend," she told him. So the neighbors were understandably pretty surprised to hear she and I were engaged.

The young mother upstairs later told me that before I started moving in, Tina used to come home stinking drunk after three in the morning. Sometimes she was so out of it that she needed help unlocking the front door. Tina told her she was coming from work.

Tina drove an immediate and effective wedge between myself and the upstairs neighbors. I saw them several times a week, coming and going, but never stopped to engage them in conversation, unless absolutely necessary. Without even getting to know them, they were the enemy, because Tina said so. After we broke up, I learned that Tina had forewarned them not to talk to me because, she told them, I "don't like people," as a way to further discourage conversation.

I also heard later about a very disturbing episode around that time. Tina had wandered, uninvited into the upstairs neighbor's apartment and picked their newborn up out of his crib. When his mom found Tina holding him, she was unable to reason with Tina or get her to put her child down. Eventually Maura was summoned and she was able to coax Tina into releasing the baby and getting out of their new neighbors' apartment.

It became pretty obvious, why she preferred an arrangement that minimized the communication between us.

It was Tina who'd urged me to park my van where I did the night before, leading to the upstairs neighbor hitting it while backing out of his garage. I usually parked in a public lot down the block in the winter. Another blow that struck the wedge deeper.

Meanwhile, Tina and her mother were full of opinions and advice on handling my mother's estate, particularly the house. For a while, they had designs to move in. When it became apparent that wasn't going to be possible, because I was adamant on splitting the value of the house with my two brothers, Maura expressed interest in buying it.

Both Maura and Tina began pressing me on the house after a while and I began to feel that they were trying to manipulate me into decisions I wasn't comfortable with.

There was a lot to work out and at first, I included Tina in all of the decision-making processes. She was often not rational about it, but I did my best to consider her point of view and tried to accommodate her when practical.

Mom's house was becoming Tina's regular home and we moved her car up from Farmington so she could get around when I was at work. We moved her ball python, Lenny, and his terrarium into the house as well, so we could more easily take care of him (or her, it seems to have turned out).

Tina became the lady of the house. It was a role she seemed to enjoy for a brief while, but eventually, it began to chafe her. That got worse when I eventually had to disabuse her of some fantasies she had about big personal profits from the sale of Mom's house. That certainly caused dire narcissistic injury and seemed to lead to a wayward shift in Tina's behavior.

Since Tina was spending a lot of time with me at the house in Minneapolis, we brought her car into town so she could get around when I was at work. She got into an accident that marred the front bumper and license plate but totalled the car she T-boned. When I asked for details about how the accident happened, she claimed not to remember where it happened. Some time later, she told me she was pulling out of the liquor store parking lot onto a busy road and somehow failed to see the car she ran into.

I know Tina wouldn't normally be one to drive drunk, but with the amount she'd been drinking around that time, I doubt if there was a moment in any given day that she'd pass for legal, even if she felt sober. You can't drink a gallon of whiskey a week and have any time without some alcohol in your blood. Livers just can't work that fast. I should point out I wasn't keeping track of the volume she was consuming at the time of the accident, but once I started paying attention, I found she was going through at least a handle of whiskey in 2-3 days time, by herself. That's more than I could have managed at my very worst, before I quit altogether. It's epic-level drinking.

She didn't want to tell me she was at the liquor store. She hid how much she was drinking, even from me and I would have understood, even if I'd not have wanted her driving.

Sometime the next day, Tina found herself irritated that the front license plate on her car was hanging askew after the accident and decided to just rip it the rest of the way off. She brought it in the house. Not more than a day went by before I found a ticket on the windshield for missing a front license plate!

Still, I didn't grouse. I paid the ticket. I fixed the license plate. I dealt with the insurance company. I tried to put Tina at ease over the incident, but Tina then began insisting that she'd never drive again and her car sat idle for weeks. My brother had an emergency situation with the family car so, with Tina's apparent blessing, I lent him the Kia, since Tina wasn't using it. She seemed to resent that later, but Jason and his family needed it. Tina had me to drive her, as usual and was refusing to drive, anyhow.

I glossed over the rough patches. I was preoccupied with dealing with Mom's estate business and I was glad to have Tina my my side, at least at first.

We were pretty much living together full time and I felt very comfortable falling back into the kind of "domestic" feeling that had (partly) prompted me to propose to Tina two Februaries past. That felt like a lifetime ago by then. Circumstances felt very different, being with Tina after I'd stopped drinking. I felt that my demons had been slain and I was confident it was going to work out, this time.

On Valentine's Day, we had errands and some Walmart shopping planned. Tina was a list-maker so I got a hold of Tina's shopping and to-do list before we set out, to add a surprise entry.

Beneath "toilet paper" and above, "mouse for Lenny," I added, "Pick out engagement ring."

She saw it while I was driving us to Walmart. "Today?!" She exclaimed. "I'm getting a ring today?" she gushed.

Her reaction almost choked me up. I was electrified, thrilled and full of loving feelings.

I immediately detoured to Wedding Day Diamonds and parked in front of a sign that read, "Reserved for nervous engagement ring buyers."

Tina was treated to a glass of champagne and picked out a white gold ring with a solitaire setting. The "promise" got an upgrade.

Our relationship seemed magical for a while afterward. I was sure the powers of the universe had blessed our reunion. Finally, we were getting it right! Nothing that I could see at the moment seemed amiss. Until it did.

Never Touch a Black Guy's Butt

Tina and I were shooting pool at the Hexagon. We went there because, of the two bars with pool tables in my Minneapolis neighborhood, the Hex was the only one that served hard liquor. The Cardinal was limited to beer and wine. I didn't drink, but Tina still loved her whiskey.

There were two very muscular black men shooting a game or two at the table next to ours. They were dressed to go out, with overly-ornate, tight-fitted button-up urban shirts and colorfully embroidered jeans. Neither could form a sentence without at least two profanities and usually, at least one was the N-word.

"I'd kind of like to play with those two," Tina told me, conspiratorially.

I didn't even want to be noticed by them. I glanced sidelong and shook my head.

They had Tina's attention for the better part of the night. It was getting late and we debated on whether to play one more game or head for home. We decided to step out for a smoke. It was chilly, so we put on our coats and started moving towards the patio door.

Our boisterous neighbors were discussing a missed shot and what the fuck the "nigga" who was shooting should have done to sink that bitch, if he knew what his partner was saying, that is.

A damnably familiar look of mischief seized Tina's face and she broke sharply left, darting away from me and towards the back wall behind the pool tables. I didn't have time to react beyond cringing. Shoulders slumped forward to lower her profile in a caricature of stealth, she rounded the second table and came up behind the guy who'd assumed the role of instructor. He was unaware of her approach until she lifted one leg and began to repeatedly bump her crotch into his butt, saying "maybe it would have worked better if he'd done it like this."

"TEE-NAH!" I shouted in horrified reproach.

The instructor first checked the beer in his hand for spillage, then very slowly turned his head to regard Tina. "Was that supposed to be some kind of gay thing?" He was calm and very still, but the air around him crackled with menace.

"She didn't mean anything by it, man. She's just really drunk," I quickly interjected.

Only then did Tina seem to grasp the gravity of the situation and she thankfully took a step back and kept her mouth shut.

"Well, are you going to buy me a beer or am I going to have to take offense?"

I froze. "Uh…" Deja vu was striking from my teen years. I was certain I hadn't been called to account for a date's behavior since then. I was caught off guard by the neanderthal notion, but figured, rather than attempt a philosophical debate about misogyny, I'd just buy the guy a beer to smooth things over and then get Tina to a safe harbor.

Watching my face, and seeming to read my train of thought, Tina preempted my reply. "I'll do it." She made a wide arc around them and came towards me, fishing her wallet out of her purse. She approached the bar.

Seemed fair enough to me.

"PBR Tall boy," he called out.

Tina bought him the beer, delivered it with a faint curtsy and the decision on whether to shoot another game was moot.

What Tina had done was so obviously wrong on many levels, but I was astonished by her take on what had gone wrong as we made our way across the parking lot to my van.

"I have to remember black guys don't like their butts touched."

Moments like those nearly forced my brain to reboot. I stammered, trying to find a response. None was handy off the shelf. I had to formulate something new.

"Especially from behind," Tina added.

My brain was trying in vain to track down a precedent. Nope. New territory and deeper afield.

"What if maybe you just didn't touch *any* strangers' butts when we go out to the bar?"

The conversation devolved into delusion, with Tina lamenting being born white, certain that her weird attempt to get recognition from random thugs in the bar was only foiled by her complexion.

This kind of dangerous and inappropriate impulsivity is a trait of cluster B disorders. Narcissists need attention and have difficulty regulating the conflicting states of inflated sense of self-worth and the inherent fragility of their egos. This results in poor impulse-control. Similarly, people suffering from borderline personality disorder are often fraught with feelings of inadequacy that result in unstable emotions, behaviors and relationships. They are unable to see how their emotions and impulses are unreasonable or excessive. A person with BPD is unlikely to consider the potential consequences of his or her actions. For the narcissist, any negative fallout is easily blamed on someone else or other circumstances, even if the explanation seems nonsensical to anyone else (that only went wrong because those black guys were racist and don't like white women).

Tina's impulsivity wasn't always destructive (but often enough for it to be a serious problem). Sometimes it was endearing, like when she'd abruptly stop during a winter stroll and throw herself to the ground to make a snow angel, or when she'd have to put a quarter into the vending machine for that shiny bauble, or needed to win a plush toy from the claw game.

"I'm having so much fun!" she gushed while we were tracing chalk outlines of each other late one summer night in Buffalo. We were making a "crime scene" that looked like people had been crushed by cars and construction equipment on the deserted Main Street.

Those child-like impulses were adorable, but I now realize that they also probably stem from terrible childhood trauma that stunted her emotional development. Her literacy was at least equal to a doctoral student, but emotionally and logically, she was hardly more developed than a 5-year-old.

Psychic Triangulation

Tina and I were introduced to one of Amber's friends at their usual haunt, the Doghouse. Jessup was a heavy-set woman with native American or Hispanic features. She presented herself as a gifted psychic. She seemed very amiable and she and I were the only members of the party who weren't drinking.

Early in the night, she said "You two are trying to conceive, aren't you?"

Tina and I weren't exactly "trying" to conceive a child, but we weren't taking any pains not to and we'd been discussing the subject in depth. Tina believed she had fertility issues and after years of unprotected sex not producing a pregnancy, it seemed one of us must have. We had just recently been discussing seeing a fertility specialist, but not until after we were married. In the meanwhile, we were rolling the dice.

Tina acted impressed by her insight, but I didn't really think she was buying into the notion that Jessup had any real powers of prognostication. Engaged couples will tend to discuss having kids!

At some point, Tina and Jessup disappeared out on to the patio for an extended conversation. After a while, I was craving some nicotine, so I wandered out onto the patio and lit a cigarette. I saw the two of them and approached, but was reproached by Tina. "We're talking about you right now," she said. "can you go back inside for a few minutes?"

I shrugged, snuffed my cigarette and went back into the bar where I tried to make conversation with Amber. It was a little awkward. She never warmed to me. After a bit, others in the gang were heading out to smoke so I joined them. I guess the private conversation was over and we all gathered together to chat.

Later in the night, Tina told me that Jessup's authoritative psychic insight told her that I was not the one for Tina. "I told her she's wrong," Tina said, "that I feel connected to you in a way I've never felt before and that I'm happier than I've ever been. I showed her my ring and told her I was going to marry you."

I smiled. That was really nice to hear.

"So she said, well, maybe he'd good for you right now, but he's not the one."

I was floored by the gall. That was exceptionally pompous and rude on Jessup's part, especially with a couple she'd just met – if, in fact, that's how the conversation went. My impression of Jessup plummeted. We weren't going to be friends. Tina mirrored my reaction. "Yeah, I don't think I like her," she said.

I have my doubts that sober Jessup was so utterly tactless, though. This exchange had the hallmarks of triangulation.

Triangulation is a manipulative tactic employed by people with borderline or narcissistic personalities to belittle their victims. The goals of triangulation (it's no accident) are to make the victim feel insecure and also to garner sympathy and turn the third party into a weapon against the victim.

Tina would often invoke her friends and family in an effort to make me feel insecure while portraying herself as my staunch defender. "My brother is worried about me," she once told me, out of the blue. "He says I haven't been myself since I got back together with you, but I told him how much I love you and he said 'well, as long as you're happy,' and of course, I am."

She told me how her dad was afraid I was going to hurt her and advised her to be careful with me.

On other occasions, she said, "Everyone says you're not right for me, well, everyone but my mom – she loves you. She's your biggest defender. And me, of course."

That night meeting Jessup at the Doghouse was probably another example of triangulation, but this time with a bizarre supernatural twist. It certainly wasn't the strangest thing to happen in the course of the Adventures of Dan and Tina.

Six-Foot-Twelve

I needed a break from the house and I made extra effort to keep Tina comfortable and at least somewhat entertained while she was staying there with me. I suggested we go out to the Cardinal to shoot pool.

I bought Tina a beer and a Monster Energy Drink for myself. Before we got a game going, Tina wanted to try her luck at the claw machine game. She blew a couple dollars without snagging a toy. Frustrated, she asked me to try. I studied the pile of plush toys and plastic balls. It didn't look very promising, but I gave it a try with a little coaching from Tina.

The claw descended perfectly over a stuffed puppy, but the prize slipped out as the crane lifted.

"You almost had it. Try it again!" Tina prodded.

My second attempt was successful and I handed Tina her prize.

It was silly, but it always felt special when I won a plush toy from the claw game for Tina. It was one of our things.

We picked out a table and I racked for a game of 8-Ball.

After playing a while, another couple started up a game at the table next to ours. The man was very tall, athletic-looking and with a dark complexion that implied a mixed racial background. His girlfriend was pretty – a petite Latina with long black hair. She looked extra tiny next to her giant of a date.

Tina was obviously fascinated. Throughout the night, she kept sidling up to the tall man and attempting to chat him up. The latina was gracious, at first, but eventually, I could tell she was losing patience with Tina fawning over her boyfriend.

"Migosh, he's so tall!" Tina gushed to me when she came back to our table from one of her forays. "He's like Six-foot-Twelve! I'm kidding. I just mean… damn, he's tall!"

He wasn't seven feet, but not far removed. I think he said he was 6-foot-nine.

Another time when she came back to me, she said, "Mmmm. I bet he just tosses her all around in bed."

I was getting as tired of hearing Tina go on about him as his girlfriend seemed to be of Tina cutting in on their date.

Tina mostly seemed oblivious to the discomfort she was causing everyone. The tall guy was becoming more curt, obviously not wanting to upset his girlfriend. His girlfriend would begin staring daggers at Tina when she'd approach.

Tina's infatuation with his height and imagined sexual gymnastics was making me feel unattractive or inadequate. It was classic narcissistic triangulation.

I didn't hear it, but from across the room, I saw Tina receiving what looked like a rebuke of some kind from the petite Latina. Tina was not good at picking up on social cues, especially when drinking. I later wondered if that lack of situational awareness could be tied to a narcissist's lack of empathy. It looked like the girl was finally getting a little less subtle for Tina's benefit and to my relief, Tina did leave the couple alone for quite a while after.

An hour later, though, as we were getting ready to leave, Tina wandered back over to the other couple. She exchanged a few words and then Tina gave the Latina girl the stuffed puppy I'd won her. I guessed it was supposed to be some sort of apology. It didn't look well-received and I'd wager the puppy ended up in a garbage bin or a slushy gutter puddle on their way home.

Tina came back to me and we got our coats on and went back to the house. I mixed Tina a drink and put some cocoa in the microwave for myself, but before it was even done heating, Tina was all over me and we ended up having sex on the kitchen floor. Her obsession with the tall dark stranger at the bar was forgotten (by myself, at least), as was the cocoa turning cold in the microwave.

The next chilly evening, Tina and I were on our way back to Farmington when Tina interrupted our chat to excitedly point out some baggage ahead on the roadside. There were three matching pieces, strewn in a way that suggested it had fallen off a moving vehicle.

"Pull over and get it!" Tina urged.

I drove on past shaking my head.

"Turn around. Go back! Hurry before someone else gets it!"

"No, Tina. That's not ours. Hopefully the person who picks it up will be the person who lost it," I said.

"That's really nice luggage," she insisted. "Do you know how expensive that is?"

"I can imagine," I said, "and can't you imagine how upset you'd be if you realized you'd lost it, turned around to retrieve it and found someone else had snatched it first?"

She grunted in frustration. "Better us than them! Hurry before someone else gets it!" she said.

Too often, I'd let Tina override my better judgment, but I had the steering wheel and in a rare moment of defiance, resisted her urging. I was disappointed in her lack of empathy for the people who had lost the luggage. Instead, she saw an opportunity to enrich herself and felt entitled. Our pleasant chat was over. She crossed her arms for the rest of the ride, occasionally grumbling about her own cheap luggage, and reminding me that we had a trip coming up.

"Tina, I'll buy you a new bag before we go," I promised, but she wasn't mollified.

I was wondering if the luggage was empty or if it was lost by travelers. I was putting myself in their shoes, imagining my distress if I was on a trip and suddenly lost all of my clothes, shoes and maybe my passport or other important documents.

When we got home, we met Maura in the apartment. Tina was bursting to tell her mom about the luggage I'd neglected on the highway.

"Mom, mom! You won't believe what Dan did."

Maura welcomed the news with an amused look.

"We saw a set of luggage on the side of the road and he refused to stop to get it."

Maura raised an eyebrow.

"It was a really nice set, too, like really expensive, probably. Dan, tell her why you wouldn't stop." Her tone was incredulous.

"Well, I guess I wanted the rightful owners to have a chance to get their belongings back," I said.

Tina's wide eyes said, "see?!" She was literally amazed by my attitude. She could not comprehend my empathetic and honest motives.

"Darn people with their good morals," Maura quipped. I took it as a joke, but couldn't really tell where Maura fell on the dispute.

I didn't take Tina for a thief, but I was learning that she was an opportunist. Her lack of empathy for other people probably bothered me as much as my failure to seize the moment bothered her. I didn't know what a narcissist was at the time, but now I can see how this incident illustrated the difference between narcissists and empaths. I was amazed that Tina couldn't see my point of view and she was just as surprised by my attitude. Ironically, as an empath, I could see Tina's point of view. I was just repelled by it and had difficulty seeing that characteristic in my partner.

Narcissists believe that deep-down, everyone is like them and everyone who appears otherwise is just putting on masks and being manipulative, just like them. In Tina's mind, if we didn't take the bags, the very next people to come along would. The original owners were already out of luck. To her, she was the victim in this story, because she was entitled to that lost luggage and I let it go to someone else.

Drunken Histrionics

It was the first St. Patrick's Day I was going to celebrate sober. It was kind-of a somber day, because it reminded me of friends I didn't talk to any more. I had to work into the evening that day and there didn't appear to be anything going on with my other friends, anyway, so Tina and I struck out on our own when I finally got home.

We we went to Kip's to see a favorite band of mine. The Tim Malloys played Irish traditional music with a hard rock twist and they'd become something of a tradition for me on St. Paddy's Day. I thought Tina would enjoy them.

Kip's was a pub attached to a Marriott Hotel and there was a ballroom across the hall from the bar. There seemed to be a wedding reception or some other kind of private-ish party going on over there.

The bar was packed, as one might expect. We arrived late into the festivities and the crowd was already well-inebriated. The band had probably exhausted their hits by then and they were playing slower music than I'm used to hearing from them, but Tina and I were having a good time, anyhow.

Tina was drinking whiskeys and beer and I had a couple Red Bulls. Eventually, the energy drinks worked through me and I had to excuse myself to the restroom. There was a bit of a line to get in to the busy lavatory, but it wasn't extreme. I was gone for maybe 10 minutes, at the very most.

When I caught up to Tina, she was lurking in the hallway between the bar and ballroom. She was peering into the crowd in the pub from aside the doorway as if trying not to be seen by someone.

I sidled up to her and put my arm around her waist. "What's up, sweetheart?"

"I'm trying to avoid someone," she said.

I was only about a quarter as surprised as one might expect. People who frequently decry drama tend to be the drama queens and Tina was such a person. I guess I was inured to it but I was also still compartmentalizing. Looking back, Tina was always stirring pots and poking hornets' nests.

"What? Who? Why?" I glanced around instinctively.

"I was dancing with this guy and then his friend… Let's go out back and have a cigarette," she said and I followed her through the noisy crowd and down a dark corridor that led to the back patio.

We lit cigarettes and Tina began to relate a very vague and disjointed story that, despite my sobriety, I can't even clearly recall, because it was so confusing.

What I gathered, was somehow in the five to ten minutes I was away, Tina had managed to dance with two other men who turned out to be friends and worked them into a jealous rage that culminated in a fist fight over her.

There were a lot of Tina's characteristic de dah de da de dahs where details were elided so I couldn't really get a grip on the sequence of events that ultimately led to the fight and Tina running away to hide.

After we finished our cigarettes, I refreshed our drinks, but Tina didn't want to hang about in the pub anymore. She led me across the hall to the ballroom. There was a very different atmosphere in there. People were well-dressed. There were disco lights and a DJ was spinning poppy electronic dance music.

"I want us to go in there and start dancing like total dorks," she said.

I was game to take Tina up on her dare and we both danced our way in like we owned the place.

That left whatever drama Tina had created in the pub well out of our way.

We danced a couple songs and ended up having a pleasant conversation with a smart-looking couple. The event, whatever it had been, was winding down around and by midnight, everyone was clearing out and the DJ was finished. The pub didn't have much appeal left for either Tina or I, so we made out way home for a record-breaking early ending to a St. Patrick's Day.

Looking back, it's impressive, in a way, that within minutes, Tina was able to triangulate two men she'd just met and then, me as well. I imagine there's quite a lot of narcissistic supply available from people fighting over the narcissist.

We were mostly staying at my mom's house at the time while I was getting some work done on preparing the house for sale, so we'd brought the terrarium that housed Tina's snake, Lenny and her car into Minneapolis.

Sometimes Maura would stay at the house with us, but sometimes Tina was left there alone while I was off at work, so I always tried to find ways to entertain and keep Tina happy when I'd get back home.

First Avenue, Minneapolis' famous Downtown Danceteria was one of my absolute favorite night spots for as long as I was old enough to get in. It was a part of my life experience I'd been wanting to share with Tina for a long time. The place was always in flux, however and recent changes to the schedules, layout and formats made it less appealing in the years I'd known Tina.

One weekend came along when there was a main room dance night with an 80s theme that looked like a lot of fun. Since Tina had been mirroring my music tastes, it appeared that she'd love the 80s music and she'd had fun playing dress-up for my friend's 80s-themed birthday party a year or so prior. It seemed like a good opportunity, so I got tickets.

It was a Friday night and I had to work the day of the event, so Tina was left at my mom's house by herself until I got back. When I did, I noticed that Tina had taken the opportunity to indulge in some pre-partying and seemed to have a decent buzz going. She'd costumed herself appropriately for the theme with blue eye shadow and big hair.

She had acquired a hair crimper somewhere along the way that she'd been eager to have an excuse to use. This was the big night.

I got into some acid-washed jeans with appropriately tapered ankles and an original red paisley Chess King shirt that had a storied history of it's own.

I was excited as we entered the nightclub. It had been a while since I'd been in the black and cavernous main room. I showed Tina around half the club and we made our way to the coat check before ordering drinks at the back bar. A double shot of Windsor with a beer back for Tina and a $7.00 can of Red Bull for myself.

I thought Tina was looking pretty hot, but it wasn't long before she was more like a hot mess.

I didn't know how much she'd had to drink before I got back from work to pick her up, but it became apparent that it was a lot.

Tina's behavior went quickly from fun party-mode to erratic and inexplicable. Back by the coat check at the very back of the main room, there was a dark, disused corridor that I think led to an emergency exit and maybe some staff only doors. Tina was drawn to it, despite being shooed out of there by staff more than once and I had to keep urging her to stay way from it. Tina attracted a lot of attention from the bouncers and it was not in any way positive. I was increasingly concerned we were going to get kicked out.

Eventually, she and I found a pocket of space to ourselves, off the main dance floor, where Tina alternated between doing some drunk girl dances and sitting down, head in hands in the international sign for girl had way too much to drink.

Again, she was attracting notice from bouncers. Seeming to become aware of that, she began exaggerated admiration of the engagement ring I'd given her two months prior. She wanted me to play along, like she was swooning because I'd just proposed to her there in the club.

We were probably there less than an hour before I realized I was going to have an emergency on my hands if I didn't get Tina out of there right away. She slunk back to the forbidden dark corridor, she fell down.

A bouncer approached me. "Yo, man, is she OK?"

"She's feeling a little overwhelmed," I said. I'm going to take her out to get some air.

That satisfied the bouncer for the moment and he held off two others I noticed were approaching from behind him.

I got our coats and managed to coax Tina out the front entrance onto 7th Street. It was chilly but the street was bustling. I lit cigarettes for the both of us and was going to lead Tina back to my van, but she decided to lie down on the sidewalk, instead.

The streets of Downtown Minneapolis on a Friday night is not a great environment to lie down in. I was immediately concerned about the kinds of attention this could bring. I never felt unsafe around there, but also knew better than to exhibit any kind of vulnerability, because there was no shortage of people looking for opportunities. There was also no shortage of cops. They'd normally leave revelers alone, but lying down on the sidewalk was the kind of thing that would raise even their jaded antennas.

I tugged, cajoled, pleaded urged and lifted Tina back to her feet and got her moving, stumbling and swaying back to my van and finally breathed a sigh of relief once she was strapped in and we were rolling for home.

I felt it is was a good thing I was sober by then. We'd had a couple nights in the past when we were probably both that obliterated, but in more forgiving environs.

In the privacy of our own home, drunken Tina was much easier to look after. In public, she could become a menace. I tried to be more cautious about monitoring her level of intoxication after that, but neither alcoholics nor narcissists take well to having boundaries.

Two Drunks Leave a Bar

Nate had barely left for his new job and home in California before he returned for a visit. I was at work when Tina informed me that Nate was picking her up to go out. She said I could meet up with them at the Doghouse when I got done.

I walked into the dive bar, very overdressed in a suit and tie, around 9:30, expecting that everyone would already be there, but I was the first to arrive. I tried calling Tina to see where she was but she didn't answer. I texted her, "I guess I beat you here" and waited in the lot for nearly an hour before I took another wander around to see if anyone had snuck in yet.

Nate was seated to the left of Tina at the bar. She had a drink before her and he was ordering food.

"There you are," I said.

"Yeah. We just got here," she said.

I wondered where they had been all that time, why she didn't bother getting back to me and where the rest of the expected gang was. It was very noisy and not conducive to conversation. I sat to the right of Tina. She was leaned in talking to Nate, but I couldn't hear either one of them. After a while, she turned to me and asked if I'd be OK with Nate taking her to his brother's wedding as his plus one.

I shrugged. "Sure."

The wedding was in a few weeks, so Nate would be back in Minnesota again, soon. "Can't get rid of this guy," I thought, a bit irked. I knew little about him, but I did know he had a (supposedly) one-sided romantic interest in Tina. Despite that, Tina assured me he was harmless and said she'd been very clear that she didn't like him that way. "He's just a good friend."

Amber, and a few of her other friends showed up an hour later. Tina seemed excited to see one of the gang: A guy who I only knew by the moniker, "purple." It was the name Tina assigned his number when she put it in her phone for reasons unknown. I'd picked up that it was a reference to purple eyeliner that had been applied to him whilst passed out, drunk. When and where, I also didn't know.

It was Jessup's birthday so I bought her a shot. Tina hit the floor to dance and Nate followed her, awkwardly dancing around her. He reminded me vaguely of one of those convulsing fan men you sometimes see at car lots and gas stations.

I made an effort at conversing with Amber. She said she was somewhat concerned because she had to work in the morning and was expected to drive the usually sober birthday psychic home, but Jessup was getting her drinking groove on.

"Bummer," I sympathized. "Maybe I could give her a lift back if you need to cut out. I don't have to work tomorrow. Knowing Tina, we'll be out late, anyhow," I suggested.

Tina and I shot a game of pool and we all chatted in the back of the bar for a while. I was surprised when Tina suggested calling it a night, kind of early. "Are you getting tired?" She asked, "want to get going pretty soon?" I shrugged. I was in no hurry and was willing to follow her lead. After a while, she approached Amber. "Well, we're going to have to get going. Dan has to work in the morning," she said apologetically.

I cringed. Why would she lie? Of course, she couldn't have known that I had just told Amber the exact opposite.

Amber shot me a quick look. I couldn't quite read her expression. It was forced, perhaps, or I didn't understand the subtext. Embarrassment, maybe? "Uh, OK," she said.

Tina picked up her purse. "I'm just going to say my goodbyes." She disappeared into the crowd, leaving me and Amber standing awkwardly together. Without further word, Amber wandered off, too. I said a couple quick goodbyes to other members of our group that were nearby, wished Jessup a happy birthday again and waited near the door. Tina came up to me saying she wanted to stay later and could get a ride back with Amber. "You can just head back. I'll meet you there." She explained that she'd been tasked with helping Amber drag Jessup out of the bar at a reasonable time.

Sadly, I recognized Tina's transparent manipulation. When she was drinking, she thought she was clever. I didn't know exactly what she was up to, but I knew she was trying to get rid of me and to say it made me uneasy would be an understatement. She was probably used to getting by with a lot of poorly executed lies and manipulations because I was rarely in a mind to question her.

I initially thought her scheming might have something to do with her interest in the "Purple" guy. It didn't occur to me at the time that it could also have been to do with the decidedly unattractive Nate.

I resolved to stick around and see what I would see.

"No. I'm cool with staying as late as you want. I don't have anything to do tomorrow."

"I just figured you weren't having any fun with my friends and would want to go," she said.

"No. I'm having a good time. It's all cool. I can hang in there… Unless you're just trying to get rid of me, then I certainly could go," I said with a teasing tone.

"What? No. Of course not," she said.

I spoke with Amber again about these apparent concerns about Jessup being able to leave the bar at a reasonable time. I offered suggestions and assistance.

"No. It's all cool. We made a deal and I'm going to stay out an extra hour and her friend is going to pick her up at my house so I don't have to drive her all the way back."

Mere minutes later, Tina, looking deflated, told me she was ready to go and I drove her home. I was mightily puzzled, but, of course, it all made much more sense in retrospect.

Avoiding Dissonance

Cognitive dissonance is a state of conflicted thoughts, ideas or realities. Or, a confused, frightening mental conflict between evidence of reality and contrary beliefs. It's a difficult, even traumatizing phenomenon that I believe my subconscious mind was trying to prevent by avoiding information that would bring the dissonance about.

Tina had been staying with me at my mom's house, with her mom coming for sporadic stays over the spring. By June, Maura hadn't been coming around as much, preferring to stay in Farmington for a while. I recall Tina saying something about her not feeling welcome there, which saddened me, because she was very welcome and I tried to make her stays very comfortable. I made up a bed for her. I set up the coffee to auto-brew for her at the early early hour she'd arise for work so she could wake up with a fresh cup. I tried to keep foods she liked in the house and so-forth. But I digress.

Tina and I were alone in the house, sitting at the dining room table. She was fidgeting with her phone, which was flat on the table before her, to find something she wanted to show me. A little circle with a face popped up on the screen and Tina swiftly put her hand up to conceal the screen while she made that go away, but I'd seen it. The quick glimpse was enough to identify it, because I'd seen it a few times before. It was an incoming message on the facebook messenger app.

"Was that Cassidy?" I asked, more to let her know that her effort to cover it up was futile than to verify, because I knew it was Cassidy.

She hesitated, uncomfortably before acknowledging it. "Yes, but I just sent that right to the trash like I always do. I'd block him, but I don't know how."

Of course, I recognized Cassidy's messenger circle because I'd seen it before. A few times, when he was trying to contact Tina for whatever reason. I saw one of his earlier messages "Wanna get together and smoke a little or something?" That one was around November, I think. He blinked up on her screen again right around Christmas and perhaps another time that I noticed. When I asked Tina about what her former sex-buddy wanted. She'd always say she just ignored him, was planning to block him and he probably just wanted to bum some weed off of her. She said he probably owed her hundreds of dollars for weed she'd fronted him in the few months they'd been together.

"When we met for Coffee back in September and decided to give 'Us' another try, I kind of envisioned some steps that would come next," I said. "For instance, I shut down my dating apps and canceled a date I had set up. I cut off ties with women I'd dated – my ex-wife being the exception – I kinda thought You'd be doing the same. I'm getting the impression that you never bothered to tell Cassidy…"

"Oh, He knows about you. Trust me on that." She found the thing she wanted to show me – some silly picture. I don't remember, exactly. Something dirty.

As Tina told it, Cassidy was a "smoke buddy" and occasional sex partner during the few months that Tina and I were not seeing or speaking to each other in the Summer of 2017. He had moved into the apartment above Tina's in the Farmington triplex. I'd met him on a couple occasions. I'd suspected he was the reason for our last falling out. He only lived in the apartment from April through August and Tina and I reconciled on September 11th, but I knew he had been over to Tina's late the night before. He was also standing guard behind Tina when I'd attempted to reconcile with her in early June. I didn't know they were a thing at the time, but I suspected. Turns out I was right. With Cassidy looking on, she'd sent me packing, dismissing me pretty harshly. That sent me into a major drinking spiral and I was hammered for days. After all that, I tried to sober up and experienced horrible, debilitating withdrawals and that ultimately, finally led me to down the road to sobriety.

Tina described her relationship with Cassidy as a "not serious" relationship of convenience. She said she didn't call herself his girlfriend and that he was pretty dim. Later on, she told me that they had never even kissed, but had sex only a couple times. Sometimes, they just spooned, she said. This was all information I didn't need. All I needed to know was that it was over. From his frequent attempts to contact Tina via facebook, he didn't seem to know that. And, those attempts are just the ones I know of – that I happened to notice when they popped up. There were almost certainly more than I saw. Tina always maintained that she never replied and intended to delete and block him when she figured out how. "I can show you," I'd offered on more than one occasion, but she always had some reason to put it off or said she wanted to figure it out for herself.

The next day was Friday and Tina told me she was feeling a lot of anxiety about Mom's house and needed to get away for a while. She said her mom would be coming to pick her up after work and take her back to Farmington with her for the weekend.

"Oh," I said, disappointed. I'd miss her terribly. I was really enjoying having her company around the house. It felt like we were a couple, a team, domesticated. It was like a trial run on marriage and I was into it. I always missed her keenly if we were apart for more than a couple days. At that time, she was my best friend and I didn't tire of her company and conversation.

After some discussion with her mom that I wasn't privy to, plans changed and she wasn't going back to Farmington after all. Yay! I get to keep my Tina over the weekend!

Things changed again on Saturday and she was desperate to get back to Farmington. I had given Tina a car for this very purpose, but she was refusing to drive it, after her accident at the liquor store.

Always accommodating, I said, "Don't make your mom drive into Minneapolis and back on her day off. I'll drive you down after I finish this work project. I was planning to run and get some materials for the bedroom, so I can stop at Home Depot on the way back."

I got to work on a writing assignment for work and Tina set to packing. She packed a lot. She tended to over-pack for trips, but she was going home where most things she needed were duplicated.

It took me a bit longer to get ready to drive Tina than I'd initially estimated, but we got on the road as dusk was falling and we listened to music loud, sang along and chatted away until I noticed a strange sound emanating from my van. Music off. Quiet. Listen, diagnose.

I determined that something had gotten caught in the suspension and was knocking on the passenger wheel well. I decided closer inspection could wait until we got back to Tina's.

I pulled into the driveway, parking behind Maura's car, because there was a red Pontiac I didn't recognize parked in the middle of the driveway, by the doorway.

"Whose car is that?" I asked Tina.

"I don't know." She undid her seat belt and hurried out of the van.

I helped Tina unload her luggage and she toted it down into the apartment while I got under the van to see what was knocking. It was a plastic shield in the wheel well that had lost a screw and was flapping when the wind caught it. I decided that wasn't urgent. My hands were dirty from my inspection and I was planning to go downstairs to wash up, and say hi to Maura before turning back for Minneapolis. It would be a very quick stop-in. I was sensing Tina needed a break from me and I didn't want to intrude on their mother-daughter time.

Tina came back out after her second trip toting her bags just as I was getting up from checking the wheel well. "Do you want to come inside and say hello to my mother?"

"Yeah," I said, holding my hands out. "I was just about to do that and I need to wash my hands."

She led me down into the basement apartment where Maura was standing in the living room. We exchanged a couple quick pleasantries and then I kicked my shoes off by the stairs and turned towards the bathroom.

"Could you use the kitchen sink instead?" Tina got in front of me, ushering me in the other direction."

I thought this was odd. I might have washed my hands in the kitchen sink when I was preparing dinner, but the bathroom was the default cleaning up room in my experience. Tina snatched a black towel off the oven door, thrusting it at me. "See? Look. It's black. Perfect for your dirty hands."

I shrugged. I set the towel on the counter and used some dish soap to wash my hands over the (dirty) dishes. I made sure my hands were clean before I tried drying them, as civilized people will do, so the color of the towel wasn't terribly interesting, except for the fact that this new dollar store kitchen towel left my wet hands covered in streaks of black lint that I had to brush off into the garbage.

Tina hurried me towards the door. Maura, standing in the doorway to the TV room never moved.

I sat on the bottom step to put my shoes back on and Tina stepped forward to give me a quick kiss goodbye and I was on my way back to my lonely bed in my mom's empty house in Minneapolis.

That night I had a disturbing dream. I was staying at Tina's and heard a strange sound from the bathroom. I went to investigate and heard the shower running. Tina was in bed and no one else was supposed to be in the house. I knew I wouldn't be peeping on Maura when I pulled back the curtain. Behind it, there was a naked man I'd never seen before, wet and soapy in the shower. He was startled and immediately moved to attack me. We struggled briefly before he ran off and out of the apartment – naked all the way.

I think I woke up as he was making his escape and never got a reaction or explanation from Tina, who had calmly observed me and him emerging wet and bedraggled from the bathroom.

I spent the weekend tinkering with improvements to the house, getting it ready to sell and come Monday, I had to get off to my driving job. I liked the chauffeur gig, but sometimes the hours were weird and sometimes there just weren't many hours to be worked.

I got done with work early and decided to swing back down to Farmington to see my one true love.

I had a key, and we were planning on cohabitating permanently once I'd sold Mom's house, so I let myself in. I found Tina in the kitchen, perusing the fridge in some jammie pants and a hoodie. She didn't seem to have heard me come in. I approached from behind, intent on wrapping her in my embrace and kissing her neck, but I didn't want to startle her, so I said "hello" as I approached.

"Oh, Hi," she said, turning towards and somewhat stiffly accepting my hug. I could feel that she was wearing some kind of girdle under her sweat jacket. Something like Spanx. It struck me as pretty odd, but I didn't call attention to it.

She may have been self-conscious about it, I thought, and I wouldn't have wanted to embarrass her.

"Have you had dinner, yet? How about I take you out to eat?" I suggested. "Just let me get changed out of this suit, first." I started towards the bedroom. Tina intercepted me, physically blocking my path. "could you change in the bathroom?" she requested.

"Um. OK… Why?"

"My room's a terrible mess. I want to clean it up a bit. Look. Clean clothes!" She quickly collected up a pair of jeans, a T-shirt and casual socks from the couch. They were neatly folded. She'd done my laundry for me. I smiled at that act of considerate kindness, but I was pretty baffled by the changing in the bathroom thing. I had become inured to the habit of not challenging her oddities. I never really told her "no." The closest I had come to that was "I really don't want to, but OK."

I took the fresh duds into the bathroom. It was a small space. It wasn't quite so bad as changing in an airplane lav, but not far removed. A bit irked, I grew suspicious. I was being manipulated, of course, but my brain fought me. I should have gone straight into the bedroom. I was going to hang my suit up in the closet in there, anyway. This is where I think my subconscious was acting to keep information from me that would have caused cognitive dissonance and maybe a fair amount of trauma.

I finished changing in the cramped bathroom and popped out. The bedroom door was open. It had been closed when Tina ushered me to the bathroom. I peered in. It didn't look at all different from the last time I'd seen it.

"I just need to hang up my suit," I said to Tina who was sitting on the living room couch. I gestured towards the bedroom.

She shrugged. "OK."

I went in, stepping over a couple bags she hadn't unpacked yet and hung up my suit. Curiosity compelled me to linger a bit and look around to see what she might have changed in the two minutes I was in the bathroom changing that was so critically "messy" that she hadn't wanted me to see it.

Nothing seemed amiss and nothing seemed an unusual mess.

I'd been conditioned and boxed in, in a way, not to challenge Tina's assertions. I was more concerned about offending her with even a hint of suspicion than protecting myself. I always gave her the benefit of the doubt, but that whole weekend gnawed at me for some time. In a way, I was protecting myself. Whatever Tina was trying to conceal, I didn't want to see it.

The next day, I was up earlier than Tina (I usually was since I didn't drink anymore and had responsibilities) and noticed the recycling was overflowing in the kitchen, so I tied up the trash bag and took the garbage and all the recycling out.

When I opened the recycling bin, I noticed a heap of mail in there, all addressed to Cassidy.

I'd been aware of the large collection of Cassidy's mail. It had been piling up in a brown paper bag in the entryway for months. Now it had been discarded, after Tina tried to hide an incoming message from him, after she had to get back to Farmington for a weekend alone, after she'd kept me out of the bathroom on one day and out of the bedroom on another. Had Cassidy been over and picked out the mail he needed, discarding the rest or had Tina merely grown weary of that bag filling up in the entryway? I never asked. I gave her the benefit of the doubt. The red Pontiac wasn't Cassidy's car. I was pretty sure of that. I'd seen him driving a black SUV with one mismatched white fender.

All trust broke down following a later incident with Nate that led to me perusing some of the contents of Tina's phone, including texts between her and Cassidy. I learned she had been texting with him at least up until November, that they had made some plans to get together and Tina was trying to get him to come over to collect all the (junk) mail that had accumulated for him since he'd moved out.

The stairs going down into the apartment were never finished. They were just raw, ugly particleboard risers and treads, so Tina and Maura let Scott's daughters write and draw all over them with colored markers – they'd eventually be carpeted over. Some time back, I'd decided to add a little Dan and Tina love message to one step and wait for Tina to notice it.

Going back into the apartment after taking out the trash and recycling, I noticed some new writing next to mine. It was a crude scrawl, reading "I was here. Please don't kill me – thanks."

Hmmm. Could be that the girls were over, again. Maybe one of them was just being silly. It didn't look like any of the other writing on the steps, but maybe they had a friend with that weekend. Was that new? Maybe it was always there and I just hadn't noticed it before…

The thought that haunts me now is what would have happened if I'd just gone into the bedroom to change. Was there a man in there? How would that have played out? It wouldn't have been good. That's for sure. Was there something else to hide? She was obviously hiding something. Why didn't I just go into the bedroom? Tina was in full control of me. In these kind of moments, my anxiety would spike, because cognitive dissonance was already setting in due to conflicts between my beliefs and deductive reasoning. I preferred to lean to Tina's explanation of the world, because I didn't want to face anything that would threaten my addiction to my drug of choice, which was her.

Ultimately, I've determined that someone was hiding in the shower when the red Pontiac was parked in the driveway and it wasn't Cassidy. Not that day. Maybe the next.

***

"I hate lying," Tina said.

That seemed an abrupt way to begin a conversion. We were driving back from Walmart on a dark Farmington road.

"Um. OK. Me too," I agreed.

"My mom lies all the time," Tina said. "It's like a problem. She lies about everything – things that aren't even important."

"Hmm."

"I mean, it's like, why didn't you just tell the truth, Mom? Now you've just complicated things and it doesn't make any sense."

"OK…"

"She's tried to get me in on her lies, but I hate it. She even made me lie to you."

Now I was was paying attention, but I proceeded cautiously.

"Oh? What about?" I used a neutral tone.

Tina paused. "Just… Like, Telling you I'm not home when I am?"

"Why?"

"Just because, look. That's not what I'm getting at. I'm just getting really upset about all my mom's lies."

She went on like that for a while, without ever really enlightening me on details or elaborating on what her mom had "made her" lie to me about.

I was mostly confused and concerned by the conversation at the time, but I later understood it as classic projection. Tina would often talk about her own shortcomings by ascribing them to other people. Maura was indeed quite a liar herself, though. I often wondered who was pulling who's strings. The two of them seemed to operate in tandem.

Later that week, Tina and her mom spent several days helping Scott's mother with a garage sale up the road. Naturally, I wondered if Doug was hanging around at all, but never inquired until a Friday when Tina came back home mid-sale to get some of her things. One of those things, I noticed, was her weed pouch. Knowing that Doug was once Tina's favorite smoke-bud, my antenna went up.

She asked me for a ride back to Lina's.

I had time to kill before work and agreed, asking if I could hang out at the sale with her for a while before I had to go.

She said "sure." and we headed out in my van.

I stopped at the gas station on the way to get some caffeinated beverages. Pulling out of the lot, I asked Tina, "So, is Doug going to be hanging around this garage sale?"

"No. I don't think so. I haven't seen him all year," she said. "He doesn't even have a license and he never goes around Scott's anymore."

We arrived at Lina's where she and Maura were sitting in the back of the garage, keeping out of the hot June sun. Dressed for work in a black suit and Tie, I was pretty warm, and definitely overdressed for a Farmington garage sale. Tina introduced me to Lina, after quietly coaching me, "firm handshake, look her in the eye." I'm a gentleman who had worked in politics for over 10 years, so I felt somewhat confident that I knew how to greet someone, but I just nodded and I stuck my hand out as I approached.

We all sat together and talked about a plasma TV Lina had for sale, but mere minutes after arriving, Maura locked in on something behind me said, "Oh, look, Lina. Your grandson has come to pay you a visit."

My heart sank. I glanced back towards the driveway and saw Doug sauntering up towards us.

"Oh my God, Mom," Tina started, "Dan was just asking me if Doug…"

A subtle look from Maura shut her up mid-sentence. I knew that censoring look.

I watched Doug closely, waiting to greet him, but he never so much as looked in my direction, let alone acknowledge me. It got pretty awkward in that garage and my blood was heating up.

"Have you met, Doug?" Lina asked me.

"We've met," I replied, far more darkly than I intended. My tone didn't go unnoticed.

"I've gotta go," I said abruptly and started down the driveway.

Tina chased after me, grabbing my arm and guiding me aside the garage, out of sight. "At least let me give you a proper goodbye," she said, leaning in to kiss me. I let her, but I was pulling away from her grasp.

"I'll talk to you later," I said, hastening to my van. I had a lot of time, still before I had to be at work but I was afraid I'd be unable to remain civil around Doug and I was very concerned that I'd just been lied to.

I texted Tina a little later. "I'm not OK with this."

"I was as surprised to see him as you. However you feel, I feel worse about it. It's like you summoned him. I'm home now. We couldn't even look at each other and he left right after you did," she replied.

I was skeptical.

When I got back to the apartment after work, Tina insisted that she had no idea Doug was coming over and went on about my amazing prognostication. It wasn't psychic power, just simple observation and inference. I knew Tina. It wasn't hard to guess. I'd just not wanted to be right.

Behind the Locked Door

I'd gotten back from work earlier than expected and found Tina in an odd mood. She seemed extra energetic and distracted. After the barest greeting and exchange of pleasantries, Tina announced that she needed some alone time. I'd just gotten back to the apartment and she explained that she didn't want me to leave. Rather, she wanted to be left alone in the bedroom to listen to music loudly in order to adjust her mood. She wasn't inclined to tell me exactly what was bothering her, but I ascertained that she meant to convey some amount of anger and depression.

"It's not that I don't want you here and I'm not trying to push you away," she said. "I just need an hour to myself with my music – that you wouldn't like anyway – and then I'll be fine."

I might have thought the situation odd, but just nodded. "You do what you gotta do," I said. "I'll be here for you if you want to talk about it. I've got to catch up on some email, so I'll just put on the tube and take care of that while you rock out."

She slipped into the bedroom, closing the door behind her. I turned on the TV and got my laptop started, but then it occurred to me that it was a good time to go to the store for a couple items I'd forgotten to pick up on my way back to the apartment. Tina's hour of solitude had just begun a matter of minutes ago, so I deemed it prudent and not invasive to check and see if she wanted anything before I went.

I could hear her excessively noisy tower fan grinding away as I approached the door. Slip Knot was playing. I recognized the song. There was a scrunchie hanging from the doorknob. I tried to give it a turn, but it was locked. Perhaps not well enough to satisfy Tina, though. Immediately, the knob twitched the other way and Tina pressed her weight against the door with a slight bang. "No!" She shouted.

"I'm just going to the store," I said. "Wanted to make sure…"

"No!" The door jiggled but did not open.

"Well, OK," I muttered as I retreated to get my shoes on.

At the time, nothing really amiss occurred to me. Tina was often on an emotional roller coaster and I did my best to be accommodating, understanding and comforting, when I could.

Only after the spell was broken did I question the locked door and noise-making devices. Once I'd seen what Tina was actually capable of and recalling how she'd once snuck me out from her egress bedroom window after a night together while we were "apart," I started looking at odd scenarios like this with a more critical eye.

Many times when Tina wanted sex while her mom was about and awake, she'd turn on that loud, dirty tower fan and sometimes her boombox, for good measure, to drown out whatever noise we might make.

I wondered, had she really needed that hour alone (when I'd been away half the day at work already) to adjust her mood, or was she hoping to get an attitude adjustment from some other company creeping through the window?

Severely advanced narcissists get a charge out of degrading their partners, sexually. Humiliating a partner gives them a sense of power and importance. A covert (or vulnerable) narcissist wouldn't want people to be certain of what they're doing, but they can't help but leave hints and clues.

While we were together, thoughts like this would have been ridiculous – Impossible, even. After figuring her out, though, it was obvious. Her behavior was actually pretty transparent – once I understood it. I just hadn't grasped how far beyond the bounds of natural human thought and emotion Tina was. Her notions were alien. That's (partly) why I couldn't perceive them as they were.

Tina confined herself to her noisy room for less than an hour. She emerged about 35 minutes later and the rest of the night passed in fairly typical fashion. We watched some TV together. Tina smoked some weed and had some whiskey with Diet Coke. She insisted we have sex on the futon, instead of in the bedroom. I acquiesced after hanging a sheet over the doorway to the TV room, but it was something that always made me feel uncomfortable when Maura was around, even though she was asleep in her room.

That's something narcissists are known to do. They continually test, push and break their victims' boundaries. It's by design that they create a sense of trepidation in these situations and it's also a way of asserting their dominance or ownership.

She tried pushing my boundaries the very first time we had sex, in fact. Her mom made an unexpected announcement that she was coming home to the apartment out in Buffalo, just as Tina and I were working feverishly to get each other undressed on the futon. Tina had insisted that we simply move to the bedroom and carry on. She'd just put a scrunchie on the bedroom doorknob and her mom "would know what that means," and give us our privacy. That was not at all how I wanted to meet her mother for the first time and I convinced Tina to alight with me to a nearby hotel, instead.

As the night with the locked door went on, I got tired and went off to bed by myself. Tina stayed up crocheting. We did occasionally go to bed and sleep together, but increasingly, she was staying up by herself. I found her asleep on the futon when I got up in the morning. The sheet was still hung where I'd left it and Maura had already left for work.

The more I thought about that night, the more certain I became that she'd snuck someone in to fuck "right under my nose." She'd certainly done it before in my van. I'd noticed towards the end that more and more, Tina liked to take risks, too. She wanted to have sex with me on on a playground. She wanted to get completely naked and bent over the kitchen sink when her mom was asleep in the other room. There'd be no bedsheet hiding that act. With considerable effort, I moved her out of the kitchen, that time. She'd told me about the time (supposedly when we were on one of our many "breaks") that she had sex with Doug in Scott's barn while Doug's fiance, Olivia was sleeping right outside the door in a tent. She'd have been expecting Doug to come back to snuggle up with her, no doubt.

Tina wanted to be in situations where she could be caught. That time behind the locked door, complete with scrunchie on the knob, was certainly one more such depraved episode.

The Men from Eritrea

There had been a few break-ups and reconciliations since I'd last taken Tina to Merlin's. After that considerable absence, we returned, triumphant, a solid, happy couple. I was no longer drinking, but was happy enough to buy Tina drinks.

Tina was thrilled to see Abraham there and she talked to him at length while I chatted with some other regulars.

That night, Tina and I had been even more flirty and affectionate than usual and I was pretty hot for her. I was eager to get her home to make love. She seemed likewise inclined and after she downed a couple double shots of whiskey, we decided to call it a night.

Always a gentleman, I gestured for her to go first as we were leaving the pub, but Tina uncharacteristically froze in her tracks and insisted that I go by first. There was a look about her. An odd, abrupt shift in behavior that set my Spidey senses tingling.

I passed by her and put my hand on the door, but looked back over my shoulder to see what she was up to behind my back. What I saw sapped all the lust and probably color out me. I could actually feel my love for Tina wash down my body and right out of my feet.

She put her hand on Abraham's chest, leaned in and so sweetly kissed him on the cheek. I know how that touch felt from Tina. I didn't at all like seeing another man bask in that soft and electrifying affection. I thought that was exclusively our shared experience. That was our love she was sharing with someone else.

I struggled with my thoughts and feelings as we walked on towards my van. I didn't say a word to Tina. It was a kiss on the cheek – I shouldn't get all bent out of shape about that, should I? It was the way she did it, though. The deliberate misdirection to hide it from me, touching his chest, the loving look on her face. The slow, lingering kiss. It was how I felt about it. It was wrong. I felt betrayed. It wasn't just a harmless kiss on the cheek – or was it?

I struggled with my thoughts and feelings the rest of the night. When we got back to the house, I told Tina I didn't appreciate it. I told her I didn't want to make love to her anymore.

I was so hot for you until that kiss. Now, I don't feel anything. I'm numb.

Well, I'm still hot for you, she said. I only kissed him on the cheek. I didn't think you'd mind.

Then why did you try to hide it from me?

Tina made an effort at seducing me despite my agitated state, but she was more drunk than I'd first realized and quickly gave up and passed out on the couch. I stayed up replaying the kiss in my mind, trying to rationalize and excuse it.

About a week later, I stopped by Merlin's by myself after work. I had my mind on having a word with Abraham. I'm not sure exactly what I expected from such an encounter, but I felt driven to pay a visit and sure enough, he was there at the bar, eyes glued to news from home on his phone. I ordered a soda and sat next to him. He didn't acknowledge me. I tried a couple times to make eye contact with him, but, though he was seated right next to me, it was as if he couldn't see me.

I did eventually get his attention and I asked him what he thought about Tina and I getting back together.

"If you think it's good, it's good, man, he shrugged."

"Yeah. Sometimes I wonder," I said. I had finished my soda. I stood. "See you next time, Abraham." I clapped him on the shoulder. He flinched.

Although narcissists ultimately want all the power, the relationship dynamic they seek and foster puts them in the position of a child to the adult, the parenting role to be assumed by their partner. They don't seem to have adult-to-adult relationships with those who are close to them.

I distinctly recall sitting on the patio at a bar with Tina when she said, "you remind me of my grandpa."

I feigned offense. "Oh, thanks a lot," I said, alluding to the age gap between us. I was by no means old enough to be her grandparent!

"No, I didn't mean it like that. It's a good thing," she said. "You'll see when you meet him."

I met him at his condo in Edina at Christmas that year. Apparently, the fact that Tina had a boyfriend had her family abuzz and everyone was interested in meeting me. The holiday gathering of Tina's extended family was pleasant, with a fun energy. Everyone was exceedingly friendly toward me, but John, Tina's maternal grandfather took a particular interest. I was flattered by how much of his time he devoted to me. He took me on an extended tour of his condominium, his own unit, the pool, sauna, gym, library and other amenities. It was a very nice and well-apportioned facility.

John, I learned, was a fairly famous coach in collegiate sports. As time went on, I found that he was universally as well loved as he was well-known. Student athletes he'd coached decades earlier still kept in touch and held him in high esteem. There definitely was something special about the man. He was kind and generous and I was indeed flattered that Tina saw something of him in me.

We talked quite a lot at that first meeting. I felt welcome and I enjoyed his company. Over the years, Tina and I would dash our relationship on the rocks repeatedly, eventually to reconcile and reunite and John was always as warm and welcoming to me as that first Christmas we met.

In the end, I came to understand that as Tina saw some similarities in personality between her grandfather and I, she expected me to approach our relationship like her grandpa might.

When I was questioning her extremely disrespectful behavior, she told me a story. Some time in the past, she'd landed in some degree of difficulty while out partying wild. She was so drunk that she could barely walk. She'd lost one of her boots and she was stranded. She called her grandpa for rescue.

"He got up and came to get me in the middle of the night. I had one bare foot in the winter and I was stinking drunk and he never even questioned me. There was no lecture. No judgment. He just helped me," she said.

It seemed that she expected the same from me.

"I'd think there's something of a difference in relationships and expectations between grandparents and spouses," I said.

Although I was often concerned by Tina's behavior or frustrated by her frequent lack of regard, I still loved her. That was beyond question. The love was unconditional and I put Tina ahead of myself, but I still needed, to a smaller degree, to watch out for my own needs and sanity. I didn't think I asked for much. Just the most basic honesty and fidelity most anyone would expect from a life partner. That's too much of a demand on a narcissist, though. Tina needed the unconditional love along with infinite and unquestioning forgiveness. There could be no boundaries or expectations placed on her. Narcissists need their close relationships to be as that of an ever-blameless child and doting parent or grandparent. Some might refer to this as "daddy issues" or "mommy issues."

Of course, romantic interests have different expectations than a grandfather might! If I were ever picking up my wife in the middle of the night, drunk, stranded and missing a boot, there would be questions.

Later that April, Tina and I went to the Hexagon, something of a neighborhood dive, but one of the few places in the area that still had what we desired: Pool tables. After a game and a half, Tina and I decided to step out for a cigarette and left our cues crossed on the table to indicate it was still in use with a game in progress. When we returned a few minutes later, our table had been reset and a thin young black man was shooting on it by himself.

It was just a game and we didn't make a fuss about it. Instead, we introduced ourselves and started a three-player game of cut-throat with him.

His name was Selah and he turned out to be an immigrant from Eritrea like Abraham. Tina was thrilled to discuss his home country with him and we had a nice time, but I was noticing that Tina was getting pretty drunk. Her usual order was a double-shot of whiskey and ice water for a chaser (as mine used to be), but I went to the bar for her and brought her back a single shot. I couldn't control her drinking, but I thought she could slow down a little bit. Drunk at home was generally no problem, but babysitting a drunk in public was something else. She looked at the shot like I'd brought her a piece of chewed gum from the parking lot.

"I guess someone thinks I'm too successful, socializing," she said to herself, but audible enough for me. Despite her disgust, she eventually downed the whiskey.

Tina didn't trust me with her drink orders anymore and asked for money to buy herself another drink. I handed her some cash and took my turn. I was having a pretty good run on the table and won the game.

When I turned back to the table, Tina was sitting across from Selah, a fresh drink and a scrap of paper before her. The tip of a pencil in her hand was pressed to the paper but when she noticed me beside her, she lamely tried to conceal the writing implements. Looking at my face, she knew I'd seen what she was doing and made a quick change of tack, pushing the paper and pencil over to Selah.

Here. Write your number on this and I can call you about the party, she said.

Selah picked up the pencil and looked uneasily at me. I tried to keep my expression neutral. I was embarrassed, for some reason and didn't want to let on about that. I also wanted to see how this would play out without any input from myself.

He hesitated, pencil hovering over the paper making nervous little circles in the air like he was trying to remember how to draw numbers.

He lifted his hand and looked me in the eye. I'm not the kind of guy who's trying to steal anyone's girlfriend, or anything like that, he said.

I kept an even gaze and gave the slightest hint of a shrug.

I was telling him about your birthday party, Tina put in. Go ahead. Write your number down. I'll call you, she prodded.

Hand shaking, he did scrawl some digits on the scrap of paper. I decided if he was going to be called about my birthday party, I might as well take possession of the number, but as I reached, Tina snatched it up and stuck it in her purse.

This was all pretty upsetting, but I didn't want to make anything of it at the bar. I waited until we got home to discuss it with Tina.

Just a month ago, wasn't it you who said you knew it wasn't right for you to get guy's phone numbers at the bars? Didn't you tell me you were sorry you did that before and promise you wouldn't do that kind of thing anymore?

It's not like I gave him my number. This way he can't call me unless I want him to.

"WHAT!?" We'd veered into crazy territory and my mind was reeling. "What difference does that make?"

"I was afraid not many people would come to your party so I wanted to invite him. He's really nice. All the people from Eritrea are so nice!"

"Why do you think I'd want some stranger from the bar at my birthday party? And anyway, before I came over, you were about to write something down. What were you going to write on that piece of paper?"

"Just... uh... Just my name."

"Your name. What, he wanted to learn how to spell Tina?"

"At least I didn't give him my number, though," she said again.

OH MY GOD.

Tina took me on too-frequent excursions to an existential crazy-town. It was taking a toll on me. I felt like I was shunted into a parallel universe.

Over the ensuing week, we actually had further debate on inviting Selah to my birthday party and *I relented*. "Go ahead and invite him if you want," I finally said. She didn't, though.

Another week went by and although I'd quit working at Bobby and Steve's downtown gas station by then, I still filled in for an hour a month to cover the counter during employee meetings. So I was working a register when our old Eritrean friend Selah from the Hexagon came into the store to buy a pack of cigarettes.

"Hey. I know you. Selah, right?"

He looked extremely uncomfortable and wasn't very talkative. Maybe he's shy when he's not drinking. "Yeah," he nodded. He got his cigarettes and beat a hasty retreat out of the store.

Over the years that I knew Tina, I'd had a nebulous notion slowly forming that began to gel as a theory after I got sober. It seemed like she became quickly and easily infatuated with other men. I may have just been an infatuation to her as well because I couldn't imagine treating the feelings of someone you truly love with such contemptuous disregard. I later wondered if Tina hadn't sent Selah in to my work – maybe to make sure I was there and wouldn't show up unexpectedly. Come to think of it, Chris showed up when I was working there the month before, too. Also, acting strangely and far from his normal stomping grounds.

Months after Tina and I broke up for the last time, I saw Abraham, that other man from Eritrea at the airport. I called out his name to greet him, but he walked right by like he didn't see or recognize me.

Photo Meltdown

In the early days of our relationship, when Tina was claiming not to have a Facebook account (she did), she had no qualms about any photos I might want to post of her and I on my Facebook wall. I had quite a collection of our adventures together going.

I didn't learn about Tina's clandestine Facebook account until much later. As it turned out, she and her mother each had an account using an alias. One of them had a name that had something to do with the Moon and the other, the Sun. I don't recall which belonged to which. At any rate, my account and her alias-bearing one were never linked as "friends" or anything else.

Sometime in February 2018, right around the time I gave Tina her engagement ring, I learned that Tina had a newish Facebook account using her real name. We linked our accounts (mine publicly proclaimed that I was engaged, but I believe Tina's kept her relationship status private) and I added Tina as a contributor/editor to the "Adventures of Dan and Tina" photos folder. At that point, she wanted to exercise some editorial control and I deleted several photos she found personally unflattering or otherwise didn't like for whatever reason. She asked me to check with her before uploading any new pictures of her. I thought it was silly, but I never denied Tina anything she wanted and agreed.

Late that February, Tina and I had gone to Washington DC for the US Supreme Court case I was involved in with work and I'd taken a lot of pictures of the trip. Some were strictly work-related and some were of Tina and I enjoying the city on my down time – Seeing the National Mall, the Smithsonian, the Library of Congress and so on. I uploaded a batch of photos to a new folder dedicated to the Supreme Court trip and, without thinking about it, had also uploaded pictures of Tina and I together. Weeks later, looking at that folder, I realized the inclusion of some couple-style pictures of Tina and I didn't fit the professional, political theme of the rest of it's contents and I moved those to the "Adventures of Dan and Tina" folder that was shared across our accounts. It didn't occur to me that those photos were not "authorized." That became an issue some months later.

In June, I received a text message from Tina. It was a screen grab of a Wikipedia entry that appeared to be about me. My picture was featured next to the name Dan McGrath, anyhow. I am a writer, but I never won any awards writing for the Simpsons. The Dan McGrath the Wikipedia article was written about had.

Tina captioned the picture, "You've been awarded a prime time Emmy for outstanding writing of an animated program. Wow."

I was aware of this Wikipedia screw-up, but assumed it would have been long-since corrected. I was surprised my photo was still connected to that other Dan McGrath.

There are, however, several people in the world named Dan McGrath. In a bizarre series of coincidences, one other Dan McGrath ended up the executive director in charge of the opposition campaign to a voter photo ID requirement that I was in charge of advancing. My job title was also executive director. This was a high-profile issue and the common name and job title was causing some degree of confusion in the press that year and years later, to a lesser degree. A reporter once suggested that I start using my middle initial to create a distinction. I was the elder Dan McGrath and wasn't inclined to change my public moniker, but it turned out that our middle initials also matched, anyhow.

I was mostly amused by the coincidences and mix-ups, though it was sometimes a headache.

"It's nice to finally be acknowledged," I wrote back, tongue planted in cheek.

I was stunned by the next message. It seemed a bizarre non-sequitur.

"I want you to take down the pictures of me on your Facebook. We can post some together. You know how I feel about this. And you have pictures of you and Jessica on there as a couple… Ummmm…"

"OK," I replied. "Every picture of you on Facebook is in a folder that you have editorial control over. You can delete anything you don't like. I'll be on my way, soonish."

My facebook account was created in 2006 while I was working on a gubernatorial campaign and I was married until 2015, so over the span of 10 years, quite a few pictures of Jessica and I together wound up posted. I had made an effort to purge those photos once Tina and I began dating, but I had hundreds and hundreds of photos in dozens of folders and had apparently overlooked a couple. Still, that was an easy solution. I'd found and deleted those before I even left work.

I got back to the apartment around 11 that night and found Tina sitting on the bed, her laptop was open in front of her. She closed it when I entered the bedroom.

I tried to kiss her forehead, but she pulled away. She was visibly upset. Examining her face, it looked like she'd been crying. I sat on the bed. "What's going on, sweetheart?" I asked. I couldn't understand why she was so distraught by a couple errant Facebook photos.

"I'm so upset with you that I don't think I even want you on my bed right now," she said.

I was in problem-solving mode. "I'm sorry. I didn't mean to cause you any upset. I already found the pictures of Jessica and deleted them. We can go through the other ones and I'll show you how to manage the folder if you don't know how."

"I'm serious. I don't want you on my bed."

"Oh." I stood. At that point, I was pretty much moved in and considered it "our" bed, but I came to realize that what's mine was ours and what's hers was hers.

"I feel so betrayed by you right now I don't even know what to think or do."

This was serious. My heart was racing and I started to tremble. I knelt on the floor, still wearing my suit from work.

"Tina, I didn't mean any harm. We can handle this any way you want to," I said. "I'll do whatever you want."

"Why, Dan? Why did you do it?" She asked that repeatedly, as if I'd deliberately set out to cause her this distress. "Why?"

I told her it was just a mistake and I apologized repeatedly. Her behavior made no sense, but I could see that she was hurt and angry with me. The reason didn't matter. It didn't need to make sense. I was just scrambling to figure out how to correct it. Having Tina that angry with me was both agonizing and terrifying. My job, as I saw it, was to protect and keep Tina happy and I'd failed.

She didn't even seem to hear me. "I mean, are you trying to take me off the market?" She went on.

My head was already spinning, but that question stunned me, splintering part of my racing mind down a different tangent. I thought you were already off the market was my initial thought, but what I said was, "no," while I was trying to decipher exactly what she meant by that.

My brain started firing off scenarios where that wasn't what it sounded like. I glanced instinctively at the diamond engagement ring she wore, as if to verify I hadn't imagined her accepting my proposal.

She started talking faster and leaping from thought to thought. "You have no idea what you've done," she said, and she blinked away tears that were welling in her eyes. "Now I'm hearing from people I didn't want to hear from. And people are going, 'who is that guy? Is that your boyfriend? If that's your boyfriend, who's that other woman he's with?' And de dah de dah da da… 'Looks like you haven't been missing any meals.'"

I was struggling to keep up but the weeds were getting thicker. "What? Who?"

Tina hesitated. "Just… Nobody. Some people from school."

Questions were starting to stack up in my head. "Who from your school? Why are they looking through all of my ancient facebook pictures?"

Tina was unprepared to answer my questions. Instead, she seemed to see me for the first time. Her expression softened into something like amusement. "Look at you, sitting on the floor. Come back up and sit on the bed."

That was a relief.

Tina began spewing word salad – talking in circles, vague notions and sentence fragments that I couldn't make much sense of. Getting further information on who was bothering her about Facebook pictures wasn't going to happen, but the most important thing was that she reversed course on her salty and teary-eyed disposition.

I offered to go through all the photos in "our" folder on Facebook with her, but she declined, saying "No. It's OK. It doesn't matter now, anyway."

I was, at first, mightily puzzled but it was clear that Tina was being deliberately evasive. It appeared that Tina had suffered some grievous injury but when she tried to express it to me, she was stymied because, I theorized, some inappropriate activity on her part would have been implicated.

This much I was sure of: Her reaction was way out of proportion with the situation as stated and she was hiding something.

I was pretty sure photos of my ex-wife and I, deep in my own Facebook archives, hadn't caught the attention of any of Tina's old classmates. It sounded like someone was being critical of her appearance. Something like that could cause a narcissistic injury, but I hadn't thought Tina was especially vain. I got a notion it could have been her mother, at least in part. It wouldn't have been the first time that Maura stirred up something toxic. Especially when it came to my ex-wife.

Around this time, the new upstairs neighbors had done some sleuthing and discovered that I wasn't what they initially thought (based on what they'd seen of Tina's behavior and her other male visitors, they assumed that I was a doped-up scumbag that they wanted nothing to do with). The wife actually posted some of her research on me to her Facebook with a sense of bemusement. I didn't see how that connected with any other dots, but it was a dot.

Cassidy, her former upstairs neighbor and sex and cuddles partner from the few months Tina and I weren't seeing each other had recently reached out to Tina on Facebook Messenger. Perhaps he'd seen the pictures of us together before Tina got a chance to change the privacy of them on her own profile. Maybe that would spoil some stringing-along she seemed to be engaged in. Or it could just as easily have been some other secondary supply source she was concerned about. I was never completely sure, but I did later confirm that Tina had been messaging with Cassidy behind my back around this time. It was shortly after when she finally deigned to inform him that she was engaged – perhaps reluctantly.

As I began to learn about narcissistic personality disorder and interacted with other people who've been victimized by narcissists, I found that social media quirks are a common theme. Generally, narcissists don't like social media posts with their significant others. Some (like Tina) had very strict rules or controls about what gets posted. Proof of a committed relationship posted publicly on the internet would interfere with the grooming and maintenance of secondary sources of narcissistic supply if sex or the promise of sex was part of the hook. Some narcissists have been known keep multiple social media accounts for carefully separated groups of friends and/or lovers. I think Tina had done that before, but eventually realized she could just control the privacy settings on everything to prevent certain people seeing certain things — until I screwed it up with some unexpected photos.

Secrecy is always a major part of any relationship with someone with narcissistic personality disorder.

Something Stinks

Tina's next door neighbors were an interesting clan and it was odd how small degrees of separation linked the interpersonal web between myself, my friends, Tina and the neighbors.

Back a ways, shortly after I'd stopped drinking, I'd met my friend Donovan after work in Farmington. I think it was around July or August 2017. We went to the establishment where I'd first met Tina so Donovan could drink some vodka-sevens while I enjoyed some cigarettes and energy drinks on the back patio of Pizza Man. I hadn't had any contact with Tina in a couple months, but I was keenly aware of how near she probably was. I missed her.

Donovan ran into a pretty young lady from his work and introduced us. She came on strong. "You're adorable," she said, taking my hand.

Before I could return the compliment, a slender and tallish man standing near her interjected, "That's high praise coming from her."

As the night went on, Donovan's coworker Carrie came around to flirt with me touching my arm, my hands. She was getting pretty drunk and pretty forward. I didn't know if the man she seemed to be accompanying was a date or a friend, so I was a little unnerved by the attention.

Brendan, I'd learned, worked down the block at a little bar and restaurant (or maybe it was Brandon or Justin/Dustin? – it was quite a while ago and there are a lot of men's names to keep track of in Tina's shadow, but this guy was in it). Carrie worked part time with him there in addition to the grocery store she worked at with Donovan. He'd suggested they go out for a drink at Pizza Man after work. He was older than Carrie, but I so was I and Tina was 18 years younger than me, so I wasn't judging! After some time, I ascertained that Justin or Brandon was hoping to get a romantic connection going, but Carrie was plainly looking at it as a couple work buddies just getting a drink after a long day.

Carrie, who'd actually seemed quite sober when I was first introduced got very drunk, very fast and by midnight, she looked on the verge of passing out, throwing up or both.

We learned that she'd ridden her bicycle to work and had it chained up a block away Donovan and I both realized that there was no way she'd be able to ride her bicycle back home and I offered her a ride.

Brendan (I'll call him) didn't seem to like the idea of Donovan and I taking his "date" away and he kept insisting that he'd walk her back. He'd take care of her, etc. Donovan and I were getting creeped out by him and questioned the purity of his motives between ourselves. Carrie was in no condition to hold off a potential predator.

Eventually, we worked it out that I'd drive Carrie home and then drop Brendan off so he could come along for the ride and be sure that Donovan and I were treating her respectfully.

We got her home with some difficulty and the whole ordeal reminded me keenly of the end of the first date Tina and I had at Gossip's. That night, I wound up with Donovan and Tina riding along to drop off an extremely drunk girl named Shayna – only she couldn't direct us to her house and we drove around Farmington aimlessly for at least an hour before Tina contacted a guy named Keith and asked me to drop her and Shayna off at his house around 3:00 in the morning. Later, on, I learned that Keith was married, his wife was out of town that night and he was a meth amphetamine dealer. Surely, there were no red flags at the end of that first date.

Carrie needed help getting up the driveway and through her garage, but we were eventually satisfied that she was safely settled in her house.

Next, Brendan had to be delivered home. He said he lived across from the grocery store. "Oh," I said. "I know right where that is – over by Tina's."

Brendan directed me to pull into the driveway with the big white truck. "Oh. Right next door to Tina's," I observed.

Donovan was well aware of that, since I'd recruited him to drop some special agates into Tina's window well just ahead of the second anniversary of our meeting. It was part of an overall grand romantic gesture that didn't really go off as planned.

"Tina? Who's Tina?" Brendan asked as I pulled into the driveway.

I gestured towards Tina's door. "She lives right next door to you. I'd be surprised if you hadn't met her. She's my on-again-off-again... Never mind," I trailed off.

Months later, Tina and I had that coffee meet-up and decided to give "Us" another shot. I was convinced that my sobriety would help smooth over any of the past kinds of problems we'd had. I was blaming myself and my alcohol misuse for everything that had gone wrong before. Tina was perfectly willing to let me assume that responsibility. As we began seeing each other again, information about the neighbors trickled out of Tina. Plenty of it was disturbing, and all of it was sketchy. There were also some other weird little coincidental connections, because, *why not, huh, universe?*

I think the first thing I heard was that Jan, a forty-ish skinny woman was a former meth addict and that Tina occasionally went with her for drinks at Gossip's, the bar Tina and I first kissed at, years prior.

Some time later, Tina told me that Jan tried to hook Tina up with her boyfriend's son. Jan assured her that the son was better in the sack than Donny, the father. She'd had sex with them both. Of course, Tina lied about so much, it could be hard to believe any of it or even piece the truth together. She had a tendency to project her own negatives onto other people. She could well have been talking about her own situation. It always seemed like something bordering on incestuous was going on at Scott's. Scandalous, at the least.

"That's some Jerry Springer shit, right there," was my first reaction. Then, "wait… was the son's name Brendan or Brandon, by chance?"

"I don't remember," Tina said quickly. "I wasn't interested in getting with anyone that meth-head was with, anyhow."

Still later, she told me about the young guy who lived upstairs at the house next door and how some time back, he'd invited Tina up into his bedroom to "watch a movie." She said she'd seen the kind of movies he liked to watch up there when he left his blinds open with pornography visible on his screen. She told me she declined. But she'd never learned his name?

Time passed as it does and after we'd been back together a couple months, I was driving us back to the Farmington apartment when Tina gravely said she had to tell me something. She was a little tipsy.

"OK," I prompted.

"You know how I told you I used to go to the bar with Jan?"

"Yeah."

"The last time I went out with her, she ditched me – just disappeared and this guy, Justin walked me home."

"OK."

"He must have misread the signals, because he tried to kiss me when we got back to my apartment."

"Uh-huh…"

"I told him I was seeing somebody, but I felt like I had to tell you because it felt like cheating."

I processed all that in silence for a moment or so and then concluded aloud, "Thank you for trusting me enough to tell me. You put a stop to it, right?"

"Yeah."

"And you told me about it. What you've described is not cheating."

"It felt like cheating," she said.

"It's not. Thank you for trusting me and telling me. I love you so much!"

"I love you more."

Later on, though, I was thinking about names and neighbors and started getting the idea that the Justin she was talking about was Donny's son, the guy Jan was trying to set her up with. I thought about Gossips, the bar we'd first kissed at and how Tina never wanted to go in there with me anymore, like she was avoiding someone. I thought back on Carrie and the guy from the bar whom I'd given a ride home to. They both worked at an associated restaurant next door to Gossips. Much later, I wondered if she'd only told me about this interaction with Justin in case the upstairs neighbors had witnessed it and might tell me what they saw.

Is this the porn movie guy? Is it the same guy that I gave a ride home to a year earlier? Is that Donny's son? I couldn't keep the names straight. Brandon-Brendan, Dustin-Justin. Might have been two different people. Maybe not.

Months went by and I never saw the guy I'd dropped off over at the neighbor's when I was around, but I had met Donny, his (according to Tina) meth-crippled elderly-seeming roommate, John and of course, Jan. I also pieced together that Jan knew Donovan, Kathy, and their daughter and had once placed a foster dog in their care. Small world. Small town, anyhow.

Then, I'd heard that Donny's son was moving back in – so, he'd moved out. That explained why I hadn't seen him around.

As Summer got underway, I noticed that Tina was spending more and more time over at the neighbor's house. I was never invited to join them. One night, Tina just left me alone in her apartment while she snuck over there and disappeared for well over an hour.

It was night time in June and I'd thought Tina was doing some tidying in her bedroom with some music playing while I was watching TV, waiting for her to rejoin me. After being left alone for quite a while, I went looking for her. The music was still on in her room, but Tina was not in the apartment. I went outside for a cigarette and to see if she was out there, but there was no sign of her. I was baffled. I went back in and waited a while, watched another couple episodes of Red Dwarf but I started feeling very anxious. *Where the hell did she go, without saying a word to me?*

I went back outside, agitated, anxious, annoyed. I lit up a cigarette and looked across the driveway. There were people moving around in the living room, I could see through the window. The TV was on. I watched for a while to see if I'd spy Tina in there. I caught a glimpse of a tangle of blondish hair from the back, but before I could determine if the hair belonged to Tina, someone suddenly closed the drapes. That was odd.

I finished my cigarette, not certain Tina was at the neighbor's, but definitely leaning in that direction. I tried to call her. She didn't answer. I felt pretty abandoned at that point and decided to head back to Minneapolis.

I was just going to disappear as she had done, but I recalled promising her years earlier that I'd never just up and leave without telling her.

"I'm leaving," I texted her.

She replied that time. "OK. Have a good night."

I was kind of blown away by that flippancy. Sometimes Tina made me feel like I was the only person who mattered in her world. Other times, I was completely disposable.

Instead of just packing a couple things to take home, I started packing everything I'd been leaving at the apartment. Maura came home while I was hauling suitcases out to my van.

"What's going on?" She asked. "Where's Tina?"

"I'm going home. I don't know where Tina is. Maybe at the neighbors. I'm not sure. She just up and vanished. She's been gone for hours."

"Why are you packing so much stuff?"

"I'm packing everything," I said.

"Why?"

"I don't know when I'll be coming back."

I drove on home with most of the stuff I kept at Tina's place and shortly after arriving, I got a text from Maura. "She is at the neighbor's. I just saw her sitting on the deck with them."

"I'm glad she's OK. Goodnight."

An hour or so later, as I was climbing into bed, my phone bleeped at me. It was a text from Tina. "I heard you think I suck."

That kind of belligerence seemed out of character.

While I was considering a reply, she added, "I probably do. Get rid of me now, before it's too late. General consensus: Tina=shit."

"Really? Is that what you heard? I'm really sad. I feel anxious, hurt and disposable. I now know that you were right next door hanging with the neighbors (didn't even know when you left or where you went at first) but you couldn't even bother to step across the driveway to see me before I left? I feel pretty unimportant."

"I'm sorry. I saw their dog and went to pet him and got pulled into weird conversations and puppy kisses."

As always, all was forgiven and after I got some work done on my mom's house, I was back out to Tina's the next day, hauling all my stuff back into the apartment. I was a little embarrassed because I felt like I'd overreacted and tried to bring my clothes and things back in a bit at a time when she wasn't watching, hoping she wouldn't notice that I had actually taken pretty much everything of mine with me the night before.

June 2018 was really when everything started going sideways. It's when she vanished to the neighbors without a word, when Doug turned up right after Tina said he wouldn't, when Cassidy was messaging Tina on facebook and when she needed that mysterious weekend away and she didn't want me in the bathroom or bedroom. Tina and I also had our first actual argument since we'd reunited in June. It was about selling Mom's house to my dad. Tina didn't approve of my decisions.

We were just getting started with June and there's more on that to come but to finish this story it's useful to jump ahead to July (another spectacularly eventful month) first.

I was off to my driving job on a Tuesday and my last run of the night got canceled, so I got back home to the apartment early (and isn't that just the oldest cliche – coming home early and finding…). Tina was nowhere in sight. I heard music coming from her mom's room, so I went and knocked on her door.

"Come in," Maura called.

I opened the door, half-expecting to see Tina in there, but it was just Maura sitting cross-legged on her bed, fiddling with her smart phone. She seemed surprised to see me in the doorway.

"Hi. How's it going?" I greeted her.

"Just fine and dandy, Dan." She seemed distracted by her phone and didn't look at me as we spoke.

"Good," I said, but I didn't think she sounded fine and dandy and she looked troubled. "Where's Tina?"

"Um. She's over at the neighbors." she gestured behind her. "If you go and yell at the fence, she'll probably come out."

I snickered at the idea of loudly berating the chain-link fence. "I never liked you, stupid fence!" I thrust my finger at the air. "Yeah. Well, OK. I'll see if I can hail her." I went outside and looked the house and deck over. No one was in sight.

I wasn't just going to start hollering. This is the modern age. I called Tina's phone.

"Hello?"

"Hi. I got back from work early. Want to go out and get some dinner?"

"Um. Sure. I'm just at the neighbor's snuggling the dog on the couch and watching Hogan's Heroes," she provided some random details.

"Well, I'm outside. Come out and give me a kiss," I said enthusiastically.

"OK."

I lit a cigarette and sat on the steps, expecting to see her emerge from the house in a minute or so, but I finished my cigarette and she still hadn't appeared. It was dusk, the sky noticeably darkening as I waited. I noticed the neighbor's TV through their living room window. There was a program on but it wasn't Hogan's Heroes. I paced down the driveway and could see into the living room. I didn't see any sign of Tina. I lit another cigarette and started getting impatient. I called her again.

"Are you coming?" I asked. "I'm waiting outside for you. Come give me that kiss and have a cigarette with me. I want to go get some pizza."

"Yeah. I'm just saying my goodbyes. We were watching American Ninja Warriors and I've got dog fur all over my lap."

"OK. I'll be out here," I said, but then I was pondering her responses. It all seemed pretty incongruent.

I finished that second cigarette pacing up and down the driveway wondering why it was taking so long for her to come out. About 20 minutes passed and as I was walking back towards the house from the street, I noticed Tina emerging from the shadows behind the neighbor's fence – from the alleyway. I never heard or saw a door open. Didn't see her cross the yard. She just appeared. She had a small green canvass tote bag looped over one arm. It didn't immediately register, but I'd seen that tote just once before: When Tina had met me for a quick "nooner" in the big Lincoln Navigator I'd rented. She'd brought her "sex supplies," including a towel in it on that occasion.

"Hi!" I approached her."

"Oh. It is you. I couldn't tell for sure in the dark," she said. It was pretty dark by then. She stood strangely away from me. I stepped up to her to give her a kiss and got a pretty lame quick peck on the lips. I was overwhelmed by the scent of baby oil. It was strong, like someone had just upended a whole bottle of it.

Tina said she wanted to change before we went out so we went down into the bedroom. I laid on the bed while she changed out of her stretch pants into jeans. Rather abruptly, her hand shot into into the open suitcase on the floor which she had still not unpacked from her last excursion. Then. she opened her underwear drawer and shoved something into it, as if she'd just then decided to take some undies out of her suitcase and put them away, leaving everything else for later.

I cocked my head but didn't say anything.

Tina was ready pretty quick and we drove up to Carbone's. I could still smell mineral oil, strongly, which was puzzling me. I didn't remember her ever smelling like that in the years I'd known her.

Walking into the restaurant, me trailing Tina, I caught a whiff of burning plastic mixed with the mineral oil smell. We got seated and the smell of burning plastic kept bothering me. It was overpowering the baby oil smell. I was looking around, trying to discern the source of the odor, without any luck.

"Do you smell something?"

"No. Like what? It smells like pizza in here," Tina replied.

"Like burning plastic. It's pretty noticeable. You don't smell that?"

"No."

"Is half of my face sagging?" I half-joked. "Maybe I'm having a stroke. You really don't smell that?" I knew Tina's sense of smell was much more acute than my own, so I was actually a little concerned.

"I don't know. Maybe a little." Then she chuckled. "I don't think you're having a stroke."

We finished our dinner as I kept trying to discern the source of these odors and then we decided to go shoot a couple games of pool before heading back home.

Tina had to put a couple quarters in the novelty vending machines on the way out of Carbone's. I don't remember what was in her little plastic bubbles, but she seemed pleased for a moment.

We drove to the Mug, a local bar we knew had a pool table. The smell of burned plastic followed us in the van and I could still smell mineral oil on Tina while we were shooting pool at the bar.

Tina had more than a couple double-shots of whiskey and got very chatty with another couple on the patio. I could tell that she was starting to slightly annoy them, but Tina was oblivious to the social cues. She pressed on, loudly repeating her insistence on the right kind of locks for keeping their new bicycles safe in Farmington.

We eventually tired of pool and went back to the apartment.

I was hoping to use the bed for more than sleeping when we got home, but Tina insisted on having a shower, first, so we took one together. Unfortunately, Tina was more intoxicated than I realized and she fell, loudly, right out of the shower, taking the shower curtain down with her and soaking the bathroom. I'd tried to catch her, but she was exactly as slippery as a soapy-wet drunk. I nearly fell on top of her in my effort to save her from injury. She was laughing and seemed unharmed and we did dry up the floor, finish our sexy shower and made love, but then Tina didn't want to sleep in bed with me. She put the TV on and got comfy on the futon, instead.

When I went to bed, I noticed the black stretch pants Tina had been wearing earlier. I picked them up off the floor to toss them into the hamper. There was no sign of any dog fur on them. They looked clean so I just put them back on the floor where Tina had left them thinking she might want to wear them again – she used those as jammie pants, sometimes.

For the following few days, Tina did not sleep. With the exception of a couple 30-minute naps, she was awake for days on end.

Some time after Tina and I broke up, I was reading an article about addiction and the smell of crystal meth smoke was described as "like burnt plastic."

Things started clicking.

Towards the middle of summer there had been other occasions when Tina would literally stay up for days on end. Then, she'd finally crash and sleep a whole day away. The upstairs neighbors later told me that she always seemed to be acting really strange if they saw her coming back from the next door neighbor's house.

I'd observed a few pretty weird episodes, myself, when Tina would disappear into the bathroom or her bedroom for a long period of time to finally emerge in a radically different state of mind.

One night that summer, Tina decided that she absolutely had to walk the neighbor's dog. "They said I can come get her any time I want," she explained.

"Tina, It's 3:30 in the morning," I pointed out.

"They said any time," she repeated. "It'll be fine. I've got Jasper's leash. I'll just go in and get her," she said.

"You're just going to go into their house at 3:30 in the morning? You might get shot doing something like that," I objected.

"No, no, no. It's fine. I promise," and Tina set off into the shadows behind the neighbor's house.

She returned not long after, without any dog. "The doors were all locked," she said, disappointed.

At the time, I considered this one of Tina's ill-considered impulses, but upon reflection, it seemed more like the behavior of a desperate addict trying to get a fix. I'm pretty sure it wasn't a dog she was craving in the wee hours.

My mom had mentioned to me that she thought Tina was on drugs sometimes. I told her that Tina used marijuana to help with her acid reflux (such was the excuse she used at any rate).

"No. It's not that," she'd said. "I've seen what druggies look like, you know," she said. "Sometimes it looks like she's on some hard drugs."

"Nah. Tina doesn't do that kind of stuff," I'd insisted at the time.

After the breakup, some unidentified person living next door (a "younger guy") reportedly went into Tina's apartment when no one was home and took several garbage bags full of unknown contents out with him. Soon after, police arrived and made an arrest at the neighbor's house. I don't know who was arrested.

Police, I was told, returned to the neighbor's house a few weeks later and that may have become a pretty regular occurrence.

I was afraid Tina's addictions and dangerous impulsiveness were worsening. The class of people she was associating with seemed to be deteriorating (or were perhaps always of that caliber but concealed from me) and it looked like she was putting herself into dangerous, perhaps criminal situations.

After I'd moved away, Antonio mentioned seeing her come home one night with "a Mexican guy whose pupils were so dilated, his eyes looked like black holes." He was sure at least Tina's date was high on meth.

Addiction is a progressive disease, it's said. Untreated, the ends are always the same: jails, institutions and death.

One important way I'm better off for having had these experiences with Tina is that I have gotten myself sober and I can so clearly see that I do not want to go down the road Tina was on.

Theft by Swindle

When it became clear that keeping my mom's house wasn't a viable option, Tina tried steering me away from using a realtor to sell the house. She said her parents had sold their old house in Eagan themselves and saved considerably on commissions. At first, Tina was talking about savings for "us," but that evolved into her wanting to act as the agent and get the commission that would otherwise go to a professional realtor.

At the same time, she was becoming less reliable. Things I'd ask her to take care of while I was at work weren't getting done and she was disappearing, sometimes for days at a time, when she'd agreed to be around to let people into the house. She wanted to get paid big bucks to be a turnkey, but couldn't even be there when I needed the key turned.

I had realtors come over to look at the house and estimate an initial listing price. I had flippers look at it. I was collecting a lot of data and many options. While Tina had convinced herself that the house was worth at least Two-hundred-thousand, professionals were estimating it between $150,000 and $175,000, assuming certain critical flaws were corrected, first.

Tina wasn't satisfied with the first realtor, so I brought in another for a second opinion. When that was essentially the same, Tina balked.

She'd been talking about how her dad had shut her mom out of the family financial decisions and didn't want to be in a marriage like that. She insisted that I be transparent with her about finances, which I was, but eventually, I realized those discussions were actually aimed at manipulating me into letting Tina (and her mother) make decisions about the sale and distribution of proceeds from my mom's house.

At the time, I was doing everything I could to include Tina and consider her viewpoints, so after she balked at the second realtor, I called up a third whom I was acquainted with.

In the end, I'd had four different realtors, a couple flippers and an appraiser over and Tina still wasn't satisfied, because none of them matched her imaginings. Tina had never owned property, never bought or sold a house. She didn't have a checking account or credit card and the only reason she had an insured automobile is because I gave her one and paid for it's upkeep. By the age of 30, she'd never lived on her own, never paid bills and didn't even manage her own medical appointments, but she insisted that she knew the value of the house over all the professionals I consulted and she had the right strategy for selling it. She wanted me to pay her $12,000 to take care of it.

I asked her if she knew how to go about clearing a house title or the legal paperwork needed to go from offer to purchase agreement to title transfer. She did not. I asked her if she knew about truth in housing disclosures and other local requirements for selling a house. Again, she did not.

Seeing that I wasn't going to pay her to sell the house for me, she changed tactics and began hinting that perhaps she should be entitled to a share of the house. She was badmouthing my brothers who were sporadically coming to help me get the house ready for sale. "I've done more than either of your brothers have," she'd often say. She didn't seem to realize that although the couple weeks she'd helped me get some things in order were appreciated, they didn't really amount to the years my brothers had contributed to helping my mom and being her loving sons. It was a simple fact that she wasn't one of my mother's heirs. My mom didn't even like Tina and hadn't been happy at all that I was seeing her again after I managed to kick the bottle.

As far as I was concerned, whatever I managed to get out of the house was going to benefit Tina, too.

If settling the estate added $40,000 to my bank account, that was a fairly significant boost to help Tina and I start our new life together, but she didn't seem interested in "ours." Instead, she seemed increasingly more fixated on what could be hers.

I'd humored Tina as far as I could. In the end, I had a duty to my mom and to my brothers to divide the estate equitably among her heirs and I had to dismiss Tina's more fanciful notions in favor of expert advise and expediency.

That did not go over well. Tina would pepper her suggestions with platitudes like "of course, it's not my place to say how you should handle your mom's estate," and "of course, it's ultimately between you and your brothers," but she didn't mean it. When I finally ended up selling the house to my dad for $150,000 over Tina's objections, and without giving her the chance to try to sell it herself and earn that big, imagined commission, it caused a narcissistic injury. Covert retaliation and devaluation began.

At one point, she asked me if I was drinking again and triangulated with her mom, saying it was Maura who suggested it after overhearing Tina and I arguing about the house. That was rich. Tina was drunk, high or (usually) both every day and increasingly irrational. She implied that perhaps I wasn't strong enough to be her husband, because I was committed to distributing Mom's estate fairly with my brothers. She said that indicated I wouldn't be able to take care of our finances, because I was "too good."

Narcissists are envious thieves. I believe they don't understand genuine love and relationships but covet some of the advantages they see other people derive from them. They may not even believe anyone is capable of an honest, loving relationship. They may think everyone is manipulating and taking advantage of everyone else and so feel justified when they use deceit to take what they want from their partners and hangers-on.

Tina knew she found something special in me. I could supply her better than many because I was limited in relationship experience and thus naive and trusting. I was generous, honest and dutiful and had already been groomed as something of a codependent. I was well equipped to provide sympathy, understanding, validation and care of any kind. I was disinclined to be argumentative and knew how to tiptoe around triggering issues.

Even still, I was never going to be enough for Tina. No one could be. She was always on the lookout for new side and backup suppliers. A visceral fear of abandonment common to all narcissists unrelentingly urged that seeking behavior on. Now I know that I was part of a male harem. I was usually her main source of supply, but she would periodically have to service the other string-along relationships she kept on the side and she'd disappear for a few days here and there. Sometimes, I'd be devalued and discarded for weeks or months while she tended her other sources of supply.

When she and I were together, she didn't have to worry about much. She didn't work and had no visible means of supporting herself, but I fell easily into the role of provider. I kept her supplied with cigarettes, whiskey, tofu (and other food that's actually edible). I always made sure when we'd be apart that she had at least some cash, in case of emergency while I was away. I took her out often and drove her anyplace she needed to go, no matter the distance.

All of that may have seemed like gifts, but in truth, it was all stolen. A theft by swindle. Tina conned me into believing she was something she isn't and that our relationship was going somewhere it never would or could.

She never extracted large amounts of cash from me and never asked, until after Mom passed away, but she was always well provided for. I couldn't account for all the thousands of dollars I spent on her over the years.

Every shot, bottle, pack of smokes, dinner, movie, phone bill paid, every ride to Cold Spring... stolen. She even stole my mom's bookcase and added insult to injury by giving it to Chris, my former friend who she'd been carrying on an illicit affair with almost since the beginning of our relationship. I suspected some heirlooms from the family cabin that went missing ended up gifted to him as well.

While we were cleaning up my mom's house, Tina was on the look out for ways to profit. My brother Steven and his wife had left their bicycles in the garage and

Tina wanted them. She asked me for Steve's number and proceeded to pester him about needing to get those bicycles out of the garage, unless he just wanted to give them to Tina, then she'd take care of moving them.

Tina told me that Steve said he didn't have room for the bicycles and she could just take them. She had me load them into my van on the very next trip to Farmington. Shortly after bringing the bikes, Maura came home with new locking bike chains and secured them to the railing next to the stoop. I never knew the combination to the locks and Tina kept those bikes after we broke up. Eventually, one of them went missing and Tina told the neighbors it was stolen, but I suspect she gave it to one of her sex buddies – maybe Doug, since he reportedly had a suspended drivers license.

Later on, Tina tried a new tack, suggesting that I should pay her and her mother for their help at the house in the wake of my mother's death. I was rather shocked by the demand, but eventually, with some degree of irritation suggested that she provide me an invoice and I'd pay them like contractors, from Mom's estate if she insisted.

Of course, if Tina had simply said, "Dan, I need money for something," I'd have asked "how much?" Then, I probably would have handed over twice the amount to be certain she had all she needed. The idea that she expected to be compensated for helping me during one of the most difficult times of my life was very concerning, however.

I had thought Tina and Maura had helped because they cared about me in my difficult time. Besides, anything that was mine was already Tina's as far as I was concerned!

Bingo

July 3rd was the day before Tina was supposed to be Nate's date to his brother's wedding. I hadn't realized when I was asked about her going that it would ruin Independence Day for us, but, Nate and Tina would have fewer opportunities to see each other with him in California, so I tried not to let that bother me. Just that day, Tina let me know she was going out to play bingo with Nate and Amber. I had the day off, but she didn't ask me to come along. Instead, she just told me that Nate was going to be picking her up.

Tina was busy doing something in her bedroom and Maura came into the living room while I was reading emails on my phone. "Are you going with to Bingo?" she asked me.

"I don't think so. I wasn't invited."

Maura didn't say anything, but turned and marched right into Tina's bedroom, closing the door behind her. I could guess at the conversation.

Tina came out a bit later. "Would you like to go to Bingo with us?"

"If you want me to. I got the idea you didn't want me to go." I felt like some snot-nosed little tag-along step-brother her mom was making her bring.

"Of course I do. I just didn't think you'd be interested. You can come if you want to, but if you want to stay here, I'll understand."

"Sure. I'll go. Then I can drive and Nate won't have to come all the way down here to pick you up."

Tina got busy texting Nate about this development, then went back into the bedroom. I followed her in and saw that she was packing an overnight bag.

"What's with the bag?" I asked, surprised.

"Oh. We're going to spend the night at Amber's and all go to the wedding from there, tomorrow," she rummaged in her dresser as she spoke.

First I'd heard of it. I was feeling a bit anxious. Something was up.

Nate was Amber's roommate at one time, so it didn't seem that out of line that he'd be spending the night with her while he was in town. If they were all going to the wedding together, it made sense, but I thought it was more than odd that Tina never bothered to mention any overnight plans to me until she was about to carry them out.

I thought it was important to give Tina her space and was leery about asking any questions that may make me seem suspicious. Tina had done a tremendous job of convincing me that I'd been paranoid and delusional, making wild, hurtful accusations in my drinking days, so I was cautious with that. I'd also made one particularly damning mistake I never wanted to repeat. I was wrong about that one thing. Very wrong. I said nothing further on the subject and decided to see what Bingo would bring.

Tina put her bag in my van and we drove out to a Cinema bar for Bingo night. We were the first to arrive by a considerable span. Nate, Amber and Shelly, a lady friend of Nate's I'd never met before joined us at the table, while Tina and I were just finishing dinner.

I bought Tina and I some Bingo cards and I won $40 on the first game. Not a bad start. Everyone at our table won at least one round, except for Tina.

Nate was enthused to talk about his new home. "California's great, but there's no Renaissance Festival, he was saying.

"Maybe not like here, but there are renaissance fairs everywhere," I put in.

"There's nothing like the Minnesota Renaissance Festival, but we do have Burning Man."

As it happened, I had just read an article about Burning Man and Tina's next weekend away from me for Rock Fest was on my mind. I also felt like probing the attitudes and mores of Tina's friends, whom I'd still not had much chance to get to know after 3 years. "Burning Man is the hookup capitol of music festivals," I said. "Bunch of alternative lifestyle folks. Dirty unwashed hippies, free love and all that." I think I let just a hint of my disdain for the notion shine through.

I had everyone's attention, but Tina lurched in first. "Then we should go there and consummate our open relationship and have a contest to see who can get the most STDs!"

"Gross," I replied. "Let's not!" That quip about 'our open relationship' stuck with me. It only seemed half-joking. Tina's behavior had been bothering me all day. She was not herself and I got the impression she was trying to manage the conversation between her friends and I.

As the drinks and conversation flowed, it became apparent that Amber was not attending the wedding, contrary to my earlier impression.

After Bingo wrapped up, Tina asked me to have a cigarette out on the patio with her so we excused ourselves. Outside, I sparked up an American Spirit.

Tina seemed nervous. She didn't light one of her own cigarettes. "I forgot something. I'll be right back," she said, hurrying back into the bar while I took a drag.

As I finished my cigarette alone, I recalled another time she'd used this smoking trick to slip away and converse with someone out of my earshot. Tina came back out and lit a cigarette just as I was extinguishing mine. "Well," she said, it's getting late, and it's getting to be about that time for us to get going." She seemed even more nervous than before. There was almost a look of desperation in her eyes.

The sun was still up. I guessed it was about nine.

"Really?" I was surprised. "You guys are calling it a night already?"

"We're not calling it a night, we're just going to get back to Amber's. We'll probably have a couple drinks there before we go to bed." She fidgeted.

"OK."

"So, I'm going to have to get my bag out of your van."

"OK."

She put her cigarette out after just a few drags and made for the door. I followed her back into the bar and we went back to our table. Nate was absent.

"Where did Nate go?" Tina asked. "I have to put my bag in his car."

"Bathroom," replied Shelly.

Tina took a seat.

"We could just go put your bag into Amber's car," I suggested, seeing her approaching the table.

"No. That's OK. I want to put it in Nate's car," Tina replied.

My suspicion level had already been elevated. Now I knew I was being managed and manipulated. Some part of my brain was putting a curtain over the big picture, though. I wanted to believe Tina's intentions were basically innocent, but I tested the waters. "Make sure and keep Tina out of trouble tonight," I floated to Amber.

"That's a tall order," she replied noncommittally. Amber had a hint of nervous energy about her, too, but I didn't know her well enough to read her face. She might have been confused.

Nate came back to the table.

"Well," Tina took charge, "if everyone's settled up, should we get going?" She half-swiveled in her seat as if to get up.

"Let me finish my drink," Shelly said.

Amber also had some beer left.

Tina turned back towards the group, engaging in a lot of chatter. I didn't say anything and I kept my ears open.

After drinks were all empty, we all made our way out into the parking lot, splitting off into different directions. Shelly got into her car. Tina and I walked towards my van to retrieve her bag and Nate and Amber had stopped in the middle of the lane to chat. It looked like a Minnesota goodbye.

"So, where's your hotel at?" I heard Amber ask.

As Tina popped open my back hatch, I spun around and stalked up to Nate and Amber. The last thing I wanted was to come across as some suspicious, jealous ogre. My heart was pounding. My nerves on end. I wasn't able to ignore that question.

I put my hands up in a "hold on" gesture. "Tina's sleeping at Amber's, tonight, right?"

They visibly froze, taking too long to respond. Nate was first to jump in with a sting of nervous "Yeah yeah yeahs."

"Um, I mean, I think so?," Amber chimed in a bit late.

"OK," I said. "Never mind." I actually felt embarrassed. Shaking my head, I started back towards Tina and my van.

"What was that about?" She asked, closing the hatch.

"Nothing. Never mind," I responded, but I felt panic and cognitive dissonance setting in.

Pulling her roller bag behind her, she gave me a one-armed hug and quick peck. "I love you. I'll see you tomorrow after the wedding," she said, making haste towards Nate's car. I got in my van, set my GPS to get me back to Tina's, which was now my only home and drove off, my mind tumbling all the circumstances of the day. Why would Nate sleep on the floor or sofa with the limited space at Amber's if he had a hotel room? Why didn't Tina want to put her bag in Amber's car? Of course, it was obvious, but I was still giving everyone the benefit of the doubt. Could Tina, Nate and Amber all have lied to me? Maybe the hotel is for tomorrow, and I'm jumping to conclusions, I thought. Seemed unlikely.

I took my phone off the dashboard and called Tina as I drove, hands shaking.

She answered right away. I could hear the noise of the road over the phone as she and Nate cruised down whatever highway they were taking.

"Say, I don't want to come off like a crazy person or some suspicious asshole," I started hesitantly. I was very nervous about getting this wrong. "But are were you planning to spend the night in a hotel with Nate?"

"You aren't being crazy," she said, "but don't worry. I'm spending the night at Amber's. It's all good."

I wasn't convinced. "Because if you were…" I considered my words carefully and I was aware that Nate was sitting right next to her, listening. "Because if you were, that's something… That's the sort of thing I'd want you to tell me about."

"You aren't crazy and I'm not staying in a hotel with Nate. We're on our way to Amber's."

"Uh, OK. Just… something wasn't adding up there," I backed out of the situation. "Alright. Have a good night. I love you."

"I love you too. See you tomorrow. Bye."

I hung up. I reexamined everything I'd observed, seen and heard. Tina was on her way to Nate's hotel. It was a premeditated lie and it was poorly executed by both Tina and Nate, but I agonized over the conclusion all the way back to Farmington.

Reflecting later, I felt that day was the most humiliating experience of my life. I'd been very publicly played for a fool, conspired against and made the butt of their cruel joke. I thought she loved me.

Maura's car wasn't parked outside and the apartment was empty when I got back and let myself in. I was disappointed. I had wanted to talk to Maura and see what she knew about Tina's whereabouts.

I took several pills prescribed for anxiety and laid down in Tina's lonely bed. I got a text from Tina at about 10:30. "I love you a LOT. See you tomorrow. Goodnight."

I drifted off into troubled dreams as the hydroxyzine began to do it's soothing work.

One Wedding Accomplished, Another Averted

It was morning the 4th of July and according to what I'd been told, Tina and Nate should have been getting on their way from Amber's house to the wedding. That wasn't exactly what was happening, but it's what I was meant to believe. In truth, Tina had spent the night alone with Nate in his hotel room and would soon be his "date but not a date" to his brother's Independence Day nuptials.

I didn't have a very restful night. I kept waking up from disturbing dreams, so I was just going back to sleep while they would have been getting their day started.

I had the day free with no work and no particular plans. Under other circumstances Tina and I would probably have gone up to the lake to see her dad, her dog and stay at her grandpa's cabin. That's exactly what we did on the last Independence Day we'd spent together, but she ended up vanishing like a ghost about a week later. We were apart, without contact for months on that occasion, but she never bothered to let me know that she was breaking up with me or why. She just disappeared. It nearly killed me. Literally.

Ultimately, I slept in pretty late, once I was finally exhausted from anxiety-tainted waking dreams. I didn't really roll out of bed until mid-afternoon. I looked at my phone. Recent messages from Maura caught my attention, first. She'd locked herself out of the apartment and was trying to get me to let her in. I never heard my phone beeping. I was out cold, but she'd managed to get herself in before I even saw the messages.

I saw that Tina had texted me a couple times, first just to tell me that she loved me more than manatees, then updating me on her and Nate's progress through his responsibilities for the wedding. Around 1:00 in the afternoon, she texted again to comment on how pretty the wedding venue was. "Thinking about our wedding. Love you!!!" she concluded.

I was expecting her back sometime after the wedding, since she'd said as much at least three or four times. I figured she'd be back late, since there was presumably a reception. I worried that she wouldn't actually be coming back at all. I wondered if she'd tell me she was going back to Amber's or something else that wasn't.

Later that evening I looked at Nate's facebook profile and saw his update, "Mission Accomplished: They're married!" and I thought, *nice work, Cupid. One wedding accomplished and one averted.*

After midnight, my phone blorped at me and my anxiety spiked immediately. I already knew who was texting, and by the time, roughly what the message would be.

"I am sleeping on the couch in Nate's hotel room. Long ass day…"

This was not a good message for Tina to transmit at this time. We'd already had a flap about where she was staying the night before and after midnight, she decided to admit to being in Nate's hotel room. If I had any lingering notion of believing Tina about sleeping at Amber's, it was gone. She had to know this would be upsetting. She had to know how this looked. She had to know that she was in the wrong. She and Nate had gone so far past reasonable boundaries that I literally couldn't see how far past the line they were. She apparently didn't care. My feelings were not even a factor.

"I'm concerned that we're at a crossroads, here," I replied minutes later. "I didn't really expect to see you tonight, but I've been waiting all day for you in Farmington, anyhow. I'm stupid."

I went outside to have a cigarette and take a walk while I gathered my thoughts and waited for her to reply.

She didn't.

I tossed around the idea of going back to my Mom's empty house in Minneapolis. I hated staying there alone since she'd passed. I noticed her absence too much. I hated everything about that house by this point, dealing with Mom's estate, my brothers and all that went with that.

Tina had violated my trust and showed me that she was willing to put our relationship on the block for Nate's sake, so I wanted to start packing my things to retreat back to home, but home was already sold. I couldn't stay there much longer. Moving in with Tina was supposed to be the next step in building our life together. I hadn't even finished moving in and that future was already in jeopardy. I was on shifting sands.

After half an hour, I tried to prompt a reply from her. "I don't know what to do here. Should I just go back to Minneapolis?"

Nothing.

I walked around the block a few times and smoked half a pack of cigarettes ruminating on the situation. An hour or so later, I'd gathered my thoughts and finished up the night with "Hopefully I'll see you soon so you can tell me your thoughts and feelings and have a discussion.

"These are my thoughts and feelings, now that I've taken some time to analyze my distress.

"With respect to a relationship, you have done an extraordinary thing by being another man's date and spending a night away with him (two nights, now). For this not to incur strife in a relationship requires a leap of faith on my part. If you were being respectful of our relationship, you'd show that faith to be well-placed instead of using deception and demonstrating by action that your words can't be relied on.

"I'd think you and Nate would have taken pains to avoid me feeling that my faith was misplaced.

"For Nate's part, a gentleman in this situation would have made certain to avoid even the appearance of impropriety. Instead, he has lost my confidence."

I didn't swear or rant or berate her. I very honestly and thoughtfully expressed my feelings. I feel I stated my thoughts very calmly and respectfully until the end, when some sarcasm came through. "But I'm probably wrong to feel this way. Why should my feelings matter, anyway?

My phone remained frightfully silent the rest of the night. I slept fitfully in Tina's lonely bed.

My phone was in hand when I woke just before noon. I don't remember grabbing it off the nightstand, but my subconscious seemed intent on gathering information.

There were no missed calls or new messages.

Irked and very concerned, I prompted her again. "Are you coming home, today?" Whatever direction our next conversation was going to take, I knew it would be better to talk in person.

Another hour passed before Tina finally answered my disconcerted messages. 12:45: "I'm on my way back to Farmington."

I'd learned that Nate's hotel was in Roseville, which was no more than an hour's drive from Farmington. I figured she'd be arriving shortly and we needed to talk. Now.

"OK. See you soon, then. I love you."

Two hours passed and there was no sign or contact from Tina. I was pacing the driveway, going through a pack of cigarettes like it was a can of Pringles.

I decided I'd waited long enough. I had been planning to head back to Minneapolis to take care of some loose ends with Mom's estate and I'd been putting it off for no productive reason. Tina was just wasting my time.

Maura pulled her silver Saturn into the driveway and brought some bags out of her car. She could see that I was upset.

"Is Tina inside?" She asked.

"Tina is in Nate's hotel room or on her way back from there, or who knows where she is."

I brought Maura up to speed on everything. "I am so pissed off right now," I concluded after a breathless recounting.

"I would be, too," Maura said. "Let me put this stuff inside and I'll have a cigarette with you," she disappeared into the apartment for a while. I was just about to go in when she reemerged and lit a menthol.

My phone blorped. It was Tina texting. "I love you lots. I just went to Barnes and Noble and now I'm eating fancy Ramen."

Obviously, she wasn't on her "way back to Farmington." Nate had to bring her to what would definitely be one of her favorite places, bibliophile that she was and apparently followed it up with dinner. Was he just trying to entice her to stay with him longer?

"Nate is going out with a girl tonight. I am going to stay here for a bit."

I related this new information to Maura. She squinted, thinking for a moment. "Ask her if she needs you to pick her up."

"Would it be helpful if I picked you up?" I texted.

"I want to swim and read and be away for a bit."

I told Maura what her daughter's reply was.

"She's probably freaked out thinking your mad at her. That kind of thing makes her want to run away."

"Well I am mad at her. This isn't cool at all and we need to talk about this."

Maura began making excuses for Tina. First, insisting that she believed Tina had spent that first night at Amber's and if she did spend a night in Nate's room, it was probably just for convenience. There's nothing going on between those two. It'd be like a couple buddies sharing a room on a road trip."

"They're 40 minutes away. It's not like crossing the Sahara to get Tina home and she's been fucking lying to me. None of this is OK." I put my cigarette out and lit another. "And Nate... I extended my hand in friendship to him, gave him my trust and he slapped me in the face. What kind of guy invites another man's fiance back to his fucking hotel room to spend the night?"

"Don't blame Nate. This is all Tina," she said, knowingly.

I resolved to make what was left of my day more productive and went back into town to take care of some unfinished business.

Feeling insulted on top of injury, I responded to Tina's belated change of plan. "OK. Thanks for letting me know. I put off business I was about to do two hours ago because I thought you were on your way back and I wanted to see you before I left. I'm heading out to do that stuff now."

I figured she'd still be back sometime that day. "I'll be back in a few hours," I added.

I went back to Mom's, trying to keep my mind on the business at hand. I'll talk this out with Tina later, I thought.

Two hours later, Tina texted again. "I am alone and reading. I love you. Amber wants to make Apple Pie tonight."

I sat on the couch in the half-packed up living room and looked around at all the work that still needed doing before closing on the sale of the house. I considered moving and storage options, but through it all, the one thought that dominated my mind was "What the fuck is up with Tina?"

"Feels like you are avoiding me. Should I just stay away?" I answered her new excuse.

"No! I want you close, forever ever! I'm eating kimchi with my fingers and reading a fantastic book… Enjoying the quiet and control of the thermostat. We're on the top floor… No upstairs neighbors."

"I need to get everything I want to keep out of the house by Monday. In other news, I don't work tomorrow." I needed some help with the house business and had been hoping I could count on my partner in life for some of that. She had other priorities.

"I will be back tomorrow."

I stared at that text and realized her message may as well have been in Sanscrit for all the meaning it had for me. A horrible sinking wave washed through me as I realized that her words had become worthless to me. I didn't believe she'd be back 'tomorrow.' I had no reason to believe her about anything.

"I'm sorry, but let me find a grain of salt and I'll try reading that again."

Clyde, my doggie, my buddy, my pal, was in my ex-wife Jessica's custody and he'd been having health problems. He was almost 15 years old and we feared he didn't have much time left. He was anemic and had a tumor in his bowels. Jessica invited me over to see him. "You don't know how much time you have left to see him," she reminded me.

When I got there, I got my usual enthusiastic greeting from Clyde. He had been given steroids to reduce the inflammation from the tumor and seemed to be doing (relatively) pretty well that day, trotting around the yard a bit, sniffing squirrel tracks. Jessica suggested we take him for a walk, but cautioned that he could usually only do half a block. He tired very quickly.

On this day, after a block, he was raring to go, pulling on the leash, insisting on a longer walk. Jessica thought it would be too much for him, but I let the tail-wagging cocker lead on for another block and we approached a new ice cream shop that had opened in the neighborhood.

Jessica told me that she'd suggested to the owners that they sell doggie sundaes, since so many people walked dogs in the neighborhood. They took up her suggestion and started promoting it, so we had to stop in and get one to treat the dog. It was a good opportunity to let him rest a bit before making the walk back to the house. He was on a restrictive soft-foods diet so the ice cream was a great treat for him. Cow's milk doesn't generally agree with doggie digestion, but he loved it.

We had a nice time and Clyde seemed to be doing really well – better than expected so I was optimistic that he'd be around a bit longer, despite the cancer.

When I got back to Mom's, planning to spend the night there alone, I realized that I'd left my computer and medications at the apartment – because I thought I'd have reason to go back there. I thought Tina was finally going to get her wayward self home. So I had to drive back to Farmington, regardless.

When I woke up the next day in Tina's lonely bed and looked at my phone. I saw that Jessica had been trying to call me in the morning. I'd taken a few hydroxyzine tablets to help me with the intense anxiety before lying down and I slept right through the phone's ringing. There was a text: "Clyde won't eat."

Then I listened to Jessica's voice mail. "Clyde really went downhill this morning. I'm going to have to take him in."

I texted her, "I'm up," then, making my way outside, I called, ready to hit the road and go to the vet, braced for the worst, but hoping for better.

"I had to put him down," Jessica's words hit me at mach one. I was not braced well enough. I staggered up the stairs. I don't remember what I said, exactly, but I felt like I had to go somewhere. Do something. It was already done. Jessica and Warren had brought Clyde in while I slept through my phone's alerts. He was my dog. My buddy. I should have been there. I stepped out onto the stoop and sat down heavily on a step as I listened to Jessica relate his condition and his last moments. It was too much. Tina gone AWOL with Nate. My Mom, my main support outside of Tina, gone. The house. My dad. My brothers. I had been pulling off some semblance of holding together, but now I fell apart. I shattered. I let Jessica go and sat there staring into the neighbor's yard, seeing their dogs, seeing my Dog.

Maura came out to smoke and asked if I'd heard anything more from Tina.

"No and I think I'm going to leave."

She told me again that she was certain that Tina had been at Amber's the first night after Bingo. She told me that Tina loves and adores me, that she says so all the time.

I was sullen; shattered; looking at pieces of my life breaking off and smashing on the pavement.

"Are you OK?" her face showed genuine concern as she looked me over.

"Clyde is gone," I said in a slow monotone. "Jessica had to put him down this morning while I was sleeping."

"Oh, no! I'm so sorry to hear that, Dan. Does Tina know?"

"No. I think I'm done talking to her."

Maura put on a sad frown. "Dan…" she trailed off. She snuffed her cigarette and went back down into the apartment.

I went down a few moments later intent on packing up my things and leaving this crazy mess. I saw Maura in the kitchen, looking down at her phone. I figured she was messaging Tina about Clyde.

Whatever. I went into the bedroom and started gathering my clothes out of the closet.

Blorp. "I'm on my way... For real," came the text at 1:00. I didn't answer. I kept packing. I filled my suitcases, I loaded my suits and shirts, still on hangars into my van.

Two and a half hours later, I was pretty much ready to leave with all of my important possessions packed and loaded. There were some trickier things I could retrieve at a later date.

I looked at the time and re-read Tina's meaningless message.

"Oh. For really real, this time? OK. Well, I won't be there... for real," I shot back.

Immediately after sending that terminal message, I noticed that I'd actually missed a call from Tina, earlier. A voice call was a rarity from Tina. Intrigued, but feeling I shouldn't, I called her back to see what she had to say. She told me how sorry she was to hear of Clyde's passing and assured me she was getting into the car to come home to me right that minute.

Some mental defect I didn't understand at the time compelled to wait a bit before heading back to my soon to be sold home. I still wanted to have words with Tina, even if it would be the last words we shared. Also, my amygdala was screaming at me to slap the piss out of Nate. I resolved to be in the driveway when he brought her back.

Between Tina and I there was apparently a fundamental disagreement on the meaning of the phrase, "I'm on my way," Which she asserted at 1:00.

At 4:05, she texted again, "Almost there."

At about 4:30, Nate's silver rental car pulled into the driveway. Tina made haste out of the car. Nate popped the trunk for her from his driver seat but made no move to get out of the car as I stared at him through the windshield.

Tina had more bags than when she left. I guess they had gone shopping. I assume Nate bought her a book. Maybe more.

Just before they arrived, Maura advised that I treat Tina gently. "Hugs and kisses, first," she had said.

My instinct had been to open the door for Tina and help with the bags she was awkwardly yanking out of the trunk. She seemed rushed. She was out and arms loaded before I could even get to her.

I gazed angrily back at Nate, considering my next action. My amygdala was still screaming at me but my super-ego was telling me not to get physical because... I'm not sure. I couldn't really make it out over my lizard brain screaming for rapid violence, but I kept my cool.

Ultimately, an angry stare was all Nate got from me, but the slightest nuance could have set off a forceful extraction from that silver car and a beating beyond my natural bounds. I was on the razor's edge. There were a lot of emotions mixing and vying for dominance inside me.

They didn't hug or even appear to exchange goodbyes. Nate backed out of the driveway with haste and he was gone, down the road while I gave Tina a one-armed over the shoulder semi-hug and followed her into the apartment so she could unload her bags before we talked.

Suddenly, teary-eyed, saying "I'm sorry," Tina pulled me in to a tight embrace and held me like that for a long time.

I'm not a hugger. When I encounter people relatively close enough to me who are huggers, I try to keep it brief. There comes a time, even with my love when a hug feels too long. I don't know if it could be measured in minutes or seconds. It's hug time. Hugging has it's own dimension of time. This was a long hug. After some murmured platitudes about Clyde, she said again, "I'm sorry."

My cheeks were wet with Tina's tears. I broke her hold on me and stepped back. "For what?" I asked. I wanted to see if she'd be honest with me. I wanted to know what she felt she should apologize for and what she was willing to confess. I wanted to know if it was a genuine and complete apology. I needed to know if she could even comprehend why what she had done was so terribly wrong. I was disappointed.

"For being away from you," she said.

I shook my head, slightly stunned. Not even close.

In the aftermath, trying as hard as I was to find a path forward for us, Tina actually kept making it worse and worse despite every opportunity and then some being offered to make it right.

Rock Fest

It was just a week after "Nategate," I was barely moved in to the apartment and even though I was still committed to making things work, Tina and I were not really on solid ground.

I was working on setting up counseling for us, but Tina had made plans with Amber months in advance to go to Rock Fest – a weekend of outdoor partying, music and camping somewhere in Wisconsin. I'd given her money to pay Amber back for her ticket, in fact.

The timing wasn't great for us, but I couldn't begrudge her for keeping her plans. As usual, Tina was broke. Amber was bringing groceries, booze and bottled water for the two of them, but I didn't like the idea of Tina heading out hundreds of miles without any cash, so I gave her another hundred dollars for pocket money before she left. Regardless of our difficulties, I loved her and wanted her to be safe and happy.

We were going to be apart for a few days, so I wanted to have some intimacy before she left, but Tina brushed me off, prioritizing packing for her trip. Then, when it was getting pretty close to the time Amber was expected to be arriving to pick her up, she initiated a romp in the sack. We'd been at it for a while when Tina told me I had to hurry it up because Amber was going to be there any minute. I obliged, but only after did I learn that Tina had left the door unlocked and given Amber instructions to let herself in, which she did. I was just in the middle of dressing when Amber surprised me by appearing unannounced in the bedroom doorway.

It was Tina's design, of course. She'd wanted to create a situation where there was a danger of being walked in on. That seemed to be her new thing. Maybe it was always her thing, but it had become apparent by then.

Tina was ready to go in a flash, but before they departed, Amber took it upon her self to warn me that Tina might be out of cellular reception range where they were going. "Just so you know," she said.

The moment felt contrived.

I spent the weekend doing some future planning and went car shopping. Just to get ideas. It was getting to be about time to replace my aging minivan. I bought myself a modest selection of new clothes and went out to shop for a gun – again, just looking. I planned to take Tina with when I actually made a new car or handgun purchase.

I did shoot Tina a couple short texts, just to say "good night, sweet dreams," or "good morning, I love you," while she was away, but I didn't hear anything from her that weekend, just as Amber had suggested.

Plugging my phone into my van's charger gave me a fright, when my phone seemed to spontaneously initiate a factory reset. It didn't actually reset, but I lost a fair amount of data and no longer trusted my Samsung J7. I drove to a T-Mobile store and saw that they had a deal on Galaxy S9s. Buy one, get one free if you add a second line. That seemed like perfect timing, since I was planning to add Tina to my account, anyhow. I decided to wait until Tina returned from Rock Fest so I could discuss it with her. My phone still worked, even though I didn't trust it to last or keep my data safe.

Maura had gone off to spend the weekend with her sister, so I had the Farmington apartment to myself. I was fairly bored and found Tina's bed a lonely place. One night, I was thinking about the promise ring I'd given Tina for Christmas a couple years prior. I'd been fond of that ring. Of course, she didn't wear it anymore, since I'd given her a proper engagement ring, but I wanted a look, so I was poking around the various baskets and jewelry containers she kept on top of her dresser to see if I could find it. I didn't locate the ring, but I did find an Atlas condom in an unfamiliar green wrapper in one of those baskets, hiding behind a little paper astrology wheel. Given that Tina and I had never once used a condom of any brand, this discovery was a little unsettling. Especially with all the other recent circumstances.

I reflected back on that day I'd come back to the apartment early and Tina insisted I change in the bathroom, because the bedroom was such a mess. Strangely, after I'd changed and needed to hang up my suit, she no longer had cared about me going into the bedroom. Whatever she'd had to tidy up only took her a minute. Could this have been part of that?

I'd seen that purple paper astrology disc before. I could remember picking it up and examining it. I'm pretty sure I'd have noticed if there'd been a condom beneath it, so it would have to have been put there somewhat recently.

Then, I thought back about when Tina had made a similar discovery in my night stand. She'd pulled a box of condoms out and asked me, "What's this about?" They were purchased while Tina and I were broken up, but never used. I pointed out that the box was still sealed. I told her I'd throw them out, since we had no use for them, but, to my surprise, she'd wanted to keep them. She said she'd like to keep some condoms in her purse to hand out to people, like "the safe sex fairy."

The suggestion made me uneasy. "I think I'd feel better if I just disposed of them," I told her.

"Fine," she'd said, crossing her arms.

There had been a legitimate explanation for the condoms Tina had found in my room, so I convinced myself there could be an equally valid reason for this green Atlas condom to be tucked away with Tina's jewelry. Like always, I gave Tina the benefit of the doubt, even when the mounting pile of evidence of serious problems was about to collapse under it's own weight and bury me. I compartmentalized and looked at each situation as an isolated incident.

I knew from experience that being apart from Tina was the most miserable experience I'd ever suffered. I felt like we were fated to be together. There was no other way to live, so my subconscious kicked denial into overdrive to prevent the dark depths of despair that would consume me if my Tina was removed from my life. I didn't understand what a trauma bond was, but that's the psychological force I was contending with. It was so powerful that with the vocabulary I had at the time, I could only attribute it to the supernatural.

When Amber brought Tina back, I had quite a lot on my mind. I let her get settled in and get some food before I brought any of it up, though. I was cautious. I still had my sights on counseling for us and I needed to make it work. We had to still be somewhat intact as a couple to make it as far as counseling, so I didn't want to kick off any big fights, but I needed to put my mind to rest on a couple things. Nate was among my concerns, but a couple others took precedence just then.

First, I asked her about her weekend, if she had a good time and all that. She said she had a lot of fun, except for the woman who'd punched her in the head.

"What? Why? What happened?" I asked.

Tina related a disjointed story to me about a couple that was camping in a tent near Tina and Amber's. The woman was upset with Tina for flirting with her husband, but Tina insisted that she wasn't flirting with him. It was one of those stories with a lot of blanks glossed over with "de dah de dah da das," and an example of how difficult it is for narcissists to take any responsibility for their part in what happens to them. After several warnings, the woman eventually brought her fist down on the back of Tina's head.

If this was the only time I'd heard one of these segmented stories, I might have had more sympathy, but things like this just kept happening to Tina "for no reason." A woman stabbed Tina with a fork at a bar for no reason. The neighbor's friendly dog bit Tina for no reason. A woman who used to be her friend just started hating her for no reason. Things generally happen for a reason.

Tina asked what I'd been doing while she was away. I told her a bit, then I went into the bedroom and emerged with the Atlas condom in hand. "I found this," I said.

"Where did that come from?" Tina asked.

"On top of your dresser," I said.

"You've been snooping," she chided.

"Hardly. It was right on your dresser, under that astrology disc thing."

She launched into an explanation of how the disc worked, and how it was from a book and that the book was a gift…

This was one of Tina's tricks, I was getting wise to. When there was something she didn't want to talk about, she'd try to overpower the conversation with a fast-talking, long-winded filibuster of subject-shifting nonsense until I'd forget what we were originally talking about and then she would re-frame the conversation. There's a name in psychology circles for this manipulation tactic. It's called "word salad."

"I'm really not as interested in the disc, as what was under it," I said. This time, I was locked on like a pit bull.

"Oh, that's been there forever," Tina said. "You're the only one I've ever slept with without a condom – well, except for that one I told you about that burned. You should be glad I was practicing safe sex when we were broke up."

"The thing is, I specifically remember seeing and picking up that astrology disc before. I think I would have noticed if there was a condom under there."

Then the gaslighting: "Yeah well, Dan, you know how your memory is. Trust me. That's been in my room since the last time Cassidy was here."

"Well, now that you mention it, when was that, exactly? Something's been bothering me about that, too."

"Over a year ago," Tina said.

"Well, I know that isn't true, because I saw him here the night before we decided to get back together, back in September."

"Oh. He still lived here, then. He wasn't coming to see me," she replied but we both knew that wasn't true. I was dumbstruck by the lie, because it was pointless. It didn't help Tina's position and I remembered that night well. I also knew that the new neighbors had moved in upstairs September 2nd, but the night in question was September 10th. Cassidy had definitely moved out prior.

There were too many open threads and I knew Tina's way of tangling them, so I didn't dwell on those details. I pressed on, past the date discrepancies.

I told her I'd been thinking about the messages she kept receiving from Cassidy and that it was bothering me. "If you aren't having anything to do with him, he doesn't seem to be getting the message," I said. "You told me that you blocked him a long time ago. Then you told me you were going to block him, but didn't know how…"

"OK. I'll do it right now," she said, produced her phone and turned on the screen. I moved closer to where I could see the screen, which made her hesitate. She waved her finger absently over the icons as though she couldn't figure out where to begin.

"That one," I said, pointing at the Facebook Messenger app.

"No, I don't think that's it," she said. "Was it this one?" She opened a notepad. "No, that's not it…"

"That one. Facebook messenger," I assured her. It was obvious she was stalling because I was watching her.

"No. Was it this one…"

"Yes, Tina. It is. This one." I reached out and tapped it.

There, right near the top of the conversations was Cassidy's face in a little circle, next to his name.

"Oh," Tina, said. "OK. Now, how do I…" her finger traced nervous figure eights above the screen.

"First, select it," I said. I reached out at tapped Cassidy's name, even as Tina tried moving the phone away. The text of their conversation sprang up as she pulled away. She really didn't want me to see something and I determined that I was going to see it.

I took hold of her phone, even as she tried in vain to wrest it away from me. I was able to hang on to it long enough to scroll quickly through the messages they'd recently exchanged.

The most recent of them was from Tina. Cassidy hadn't bothered to respond. It said, "Oh, and, um, I'm engaged. He doesn't smoke, so I have lots."

"There, see? 'I'm engaged.' I told him," Tina said defiantly.

I scrolled a little further and saw they'd been chatting about getting together to "smoke some weed and do some other stuff." until Mid-June. There was more, but I'd seen enough. I let my grip on her phone relax and she pulled it away from me.

I stood up.

"Where are you going?" She sounded alarmed.

"Right now, to the bathroom," I said. I went in to relieve myself. I'd suddenly had an urgent need to go. I noticed I was shaking. I stayed in there for an extra minute or two to compose myself.

"There. See. I deleted him," she held up her phone with the Messenger app open, when I came back out.

I was pretty sure she hadn't deleted anything but the conversation and he would still be in her contacts, but didn't choose to press that point just then. "You said you never answered his messages," I reminded her.

"He was just looking for weed," Tina said.

"You lied to me."

"He was going to buy some weed from me," she said.

"Really? Where was that conversation? I didn't see that in your messenger."

"Just, uh…"

"Did you talk to him on the phone?"

"No. It was just… another message app."

"You changed apps to carry on a text conversation? Where's that one?"

255

"I don't know… I don't have it any more. I deleted it. You probably cost me a couple hundred dollars." she changed her tone and went on the offensive. "He owes me money and was going to buy more weed, but now that you made me delete him, I'm going to be out that money."

"You told me you were going to delete him eight months ago!"

Snapcheat

It had always bothered me how the media just lazily tacked "gate" onto the end of some pertinent word to denote a government scandal. Watergate (the first "gate" scandal) was the name of a hotel. The Nixonian scandal involved a break in at DNC offices at the Watergate Hotel, so it was the "Watergate Scandal." "gate" has nothing to do with scandal. That said, "Nategate" works for me in describing Tina's illicit 3-night dalliance with Nate. It was scandalous. It involved Nate. It rhymes and it happened at a hotel. Close enough.

A week after Nategate, Tina was gone for another few days with Amber for Rockfest in Wisconsin.

The Sunday after Tina returned from that dubious road trip, she and I went to get new phones. I wanted to add her to my plan, since I'd been footing the bill for her pay-as-you-go phone, anyhow and adding her to my plan would save a little money. I also needed a new phone since mine had nearly wiped all my contacts, texts and emails in a bizarre charging mishap and I lost a newer chunk of photos that never got backed up. I no longer trusted my J7. T-Mobile had a deal on the new Samsung 9 Plus phones, the top of the line model: Buy one get one free if you add a line. Perfect! Tina and I both got new phones, cases and accessories. We got to work setting up our new phones and transferring data and pictures over from the old ones and after a couple hours had them in decent working order with some details left to iron out later.

Monday morning, while Tina was still in bed, I was tinkering away with my new phone and it occurred to me that I could recover at least some of my lost photos from Tina's old phone. They were the most precious kind of memories: Pictures of Tina and I having fun together and she had either taken or had copies of many of them. I picked up her old clunker, which was still powered on and would be functional for another day before her plan ran out. I turned on the screen to hunt for her gallery and noticed a red number 3 on her Snapchat icon, indicating new messages.

After Nategate, my trust level was at an all time low. I'd always considered Snapchat a shady app and had heard people refer to it as "Snapcheat" because of how it's designed to automatically burn all messages after reading. Still, I had the app installed (only for the Bitmoji add-on and because Tina did) and I knew her Mom also used it. My curiosity got the best of me and I tapped the icon to see who was snapping her and my heart immediately sank.

There were 3 new snaps from Doug. If I had to pick the name I'd least like to see pop up in Tina's Snapchat, that was it.

Knowing a bit about the app, I knew if I opened the snaps to see what he had to say, a couple things would ensue: 1. Doug would see that his messages were read and 2. The messages from Doug would get deleted before Tina could see them.

I was in a moral quandary. Tina's lies about Nate and Cassidy were very fresh in mind. I agonized about opening the messages for about an hour, sitting on the stoop puffing cigarettes like a lab rat in a cancer study.

Finally, my mistrust and need to know outweighed any moral or practical dilemmas I'd face and I tapped Doug's icon, bringing up his three unread messages. Two were from Sunday. One had just been sent a couple hours earlier.

The messages were cryptic, at best. The first two were nothing but a question mark. The most recent just said, "hey."

It looked odd to me. When I had something to say or a question to ask someone by text, I just came out with it. I didn't ever feel like I had to hail them for attention, first. More agonizing. What I contemplated next definitely crossed a moral boundary. If I was going to find out what he really had to say, I'd have to impersonate and answer for Tina. After another hour of moralizing and rationalizing, hands shaking, I responded to Doug. His last message was "hey," so I found a Bitmoji of Tina's avatar saying "Hey you!" and sent it back to him.

Doug shot a message back immediately and it only got worse.

"What's up, beautiful?"

It felt like my heart stopped beating and my anxiety over my clandestine skunk op changed to full-blown panic. I tried to think of a response and see how far he'd go.

"Just rolled out of bed," I snapped back in Tina's name.

"That's when you look the best."

Ugh. This didn't look good. Not at all.

I sent a silly-faced emoij back, then must have tipped my hand with my next missive: "It's lonely here."

The entire catfishing expedition instantly vanished from the screen. Doug had aborted the conversation and covered his tracks before I thought to take a screenshot of any of it.

Now what?

I didn't try to prompt him into further conversation. I knew then that I'd have to come clean to Tina about my snooping and see what she had to say about what came of it. I was feeling pretty shitty about what I'd done and I was feeling pretty shitty about the overtly flirty and suggestive messages I found Doug was sending Tina. It just kept getting worse.

Tina was just rousing from sleep when I went back down into the apartment. I told her about my brief exchange with Doug in her name and that I was pretty concerned by his tack. I told her that I was ashamed of impersonating her and I was sorry. I described the exchange verbatim.

Tina was pretty upset about my impersonation and pressed me on that, rather than acknowledge the substance of the exchange. Tina maintained that since she never saw the messages herself, they didn't exist.

Maura came into the apartment while Tina and I were having an unpleasant conversation about the whole situation and asked what was wrong. Tina looked to me to explain and I did.

"What did he say?" Maura asked.

"What's up beautiful?"

"Well, yeah. He always thought Tina was pretty."

"And about how she looks the best when she's just rolled out of bed."

"I'll leave you two alone to work this out." Maura extracted herself to her bedroom.

There wasn't much to work out. Tina was simultaneously pretending that Doug hadn't sent her any messages and being mad at me for reading them. Later, she offered an explanation.

"I know why Doug was contacting me," she said out of the blue. "It's from when me and Amber were having breakfast after Rock Fest. She knows I don't have many friends and she was trying to help me get more social, and she had my phone and was just adding people to my Snapchat, like. Oh. You know him: add. And you know her: add. And you know Doug: Add."

The story seemed unlikely and didn't do anything to assuage my dismay over the tone of Doug's messages.

A few days later, Maura and I were outside smoking. She asked how Tina and I were doing and I explained my frustration that she was completely unwilling to take any steps to make right the untenable situation she'd created with Nate.

"Tina's not a cheater, Dan. She tells me everything. Trust me. I'd know. You wouldn't have cared about her spending the night with Amber, would you? Nate's just a buddy."

"I would have cared a lot if she lied to me about it. If everything's on the up and up, why would she lie?" I brought up the snapchats from Doug. And said I also wanted her to ask him to stop contacting her.

"Now, see that would just be weird," Maura said."Sometimes when we visit, Doug is over there. I mean she can't just avoid him. And sometimes, we spend the night, so Doug's seen her waking up, just so you know."

"Tina told me Doug never goes over there anymore and that she hadn't seen Doug in a year, except when he showed up at Lina's."

Maura didn't have an answer for that.

"She said that Doug's a dirtbag and has no problem cutting off contact with him," I went on.

"She shouldn't have to do that. Just because he's a guy... Besides, he's with Olivia"

"So? What does that matter? Tina tells me he cheats on Olivia." I paused and looked closely at Maura. "You do know Tina and Doug had a sexual relationship, don't you?"

She seemed uncomfortable. "I wouldn't know. I don't ask about that. Maybe when Doug and Olivia were broke up that one month..."

You literally just said Tina told you everything, so you'd know if Tina was a cheater. "Well, Tina told me. And..." I thought about the time Tina told me she'd had sex with Doug in Scott's barn while his fiance Olivia was on the property, sleeping in a tent just outside, mere feet away from the action. I decided not to relate that story to Maura just then. Tina seemed to be ashamed of it. I left it at that.

"Well that was probably just..." She seemed to struggle for a fresh lie or excuse. Finding none handy, she trailed off with "sex..."

Probably just sex. Yeah. When they had sex it was probably sex, Maura!

I was a bit stunned to see how vehemently Maura would stick to a narrative, even when it was so plainly bullshit. I could see where Tina got it from.

I knew that for all her feigning ignorance that Maura was certainly fully aware of Tina's sexual relationship with Doug. I was pretty sure that Maura actually encouraged it, despite the all around disgusting, immoral, deceitful infidelity of it all. Tina once showed me a series of texts from her mom, trying to entice her to come over to Scott's for the weekend. "Doug will be here," one of the messages said. "No Olivia."

Only after I read the messages, did Tina re-read them herself and think to address that last bit. "And I don't know why I should care if Doug is over there or has Olivia with him or not."

Although she insisted she didn't want to go over there, she did end up with her Mom's at Scott's. With Doug. No Olivia and there had been yet another breakup with me, at least in part, because of it.

Narcissists give themselves away, once you learn to speak their language. They'll tell you about their misdeeds, but they'll project them onto other people, like when Tina would complain about her mother's pathological lying. They'll tell you about their habits by telling you the things they "never" do. Never means frequently. They might tell you what they have done by telling you what they haven't done. For example:

During the time that we were on the rocks after everything coming to the surface with Nate and Doug and Cassidy, Tina and her mother went up to the cabin for the weekend of Zappfest. That was an annual music festival that was put on by friends of Tina's family up on Big Watab Lake. Zapp was involved in business revolving around extreme sports and was evidently pretty successful with it because he put on a pretty extravagant event, from what I'd heard. I'd been hearing about Zappfest from Tina for years. Tina had invited me to join her and her mother at the cabin and attend the party when I got done with work, but just as I was getting ready to hit the road to join them, Maura texted to tell me not to come. Some other family members had also gone to the cabin and there wouldn't be room for me, she explained.

Well, wherever Tina was sleeping, I expected she could snuggle me in and there was always Tina's entire bedroom and some spares across the bay at Tina's dad's house, so I wasn't really convinced that space was the reason I was dis-invited.

I heard a bit about it from Tina when she came home the next day.

"I was feeling overwhelmed, and had gone into the kind-of backstage tent to cool down," she began. "I was talking with a couple of the musicians who came by and it was all cool and I had permission from Zapp to be in there, but his big, fat security guy came in yelling at me, 'You! You gotta get out of here. You're banned from the event!' he says."

"You tell him you're friends with the organizer?"

"Yeah. Well, I'm sure he knew. I don't know who told him to kick me out. Probably Shooter."

Shooter, I knew was Zapp's son and Tina's brother's best friend on the lake. I didn't know why he'd have a beef with Tina.

She went on. "I'm like, I'm not doing anything. Just chilling out, here, sitting down for a minute. I mean, it's not like I was out getting wasted and hitting on other girls' boyfriends or something and he's all 'de dah de dah da dah you gotta go!' So I called it an early night and just went back to the cabin, but then. I got to go skinny dipping with my cousins. Those girls said they never did it before, so I got 'em out in the water naked with me."

That was a sudden turn. I was still trying to decode Tina's Zappfest story. It was another example of things just happening to Tina for "no reason," but I think she gave me the reason.

Helpful Nate

I think I was going above and beyond in the patience and understanding departments. I entertained several options to correct the damage done to our relationship by Tina's imprudent actions.

Tina was reluctant to cut ties with Nate.

I told her I would never dream of asking her to cut him out of her life forever, but "right now, he's in the way of mending us."

"He's helping me through these problems with our relationship," Tina told me when we were standing outside by my van one day.

I didn't think people really pulled their hair in frustration, but I could only grab fistfuls of mine in response to the insanity I was hearing. This is what it feels like when trying to apply reason and understanding with someone who's gaslighting you. "Tina, Nate isn't helping! Nate is the entire reason we're having these problems. Nate isn't the solution. He is the problem."

"I need him right now."

"What about me?"

In a mind-bending exhibition of double-standards, Tina asked me not to talk to any of my friends about the situation with Nate. "I don't want to give them more reason to hate me," she said.

"Tina, you're going to Nate for help with the situation with Nate..." My mind had to contort in ways that would make a pretzel blush. "Don't I have a right to consult with someone about all this? Who do I get to talk to?"

She wanted to know who I might discuss it with. "I don't know. Maybe Bergt," I said.

"OK, Only Bergt?" She gave her reluctant blessing for me to discuss the situation with Bergt.

Over the course of a month, two mental health professionals we met with said that contact with Nate needed to cease. I proposed a temporary break from him, since Tina had allowed her relationship with Nate to become inappropriate. I didn't think this was very much to ask at all. His continued interference was a huge detriment. Where were her priorities?

At one point, I mentioned that I had some things I'd like to say to Nate. Tina wanted to know what I'd say and I said that I'd conclude my remarks along the lines of "Tina needs good friends in her life and I want you to be her friend, but the romantic overtures are not welcome."

Tina warmed to that idea. She suggested I compose a message to Nate to get the discussion going and she'd follow up to talk to him about it. I felt a sense of relief. Maybe a solution was finally in reach!

I was just on my way out the door to work when this came up, so I told her I'd work on something on a break and let her see it before I sent it to Nate. "This will be good," I said. "We can get everything out in the open and deal with this, all three of us." I kissed her and went to work feeling great.

I composed a very frank message that conveyed what I felt was necessary to assuage my anxious misgivings and ensure appropriate boundaries that respected our relationship would be enforced. I thought it was very mild, given the circumstances. I was trying to work with Tina on a solution.

The message read:

Nate,

First, I apologize for the tone and nature of my last messages to you.

There are some things that need expressing and so you know, Tina has read and approved of me sending this message (she has read our prior exchange as well). She will be calling you.

I've been thinking about your characterization of me as a 'manipulative control freak.'

It's natural that you'd imagine me in a bad light, given the circumstances.

Tina and I have our difficulties to work through, but do you really think so little of her that she'd invite such a monster to live with her?

I don't wield any sort of power over her. We're just in love.

Tina and I spend nearly every day and night together. Don't presume to have a full picture of our relationship.

I tried to extend my friendship to you because Tina told me of your good nature. I gave you my trust because Tina vouched for your good intentions.

I brought her to you when you wanted to hang out. I dropped her off at that restaurant so you two could have dinner together.

Does that sound like an insanely jealous control freak?

I was accepting of your friendship with Tina until last month.

I'm still willing to try to be friends, but it's not necessary. I just want her to be happy.

Tina needs good, supportive friends. She thinks very highly of you. Please be a good friend to her, but I'm going to need you to leave off the romantic overtures and respect the bounds of our relationship.

Sure. Tina and I have issues to work on together and some of it is hard. We get angry with each other sometimes. We need to vent, sometimes. We've both made mistakes. Maybe we even bitch about each other on occasion, but we love each other so much that we're both willing to do whatever it takes to get through it all and improve our life together.

We're working hard on us because we both believe it's worth it. Neither of us will stand for anything or anyone coming between us.

Tina fervently desires your continued friendship, but she's made clear that there will never be anything more than that between you. Please respect that and be a great friend to Tina.

Maybe someday you and I can be friends, too. Who knows?

- Dan

"NOPE." Tina texted after she'd read it. "Don't send any of that. Please?"

I called her to find out what she was objecting to and to discuss how the message could be edited to suit her preferences, but she had abandoned the whole notion. "I'll deal with Nate myself," she said. "Don't contact him."

When I got done with work, I pressed for more of an explanation.

"It makes you sound possessive," she said.

Aside from not exactly prioritizing my image with Nate, I said, "I think it's pretty tame. I'd like to tell him quite a lot more. Anyway, a certain amount of possessiveness is normal in a relationship."

"You didn't have to write a novel," she critiqued. "And, 'there will never be anything more between you?' That's just going to hurt him. He already knows that."

"What about how I feel? Does that matter? And, he doesn't seem to know that. Not at all. If anything, he's emboldened. I wonder if that could have anything to do with him seeing you lie to your fiance to spend three nights in his hotel room?"

"I told you I'm not attracted to him. I told you about how he smells like sauerkraut, even when he hasn't been eating sauerkraut. There's no chemistry. I've told him I'm with you and only you. I'll talk to him."

"When? Are you going to establish and enforce some respectful boundaries? I need you to show me."

"I did text him after I read your message and asked him to block you."

Non-sequitur. "Huh?"

"I don't need you sending him any more crazy messages."

Openness and honest communication was what I thought was needed in this situation. Tina seemed to believe the opposite.

It was too much. Counseling was the last thread of hope I could hang onto. I used to feel like I understood Tina on a supernatural, quantum level, but she was making zero sense to me.

On my way to work the next day, I dropped Tina off on a country lane in Farmington, where she was to help with some wedding planning. Whitney was one of Tina's mysterious friends. I'd only rarely heard her name and had never met her during the three years I'd known Tina. If my recollection is correct, Whitney was the daughter of one of Scott's friends named Mark, who I'd met at least once, out in Scott's barn. Also, if memory serves, he was one of the guys who'd said he'd pay to see Tina strip. It was Whitney's birthday that Tina and Shayna had been out celebrating the night Tina and I first met at Dew Days in Farmington (something I learned much much later). Tina had been occasionally involved in helping Whitney prepare for her upcoming wedding during that turbulent summer when Tina and I were transitioning to living together.

That evening, Tina had just returned from helping Whitney as I was getting back from work. We were out on the driveway having a cigarette and catching up on each others' day. "We had a lot of laughs," Tina told me about her time with Whitney and the other girls involved in the wedding preparations. "In fact, we were laughing about Doug," she mentioned.

That received one raised eyebrow. "Oh yeah? What was funny about Doug?

Tina faltered a moment then offered, "That he's been beating Olivia."

I didn't find anything funny about that.

"Turns out He's an abusive dirtbag," Tina said. "So, he's out of the running…"

The running? I guess engagement isn't quite the end of the race.

Tina was irked when I called the other men sniffing around "her suitors." I considered Doug one such and reiterated that I was still bothered she'd not taken steps to demonstrate good boundaries with him.

"They're not suitors," she insisted.

I could see that none were likely to propose marriage. What they were, which would have been impolitic of me to say at the moment, was a bunch of "hard dicks" sniffing around, that Tina was keeping on a string.

Just Like Tom

"I think it's funny that you feel threatened by Nate. Nate is no threat to you. Not by a long shot," Tina said.

I realized the similarities with the relationship my ex-wife had with a friend of mine. Those two had their buddy dates with increasing frequency towards the end of my marriage. It was beginning to make me uncomfortable. I knew Warren always carried a torch for Jessica. I imagined he helped push her along into divorce territory and once we were divorced, Jessica and Warren committed the cardinal sin of beginning a romantic relationship. Warren and I aren't friends anymore. That situation also served to help alienate me from my core friend group. If Warren was going to be at an event with Jessica, generally speaking, I wasn't going to be.

"He's your Warren," I said emphatically. "He's worse, actually. Warren would never have even dreamed of asking Jessica to spend a night with him when we were still married. Never in a million years. Where I come from that kind of thing gets your ass kicked."

She seemed disturbed by that notion. "I asked him."

"What?"

"I asked him if I could stay at his hotel."

I didn't believe her, but said "Where I come from, That gets you broken up with."

She nodded silently.

"Am I missing something? Is this a generational thing? Fuck, you're making me sound old, but in my day, none of this would be considered even remotely OK."

"No. It's not a generational thing. My friends would feel the same way."

"Then what the hell, Tina? Is this your way of forcing me to break up with you?"

She shook her head.

"It's working. I don't understand what's going on here."

Maura came into the room. "Are you guys doing OK, here?" she asked, concerned.

"No. We're not OK," I said. I briefly told her a story about a woman I'd met who had made sexual advances on me, but I'd only maintained a friendship with and asked Maura what advice she'd give Tina if I told her I was spending the night at my friend Donovan's, but she found out I was really in a hotel room with that woman who I'd turned down for sex.

"But she wants to fuck you," Maura said.

"Yes. I've only been friends with her, but she wanted me sexually. What advice would you give Tina if she found out I lied to spend the night with her?"

"But Nate doesn't want to fuck Tina." Maura didn't want to answer that question. Of course, it was obvious and meant to be rhetorical to help them understand my feelings. For all they let on, they were oblivious to the obvious.

"I mean, he would if I'd say yes," Tina said, "but I could go into a bar any night of the week…"

Maura's eyes flashed daggers at Tina.

"You're a grown woman and you can do whatever you want," I said, "but if what you're doing is hurting me, I can't be near you."

"No. Now, that's just not right. You can't say that, Dan," Maura jumped in excitedly.

I was taken aback. That really offended my sensibilities.

"What?! Of course I can. I have a right to protect myself. If something is hurting me, I have every right in the world to say something and to get away from it! I have feelings, too! I'm a person. So, what, My feelings aren't supposed to matter? I'm just supposed to shut up and take it?"

"Oh God," Maura sounded incredulous. She was getting personally invested. "He sounds just like Tom. Just like Tom! Doesn't he sound just like your dad, Tina?"

Tina, sitting cross-legged on her bed, nodded emphatically, her eyes lighting up with recognition.

"Of course," I said, realization dawning on me. All kinds of stories I'd heard bits and pieces of about the disintegration of Tina's family started to fall into place. "Of course," I repeated. "Of course Tom would act like this if his own wife and daughter were both lying to him all the time."

The California Caper

After Tina returned from her extended stay at the Nategate Hotel, she told me some things. First, after some tears and apologies for "being away from me" she told me that a big part of the reason she stayed those three nights with Nate was that she was binge drinking and didn't want me to see it. She said further that she thought it was time for her to quit drinking and wanted to seek some counseling.

She said she'd discussed it with her mother and got a commitment of support on her new determination to give up the bottle, which she was blaming for her abhorrent behavior. She insisted that she had spent the first night with Amber and that she'd gone back to Amber's for the third night to make Apple Pie Moonshine. It was Nate who dropped her off. I didn't believe her about that.

Once she'd said she wanted support quitting drinking, that put a stop to my pressing her about her stay with Nate. I refocused on how I could help. I knew it would be a long shot, but I felt some sense of optimism in that moment. I told her I forgave her and wanted to help in any way I could.

Later, while Maura and I were smoking outside, I suggested, "I think it would be a good idea if you didn't keep any alcohol in the house for a while."

I was under the impression that Tina had discussed this with her mom already, but Maura's eyes spoke of confusion instead of understanding. She nodded without comment. The alcohol in the house stayed right where it had been.

Later on, Tina told me that she'd been talking with her brother Nick who'd recently relocated permanently to Colorado with his girlfriend, Kelly. Tina's dad had been out to visit them and she was upset that she didn't have the opportunity to go, so she'd been discussing it with Nick. She hoped to go soon.

"I'd be happy to take you out to Colorado to visit Nick," I told her.

She dropped the subject after that.

I'd been planning to get her added to my phone plan since I was paying for her by-the-month plan already and it would save a bit of money and hassle.

Although things were rocky with us, I was maintaining optimism and didn't want to lose any forward momentum. We had a house to buy, a wedding to plan, probably a car to buy and getting our phones straight was part of the overall future plan.

T-Mobile had a buy one, get one deal going on the top of the line Samsung Galaxy phone, so Tina and I both walked out of there with a spiffy new toy. We weren't able to keep her old number, but Tina said that was probably good, so she could slip away from people she didn't want contacting her anymore.

Back at the apartment, we spent some time setting up our new phones and had some fun customizing our cartoonish Bitmoji avatars for Snapchat.

We went to bed early, curled up together nice and cozy.

My subconscious was hard at work over that night and when I woke, I didn't feel quite so forgiving. I had a lot of misgivings. I had a lot of anxiety. I realized that I didn't trust or believe Tina at all. I confronted her again when she woke. I was set on having the truth.

"You never went to Amber's at all, did you?"

"Yes, I did. That first night and last night," she insisted, but her story fell so hopelessly apart under questioning that she finally admitted that she spent the first night at Nate's hotel, too. Oddly, she persisted in her assertion that she'd gone to Ambers the last night.

"I don't believe you," I said plainly. "You were planning to spend all those those nights with Nate all along, weren't you? You lied to me at Bingo. You lied to me every day you were gone and you're still lying to me."

She started crying. "I wasn't lying all along. I meant to come back. I was only going to spend two nights at the hotel. I was going to go over there, but Amber wanted me to go pick up the stuff in Wisconsin and it was too much hassle, so I stayed on the couch in Nate's room and read instead."

"This is bad, Tina. You've really put me in a bad place here. I don't know how I'm ever going to trust anything you say again and if I can't trust you, I can't begin to fathom how we're going to have a relationship. How am I ever going to be able to trust you again?" I was genuinely looking for a lifeline. I couldn't see a way to fix this and I was madly asking Tina for a solution.

"You can put a tracker on my phone," she said. "I promise I'll never lie to you again. I can't lose you. I don't know what I'd do if I ever lost you. I want to get into counseling. All that lying my mom made me do with my dad really screwed me up."

She was gifted at turning a situation around to garner sympathy. I softened.

"Fine," I said, switching to problem-solving mode. "Your insurance should cover counseling. I'll set it up. I'll set up couple's counseling for us so we can work on rebuilding trust and we can get a recommendation for a therapist for you at my clinic."

She agreed emphatically, relief washed over her teary face. "I'll quit drinking. I know it's a problem."

"I think you should get into treatment."

"I want to try it by myself, first."

I considered that. I felt like I needed treatment to help me quit, but I'd managed a month sober on my own before I got admitted and I never followed up with recommended AA meetings. I relied on individual therapy, which Tina was on board for. It'll work if she wants it to, I figured.

"I might have to smoke a little more weed in the meanwhile."

I calculated that would be less harmful to her and our relationship than the drinking.

"If I'd had easy access to it, I probably would have been tempted to smoke some, too when I first quit drinking. The withdrawals were terrible," I agreed.

Tina and I set out to get her some healthy foods and beverages to help I spent over $100 on fruit, salads, easy-to eat foods, Gatorade and Slim Fast shakes, in case she couldn't stomach solid foods right away. After I put her back to bed, I went back to my Mom's house and collected up my left-over detox medications and supplements to bring back and get Tina started on her journey towards sobriety.

The next day was moving day. Tina had agreed to help me get the last items out of my mom's house. I'd arranged a storage locker near Tina's apartment in Farmington and rented a truck. There were a few items too heavy for me to risk lifting with my injured back. At the last minute, I coaxed two of my friends to help load those few items into the truck, but unloading was still going to be a challenge.

Tina was a trooper. I could see that she was suffering alcohol withdrawals. She was shaky and sweaty. I honestly don't know how she managed any labor at all in that state. When I was going through withdrawals, just walking could be a challenge. I later learned that she was already drinking again, which would have alleviated the symptoms, but that day, I marveled at how tough she could be.

We loaded the truck and my friends left us to it. I was hoping to recruit another friend to help with the unloading, but he turned out to be drunk beyond usefulness that day.

There were only a couple items I thought were going to be dangerous for Tina and I to unload ourselves, so we unloaded items destined for the apartment and put our brains to work on getting the heavy stuff done.

"The only people I can think of are Scott and Doug," Tina said. "Or I could call Cassidy... Oh, but I don't have his number anymore... And he works out, so..."

"You're killing me, Tina," I said.

My back injury made me feel like an incomplete man when I couldn't do tasks like this. Suggesting recruiting help from former lovers made me feel pretty small. I didn't really care if Cassidy worked out. Good for him. Tina seemed a bit hostile when she quickly tacked on that bit about not having Cassidy's number anymore. It sounded smarmy.

It was she who kept asserting that she had no contact with him. She insisted the only reason Cassidy was still contacting her was to get weed and she just didn't know how to block him on her phone. She'd had no difficulty blocking me back when we were broken up!

Maura came home from whatever she'd been up to for the day and with some creative engineering, the three of us managed to unload the rest into my storage locker. To show my appreciation, I took Tina and her mom out for dinner.

Sitting at the table, Tina again brought up her desire to go visit Nick. She told her mom that she felt bad that her dad had chosen to take his girlfriend Karen with to Colorado instead of Tina.

"I'll take you to Colorado to visit Nick," I said again.

"Oh, will you?" She shot me an angry look. "Because I'm going to go to some brew pubs."

Her look, tone and words felt like a hard slap to the face. The sting must have shown.

"Is something wrong, Dan?" Maura asked.

I looked at my plate, unsure where to begin. Scarcely a day had passed since Tina announced her intent to quit drinking and she was angrily declaring her intent to drink in Colorado. I took it that she was acting salty because she resented me for her decision to stop drinking. Her hostility about blocking Cassidy and now about going to breweries was stunning.

"Are you just worn out?" Maura persisted.

"I'm pretty tired."

"He's upset because I said brew pub," Tina chided.

"I never asked you to stop drinking. You said you wanted to. I don't understand this hostility," I said.

"I'm not being hostile. I never said I was was going to quit drinking forever. I just don't want to be a drunk. There are some really good micro brews in Colorado, that's all."

I never cared if Tina drank in my company. We often went to bars together to shoot pool. I bought her whiskey. Of course, I didn't like it when she got so drunk as to be dangerously impulsive or embarrassing to be out with, but besides futile efforts to curtail that aspect, I'd never interfered with her enjoyment of alcohol. I was disappointed that she was already abandoning her plan to get sober, especially since that was a big part of her proposed solution to the problem she'd created between us by taking off with Nate.

I was reeling a bit, but I was actually too tired to discuss it further, especially in front of Maura. I let it drop. I wondered if moving in with Tina could be my undoing. Somehow, I'd just have to make it work. It's the course we were locked into.

What I didn't realize at the time was that the whole notion of going to Colorado was itself a ruse and if I accompanied Tina, it would have spoiled the real plan. In retrospect, that explained the unwarranted hostility.

Something I should have come to grips with much sooner was that when Tina's words or behavior seemed irrational or inexplicable, deception was in the works.

We retreated to her grandpa's cabin to get away from everyday concerns and have some together time. It was a pleasant weekend for us. We took her German shorthair, Jasper, to the dog wash and gave him lots of treats.

Tina's kinky side was on an upswing and I felt like I had to step things up to keep her excited about me. I felt like she was slipping away, sometimes. That night, I tried things a bit differently – in a way I wasn't completely comfortable with, but speculated she'd enjoy.

"I loved everything you just did," she said breathlessly, afterwards. I went out for a cigarette and she had fallen asleep before I returned to the bed.

I was still pretty alert, so I stayed up for a while doing crossword puzzles. I noticed Tina's new phone sitting next to her old one on the counter. I wondered why she'd brought them both to the cabin. Her old one was deactivated and the new one didn't get any reception there. I was reminded of her two-phone situation from years before. Back then, I'd also provided her a smart phone which I paid for, but she was still maintaining a second one that her dad paid for. Watching Breaking Bad together and observing Walter White's surreptitious use of two cell phones, I asked, "is that why you keep two phones? Are you running a meth business?"

"No, Dan. It's for my prostitution business," she'd replied glibly.

Reflecting on all my past misgivings about her double-phoned life in the past, I snooped. Her old phone was off and nothing seemed unusual about it, but her new phone revealed a disturbing text exchange between Nate and Tina. They were discussing plans for her to fly out to California, "The earlier the better," Tina wrote. She followed up later with a caveat that she had to go to Colorado to see Nick, first. Nate offered to foot the bill to fly her to California from there.

She'd said nothing to me about any plans to go to California, except that before Nategate, we'd discussed going there together to visit my friend Bergt, come winter. At that time, I still believed Nate to be a platonic friend with innocent intentions and offered to make it a "two-fer" trip. We'd visit Nate and Bergt while there. They lived relatively close together. I offered to take her to visit Nate. Why was she making plans to go to California behind my back?

I put the phone back on the counter and sat in a chair in the dark, quiet cabin and I wept.

Things with Nate just kept getting worse. I felt betrayed, again. I realized that Tina and I were on the verge of break-up and speculated that she'd made these plans while we were arguing. *Maybe she's dropped it now that we have a plan to get counseling*, I thought.

Tina came out from the bedroom and saw me sitting in the dark. "Is something wrong? Are you Ok?"

"I'm feeling very sad and worried," I said. I decided not to mention what I'd seen on her phone and wait to see where that went.

"It's all going to be OK, Dan. I love you. So much. You don't even know. Come to bed."

Some instinctive part of me wanted to fuck again. Like the time Tina asked me if I was trying to "fuck the Doug out of her," I might have thought I needed to fuck thoughts of Nate out of her. Sex seemed like a way to cement our relationship. That rather unhealthy thinking was probably borne from desperation. I was at a loss.

"Since you're up, I could go again," I offered.

"That was wonderful, but I'm wiped," she said. "I just got up to use the bathroom. In the morning, for sure. Let's go to sleep."

I laid down with her and drifted off while trying to assemble all the pieces of an increasingly complex-seeming puzzle. It wasn't really that complicated, but at the time, I couldn't see the forest for the trees.

A week or so later, Tina had a doctor's appointment up in St. Cloud, so I took a day off of work and we drove up to the cabin to spend the night before her morning appointment. It was a chilly, rainy day so we didn't have much enthusiasm to stay at the lake afterwards, but Tina wanted to get some things from her dad's, so we drove over there. Her dad came back from work as we were about all packed up and ready to head back to Farmington. We only exchanged a few words and Tom said something about going to see Nick. My ears perked up, since we'd been discussing that. I was about to mention that Tina and I were talking about going out to Colorado to visit Nick, but Tina made a swift topic change and started rushing us out of the house. Something was off, but I chose to ignore it.

Taking a Narcissist to Couple's Counseling

Tina and I had prior visited my therapist together to figure out our best course to move forward on relationship counseling.

At the time, Tina appeared committed to repairing the critically damaged trust between us. Jeff, my therapist had asked her about why she had lied to me when she snuck off with Nate to spend three nights in his hotel room. She insisted that their relationship was platonic, and said at the time that she reasoned it was "easier to ask for forgiveness than permission."

That was a pretty significant mis-estimation.

Her narcissistic brain didn't really grasp boundaries or consequences well. The truth was Tina simply felt that she could do anything she wished and whatever my objections may be were of little consequence. I'm sure she was supremely confident that I'd suffer endlessly, with minimal fuss for her. The idea that I might leave her probably never seriously crossed her mind.

Jeff had suggested that while we were sorting all that out, maybe it would be a good idea to put her friendship with Nate on hold. That seemed like the most obvious first step, to me. Tina didn't commit to it, there and then, in Jeff's office, but later raised it at home, as though it was her idea.

"I'm thinking I should stop talking to Nate for a while," she told me when we were getting ready for bed that night.

"Well, you know, I wouldn't ever ask you to cut him out of your life forever, but for now, I think that would be a good idea. We can't afford to have disruptive, contentious or unsupportive people in our lives, at the moment. If we're going to get through this, we need to surround ourselves with positivity and get rid of distractions that could divide us."

Besides, it seemed supremely obvious to me, that for someone who wanted to preserve their relationship after getting caught sneaking off to another man's hotel room, breaking off contact with that other man would be the very first order of business.

Tina agreed. I felt optimistic. In fact, I felt supremely confident that our love would triumph over this temporary adversity and we'd come out of it stronger and wiser. I did not understand what forces I was contending with. I hadn't even the faintest notion.

Ultimately, Jeff had recommended that Tina begin seeing a therapist of her own to deal with anxiety and depression. Tina urged for someone who was experienced in dealing with chemical dependency. Jeff felt he had the perfect match in mind and scheduled Tina a recurring appointment with Aljandro that coincided with my regular appointment with Jeff, so I could easily drive us both every week.

For relationship counseling, he recommended Adeline, who specialized in couples therapy. She was in demand and it would be a couple weeks before we could get in for our initial consultation with her.

Tina seemed initially excited about our path forward. I felt good about it, myself. "We'll have advantages other couples don't," I mused aloud. "With both of us working independently on our own issues and the opportunity to check in regularly in couples counseling, I think we'll be stronger than most anyone else."

In retrospect, my thinking seemed delusional, but again, I did not understand the inexorable power of a personality disorder, or even that I was up against one.

The next morning, I needed to take my van into the shop for some work and it would be there a couple days. I was thinking about upgrading my vehicle, so I had rented a big fancy SUV to try it out while the van was at the garage. I still had ample time before I had to be to work after those errands. Still feeling good about the apparent turn for the better things had taken with Tina, a naughty idea struck – something I knew Tina would love.

"Thinking of you… I'm getting an idea… I have some time before my first run." I texted Tina before I started back towards Farmington. 'An idea' was an inside joke between us meaning 'an erection,' since it only has one idea.

"My mother is here," she texted back.

"Do you think you'd be up for a 'nooner?' Come out and fuck me in the back of this big ol' Navigator?"

"Yeah! Yes," she replied. "Give me a 10 minute warning." She sent a few other misspelled and garbled messages.

"Flustered?" I teased and then set off to make haste back to the apartment. The clock was ticking.

From a stoplight at the outskirts of Farmington, I texted, "I'm about 10 minutes away. Don't forget to bring a towel," South Park references were a part of our personal language.

She sent back a series of emojis with hearts and kissy-lips.

Tina came out of the apartment looking giddy, a green canvas tote bag slung over her arm. *That* green tote. The only other time I saw it was when Tina came back from the neighbor's reeking of mineral oil.

"My mom knows. She gave me this look and asked me what I was up to," Tina said as she climbed into the SUV.

We found a secluded spot to park and had a very passionate time in the back seat on the towel Tina produced from her sex kit.

I still needed to get to work and time was a pressing matter. I dropped Tina back off at the apartment, blushing and giggling.

We exchanged a series of silly, lovey-dovey messages while I worked. It was a really good day.

I got home from work in the evening and made my way down the bare, graffitied steps into the Farmington apartment. I sat at the bottom to take my dress shoes off. I could hear Tina's voice coming from the bedroom. The door was closed and I couldn't make out what she was saying, but it sounded like she was talking on the phone.

Tina's voice became more distinct as I neared the door. I could hear her laughing heartily. "OK," she said, mirth still in her voice, "Thank you for everything. Talk to you later. Bye."

I opened the door and strolled into the room with a "Hello, my love."

I pulled my tie off and hung it up. "Who were you laughing with?" I asked casually as I put my suit coat on a hanger. I had a suspicion, but hoped I was mistaken.

There was a long silence before Tina sheepishly replied, "Nate."

I froze, still facing away from Tina, into the closet.

"I was talking to my Mom about it and she doesn't think I should have to give up my friendship with Nate," she went on to explain.

I didn't look at her as I resumed stripping off my work clothes. I didn't have anything ready to say, either.

"I have few enough friends as it is," Tina continued.

My former optimism flagged. "Yesterday, we were in agreement on this. My therapist agrees. If we asked anyone on the street, they'd agree. After what happened, your continued contact with Nate is hugely detrimental to our relationship. What are you going to do if our couple's counselor also agrees?"

"I don't know," Tina said. "I'll evaluate her advice after I hear it."

I couldn't fathom how Tina could think this was anything close to OK. How could she possibly think that after being caught lying to sneak away to another man's hotel room for three nights, she could just carry on seeing and talking to that guy unabated, and keep her relationship with me in tact? I could not imagine that any sane person would see things her way, but Tina and her mom waged a

277

campaign to try to convince me that I was the one who was out of step on this. I let it drop for the nonce, hoping it could be settled in therapy.

We decided to go up north again to the cabin to have some time alone together, but mail arrived just as we were departing. Tina had received a letter. From Nate. She tucked it in her purse, but not before I saw the return address. I let it lie for the nonce and drove pleasantly us up to the cabin as planned. We were up until the sun was starting to peek over the horizon. Tina was extremely drunk by then and she was getting salty about Jason's family using the car that she had said she'd never drive again.

She wanted me to drive her over to her dad's to ask him about getting one of his cars to use. Drunk, at seven in the morning. I pointed out how amazingly terrible this idea was and we went to bed, instead, but as soon as I was asleep, she decided it wasn't time for me to sleep and she woke me up by violently shaking me and shouting. She had been harboring a grudge because I'd woken her up a few days prior to see if she wanted anything from the store before I went there. This was her revenge.

She did eventually settle down and go to sleep, but I'd been jarred awake so forcefully that adrenaline was pumping and I couldn't fall back asleep.

Everything went from kinda shitty to a fucking shit storm from there. I found the letter Nate had just sent her. She'd already opened it. That must have been during the very brief span I was permitted to sleep. So, I read it. I didn't feel in the least bit ashamed after the lies I'd caught my fiance in about her rendezvous with this supposedly helpful and well-intentioned friend. I had a right to know what was going on before marrying this woman.

Nate, who was supposed to be this platonic buddy with no romantic designs, who she'd lied to spend three nights with at his hotel had sent her what can only be described as a love letter and in it, he wrote about taking her back to California with him, where, if there was any breast-grabbing, it would be "tasteful and distinguished or lewd and inappropriate, anything but awkward and confusing," and because his bed was "meant for pants-on canoodling" and that purpose was "going unfulfilled." He further proposed dancing and awkward kisses after awkwardly professing his love and affection for her.

To say this letter was disturbing would be like saying the sun is warm. I had a slight melt down, swearing to myself, nosily stomping and banging around the cabin before going out for a smoke. I walked around outside a bit and debated just getting in my van and leaving Tina there. I nearly did, but I remembered promising her that I'd never leave without telling her, first. I took my promises seriously. I went back in, wrote "What the FUCK?!?!" on a piece of paper, left it on top of Nate's letter and asked myself if that was a good enough explanation. I figured it was, but I heard Tina stirring in the bedroom, so I decided to speak to her directly.

That became quite an unpleasant scene and my head was spinning from the rapid-fire of outlandish lies Tina began shooting at me.

"You're going out to stay with him in California?" was just one of my many questions.

She insisted that she wasn't. She told me just the night before, she'd asked Nate to stop contacting her. She told me that the letter wasn't meant for me.

"I beg to differ," I'd said. "This is exactly the sort of thing I should see."

At one point, she told me that the letter from Nate wasn't genuine. She claimed it was a ruse they'd concocted together to test me and see if I'd snoop her correspondence. Evidently I failed the test.

She eventually asked me to leave so I started collecting up my things while Tina went to the bathroom. I retrieved the half-gone half-gallon bottle of whiskey I'd bought for Tina from the freezer. She was more upset that I was taking the bottle than she was that I was removing myself and she put up such a fuss about it, I relented and let her keep it.

I left for a couple hours, but didn't go far. I talked to Maura on the phone and she ultimately encouraged me to go back to Tina at the cabin. Things had calmed down and Tina didn't send me away again, but what ensued was a dizzying array of disjointed, half-baked and nonsensical excuses crazier than anything I've ever been confronted with. I could tell that I was witnessing the beginning of some kind of a mental break. Tina was falling to pieces, scraping desperately at the bottom of her barrel for some lie that would make her world safe again.

I felt love and sympathy and felt a need to proceed gently. I let a silence fall between us as we sat on the steps overlooking the lake.

My brain worked at it, but I couldn't, in the moment, think of a diplomatic way to say it, so, finally, I just said it. "What's with all the lies, Tina?"

Then, I saw something that I realized in that moment I had not seen for some time. It was Tina. Lies exhausted, ammunition spent, her mask fell and she transformed before my eyes. Her voice and visage softened. I got a sense of a scared, sad, almost pleading little girl. All hope nearly lost. "You knew I was like this when you fell in love with me."

I thought it may be something she'd told herself so many times that she almost believed it. There was a lot to unpack in that sentence. It stopped me cold. All I could do was shake my head.

She lied so often and casually, I couldn't really know anything about her for sure and if I didn't know her, how could I love her? That was when I really began wondering about exactly what misfiring psychology was going on in Tina's head.

I sat next to her staring at the lake in silence for a long time. Counseling was my last lifeline. She'd agreed to proceed with counseling. We were still fighting for us — or so I thought. I was, at any rate.

After taking a ride on her dad's double-decker pontoon and checking out the turtles swimming in a bay, we spent another night at the cabin together. Sitting across the living room from one another, we chatted about things of no consequence. I was consciously trying to avoid any further controversy. I thought it best to wait to deal with that in therapy.

"We can stay together if you'll promise not to look at my phone or mail any more," Tina suggested during a long silence.

My heart sank a little more. We weren't on the same page.

"That's fine, Tina, but I still need you to do something. I need to see that you have established and will maintain respectful boundaries with Nate and Doug and Cassidy." Chris wasn't even on my scope just then.

Tina scowled. She was trying to turn things around to me but she had finally found my limits. I wasn't budging and narcissists hate boundaries. "I'll think about it," she said darkly.

Whatever progress I imagined had been made earlier evaporated.

"It occurs to me that we never really discussed exactly what our expectations are from this relationship. I assumed some things didn't need saying, but maybe I was wrong," I said. "I don't think we are in the same relationship."

"I mean... I thought we were," Tina replied.

"I'm not very sure about that. I think we need to define, explicitly what we expect from one another," I said.

Tina had no interest in taking up that subject just then."I think we should talk about things we're thankful for," she said.

Ultimately, after considerable drama, we remained committed to pursuing therapy together, but after that fell apart (mostly over Nate), we broke up (again). I asked her again if she was planning to go to stay with Nate in California. She again insisted that she wasn't going to do that. "He asked me to come stay with him, but I don't want to do anything to lead him on," she'd said.

I was never completely sure when the California plans were formed. I initially guessed that she'd discussed it with Nate when Tina and I were on the verge of breaking up. Bergt had a different take on it when I related the story to him. He was sure it was already planned before that. He figured it was planned out while Tina was at the Hotel with Nate and she was lying to me about it all along. Colorado was a ruse – a way to get away to California without me knowing where she was really going. Bergt was most likely right.

August 10th, 2018 was the big day for our first consultation with Adeline. Tina had been staying at Amber's, ostensibly to watch her pets while she was away attending the nuptials of her roommates, Kenny and Kammy. I picked Tina up there early that Friday afternoon. She seemed a bit sluggish and said she was nervous.

"Don't be nervous," I said enthusiastically. "Just remember we're doing this because we love each other and our therapist only wants to help us. What's to worry about? This will be a good thing." I was painfully naive.

In the clinic's lobby, I slid my parking ticket into a little machine that stamped it with an electronic code that would let us out of the ramp for free.

"I already like it here," Tina quipped. "Instant validation."

We laughed. Our fingers were entwined. Our new therapist called us in to her office.

Adeline was a young black woman who came off immediately as a no-nonsense person who spoke plainly and with a blunt air of authority.

I started out, saying that we'd been having some difficulties, but that we both loved each other so much that we were willing to do anything to make it work between us.

"He's my best friend," Tina added. "I've never felt so close to anyone else before and he's the only person whose company I never get tired of."

I nodded and squeezed her hand reassuringly. My feelings mirrored that sentiment, exactly.

Conscious of how quickly an hour can go by, I tried to be efficient with our time and summarized events that led to us deciding to seek professional help.

"Whatever the actual details of Tina and Nate's hotel stay, with all the lying and sneaking around, it feels like an affair to me," I concluded.

"An emotional affair," Tina added. She explained that she felt a lot of her troubles stemmed from her upbringing. "I think all the lying my mom used to make me do really screwed me up," she said.

After hearing a bit of our story, Adeline said, "I think I can help you, but you both need to do exactly what I tell you," she said. She explained her rules for couples therapy. Secrets were out. Open communication between the three of us was key.

Tina's recent disappearing act with Nate was the primary reason that we were in counseling, so that was the first order of discussion.

"You can't be talking to Nate anymore if this is going to work," Adeline eventually told Tina.

"I don't have many friends," Tina said. "He's been helping me with all of this. He's my best friend," Tina objected.

"I thought Dan was your best friend," Adeline observed, "and that sounds like a self-esteem issue that you should start working on with your own therapist. You have an appointment with Aljandro coming up, right?"

"Well, Dan's the one who almost cheated on me with his ex-wife," Tina's tone became defensive and I was fairly surprised to hear that come up. She was talking about an incident from the very beginning of our relationship, three years prior, that I considered long behind us.

"That was years ago," I said. "I told you about it – it's not like it was a secret and I took steps to remedy the situation." I had agreed to always inform Tina when I saw my ex-wife for any reason and I'd kept that agreement.

"OK, is this a tit for tat thing?" Adeline interjected.

Tina shook her head. "No," she said rather quietly.

We discussed Tina's other suitors. Besides Nate, there was Cassidy and Doug. Since both were former romantic interests and sex-partners, I had misgivings about discovering recent surreptitious communications between them and Tina.

"That's another thing, though," Tina interrupted, "I feel like I can't have any privacy, because Dan was looking at my phone."

"I am all about respecting your partner's privacy," Adeline began. Tina's expression immediately looked more receptive, but Adeline went on to say, "until something is done that betrays your trust, then all bets are off, because you have a right to know what's going on. My husband and I don't have any problem answering each other's phones because we both know we don't have anything to hide."

I could tell Tina wasn't happy with that statement. She was becoming more defensive and complained that I "wouldn't let her" talk to her "friend," Cassidy. She tried to make it out like I was controlling, but failed to mention that Cassidy was a former lover. I had to reiterate that detail. I'm hardly in the minority, being uncomfortable with my future wife buddying up with exes – especially when she was trying to hide it from me!

Tina made a few confused attempts at explaining her actions, but what may have seemed like righteous justification in her own mind completely fell apart when put into words.

At the end of the session, Adeline admonished us both, "No contact with any former boyfriends, girlfriends, ex-wives, sex partners or whatever. That includes on social media. Start with that and we'll talk again in a week." She looked over her calendar. "Is that how we're doing this? Once a week?"

"Yes," I said. "We figured we'd start with weekly while we're kind-of in crisis, and maybe go down to every other week or once a month once we're on more stable ground."

"That sounds like a good plan. I think that's exactly how we should do it," Adeline agreed.

Tina wasn't very talkative after we'd left Adeline's office. She was yawning a bit.

"What do you think?" I asked her.

"Well, Mrs. Adeline Taylor seems like a no-nonsense kind of person who will call you on your shit," she said. "I guess that's good."

"I suppose it is," I agreed.

On the way to the clinic, We'd passed by a little Italian sandwich and pizza joint Tina mentioned she was interested in trying sometime, so I stopped there on our way back to Amber's. It was a sleepy, dim-lit restaurant with sticky, red and white checkered plastic tablecloths. It was a pretty old-school hole in the wall that made generously portioned, delicious, yet inexpensive hoagies.

We ate, mostly in silence, with Tina yawning more frequently and avoiding eye-contact. I thought it was pretty important we discuss our first counseling session, but Tina plainly wanted none of that.

We left, with Tina taking about 3/4 of her sandwich with her in a box and I dropped her back off at Amber's to resume her pet-sitting duties and presumably, to take a nap. I was anxious and felt uncertain about the future.

At first, I wondered if a gentler approach from the no-nonsense Adeline might have produced better results, but after hearing the stories from so many other victims of narcissistic abuse, I realized there could be no good outcome from taking Tina to therapy.

Getting a narcissist into counseling is no small feat, because they generally don't believe there is anything wrong with them. If they do go, it's either to deal with problems other than a cluster B personality disorder, like depression and anxiety, or it's simply a ploy.

It appears that couples counseling with a narcissist goes one of two ways. Therapists are only human, too and often, a clever, charming narcissist can win them over. Weaving tales of difficult childhoods or traumatic events can garner sympathy and a therapist may be used as narcissistic supply and can even end up being used to triangulate and help gaslight the narcissist's victim. That outcome is frequently reported by survivors of narcissistic abuse.

The other way it goes is how it did with Tina. The therapist wasn't won over and Tina was forced to confront the flaws in her internal justifications. She didn't like it and ultimately rejected the entire endeavor. Overt narcissists might respond by raging when they get home after a session like that. They might swear, threaten, possibly even become violent. A more vulnerable, or "covert" narcissist like Tina would be more inclined to passive-aggressive retaliation or withdrawing into a silent treatment or ghosting – which is exactly what Tina did.

I spent the rest of the day fretting about our next steps. Fortunately, I had a task to complete that kept my mind occupied for a while and I got to work on replacing the side-view mirror on my van. That would help pass some time while I waited on word from Tina.

The Total Destruction of Life, the Universe and Everything

The Irish Fair in St. Paul was an event I looked forward to annually. It was taking place on Harriet Island the weekend that Tina and I had our first and last session of couples' counseling. I was planning to take Tina to it, but after counseling, I'd had to take Tina back to Amber's because she was on pet-sitting duty over that particular weekend and Tina was entirely unsure of when Amber would be returning. That was one of the things I planned to discuss with her when I called later on. We hadn't really had an opportunity to talk since leaving the counselor's office and I considered that of utmost importance.

Tina had effectively isolated herself from me, though. When Tina was packing to go to Amber's she'd said to me, "You know you can't come over, right?"

With everything we had going on at the time, I figured Tina could use some time to herself, but being told that I wasn't welcome came as a slap in the face. I was fairly confident in my recollection of being told earlier that I was welcome. Tina's assertion caused doubt, which is exactly what gaslighting is all about. "OK, that's fine, but why?" I asked.

"Because Kenny and Kammy don't know you," Tina said. "They don't want strangers in their house."

They didn't know me well, but I'd met the betrothed couple a few times and I got along well with them. I couldn't imagine a scenario when any of my friends would ask me to house-sit and tell me that my fiance wasn't welcome or couldn't be trusted at their home (not even Tina). I was stunned.

I also recalled some discussion of this ahead of time and had a fuzzy memory of Amber explicitly telling me I could hang out over there to keep Tina company.

I'm a very easy going person and I get along with people of all walks of life. I'd never actually been told I'm not welcome somewhere by anyone, ever, before meeting Tina. Scott's house, the place Tina and Maura spent the majority of their time away from home became a no-go zone for me after a series of circumstances created a hostile rift between Scott and I. This was where Tina and Scott's son Doug did their illicit fucking out in his barn, whether his fiance Olivia was around or not.

I theorized that Tina maintained separate realities with different groups of people and needed to create rifts and mistrust between people to prevent her incompatible worlds from colliding. She went to considerable lengths to prevent communication between different people in her life.

She definitely saw honest communication between Nate and I as a threat. She made the rather bizarre request of him to block me on his phone to prevent any further communication from her own fiance reaching him.

For the first two years I knew Tina, she never mixed me with her friends. She rarely spoke of them, in fact. She brought me around her family, whose company I enjoyed a lot, but I'd only met Shayna (nicknamed Shayna Sidewalk) Keith, the Meth Dealer, her mom's sort-of beau Scott and his son Doug, Tina's ostensibly former bang-buddy. Doug was oddly evasive. When I was first introduced to him, he wouldn't look me in the eye and he shook my hand with his left, which I took as an immediate sign of disrespect. Only after that first meeting did Tina inform me "I slept with him once." As time went on, of it became apparent that "once" was a bit of a miscount.

Scott and Doug were both hostile towards me almost from the beginning and it wasn't long before I was told I wasn't welcome at Scott's.

I'd never been introduced or invited over to the next-door neighbors Tina had been spending more and more time with.

I was thinking about all the no-go zones that existed for me in Tina's life, but there were much bigger issues to deal with just then and on top of that, I had a mirror to replace on my van, so I went to work on that and pass some time.

The parking situation in Farmington could be a challenge. Especially in winter, but partly because of Tina's intrigue, it was complicated year-round. I was always having to park my van in different places to keep peace in the neighborhood – and in Tina's world. For a time when we'd first got back together, after I'd stopped drinking, she didn't want me to park in the driveway, so I'd been in the habit of parking around the corner on the opposite side of the triplex. Then, Tina began asking me to park on the other side of that street, because the neighbors, she said had taken "too much of an interest in who's van it was," and she said something about them being "invested."

She had been trying (and largely failing) to keep my presence a secret from a number of people. As to the neighbors being invested, I think they had a connection to Cassidy, who'd previously lived adjacent to them in the triplex and I'd guess Tina didn't want him to know about my return.

On this particular day, I'd parked in front of the neighbor's door (they had their own driveway), like I often did, once Tina took the secrecy down a notch. Christie came out and approached while I was unboxing my new mirror.

"Hey, Dan. Can I ask a favor?"

"You can ask," I said with a bit of humor in my tone.

"Can I get you to park up there?" She pointed to the other side of her driveway. "See, I have a hard time seeing around your van when I'm pulling out and I almost got hit the other day."

I sighed. "Sure, Christie. I'll try to do that."

"Thanks. I'm not trying to be a bitch or anything. I just really appreciate it."

"Yeah. OK." The humor was out of my voice. I set to work on replacing my mirror.

When I was finished, I took a picture of my reflection in the new side-view mirror, sticking up an accomplished thumb. I sent it to Tina.

After I packed up my tools, I moved the van up to the other side of the driveway like Christie had asked, and as soon as I shut it off, the neighbor from across the street burst out of his house, yelling at me. I looked up and saw the older man coming, unsteadily, towards me, literally shaking his fist.

"Why are you parking there?! You know Mike likes to park there! You come in here acting like you own the whole fucking place... I put up with your shit all last year," he shouted.

I was completely baffled and more than a little agitated. I didn't even have the faintest idea who Mike might be.

"I'm just doing what Christie asked me to do," I hollered back. "I'm fucking trying to be accommodating, here! I just need a place to park on the public street. There's no reserved parking, here."

"I don't give a shit. Find somewhere else to park that piece of shit," he said.

"Fine." I was seething, but I turned the key and started my van back up.

He went on ranting.

"I said, 'fine!' I'm moving it, ya lunatic," I bellowed. I moved my van forward another ten feet to mollify the crazy old man, making my walk back around the corner to the apartment door progressively further. At least it was nice out.

I couldn't figure out what the old man meant about all of last year. I might have parked in front of his house a time or two. Insanity swirled around that place.

Tina texted back to say "nice mirror" and I told her what had happened with the neighbors.

A minute later, she replied, "What the fuck? I hate people."

"How are you?" I texted back.

She didn't answer.

I tried again an hour later. It was about ten at night by then. "Call me tonight?"

Half-an-hour later, she replied, "I'm good. Just reading on the couch. I am all talked out for today, my lovely Dan. I will call you tomorrow, mmmmmmkay?"

Another text followed momentarily, "XOXO."

"Alright, sweetheart. Let me know when you're up and at 'em for Irish Fair, Tomorrow. I love you. I miss you. I want to caress and kiss you..." I sent the text with a cartoon of a love-struck squirrel.

I had a hard time sleeping that night. I was on edge about Tina's reluctance to talk with me since counseling. I ended up taking some anti-anxiety pills to help me fall asleep on Tina's lonely bed.

I woke up late Saturday morning. Almost as soon as my eyes were open, my phone was in hand, checking to see if Tina had messaged. She hadn't.

I went outside to have a smoke. I was hoping to pick Tina up and take her to Irish Fair at some point. I sent a text to my wayward love. "How about we get some lunch?"

It was almost noon by then, though, so time was of the essence. When half an hour went by without a response, I tried calling her. I was somewhat surprised she answered. The conversation was brief and frustrating, however.

I asked her about Irish Fair and she told me that she didn't know when she'd be able to leave, because, "Amber's coming back, today."

"Great, then you should be off the hook. I'm sure her pets can get by without you until she gets back," I suggested.

"No. I want to talk to her when she gets here," she explained.

"OK. Well, when's that going to be?"

"I don't know."

"Kinda hard to plan the day..."

"I'll try to find out. I'll get back to you when I know something," she concluded the call.

Tina texted me a couple hours later with a not-too-enlightening update. "I am heating up some boiled peanuts and going on a poo-pick-up mission. Amber hasn't responded yet, but as soon as she does, I'll let you know what's going on today. Love you!"

It was 2:00 by then. "I'm going to Irish Fair," I replied, irked.

"Alright, Have fun," she replied. "I'll let you know when I hear from Amber and when I'm done here."

I got dressed and made it as far as my van in my quest to attend Irish Fair, but that's where I gave up. I really didn't want to attend alone. There was still one more day of the fair. Maybe Tina would be ready to go with me on Sunday. I was still very anxious and had the feeling that Tina was avoiding me. I still felt strongly that we needed to talk about our counseling session. I needed to know we were on the same page.

I got back out of the van and slunk back into the empty apartment. I made myself a sandwich and tried to watch some television, but I was too distracted and worried to enjoy it. A foreboding feeling was looming darker as the day went on. The hours crept by without further word from Tina. I wondered what she was up to. I had a growing suspicion that she was talking to Nate while she seemed to be avoiding any meaningful conversation with me. I was being kept on hold.

I tried calling around six that evening, but she didn't answer. Then, I texted at ten to try to prompt her. "So…"

There was no reply. I tried again at 11:30. "What's up?" I wrote.

There was still no reply.

By midnight, I was at wits-end and fired off one last message before I took some anti-anxiety pills and went to bed. "I've been having the distinct impression you're avoiding me and it's freaking me out. Correct me if I'm wrong, but I assume you've been talking to Nate," I began. "I'm feeling very much in the dark. Is that it, then? Therapy is a bust, have a nice life?"

I must have dosed myself pretty good, because I didn't wake up until after noon. Again, the first thing I did was check my phone. Tina had finally messaged back around three in the morning, while I was in a deep slumber.

Her first message read, "I am okay. I read and slept… I've been talking to Amber and my mother. Is that a problem?"

Another message stamped 3:15 AM followed it. "She is back now. We are watching a horror movie and going to bed."

I was still trying, but I was full of dread. That first message didn't sit well with me. 'Is that a problem?' I was increasingly suspicious she'd been talking to Nate while avoiding me.

Still, I tried normalizing things and texted, "I never did make it to Irish Fair, yesterday. Any interest in going, today? Maybe Amber would be interested?"

Hours passed without a response. Her snippy middle-of-the-night text was eating at me. I didn't believe her. It dawned on me that I could probably actually see who she'd been talking to. I opened my laptop and pulled up T-Mobile.com. When I clicked on Tina's line, I was floored. I was right that she'd been talking to Nate, but the sheer volume of text messages and calls and minutes exceeded any weekend of conversations Tina and I had ever shared on the phone. By a country mile. There were over 40 text messages each way and a dozen phone calls that totaled hours and hours of talk time over the past two days. Friday night, immediately after Tina had texted me that she was "talked out," she had called Nate and talked to him for two hours.

For a while, the room was spinning as I sat on the bed staring at my screen in astonishment. My vision blurred and I realized I was crying when tears spattered on my keyboard.

I knew it was the end for us and that felt like death looming at my door. I'm not sure how long it took me to pull myself together, but once I was standing again, I sprang into action, packing. I'd done this before, but I was fully moved in by this point. It was a considerably larger task than last time. I quickly realized that I wasn't properly provisioned for the job. I drove to Walmart to buy some plastic totes. When I got back to the apartment to resume packing, my phone bleeped. Expecting that it was a message from Tina, I ignored it, at first and kept working on gathering my belongings.

When I did stop to look at my phone, it was like a fresh blow to the head. The text had come not from Tina, but from her mother. "I'll be home in an hour or so. Tina and I have a friend to visit, just so you know. I'm thinking you may want to look for another place to live… I'm looking to move out of Farmington by September 1st."

I laughed humorlessly, then texted back, "I'm already packing."

"Oh." was all she sent back.

Minutes later, Tina finally texted herself. "I am just getting up," she wrote, "Can I call you in a bit?"

"Why?" I texted back, indignant.

"I am on my way back to Farmington," she wrote.

I turned my phone off and numbly got back to work. I think I was in shock.

I had half-filled boxes and totes and bags all over the place when Tina came down into the apartment. I kept packing and tried not to acknowledge her at first. Tina stood in the living room, seeming not to fully register her surroundings.

I finally stopped what I was doing and looked at her. At that point, she took a breath and said, "I'm not happy in this relationship anymore."

I scoffed. "Oh. Really?" I went back into the bedroom to get some things off the bed.

"I feel like you're trying to 'fix' me. I don't want to be fixed. My mom and I are moving to Colorado," Tina said, when I came back into the living room.

"Wow. When did you decide that?"

"Just today," she said. "We're going to stay with my brother."

"Uh-Huh. When you get there, get into some therapy, get a job and get away from your mother. She's keeping you sick," I advised. I didn't know what a narcissist was at the time, but I had recognized Maura's role in infantalizing and warping Tina.

"I'll never leave my mama. I love her too much," she said.

That's something I'd suspected for quite a while.

The insanity of it all had my head spinning. On the spur of the moment, they'd decided to move out of state in a couple weeks or so and this was how I was learning about all of it.

"And I think I should be able to keep my ring," Tina said, "but I'll give it back if you want it." I had the feeling she'd been coached.

"Hell yes, I want the fucking ring back," I said. There was no way I was going to let her profit on our phony engagement after all her lies and betrayals.

Tina took it off her finger and handed it to me. I slipped it on to my pinky, facing the diamond setting downward, so as not to lose it.

"All I ever wanted from you was honesty, Tina," I said.

"And fidelity and I can't give it. Me and my mom are going to visit a friend. We'll be gone for a while," Tina said.

I hadn't said anything about fidelity. Just honesty. Sadly, I was so hooked on her that honesty might have been enough to keep me around, for a while at least. Even if that meant accepting her sexual escapades with other men. It would have slowly killed me, though.

"Hopefully, I won't be here when you get back," I replied. "You know… I am a good man, Tina."

"Yes, you are," she said quietly.

"I deserve better treatment than this."

"Yes, you do," she said.

"Now, at the end, could you be honest with me for one minute?"

"Sure."

"How many times did you cheat on me?"

"Never," she replied.

I shook my head and carried on packing. I had more to say. I opened my mouth, but thought better of it. "Never mind. You're not worth it," I said aloud, instead.

Tina disappeared up the stairs and left me to it.

I had no idea where I was going to go. I was really wishing my Mom hadn't left this world behind. I wanted to retreat to her shelter. I felt like Tina had been the last harbor for love in my life and I was cast into a dark and indifferent sea. Staying sober felt like a bigger immediate challenge than finding a place to sleep. Tina had been a major consideration in my decision to quit drinking and stay sober.

At one point, I found myself on my knees on a dirty spot of floor between the stove and a corner, sobbing uncontrollably. I gave up on trying to recover my things from the kitchen. I wasn't even sure what all Tina had taken from my Mom's house.

I ran out of boxes and totes, but time was unrelenting and I didn't want to waste any more of it driving back to Walmart. I knew Maura had some sturdy empty totes in a closet, so I used a few of those to finish up. I left $40 behind to pay for them.

Eventually, I called it "done" and locked up the apartment. It had gotten late. I was surprised to find it growing dark outside when I climbed into my van.

I found myself in a liquor store parking lot, without ever making a conscious decision to go there. I turned off my van, got out, started walking towards the door and didn't even realize where I was until I looked up at the sign. It spooked me. I got right back into the van and drove off.

A few blocks down the road, I pulled over to pull myself together before continuing.

I drove to a couple different motels in the area before I found one that wasn't too seedy with a vacancy. Once I got checked in, I texted Tina. "I've moved everything out. I just need my phone back and my 'heart,' the dolphin agate."

The agate had been given to me by my counselor when I quit drinking. Tina had an extraordinary affinity for agates and there was a gold foil dolphin stamped on this one. Dolphins had been a subject of conversation the night we'd first met, so I had seen some cosmic significance in that stone and given it to Tina one night, with a little bit of prose that I'd originally penned for our two-year anniversary when I meant to give her a heart-shaped agate, but she said she'd never seen that. The dolphin agate became its replacement.

Tina,
This is my heart;
You already own it;
I gave it to you;
Or you stole it;
Treat it well;
And it is yours forever.

The symbolism of it felt powerful and I needed to wrest it back from Tina.

I was moving alone, so I hadn't been able to move the dresser or bookcase that I'd inherited from my mother, or my big, fancy grill – I'd hurt my back a bit trying to move that by myself. There were a few loose ends, unfortunately, and that kept me in contact with Tina for some time after moving out.

Ultimately, the dolphin agate ended up back in Tina's possession. I realized it was no longer any good to me. I felt that both my metaphysical heart and the symbolic representation of it were worthless to anyone else and I hoped that Tina could take inspiration from that symbol of my sobriety to one day give up the drugs and alcohol that I deemed a destructive force in her life. Even then, I still cared about her.

Thus began a months-long decent into darkness and despair that felt like the end of my world. A severely wounded animal without even a cave of my own, I retreated to a hole in the ground. I was breathing but not living. I barely existed. I didn't have even the faintest notion, nor did it remotely feel like it, but that was when long-overdue healing finally began.

Mirrorshades

A few weeks after moving out of the apartment, I was getting ready to fly to Miami to visit an old friend in hopes of resetting my mind. Going to Ireland after my divorce had worked some magic I hoped to at least partially recreate in Florida.

I was living in a motel and my mail was still being delivered to the apartment in Farmington, so I needed to drop by from time to time. The night before I was flying out, I stopped over to see Tina and collect my mail. I was at that time still trying to maintain some kind of friendship and I was still trying to encourage her to get into some kind of counseling.

I hadn't seen Tina for a couple weeks. In the meantime she'd gotten stumble-drunk at Whitney's wedding and I knew she'd been languishing with a very painful broken arm from that event. I was surprised, then, when I arrived and found her well-dressed, wearing dangly earrings and makeup. Her hair was braided. She looked very pretty and put together. It put me off a little. Her right arm was in a sling. I gave her an awkward hug.

"You look nice," I said. "Going somewhere?"

"No." she gave a nonchalant shake of her head.

"Nice" wasn't normally a word I'd apply to Tina. She considered it less than faint praise, but "beautiful" felt awkward in our circumstances. I guessed she was making the effort for my sake. She retrieved my mail from a drawer in my mom's dresser that was still in the living room where I'd left it. I said a quick hello to her mother who was watching TV in the other room and Tina and I decided to get dinner together and catch up. I really had no idea where that conversation might go.

I drove us to Carbone's Pizza and just as we were pulling into the parking lot, my van began to malfunction. The lights dimmed. The alternator light came on. Mechanical problems the night before I was set to both move out of my motel room and fly to Miami was considerably less than optimal. I for sure didn't want to get stranded in Farmington.

I decided to drive to the nearest auto parts store before having dinner. I was looking for an emergency jump-starter pack, which I found for sale. Problem was, they didn't come charged. I bought ordinary jumper cables instead, hoping for the best and drove us back to Carbone's. The van had started and drove fine for the trip back to the pizza joint. Crossing my fingers, I shut the van off and we went inside. We'd been to this pizza joint many times (there weren't a whole lot of dining options in Farmington). It was familiar and awkward at once.

We made small talk and ordered food. While waiting for our pizza, I asked her if she'd figured out what she was going to do about counseling, since she'd canceled all her appointments at my clinic.

She said she'd been looking at other places closer for her to get to, but shut down further inquiry, saying, "I really don't feel like giving you a progress report."

I still considered therapy of critical importance for her, but I left it at that and steered our conversation into more tranquil waters. I'd say we had a nice time. We didn't get very deep.

After Dinner, we walked out to my van and I opened the passenger door for her. I noticed the dome light didn't come on. "Fuck!"

I went around to the drivers side and tried my key in the ignition, anyway, but, of course, there was no power. Not even a click.

I went back inside and asked around for the person who owned the pickup truck that was parked facing my stranded van. He turned out to be an employee who was just on his way out and he obliged me by letting me connect my new jumper cables to his battery. The van started and I got us back to Tina's apartment, but now I was in trouble.

I needed to drive back to my motel to finish packing up my things. I was expected to check out in the morning and I had been planning on storing the things from my room in my van while I was in Miami and finding a new place to stay when I got back to Minnesota. I needed to get back to Burnsville and I needed to get my van towed to the garage.

Maura lent me her Saturn to go back to my motel and offered to give me a ride to the airport in the morning if I wanted to spend the night in Farmington. I felt awkward about all of that, but I accepted the offer. It certainly solved my immediate problems. I called the garage I used to work part-time at and arranged for my van to be towed into town and Tina accompanied me in her mom's car to my motel. I guess she wanted to see how I'd been living. It wasn't pretty.

I had been attempting to do a small amount of work in my room, so I'd brought my big office printer over from my storage locker. That didn't fit easily into the small Saturn, but after rearranging things, I managed to get it and my suitcases loaded. Tina noticed that the rubber baseboard was peeling off the wall in my bathroom and wanted to pose for a picture with it. I guess she wanted a memento of how low I'd fallen.

We got back to the apartment and without much else said, Tina, Maura and I were off to our separate beds. "I'd let you sleep in bed with me, but..." Tina indicated her broken arm in the sling.

The notion hadn't even crossed my mind. "That's fine," I said. I slept on the futon in the TV room.

In the morning as we were about to ride to the airport, Tina picked up a pair of mirrored aviator-style sunglasses off of my mom's dresser. They had silver rims with some kind of woven pattern on the temples and seemed a bit on the flimsy side. She handed them to me. "When you're in Miami, can I just ask one favor?"

"Sure," I said. I was still conditioned. Anything for Tina.

"Can you take a picture somewhere with these on and send it to me?"

I thought it was a pretty strange request, but harmless. "Sure," I said again. I tucked them into the suitcase I was taking to Miami. My other belongings were being left with Tina and Maura.

With her broken arm, it was difficult for Tina to get in and out of the small coupe, so she sat in the front seat while I wedged into the back for the trip to the airport. I bought coffee for the three of us on the way.

On arriving, Tina hugged me goodbye, reminded me to send her that picture and I thanked her and Maura for the ride and help with storing my things while I'd be away.

Our flights got in at about the same time, so I met Bergt at the airport and we took a cab together to the AC Hotel in Miami Beach. After getting checked in, we went up to the roof, where there was a swimming pool, patio and a nice view of the ocean. I put on the mirror shades and posed for a picture for Tina. The lenses, I noted, had seen better days. They were a bit scratched up. I sent the photo to her and her mom and posted it on facebook to announce the onset of my mini-vacation.

Seeing Bergt and soaking in the tropical weather put me in a better mood and we set off on an adventure exploring Miami Beach. Tina was out of mind for a while, until one of her flying monkeys reached out to touch me through the ether.

My friend and I were walking down a bustling street. Music was coming from everywhere. The humidity was palpable. The smoky scent of Cuban food cooking wafted by. Well dressed men and less-dressed women crisscrossed the sidewalks. Miami nightlife was in full swing. My phone vibrated in my pocket. Like Pavlov's dog, I was conditioned. Whenever my phone made the slightest murmur, my heart would still skip a beat in anticipation of word from Tina. Maybe a comment about my mirror shades picture?

There was a new text. "So Dan, I hear you have an issue with me? Is that true? I'm a great dad and amazing friend to Tina."

I couldn't immediately tell who the message was from, but I guessed it was Scott. I had deleted his number some time back, but past text exchanges with him were still there, so I confirmed it pretty quick.

I stopped walking for a beat. Bergt looked back, noticing that I wasn't keeping up while I pondered this message. Bergt snapped me out of it and we got back on our fun-seeking mission, but Scott's out-of-the-blue message wouldn't get out of my head. About a half-hour later, we were at a little dance club called "Do not sit on the Furniture" that featured a mirrored disco shark instead of a disco ball and no furniture that I can remember. I stepped outside for a cigarette and typed up the first reply to Scott that had been percolating in my head.

"Actually, Scott, the last time I can recall your name coming up, I was telling Maura and Tina that I thought I should offer you an apology for my past drunken ravings. Tina suggested that I buy you case of beer. The circumstance just never arose, so I don't know what you're talking about.

"I'm having a hard enough time since I broke up with Tina. I'm heartbroken and I don't need you trying to stir up drama. Peace be with you."

He wrote back right away. "Peace? You should've thought of that before you disrespected all of us… And you're heartbroken? Hmmm…"

All of us? All of who? I couldn't make sense of that, but guessed that Tina or Maura were over there trash-talking me to explain the breakup. I realized it was a fools errand to try to reason with Scott. I considered that Tina had lied to me about Scott and certainly also lied to Scott about me, so there was nothing but angry confusion there. I ceased that conversation, but I texted Tina and Maura to ask them why Scott was picking a fight with me. Neither bothered to reply. Sadly, I allowed that sliver of lunacy to spoil my mood and I ruminated on it. Late that night, I drafted a lengthy follow-up message. I decided against continuing the crazy and didn't send the message, but here's what I was thinking:

Scott,

We don't really know each other. I'd say 99.9% of what I know about you I've heard from either Maura or Tina, so if I have a negative impression of you, where do you think I got it from?

One reason I never trusted you was that Tina would often leave your house with fresh marks on her body, some of which she attributed to you.

One weekend that Tina was spending at your house, she sent me a photo of herself in nothing but panties and there were bruises all over her inner-thighs, all the way up to her private business. The message that accompanied it was something of a cryptic apology, but she didn't offer an explanation until I saw her the next day. Then, she told me that you had caused those marks on her. She tore her pants off in front of her mom and I and made a big, dramatic show of it, demanding that Maura talk to you about how you mistreat her. Maura just said, "OK I'll talk to him" like it was no big deal or surprise.

If I had offspring who showed me those marks and said my romantic partner was responsible, I'd have had a pretty strong reaction and a lot of questions for everybody involved.

Looking back on it, it was a pretty ridiculous production.

Just this last July, after she'd been over to your place, she had a wicked, huge black bruise on her arm, just above her elbow. She initially said it was from helping me move stuff out of my Mom's, but later on, she 'admitted' that you were responsible and she didn't want to tell me so I wouldn't get pissed off at you.

Now, I figure it was actually rough sex with Doug in your barn that caused all those marks, but I never knew what to think – only that Tina was often all fucked up both physically and emotionally after visiting your home and at least one of these two things was definitely true:

1. You were physically abusive to Tina
2. Tina was cheating on me on your property

Either is a very good reason for her fiance to be uncomfortable about her visiting your house!

What little I personally witnessed of your behavior was concerning, but what Tina said about how you spoke to and manhandled her was one reason I didn't like her hanging out at your place.

Bottom line, if you want to know why I don't like you, maybe just ask Tina what she told me about you. If you don't like how you come across in her stories, talk to her about it.

I'd be amazed if you haven't figured out by now that Tina and Maura are both compulsive liars.

Regards,

Dan

Hanging out with Bergt in Miami Beach was a slight distraction, but wasn't the pick-me-up I'd hoped for. My woes still loomed too large and had followed me to the otherwise beautiful beachfront city.

When my flight landed back in Minneapolis, I took a taxi straight to the garage to pick up my van, then made a quick trip down to Farmington to recover my belongings. I returned the sunglasses to Tina, but I didn't linger. I had a tight schedule to keep. First and foremost, I had to find a place to sleep!

For quite a while, I told myself that it must just be a coincidence, but when I saw the picture on facebook of Chris sitting in an airport wearing an identical pair of aviator sunglasses a couple months later, I was floored. I'd never thought to ask Tina where she'd obtained those rather masculine sunglasses that I'd never seen in her possession before. They certainly weren't a new purchase, judging by their condition. It was so bizarre and surreal that I just went numb. I didn't know how to process what I was seeing.

Trying to understand the value a diseased mind finds in that kind of "prank" is a treacherous road to turn down, but my best guess has to do with feeling powerful.

Even though covert narcissists are by definition secretive, I think they ache to talk about their machinations as if they were accomplishments to be proud of. Because of that, they tend to give themselves away. Their victims just don't tend to immediately recognize it because of the manipulative gaslighting tactics that were employed to cloud their reason and better judgment.

Tina, I believe, relished hiding in plain sight. Triangulation is the other likely motive. Narcissists triangulate their supply-sources to keep them off balance and feeling vaguely threatened. The mirror shades provided all of that while leaving Tina an avenue for gaslighting, plausible denial if confronted about it. "You're crazy. Everyone has those glasses. You're being paranoid," she could say. To either of us.

It does seem crazy. It is crazy. Without the proper context, telling a story like this can make one sound crazy. That's gaslighting. That's crazymaking. That's what narcissists very deliberately do.

Regression on the Path to Healing

It was a herculean struggle to understand my own psychology in my relationship with Tina.

How could I have been so blind? Was it willful denial?

Maybe in part. At the core, it's a problem with first principles.

Everything I thought and observed was seen through a prism predicated on the notion that Tina loved me.

Believing as I do that the Earth is a sphere with gravitational pull, if I saw someone levitating or heard of a ship sailing off the edge of the world my mind would reject what I saw or heard. I would dismiss as untrue such phenomena, or at least seek alternate explanations.

The core flaw in my reasoning was the unshakable belief that Tina loved me. Since someone who loved me could not possibly be capable of the misdeeds I observed and inferred, my mind rejected reality, compartmentalized or deleted memories and readily accepted alternate, if unlikely explanations.

I came to mistrust my own eyes and ears. I doubted my own ability to reason. The core principle at the center of my universe was that Tina loved me. My perception of reality had to comport to that fundamental law.

I suppose it didn't help that I'd ultimately put myself in the hands of *two* practiced and compulsive liars and manipulators who were long accustomed to working in tandem.

I had been nervous about moving in with Tina after selling my Mom's house. I was aware I'd be dependent on her and her mother. I asked Tina several times if she was sure about the arrangement. She continually assured me that it was the best course of action for us, for now – until we began the hunt for our more permanent marital home. I had to make that leap of faith. I was fully committed to our future, together.

Tina kept reminding me to have my mail forwarded to the apartment in Farmington. She figured out what items from my Mom's house would be useful there, and we moved those things in.

It was when I had made myself the most vulnerable and dependent on Tina for a home that she showed me her most blatant betrayal. I'd provided a kitchen full of groceries, gave her mom a check for more than half the rent for the month and moved all of my worldly possessions to Farmington. No sooner than I had my mail forwarded was I forced to flee the new living arrangement. I found myself homeless and despondent. My only immediate option was a motel, but at $150 a night, it wasn't a practical long-term solution. I eventually moved into an extended stay motel, which was moderately more affordable, but I was hemorrhaging money.

When Tina found out how much I was spending on motels, she tried to convince me that I shouldn't have moved out. "My mom could have used that money," she said. "It's not like we kicked you out."

I was only slightly stunned.

"Oh, yes! I should have paid your mom to stay with my ex-girlfriend while she runs around with other guys – for what? Another week, was it?"

The day I moved out of the apartment, Tina and Maura announced to me that they were moving to Colorado in less than two weeks! That came as more than a surprise. As it turned out, they didn't move for a few more months, but regardless, there was no way I was staying under those circumstances and my sensibilities were duly offended that my money was Tina's only motivation for wanting me to come back.

While living out of bags in a rundown motel, my future in ashes behind me, I was too depressed to work much. The complexity of my political work was too much for my bleeding brain to handle at all, so I completely avoided that for months. That cost me thousands in income, but it couldn't be helped. I was simply rendered unable.

My part-time driving job was more manageable, since it didn't require much of my over-taxed brain power, but I only went to work a couple days a week and eventually stopped even that much. I realized I needed to stabilize my living situation before I could start working on stabilizing my mental health and life in general.

I'd also had a pretty big setback in my healing when I learned that Tina was in the hospital. With very little information, I was sick with worry. What little I initially heard sounded dire and led to renewed attempts to keep in touch with Tina. Of course, it turned out to just be the broken arm she'd suffered at Whitney's wedding.

I was foolishly hoping with continued friendship, maybe she'd begin to get some help for her chemical dependency and deep-rooted psychological problems.

That notion had to be abandoned before I could stabilize myself. I realized I had to forget about her well being, or indeed the well being of anyone who wasn't named ME. Selfishness is not in my nature. It was really difficult to arrive at and stick with that conclusion, but entirely necessary.

My uncle put me up for a while after I took that little vacation to Miami. I paid my uncle a modest sum to rent a spare bedroom, which was far more economical than the motels I'd been staying in and I was very grateful for the help, but, even if I wasn't fully aware, I needed my *own* space.

Eventually, a friend in Minneapolis came to my rescue by renting me a condo unit at a good price. I say friend, but really, she was more of an acquaintance – someone I knew from some years-back political activism, but she sure became a friend in deed by stabilizing my housing situation. That was an absolutely essential beginning and I was so grateful. I was making a weak effort to find a place, but I was in no state to be truly effective. I was wallowing, near nonfunctional. It might have taken months longer to find my own place.

I moved in October 1st. I occupied myself making the space my own. I spent a lot of money on new furnishings.

I was dealing with acute symptoms of PTSD and I needed isolation. I became a hermit. I did manage to get myself back to work at the driving job after about a month of not working at all. Eventually, I went back to some limited political work, too (that ceased when new revelations about how some friends were co-conspirators in the abuse I suffered caused another setback), but it took time. It was gradual – over months.

My therapist and a lot of online sources say that isolation after narcissistic abuse isn't healthy, but I've observed that it's 100% common to victims and I'm convinced that it's a necessary part of the healing process. Once I finally had my own space, I often just wanted to be left alone in my "cave." It's probably not good if that instinct prevails for more than a few months, but for a while, I think it was natural and helpful.

Tina had pulled something amazing out of me that I didn't know existed and then she killed it. And when that special something was killed, so too was my capacity for love, affection, trust, faith and optimism.

It's as if my affection was an organ, bloodied and battered from abuse and it was raw and painful to be touched. I didn't want to be touched by anyone. I didn't want to be close to anyone. It hurt and when the pain finally abated after almost a year, what was left was dull and unfeeling. Deadened.

I had preexisting issues I was unaware of. I was raised in an on-again-off-again broken home with an alcoholic father. I suppose I was inadvertently raised to be somewhat codependent. My past traumas made me kind, patient, helpful, accepting and accommodating. I was conditioned to be tolerant to abuse and my memory of distressing events susceptible to suppression. My troubled past apparently also made me far more gullible than I thought I was.

My nice-guy, codependent personality made a match with a cluster B personality type like Tina seem supernatural in it's power.

My whole sense of reality and faith in my own ability to reason was then destroyed by years of gaslighting, lies and manipulation. My faith in my fellow humans was lost. I didn't trust anyone or believe anything.

My understanding of morality was compromised because part of my coping strategy had been rationalizing Tina's misdeeds when I couldn't erase or explain them away. My whole world had been turned upside down and inside out. Right and wrong didn't have the same meanings.

I know people wonder why I couldn't just get over it and move on. I asked myself that. A lot. I was used and abused by a terribly sick person. Just leave her in the past and move forward, right? The damage Tina and her mom inflicted on my psyche didn't merely linger, though. It affected me through and through. It was emotionally and mentally crippling.

I was suffering a form of post traumatic stress disorder. Some call it Complex PTSD some call it narcissistic abuse syndrome. I was riddled with anxiety and depression, angry and sad and most of all disappointed in myself – for being so fucking stupid as to allow all of this. At the same time, something like Stockholm syndrome haunted me. I could still feel a pull towards her!

Through study, I discovered that the debilitating symptoms that plagued me were at least partly (if not mostly) physical. Long-term narcissistic abuse causes chemical and physical changes in the brain. The actual, physical shape and function of the brain's hippocampus and amygdala regions become damaged from constant exposure to stress hormones like cortisol. The trauma bond caused by such an emotionally manipulative and abusive relationship is a powerful addiction, which is also a physical phenomenon.

When we broke up, I was wondering aloud why I'd put up with so much shit from her for so long to that point. "You're not worth it," I said as I packed my things. She later said that I had I called her "worthless." I don't remember saying that and I don't believe I called her that, but she said she felt worthless. I was sure she misheard me. She's not worthless, but the way she'd chosen to avail herself has no currency in my world. As I saw it in the immediate aftermath, the way she chose to avail herself to humanity was as little more than a fuck hole for dirtbags and, I figured that as long as she goes untreated, that's all she'd ever be. Where I was probably mistaken was in believing that therapy might offer a way for her to change for the better.

On more than one occasion, Tina said "sometimes I feel like the only way I could make a living is on my back." She also spoke of "considering" stripping as a vocation. I didn't take her literally on any of that, but perhaps she was telling me a truth I preferred to ignore and perhaps she was exactly correct.

She was completely unable to hold a job in the three years I knew her. She was full of excuses about why, but the one she used most often was that she had a compromised immune system. She said she didn't want any job working with the public because she was afraid of falling ill, but she had no problem hanging out in crowded bars, where hygiene standards were probably not too much superior to clinic reception areas.

In general, I've found tattoos unattractive, but in a way I also appreciated face and neck tattoos because they so clearly marked a person as someone for me to avoid. I wished Tina carried an obvious mark, along the lines of a scarlet letter, not to mark her as an adulteress (even though she is), but to warn good people away from her covert, narcissistic evil.

As I learned more about borderline personality, narcissistic personality disorder and other "cluster B" disorders, I was amazed at how other people's experiences mirrored my own. My emotional connection to Tina seemed more intense than anything I'd experienced before. I thought there was something cosmic about it – that it must have been meant to be. We were a perfect fit, drawn together like magnets, connected like complex puzzle pieces and inseparable.

Now I see that in a way, we actually were made for each other, but it wasn't a match made in the stars. Our personality types, each shaped by earlier traumas made a "perfect," irresistible match that (lacking some enlightened intervention) was psychologically preordained to play out in exactly the way it did for us. We fit like a key in lock and it could only open the one door. It was like we were each only half a person, emotionally, but together, we felt complete. I know that cheesy sentence calls Jerry McGuire to mind, but I actually did feel that way. I believed Tina did. She said she did, but now I know that's extremely unlikely. Narcissists aren't generally thought to be capable of that kind of connection.

Thank God I had stopped drinking before the bitter end arrived. I'm certain sobriety played a major role in my ability to survive and begin healing. I was a year sober when Tina and I split up for the last time, so I was finally able to see the situation with some clarity. When we'd broken up in the past, I was still drinking and the trauma of breaking up spurred even heavier drinking that clouded my understanding of circumstances and opened me up to easier manipulation by Tina. She could practically rewrite my memories when I was drinking. Relying on any mood-altering chemicals would definitely delay and perhaps even render impossible any healing from narcissistic abuse.

During those initial months of living alone (for the first time in my life), I found myself reverting to an earlier version of myself. My therapist called it "regressing" but I saw it more like restoring the last backup state known to work. I had to go back a ways to get past the traumas I'd experienced – not just with Tina, but from much earlier. I bought a Play Station and got into video games. I found myself buying Cookie Crisp cereal and Eggo waffles for breakfast and binge-watched old

Doctor Who. I re-watched every Star Wars movie. I relived some of the excitement I felt in the late 1970s, re-watching every episode of the original Battlestar Galactica.

I had to rediscover myself in a lot of ways. I had to kind-of re-raise myself. I located and decorated my home with a lot of mementos from my youth. Pictures and artifacts from times and events that had shaped me – the old me, from before the abusive relationships and before I turned, self-destructively to the bottle for solace.

I surrounded myself with bittersweet memories – things that made me happy once. The bitterness only stemming from their loss. Pictures of my mom and grandma went up. A picture I drew of the family cabin before it burned. Leo, the plush lion who used to guard that cabin from atop the mantelpiece went on display. I printed an enlarged photo of an enchanting waterfall I'd seen when visiting Ireland and framed that. Pictures of my nieces and nephews helped remind me of reasons to carry on.

A somewhat more daunting task was locating and disposing of mementos that reminded me of Tina. It was difficult, both because of the emotion conjured by those memories and because those objects were legion. Tina was woven through the fibers of my life. Extracting her was no small chore. Even after a concerted seek and destroy mission, I was still coming across "Tina-things," months on. The pair of Star Wars boxers she'd given me for Christmas turned up in a bag I'd forgotten to unpack. A brief love note she'd hidden in my briefcase had remained unread until after we'd been separated for almost a year. Odds and ends like that continued to turn up and I found I had a dilemma. What to do with Tina's sparkly diamond and white gold engagement ring? It was tainted. Poetically, I considered disposing of it in a septic tank, since I'd be better off marrying an actual piece of shit than a selfish lying addict doing her best impression of one.

As significant as the objects to dispose of, objects missing because of Tina were glaring in their absence. I'd recovered my mother's dresser from the Farmington apartment after Tina and Maura moved out, thanks to the kindness of the upstairs neighbors, but I also learned from them that Tina callously gave the matching bookcase to one of her side guys. Specifically, my old "friend" Chris. They had pictures to show me from their home security cameras. That pretty clearly verified that she and Chris had been carrying on an affair behind my back (and presumably his wife's) for years – almost as long as I'd known Tina and it was still going on. That also meant that other friends I used to love had probably been lying to me.

Tina's mom had promised to get the dresser and bookcase back to me when she and Tina moved to Colorado, but instead, the dresser was broken and abandoned while evidently, my "buddy" Chris showed up in his blue and gray Dodge pickup to collect my mom's bookcase for himself!

The upstairs neighbors also mentioned that "the revolving door of men" that they'd observed when they fist moved into the triplex had resumed right after I moved out. Chris, who's married, with children rarely spent the night, I learned. He wasn't there "during times when people would be with their families," but there were reportedly at least four other men who did spend nights there in the aftermath of my departure. That's either pathological or professional. "We always assumed they were running a brothel down there," the neighbors told me.

"Her knees were always all bruised up," Antonio mentioned.

For some time, I noticed the absence of my mom's bookcase daily with no small amount of annoyance. Every day, that reminded me of how Tina turned my own friends into accomplices in her abuse. Astonishment, anger and disbelief eventually gave way to acceptance and a new paradigm of understanding, though.

I also noticed the absence of some heirlooms from the old family cabin. While I was working, Tina made decisions about a lot of what to keep and what to dispose of in my mom's house. She did some of the packing alone. I thought she was being helpful.

In my room, I had a box of cabin artifacts — mostly nick-knacks of modest monetary value (a ceramic Paul Bunyan, a deco-style brass desk calendar from the 1920s, some bear sculptures and the like), but all tremendously sentimental. When I noticed several items missing from the box, Tina said she'd repacked it. She told me she thought such important mementos should be wrapped up safer before going to storage. I thought the box they were in was secure enough, but I trusted her with that.

She designated several boxes to be donated Savers, a thrift store benefiting Disabled American Veterans and other charities. Some other boxes were destined for the apartment and the remainder were supposed to go into my storage unit.

The box of cabin artifacts was either stolen or donated, because after a thorough search, through every box in my possession, they remain missing. Trusting Tina with anything at all proved to be a mistake.

It's remarkable how some of these revelations could still reach out and hurt me a year later and more, but eventually, I knew I was getting close to reaching the bottom of that unsavory barrel.

Coming to understand my friends' involvement in the assault on my psyche was a brutal blow to my ability to trust anyone whatsoever. It was a fresh setback in my progress in finding relief for PTSD-like symptoms, but only temporarily. Regular application of therapy and study of narcissistic abuse syndrome helped brace me and helped me more quickly process that new information. I became pretty jaded. Areas that used to be emotionally vulnerable became callused — which some may see as an improvement. I lament the loss of sensitivity, even if it helped me cope in the short term.

In the world of what's written on narcissistic personality disorder and the victims of people possessed of it, there appears to be an imbalance of genders. Most writing on the subject chronicles male narcissists tormenting female empaths – at least in the context of romantic relationships.

It's my studied opinion that the apparent gender bias is a result of cultural pressures that make it more acceptable for women to share stories of mistreatment. I believe that NPD occurs about equally between the genders, but men are more typically shamed into silence when they are the victims of creatures so-afflicted. Society still doesn't allow men to be the victims. Admitting to being used, abused, tormented and manipulated by a woman can be tantamount to proclaiming oneself weak, incompetent and essentially, unmanly.

That cultural stigma held me on the fence for some time before I decided to make my own stories public. I was ashamed of what I'd allowed to be done to me. Once I published my first few stories, Chris, who I once thought of as a friend, began attempts to torment me – mocking and ridiculing my pain. He referred to me as a "whiny beta cuck" and sent rude messages assailing my manhood. Of course, it became plainly revealed that he had been carrying on an illicit affair with my narcissistic ex and had been a party to my abuse almost from the very start. He had joined Tina's harem and became one of her flying monkeys.

A mutual friend, while not "agreeing with" Chris' "tactics," still told me he thought I'd said "too much," when I published that DanandTina.net blog of mine. "Sorry if wasn't playing by the 'rules,'" I told him, "but it's not been a game to me. It's my life and well-being I've been dealing with."

It's astounding that abusers expect their victims to remain silent, and they often do.

These are just some examples of why men aren't so inclined to share their stories of being abused by women. On the surface it looks like women are more commonly the victims, but I believe the numbers are about equal. Anecdotally, it appears that men are more likely to seek one on one therapy and other professional help for narcissistic abuse but women are more willing to openly discuss their experiences.

I've found reading other people's stories about narcissistic abuse tremendously helpful. Most of what I've read has been written by women. I simply reverse the gender of the pronouns in the stories and generally find them immensely relatable. At their core, all narcissists are pretty much the same. The same scripts play out over and over across millions of doomed relationships, with only the minor details differing in the overarching story.

Aside from reverting to my younger, more innocent mind, an important part of healing from narcissistic abuse was learning about it. I studied narcissistic personality disorder (and related cluster B disorders) in depth. I read stories from other victims. I watched their videos. I documented my own experiences on my blog and in this book. All of this was essential to making progress towards recovery – towards normalcy. I found that writing my story was instrumental in unraveling the illusory and massive tangle of lies and confusion I'd been navigating blindly for years.

I'd seen some articles advising victims not to spend too much time plumbing the depths of narcissism, but I'd also observed that everyone seems to do it anyway and concluded that those writers are wrong. It is absolutely an essential part of recovery. It's also pretty important to know how to avoid being ensnared by a narcissist again. I can spot them easily, now. That's important to protect myself in the future. My own empathetic personality seemed to make me look like candy to a narcissist. I realized others had tried worming into my life. I was better prepared, after Tina, to fend them off. In fact, I was pretty proud of myself for recognizing the traits early and dodging that bullet.

Finally, an ingredient in my recovery formula that can't really be controlled: Time. Knowing that time is a crucial element in healing helped provide the patience and perseverance to keep going, even when it got difficult and even when there were setbacks. Each week, each month, each year that passed carried me closer to peace.

Storage Locker Blues

For over a year, I maintained a storage locker in Farmington. It wasn't a convenient location for any more than a month. It had made sense at the time Tina and I decided to rent it, since I'd just sold my Mom's house and was moving in with Tina as a stepping stone towards getting a new home together.

After Tina and I ultimately parted ways for good, I eventually landed back in my home city of Minneapolis. For a time, I largely ignored the existence of the storage locker, with more pressing concerns cluttering my mind, but I was paying for it. One day it dawned on me that I'd paid over $2,000 to store possessions I'd not seen in a year. Not much in there was worth that much. I'd be better off buying replacements for just about anything in there than paying to store it any longer, I reasoned, so I began to go through it all, moving some things to my condo and throwing some things away, with the goal of closing that money-drain.

Every 30-mile trip to Farmington to work on that storage locker stirred up anxiety, sadness and anger. After searching in vain for family heirlooms from my grandma's cabin and realizing that Tina had really managed to permanently remove them from my possession, going through what was left became even more depressing. I was always aware of what should have been there and wasn't. Tina's immaculate handwriting was still on some of the boxes and bins. "Dan's Sweaters," "kitchen stuff" and the like. Those labels echoed the false future I'd once eagerly believed in – the life Tina and I were preparing to build together. Those labels mocked me.

It was always stressful, returning to Farmington. Besides being a town brimming with ambivalent memories of Tina, it was a frightening place to visit. I never returned without extra vigilance. I was in a heightened state of awareness, surveying my surroundings, paying attention to faces, adrenaline elevated, ready to defend myself. I had no idea what threats could still be lurking there – what people Tina had turned into flying monkeys who might mean me harm. She appeared to be involved with a criminal element in one of her secret lives and she'd previously intimated that I was under threat from Scott (Scott himself backed that up when he suddenly started sending me provocative texts while I was in Miami licking my wounds from the breakup). Scott lived just down the road from the storage facility. I could easily encounter any number of other people I wouldn't want to see while visiting that little town.

It's ironic that Tina expressed fear of "dangerous Minneapolis," when I'd first met her in Farmington and I felt far more fear in that little town than in the big city sometimes billed "Murderapolis."

Every trip to that storage locker reignited anger at Tina for her causing me to move my entire life to Farmington where I was immediately dropped on my head, leaving me homeless, bewildered and devastated.

Disposing of the storage locker was unfinished business in the effort to eradicate Tina from every corner of my life.

"Future Faking" is a particularly destructive game narcissists play and Tina knew how to use it against me all too well. Winding up homeless and stuck with a storage locker in the boonies was only the latest time she'd pulled the rug. I drew analogy to Charlie Brown always trying to kick Lucy's football. He kept falling for it and so did I.

Living together in Farmington wasn't the first or even second time we'd planned cohabitation. Every time it came time to actually do it, though, Tina either acted out to sabotage our relationship or simply vanished. Before, she might have just ghosted on me right before the moving date, but this time, I was already moved in and had keys, so she ran to Nate's hotel room and she hid out at her friend Amber's, leaving me with her mom as a roommate – until I finally snapped and the floodgates of reality opened.

Not more than a month or two prior, Tina and I had been sitting on the patio at the Mug bar with another man and woman. They were just friends and the woman was telling her tale of woe. She'd moved her entire life to Minnesota for her boyfriend only to have him abandon her to live with another woman as soon as she'd settled in with him. Then he tried stringing her along so he could date them both. Tina and I expressed sympathy, joined in calling the offending ex-boyfriend a douchebag and the like. It was like a harbinger – or really just an example of another narcissist destroying his victim with a little future faking and perhaps Tina was taking notes.

About three months after I moved out, I drove past Tina's on my way to the storage locker I had unfortunately located in Farmington. I happened to notice a familiar, hooded dirtbag puffing a smoke out on the driveway. Go figure. Tina's barn-banging fuck buddy is already coming around, I thought.

Douglas. her mom's sort-of-boyfriend's son had recently earned himself a third DUI and according to Tina, he'd been hitting his pretty little fiance, Olivia. Of course, Tina lied to me so much, it's hard to know what's true. She may have just been trying to put me off the scent of infidelity after I'd expressed misgivings about discovering the surreptitious messages from him on her Snapchat.

Tina told me she hadn't had any contact with Doug in a year and didn't want to, because, in her words, "he's a scumbag." I suspected otherwise. I knew otherwise.

And there, he was.

I was still setting up my new bachelor pad and had to visit my storage locker again the next day and... lo and behold! Glancing ruefully at Tina's place as I drove past, I scoffed to myself. There he was again! Doug, unshaven and unkempt was alone in Tina's driveway tapping the ashes off the end of a cigarette. He must have spent the night, I figured.

I wondered if maybe Olivia caught him banging Tina and forced him out of the house, so he had to bunk with his mistress for a while. It seemed likely, but there are certainly plenty of other reasons he could have been put out on his ass, or maybe he said he was somewhere else. I wondered if Olivia knew where he was. I wondered if she'd care. This younger generation, at least in Farmington, didn't seem to get as caught up in quaint old notions like honesty and faithfulness.

For her part, Maura hadn't seemed to think Olivia would have minded if she knew Doug was snapping flirty messages to Tina, or so she told me when I asked. I thought she probably would, but maybe that's just because it offended my silly out-dated morals.

Learning what hate Means

I thought I understood what hate was. I'd used the word – probably numerous times, to describe a someone I disliked, who angered me or perhaps a person I just found particularly disagreeable. "God, I hate that guy," I can remember saying more than once. I had no idea what I was saying. I had no idea what hatred really entailed, until Tina. Since I'd glibly engaged in hyperbole tossing around the word hate without grasping the depth and torment of the emotion, I felt a sufficiently horrible word had not yet been devised to describe the sad, angry and ever-present black loathing I was feeling.

Hating Tina became a second full time occupation. I found that the emotion had the same fervor that my love used to, which was beyond anything I'd previously experienced. Flipping that emotion into reverse stirred up a dark side of me I was astonished and somewhat frightened to discover.

A good friend, who has heard about everything I've ever had to say about anything in the forty some years I'd known him was taken aback by the vitriol I sputtered whenever I spoke about Tina. He chastised me over my choice of words.

"What? She's a fucking whore," I defended my rants.

"That may be," he said, "but I've never heard you speak about any woman that way, ever. That isn't you, Dan."

I explained that a nasty enough word to name her didn't exist and words like cunt, slut and bitch didn't even approach the order of magnitude required to express my disdain. Therefore, I felt no remorse in uttering those words. They were kind by comparison to the word I wished for – the word yet to be invented. I refused to accept his rebuke.

I've learned what hate is and I'm glad it's not something I'd really experienced before. I hope I never do again. It's poison. It ate at my mind and soul, blackened my heart and stole my innocence. I believe to truly hate someone, one must know the person intimately. The object of my hate got close to me. So close, I took part of her into myself. Only then could she inflict the repeated painful injuries and humiliations needed to churn my font of love and affection into bitter acid.

Hatred is not a satisfying emotion. It hurts. It's like a traumatic wound that won't heal, with persistent pain as fresh as when first acquired. All that hurt is personified. The person becomes pure, sickening, maddening evil. All of the wounds Tina ever caused were replayed over and over and over again. I couldn't escape the torment of hating. I wanted desperately to forgive her, just so I could relieve myself of the burden. The hatred was so overwhelming it was crushing the spark out of me.

Mommy, Where do Narcissists come From?

Or:
Narcissists are Dung Beetles

The dung beetle is a fascinating, but bizarre creature. Its life revolves around a literal ball of shit that it rolls or carries with it everywhere. Most creatures, especially humans, find rather repugnant the idea of carrying around a ball of shit. The notion only becomes more repellent when we learn that the beetle uses it's ball of animal scat as food, housing and breeding chambers. To the dung beetle, however, that ball of shit is everything!

When I first began to learn about narcissistic personality disorder, the lowly and lonely dung beetle sprang to mind. Narcissists also carry with them a ball of shit that the rest of us would be repelled by. To the narcissist, it is everything. It is precious, and guarded above anything else. Their ball of shit is what motivates them. It's not made from manure, though. Instead, it's a filthy ball of envy, shame and lies.

Sometimes, we can smell it. We know something's off, but with the mind clouded from narcissistic abuse, can't quite pinpoint it.

These human-shaped dung beetles love their dung but they also want to fit into society, so they undertake great pains to hide their ever-growing balls of shit.

As long as no one truly sees them, they can imagine themselves as something greater than the dung beetle. This is why they wear their masks, adorn themselves with lies and obfuscate their shit with gaslighting and projection.

I think it's a pretty fair analogy, but probably the more precise way to look at narcissists is as the scared, hurt and neglected children they were when some awful trauma halted their emotional development. Maura once texted me a picture of Tina as a little girl – maybe 3 or 4 years old. It was about the cutest thing I'd ever seen. She was sitting in a brown paper bag on the floor like her mom had just picked her up at the grocer. She had a shaggy-cropped head of blonde hair and the smile of a kid semi-conscientiously posing for a camera. It was fucking cute.

The conventional theory is that narcissistic personality disorder results from severe early childhood emotional trauma (attachment trauma, abuse and/or neglect) that freezes emotional development – probably right around the age Tina was in that picture.

When not imagining Tina guarding her precious ball of shit, I'd sometimes see her as that little girl, in a soiled white shift with matted, neglected hair and bare, dirty feet. Scared and alone in the dark, she has to learn to fend for herself. She has to raise herself and eventually pretend to be an adult to survive – but she's still ever that wounded little girl.

When I'd think about her like that, it made me sad and I wanted to curse the world for its cruelty, but I can no longer afford any compassion for my abuser. I did often wonder, though, what untold trauma did Tina in. There was no one thing I was certain of. Maybe she was just born like that. Some theories pointed to a genetic component or a combination of nature and nurture (or lack thereof). I sometimes theorized a connection to Munchhausen Syndrome by Proxy might even have been involved.

Then, I happened to read about a newer theory that doesn't seem well circulated or widely accepted as yet. The newer theory puts the disorder in the physical realm, attributing it to brain damage, either congenital or by injury – even just from being hit on the head. Frontal lobe or prefrontal cortex damage is what's implicated. That caught my attention, because Tina said she'd actually suffered numerous concussions and was at one point told that another could kill her. It's only anecdotal, but it fits terribly well.

The reported symptoms of frontal lobe damage are a fair analog to cluster B personality disorders: impaired moral judgment and comprehension of consequences; emotional and behavioral dis-regulation; disorganization; loss of motivation, loss of emphatic reasoning (empathy); trouble picking up on social cues, as examples. Each of those symptoms describes a troublesome aspect of Tina's personality.

I'm not a doctor and I can't claim to know what made Tina behave as awfully as she did. I used to wish I did know for certain. All victims of narcissists ask "why?" Some of us might come up with answers enough to satisfy ourselves. We'll never get the answer from a narcissist, but for me, somewhere in this batch of theories lies something close enough to the truth.

Munchhausen by Proxy?

As I've already noted, it's impossible to know with certainty what made Tina the way she was, I did eventually develop a working theory that seemed consistent with the facts I had at my disposal, however.

There is a strong correlation between Factitious Disorder Imposed on Another (more commonly known as Munchhausen Syndrome by Proxy) and Cluster B Personality disorders.

According to the psychological manuals, the victims often become perpetrators themselves and develop depression, emotional detachment, abandonment issues, anxiety, addiction and PTSD.

It seems obvious to me that someone close to Tina betrayed her in a major, extremely harmful way in her early years. That trauma, whether acute or prolonged (more likely) slammed the brakes on her emotional development, so that even though she is extremely intelligent and knowledgeable, she seems to possess the emotional maturity of a 7-year-old.

Tina, still unable to function as an adult apart from her mother, had the most bizarre and tortuous medical history in youth that I'd ever personally heard of. From what I've been told (however reliable that may be), her father was oddly disengaged from Tina's treatments, sometimes reluctant to pay for them. By Tina's account, he seemed skeptical of the need. I didn't know him well, but my impression was of a hard-working, responsible family man and a capable provider. That didn't add up.

Although Tina was 30 years old, her mother still scheduled all of her doctor appointments, managed all of her prescriptions and regularly made changes to Tina's treatment plans without her consent. She picked up and distributed Tina's medications (and they are beyond numerous). I always looked at this arrangement with some degree of skepticism. It looked to me like Tina was being infantalized. Maura had control of Tina's medications and I recall one instance when Tina was in a panic because her Mom had "taken off" with all of her medicine and was unreachable for a time.

Tina had a strange relationship with the medical profession. She was well versed in medical terminology, expressed dismay that she hadn't finished school, because it had been her desire to be a medical doctor, but she had phobias about going to the doctor. She'd also kept her pediatrician as her primary care physician long after she became an adult.

Further complicating her dream of practicing medicine was her reported immune deficiency. I was told she had a genetic mutation that rendered parts of her immune system impotent, making contraction of disease or infection a high risk for her. This deficiency was often cited as a reason not to apply for work – fear of germs in the public space – but for all her bubble-boy concerns, she had no qualms about crowded rock concerts, camping with thousands in music festivals, sharing joints or pipes with strangers, hanging out in bars or being wildly promiscuous.

She didn't seem to contract viruses any more frequently than I did. When she did, her mom would order up a prescription for antibiotics for her – which is, of course not useful to fight a virus, but ostensibly was still deemed necessary to prevent bacterial infections while her immune system was preoccupied fighting the virus.

Piecing everything together, I began to develop a theory, but it's no more than that. I wondered, could Tina have been a victim of Munchhausen by Proxy? That was just a loose theory based on my own observation and some research that I played out as a possible explanation.

With this mental illness, a person acts as if an individual he or she is caring for has a physical or mental illness when the person is not actually sick. The (usually) adult perpetrator has the diagnosis and directly produces or lies about illness in another person under his or her care (usually a young child). Factitious Disorder Imposed on Another (FDIA) is considered a form of abuse by the American Professional Society on the Abuse of Children. However, cases have been reported of adult victims, especially the disabled or elderly. FDIA was previously known as Munchhausen Syndrome by Proxy.

People with FDIA have a twisted need for the other person (often his or her child) to be seen as ill or injured. It's not a scam done to obtain a tangible benefit, such as financial gain. People with FDIA are even willing to have the child or patient undergo painful or risky tests and operations in order to get the sympathy and special attention normally given to people who are truly ill and their families.

Tina had a number of surgeries chasing mystery ailments as a child and none of them got at the cause. Her problems persisted after numerous torturous hospital stays and doctors were flummoxed. She had organs removed without apparent benefit, but caused her digestive troubles later in life. Always at her bedside, her diligent mother.

The Diagnostic and Statistical Manual of Mental Disorders 5, is the standard reference book for recognized mental illnesses in the United States. It describes this diagnosis to include falsification of physical or psychological signs or symptoms, and induction of illness or injury to another associated with deception. There is no evidence of external rewards and no other illness to explain the symptoms.

FDIA most often occurs with mothers. A person with FDIA may use the many hospitalizations as a way to earn praise from others for their devotion to the child's care. They may use a sick child as a means for developing a relationship with a doctor or other health care provider. The adult with FDIA often will not leave the child's bedside and will discuss in detail symptoms and care provided to demonstrate that he or she is a good parent or guardian. If the symptoms go away in the hospital, they are likely to return when a caretaker with FDIA is alone with their victim.

People with FDIA might create or exaggerate a victim's symptoms in several ways. They might simply lie about symptoms, alter diagnostic tests (like contaminating a urine sample), falsify medical records, or induce symptoms through various means, such as poisoning or injuring. The complaints may also be about psychiatric or behavioral problems.

When Tina and I broke up, one of the things I remember saying to her was "When you get to Colorado, *please*, get a job, get into therapy, get away from your mother and live on your own as soon as possible. She's keeping you sick, Tina." That last sentence sprang up from a place of instinct. My subconscious appended that part without my even thinking about it until after I'd said it.

She replied, "That'll never happen. I love her too much."

"This isn't healthy," I told her. I recognized something was very wrong with that relationship. Tina's inability to look after herself was concerning and I occasionally wondered if it wasn't by her mom's design.

As unbelievably hurt and angry as I was at that moment, I still cared. I still hoped she'd be OK, but it wasn't looking good. The abrupt plan to move to Colorado was bat-shit crazy.

The words I chose that day, "She's keeping you sick," continued to ring in my mind for some time. I was speaking of mental health, but my statement echoed part of the film The 6th Sense, when a father finds out his wife, in the throes of Munchhausen by Proxy, had been poisoning their (now deceased) daughter. "You were keeping her sick," he said. I wonder if my subconscious had already pieced this theory together long ago. My subconscious seemed to know a lot about Tina that my conscious mind chose to overlook.

Even if not attributable to mental illness or abuse, all that early medical torture probably had some effect.

Whatever it was that happened to Tina, it was undoubtedly terrible and It's a shameful tragedy that things like that happen to children. At some point, however, Tina transitioned from abused to abuser and I had to remind myself that I owed no more sympathy to my abuser.

Lasting Damage

After the grand finale with Tina, I developed or experienced more keenly, a cluster of symptoms that's been associated with Complex Post Traumatic Stress Disorder (C-PTSD) or more specifically, in my case a variety of C-PTSD sometimes referred to as Narcissistic Abuse Syndrome.

Narcissism as I use the term here is kind-of a catch-all because I couldn't say for certain where, exactly, Tina landed on the spectrum of Cluster B Personality Disorders. She exhibited destructive traits that overlapped into antisocial, borderline, histrionic and narcissistic personality disorders, but as far as the damaged state induced in a long-term partner of someone suffering a cluster B disorder, it's pretty typically the same result.

Of course, Tina had co-morbid substance abuse issues and it's been said that all addicts are narcissists. So, it's also not possible to tell what behaviors stemmed from what disorder. My therapist advised that it's hopeless to try to pinpoint it, but it's a natural instinct of many who survive this kind of abuse.

Perhaps the worst and definitely the most persistent aspect of surviving narcissistic abuse and gaslighting was loss of confidence in my ability to reason.

I experienced decision paralysis. For a while, I was constantly second-guessing myself and as a result, everything took much longer to accomplish. A lot of things had to be sidelined. Even simple decisions could become mind-benders. I was standing in the bakery section of the grocery store, deciding on a treat. I picked up a box of tasty-looking donuts. I noticed apple fritters. *I haven't had those in a long time. Do I like apple fritters? I think so. Maybe I should just get the donuts…*

I stood, contemplating the two boxes for a good five minutes before I became aware that I must have looked pretty odd just standing there, staring back and forth between two $4.00 boxes of pastry. Even realizing how long I was taking, it still took another minute or two to break the decision paralysis and put the apple fritters in the cart.

That's just one example. It was a daily struggle. I lost confidence in my ability to do complex work and ceased all political involvement, for example. I couldn't even fathom how I used to give speeches, testify to the legislature, devise legal arguments and strategies... When I'd think of those things, I'd feel overwhelmed and asea.

Gaslighting is no small thing. It's extremely harmful. It warps a person's whole sense of reality and destroys confidence in their mental prowess. It can take years to dig out and recover from this kind of psychological and emotional abuse.

Tina had managed to convince me that I was the problem – that it was in my head. I was misinterpreting what I saw and heard. I was being paranoid, possessive, jealous.

When she was getting phone numbers from other men at the bars, there was a perfectly valid and innocent reason for it. When she wanted to spend weekends with her "former" sex partner, it was just to spend time with his sisters. When she came back all marked up with intimate bruises or bite-marks, that was Scott just worried that his hands weren't strong enough to inflict pain and bruising on a woman anymore. Perfectly innocent. How dare I question it?!

I was essentially trained over a course of years to doubt my own judgment. "Word salad" and gaslighting kept me confused and off-balance. It's especially malevolent behavior that causes lasting harm in order to rob a person of their free will, manipulate and control them.

The situation was made worse because of one time I was wrong. I was very wrong about one situation. Spectacularly and embarrassingly wrong. The pocket-dialed voicemail incident really caused me to question my own judgment. It made me fearful of being wrong about other things, or even being perceived as suspicious. I became hyper-vigilant with my assumptions and deductions and Tina used that to her advantage.

Tina convinced me that I needed anti-depressants because I was sad and confused and terrified about Tina's relationship with Nate becoming inappropriate. I was happy when we were in agreement about how to move forward, and then devastated when she continued to refuse to take any steps at all to correct the situation and alleviate my justifiable discomfort.

Going from questioning Tina's faithfulness to becoming convinced that I was crazy (or just a dumb drunk) to accepting responsibility for everything that had gone wrong after I stopped drinking to needing to suppress and compartmentalize information that would cause dissonance or anguish, needing to avoid questions that could be perceived as suspicion to realizing that I was essentially right in my instincts all along was quite a wild and convoluted trip.

In the years away from Tina's influence, I had to reassess numerous past incidents with eyes newly free of scales. Behind every door, it seemed, there was fresh torment, humiliation and chagrin as difficult realities slowly replaced the warped and contradictory memories of cognitive dissonance or the semi-conscious avoidance thereof.

New revelations came unbidden, often enough that it caused undue rumination. Documenting all of this is one way I coped with it all and tried in particular, to dispel the feelings of shame and embarrassment.

I thought of myself as a pretty intelligent man. I got far on my wits so I struggled with understanding how I could have been so astoundingly stupid for so long. How could denial and loyalty to someone who had so little regard for my feelings override the advice and urging of truly caring friends and family? I'd seen other men in similar situations. I judged them harshly for their willful ignorance and tolerance of obvious abuse. But I became that poor sap. My pride made that hard to accept.

I knew this much: Before I met Tina, I didn't drink myself to the point of withdrawals. I hadn't ever felt the need to get counseling and I wasn't taking any medications for anxiety or depression (I called those temporary interventions 'my Tina Pills' for years). The relationship was toxic. Tina was worse for me than booze, but harder to quit.

Narcissistic abuse can cause reduction in self confidence and decision making ability. That can make it difficult to perform any work, but complex work that engages higher mental functions can be especially hampered. Losing faith in my own mental prowess was a small but significant factor in my withdrawal from political work.

One big reason political work became so difficult for me is that it became extremely anxiety-inducing: It's dealing with liars. Being forced to use logic and truth to refute falsity after falsity is exhausting after spending years doing that on a personal level. It triggered the same feelings I experienced while attempting to unravel Tina's gaslighting. It was like reentering combat while still shell shocked. I felt anxious, sometimes even panicked when confronted with lies.

As cliched as it may sound, I found I'd also lost faith in humanity. I didn't even trust my friends anymore. Some cynics might think that's a good thing, but to me, the world had become a much darker place. My newfound inability to trust was not really a welcome change.

Impassioned work in politics stems from a belief that one can make society better. Part of the mental block I had with political work was a newfound belief that the world was not worthy or able to be improved. Attempting to inject integrity was futile. I've never been able to sustain any work for long that I didn't have an interest in.

According to studies by neuroscientists, long-term exposure to narcissistic abuse leads to physical damage to the brain as well as the psyche. Those physical changes in particular can account for some irrational anxiety, panic and aversion.

Being honest and honorable was very important to me and I abhor the dishonesty that is endemic in political discourse, but I'd always had faith that logic, reason and the truth would ultimately prevail. I was good at refuting falsehoods and proving with words where dishonesty or inaccuracy were being applied. After Tina, though, reading a legal brief, white paper or op-ed filled with obvious sophistry no longer triggered instincts to refute the offending piece. Instead, upon recognizing deliberate dishonesty, I'd feel a strong and immediate pull towards avoidance. Stress hormones pumped into my veins and fleeing felt like the only option available in the fight-or-flight response my body was reacting with.

Recognizing for myself that what I was facing was patently false was enough. I no longer had the drive or energy to prove it. In part, I believe that's because I'd concluded that the truth didn't matter to enough people to make much difference. Society at large didn't want or have much use for the truth, so any energy I'd expend advancing it felt like it would be wasted.

Where I used to almost relish the opportunity to destroy falsehoods with truths and facts I was confidently in command of, I found it required exponentially increasing expenditures of mental energy to even consider that kind of work. I could only manage it in small doses.

I almost entirely stopped watching or reading news.

I simply didn't want anything at all to do with liars anymore and in politics, liars and narcissists are legion.

I still dabbled here and there with critical issues from a sense of obligation or proprietorship and eventually, the black curtain around everything political in my mind drew slowly back, but never completely.

Symptoms of Narcissistic Abuse

How do you tell if you're a victim of narcissistic abuse? Most everyone would agree that breaking up up sucks and finding out you've been cheated on hurts. Being psychologically and emotionally abused by a narcissist isn't the same as a bad break up, though. It's not just an indiscretion or incompatibility. Unless you've experienced it, it may be difficult to fully grasp, but the trauma suffered by a narcissistic abuse victim can be just as damaging to the psyche as any physical, violent or sexual abuse. Even more so.

The symptoms of narcissistic abuse (victims) syndrome I experienced persisted acutely for several months and even after a year of no contact and conscious effort toward recovery, hadn't fully abated.

While many of the symptoms might seem obvious, some were initially hard to understand. Jumpiness is a symptom I experienced and found the oddest. At first, I couldn't understand the mechanism that made me wake with a start, flinch at sudden sounds, nearly jump out of my skin if I encountered another person when I rounded a corner or opened a door. After a lot of research, I finally understood the reason.

Name it PTSD, Complex PTSD or Narcissistic Abuse (Victims) Syndrome, it's all pretty much the same, with some slight nuance. These conditions aren't purely psychological. There is a significant physiological component.

Along with hyperarousal (the jumpiness), common symptoms include:

- Anger issues and rage
- Low self-esteem, loss of confidence, self-loathing
- Anxiety and panic attacks
- Depression, thoughts of suicide
- Denial, dissociation, memory loss
- Confusion / mental fog
- Difficulty making decisions
- Flashbacks and rumination
- Loss of faith in humanity, distrust, self-isolation, difficulty forming close relationships
- Shame and guilt
- Desire for revenge
- Eating disorders, substance abuse, alcoholism, hypersexuality
- Chronic pain, migraines
- Cardiovascular and gastrointestinal problems

To some extent, I experienced all of the above symptoms throughout the course of my relationship with Tina. I had quit drinking a year before, but aside from chemical abuse, the symptoms were the most pronounced after the grand finale discard. Without Tina's manipulative influence, reality and awareness of how sick I'd become began to set in.

The trauma bond formed to one's abuser is like a potent addiction that's been compared to heroin and nicotine. Once a victim is separated by no-contact, a physically and emotionally brutal period of literal chemical withdrawals begins. I had a bit of an advantage in dealing with this aspect of recovery because I'd already experienced chemical withdrawals before. I recognized the symptoms and I could reason my way through it, knowing that this particular kind of suffering was necessary to begin healing.

Some symptoms are psychological, some physical and some are a combination. The physical and chemical changes that occur in the brain are a result of an excess of stress hormones, like cortisol. This physical brain damage is insidious because in a vicious cycle, it makes a person even more susceptible to narcissistic abuse. At the same time, it amplifies and prolongs the detrimental symptoms of that abuse.

The fight-or-flight response built into humans and all other animals is designed to operate in short bursts. Adrenaline pumps into the blood stream, senses and reactions are heightened and the primitive "lizard brain" amygdala asserts control over higher functions. That helps us defend our territory from a neighboring tribe or run from a pride of lions that would otherwise surely kill us. When that system ends up being engaged for prolonged periods, however, our brains actually begin to change shape to adapt. Marinading in cortisol triggered by abuse, the brain's amygdala physically changes and becomes more dominant, while the logical, mapping, boundary-defining and memory-forming hippocampus region shrinks and weakens. Accustomed to the stress response, the body develops a hair-trigger to produce more cortisol until a person is almost continually aroused into that fight-or-flight state. The resulting vicious cycle is like a feedback loop: stress causes physical changes and the changes make it easier to trigger stress.

Coming to understand that process finally explained why I was so jumpy, even though I'd never had reason to feel physically afraid. Hurt is hurt and my amygdala wasn't making any distinction between physical and emotional pain. It was all a threat. Understanding that helped me develop some new strategies to address the physical brain damage on my own.

Aside from depression and anxiety that may be near-debilitating, another very common complaint of narcissistic abuse victims is rumination. Memories of certain instances, conversations or discoveries play over and over again, relentlessly. This can be accompanied by intense emotional flashbacks that exactly replicate the feelings of the original moment. Reliving some trauma over and over again, is if it were happening fresh is a torture most victims suffer to at least some degree. It's a PTSD-related response that can have any number of triggers. Identifying and avoiding those triggers is one way to begin reducing the occurrences and learning to distract yourself into another train of thought can help, but therapy might also be needed.

Of all the psychological fallout that comes from narcissistic abuse, the loss of faith, trust and ability to be open to others might be the cruelest. For myself, I felt like the part of me that was designed to love had become no more than a burned-out shell. There was a loss of innocence involved in breaking free from and waking up to narcissistic abuse. I found that forming close bonds with other people was no longer possible. Everyone stayed at arm's length.

When I'd have notions about expressing love or affection in ways that used to come naturally to me, powerful injunctions from more obscure regions of my brain would freeze me in my tracks.

There is a lot of damage that needs repair after narcissistic abuse. People who haven't been through it may not understand and may be dismissive of the real harm and ongoing suffering that victims endure, but it's very real and excruciating to live with. Sometimes it can feel overwhelming and hopeless, but healing is possible. The most important thing I learned about it is that healing the wounds of narcissistic abuse requires intervention. You can't just wait for these wounds to heal. It takes work and it probably requires some degree of help.

Things can change back. As an odd example: It didn't comport to my prior understanding of hair coloration, but after nearly a year with absolutely no contact with the vampiric Tina, my shock-white hair had reverted to a silvery mix of black and gray – what it had looked like years prior, when I first met her.

Towards the end of my dealings with Tina, I'd noticed to my dismay that I was looking washed out, literally from head to toe. I was drained of color. My still thick head of hair was white as snow. There were perpetual dark circles under my eyes. The former upstairs neighbors observed that I looked healthier than they'd ever seen me, just a couple months after I moved out. A year later, even my hair looked younger and livelier.

It had been my understanding that hair color was determined by special pigment stem cells in the follicle that could reproduce a finite number of times and once they were gone, they were gone. Irreversible, except by dyes.

Intrigued by seemingly impossible change in my hair coloration, and wondering if it was just a matter of perception, I did a bit of research. I found out that under extreme stress, the body produces hydrogen peroxide, which in bottled form can be used to bleach hair! Energy vampires like those affected with borderline or narcissistic personality disorders actually can drain the color out of a person!

It took a long time before I felt I was becoming my old self again, and when I did, even my hair was healthier!

There are a number of psychological treatments for Narcissistic Abuse Syndrome or PTSD. For clinical therapy, Cognitive Behavioral Therapy and Eye movement desensitization and reprocessing (EMDR) are typically recommended.

Get Help for Narcissistic Abuse Syndrome

Narcissistic Abuse Victims Syndrome or just Narcissistic Abuse Syndrome is not included in the current, official Diagnostic and Statistical Manual of Mental Disorders in the United States. The unofficial diagnoses are rather an observation, by numerous mental health professionals, of the same cluster of symptoms in people they've treated who were in relationships (romantic, family, friendship or professional) with suspected or diagnosed Cluster B disordered people. The cluster of common symptoms is sometimes diagnosed as Post Traumatic Stress Disorder (PTSD) or Complex Post Traumatic Stress disorder (C-PTSD). There is little to no difference between the symptoms of these conditions. The primary difference in diagnosis may come primarily from the specific cause. See more about this in "Symptoms of Narcissistic Abuse."

Whatever you choose to call it, the aftermath of emotional abuse can be debilitating and often requires some kind of professional help to process and recover from it.

There are psychological, emotional and physiological causes underlying the symptoms and there are several treatment options available.

Find Psychotherapy

For clinical, psychological treatment, Cognitive Behavioral Therapy (CBT) and Eye movement Desensitization and Reprocessing (EMDR) are typically recommended. Other styles of talk therapy can also be of some help processing emotions. Although our collective knowledge about narcissistic abuse is increasing rapidly, finding a mental health professional experienced in treating victims of narcissistic abuse can be challenging. Fortunately, there's a great tool for finding the help you need. That and links to all the other resources mentioned in this chapter can be found online at **www.danandtina.net/get-help-for-narcissistic-abuse-syndrome**

Free PTSD Coaching App

The Veterans Administration offers resources for people suffering PTSD, including a free PTSD coaching app for your smart phone. There's also a desktop version. The VA's PTSD coach offers help for:

- worry or anxiety
- anger
- sadness or hopelessness
- sleep problems
- trauma reminders
- avoidance of stressful situations
- disconnection from people
- disconnection from reality
- problem solving skills
- direction in life

Personal Healing Strategies

Through my own research and trial and error, I developed several strategies to address my own (largely physical) symptoms, which are detailed in the chapter, "Healing Strategies After Narcissistic Abuse."

Psychiatric Treatment

I experimented with psychiatric drugs on advice of my therapist and found some temporary use for anti-anxiety and anti-depressant medications, but would give them mixed reviews. Gabapentin (used off-label), hydroxyzine and Propranalol (off-label) are mild, non habit-forming medications that aren't SSRIs and didn't require ramping up or weaning off of. I found them moderately helpful for anxiety and not at all dangerous.

Other medications commonly prescribed by psychiatrists for treating symptoms of C-PTSD are:

- Sertraline (Zoloft)
- Paroxetine (Paxil)
- Fluoxetine (Prozac)
- Bupropion (Wellbutrin)

These are heavier-duty medications that may have long-term or even permanent effect on brain chemistry, even after cessation. They may take months of gradual increasing dosages before they begin to work and may require lengthy tapering-off periods to safely stop taking them.

Not everyone responds the same way to these types of medications. For some people they may be positively life-changing, but they may make things worse for others. It can take some experimenting with different combinations and dosages to achieve the desired affect. All require a prescription.

OTC Medications

Antihistamines have been found to have a mild sedative effect that may reduce anxiety. Hydroxyzine is a prescription antihistamine sometimes prescribed for anxiety, for example, but non-prescription antihistamines can also work.

Diphenhydramine, also known by the brand name Benadryl is one such over the counter medicine that can help with anxiety and sleeplessness.

There are a number of nutrition supplements and holistic remedies that are purported to help with anxiety and depression. I wrote about my experiences with some of those in the article, "Healing Strategies After Narcissistic Abuse."

Self-Help Books

Besides my own musings, I recommend checking out these couple books to get started understanding narcissistic abuse and its aftermath.

- The Body Keeps Score: Brain, Mind and body in the Healing of Trauma by Bessel Van der Kolk
- Complex PTSD for Beginners by Dr. Gerhard Christianson
- Psychopath Free – Recovering from emotionally abusive relationships with narcissists, sociopaths and other toxic people by Jackson MacKenzie

Healing Strategies After Narcissistic Abuse

Healing from narcissistic abuse is no small matter. For the first couple months after I left my abusive relationship, all I could really do was survive. I was having a moral and spiritual crisis and I was viewing the world with new cynical and suspicious eyes. I retreated. It wasn't until I began to look at my condition more scientifically that I realized it wasn't only a "time heals all wounds" situation. I could take steps to help the healing process along.

I tried a lot of things, even things I was skeptical of. I wanted desperately to feel normal again. Some things worked better than I imagined they would and some things were about as effective as putting magic crystals on my head. I was fairly unimpressed by aroma therapy, for example.

I was adrift for too long and didn't immediately appreciate how important stabilizing my housing situation was to my well being. Living out of bags in motel rooms was not at all conducive to healing. I needed a space to make my own.

I had to come to grips with what had happened. Realizing the depths of deception and depravity I'd been entangled with led to deep shame. I was so disappointed in myself for being deceived and manipulated. I didn't trust my own judgment anymore. Getting that back required learning about cluster B personality disorders and connecting with other people who'd suffered narcissistic abuse. I read so many personal stories and began to see how similar all those experiences were to my own. I wasn't alone. Coming to understand how the pattern of behavior plays out helped me forgive myself for becoming entrapped and then debilitated by narcissistic abuse syndrome.

Even understanding the darkness of narcissistic abuse that I was dealing with, I still suffered from intense feelings of loss and loneliness. This was no ordinary breakup. The relationship was more like an addiction than love. That's a trauma bond and it had to be broken.

I had firsthand experience with chemical dependency and I recognized that just like quitting smoking or drinking, I was going to have to commit myself to a period of suffering in order to break free and begin recovery. Maintaining no contact was first a physical endurance challenge.

I came to learn that narcissistic abuse leads to physical brain damage. The hippocampus shrinks while the amygdala grows. This leads to chronic confusion, short-term memory loss, anxiety, anger, panic attacks and even bouts of rage. Reversing that damage is crucial to recovery and that's not a matter for magic crystals. It's scientifically, physically quantifiable. It's all about stress hormones, which a person's brain is continually marinading in while in a relationship with someone with a cluster B personality disorder. This physical change explains why I found myself very jumpy after leaving Tina. I was never physically afraid of her, so I couldn't understand why my complex post traumatic stress disorder was manifesting as if I'd come out of a bloody war zone. I never had to dodge bullets, so I didn't get why I'd jump so easily at certain sounds, wake up gasping in adrenaline-pumping fright or jump backwards like Jason Vorhees had lunged at me with a machete, just upon noticing people I wasn't ready for. It's because the amygdala controls the fight-or flight response and thanks to a steady diet of overflowing cortisol, mine had grown out of control. These reactions aren't psychological. They are physical! They are chemical. The amygdala doesn't distinguish between physical and emotional. A threat is a threat. That revelation changed the course of my recovery.

I began to study what causes increased cortisol production and what can mitigate it. Stimulants are an obvious culprit. Caffeine, nicotine, taurine, etc. All of those (and illegal drugs like methamphetamines or cocaine) elevate stress hormones. Those chemical precursors had to be eliminated, or at least curtailed.

I had to evaluate situations that induced any physical stress or anxiety. That required really paying attention to what was going on in my body. I realized that I was producing a stress response sometimes just by playing intense video games. From that, I learned how to identify other things that were stressing me out and then to limit their impact on me.

Physical exercise is a proven stress-reducer. It doesn't have to be intense. Just taking a long walk can have a beneficial effect.

I was happy to learn that there were other things I could do beyond just changing some habits. Fish Oil, for example is an effective cortisol-reducer. I began taking it daily and found it almost immediately beneficial. Magnesium deficiency is a common culprit for elevated stress hormones, so magnesium supplements can also help. I was already taking magnesium as a migraine preventative, but I dabbled with some other supplements for stress-reduction and found some use for Kava Kava and particularly, ashwaganda and vitamin D (also helpful with depression).

I'd learned earlier that, unlikely as it sounds, over the counter pain relievers, like aspirin and ibuprofen can ameliorate heartache (don't just take my word for it – there's research to back this up). In case of acute anxiety or panic, diphenhydramine is a surprisingly effective over the counter solution. It's an antihistamine. The most commonly known brand name is Benadryl. It's also marketed as a sleep aid. In my personal experience, I'd take two (25 mg capsules) to sleep or just one to kill a panic attack. Bear in mind, I'm not a doctor. This isn't medical advice. I'm just relating my personal experience.

I gave up energy drinks, but couldn't quite manage without a cup or two of coffee in the morning, so I allowed that much for myself, but in the evening, I found Hawthorn Tea to be particularly soothing.

Quitting nicotine required a compromise of sorts. I had to forgive myself for gaining some weight. Snacking replaced smoking and vaping, for a few months. That was hard. It was almost three months before the cravings were gone, but it wasn't as hard as breaking the trauma bond. If you can do that, you can do anything!

Having undertaken some steps to repair my enlarged amygdala, I began to research ways to address an impaired hippocampus. Many years back, I'd seen a documentary about London taxi drivers which claimed learning the haphazard maze of roads in that city caused a measurable increase in the size of drivers' hippocampi. So, I knew deliberately, physically changing this part of the brain was possible. I'd had a part time job driving limos for some time and I found it satisfactory, so I was already engaging and exercising my hippocampus with that occupation. I also had an affinity for crossword puzzles and with an app on my phone, I finished at least one a day. Little did I know I was perhaps instinctively engaging in the very activities I needed to repair my hippocampus. Crosswords and logic puzzles are cited by doctors as activities to strengthen that region of the brain!

Light therapy sounds like new agey hocus pocus, but it's actually helpful for depression. Getting outside on a nice sunny day is best, but when that wasn't possible (like dark winter days), natural daylight simulating full-spectrum lamps made a noticeable difference for me.

I needed a lot of alone time at first, but as I gradually began to grow stronger and more confident again, getting supportive friends and family back into my life accelerated my recovery and tipped the balance of good and bad days or even hours in my favor.

During the deep depression that set in when I'd first left Tina, my body atrophied. I eventually had to force myself into physical activity. I began getting some light exercise every day (or at least every other day). As I mentioned above, that's also a good way to reduce stress!

After I got settled into my condo, making improvements to it were like an analog to improvements I was making inside myself. Putting up decor that reminded me of my history – of who I am – mirrored and reinforced the reconstruction of my very personality.

I gravitated to a lot of elements from my youth. My therapist called it regression, but that seems to have a negative connotation. I restored my operating system to an earlier state that was known to work! I was buying Cookie Crisp cereal and Eggo waffles like I used to eat before school as a kid.

I was binge watching 70's science fiction television. Star Trek, Doctor Who, Battlestar Galactica. The old stuff was good. It had a straightforward morality to it. The good guys always won and there was nothing too vicious that could trigger an overblown response of stress hormones. Those kind of things also helped me remember who I was – before the narcissist took over my life. Immersing myself in things that I enjoyed before the trauma helped me reconnect with my good, less damaged self (see also: Regression on the path to Healing).

If I wasn't watching nostalgic sci-fi, it was comedies – just not the romantic varieties.

I had to avoid a lot of music for a while, because most songs are love songs and every love song was about her. Fortunately, I like electronic dance music, because a lot of that is just instrumental.

Writing proved to be essential in setting order to the swirls of gaslit confusion in my bleeding brain. Writing my stories helped me reestablish objective reality and hold on to it when emotional and trauma-bonded responses would try to convince me otherwise. It also helped me to segregate the emotions connected to those memories and thereby reduce their impact.

My therapist always counseled patience and self-forgiveness, which are easy enough words to say, but surprisingly difficult to put into practice. I did eventually learn. I was eventually ready to be patient. Though I've learned that time isn't the only factor, it's still an important one. There is no rushing some healing.

I discovered that I had some delayed mourning to do. I was so wrapped up in all the chaos and confusion of Tina's making as well as the responsibility of dealing with my Mom's estate that while still embroiled in the relationship, I never allowed myself the time to fully accept and mourn my mom's passing, or losing my dog, Clyde to cancer. Delaying the processing of that kind of grief had the unfortunate side effect of prolonging it.

I still practiced kindness and generosity. That's just who I am, but I gave myself permission to set limits and even to be selfish. It's OK to be selfish sometimes, especially in times of need. My wellness and comfort could come first. I doubt I'll ever be exactly the person I was but after a year, I found myself stronger, more confident and having more good days than bad ones. That's pretty good progress for only a year after narcissistic abuse. I'm certain that being proactive about my recovery instead of just waiting for it made a huge difference.

I'd had my doubts that I'd ever be ready to become romantically involved again, but I'd even started dating after 6 months or so. I discovered that some superintendent of safety in my brain still has some areas cordoned off and I'm not able to fully trust or let people closer than a metaphorical arms-length, but I still consider that progress!

After coming to better understand cluster B personality disorders, in a way, I felt safer in the world because I knew how to recognize them and knew to stay away. On the flip-side, knowing that these people exist and in larger numbers than I would have imagined (6 to 15% of the population, depending on the study) made the world seem a darker place.

Ultimately, though I still had some work to do, particularly in areas of trust and intimacy, I emerged healthy, strong and happy. I kicked alcohol and tobacco, learned to keep narcissists at bay and I got back into many creative pursuits, including writing, music and video production, art, and I even began school for a pilot's license. No day is too bad when you get to fly an airplane!

Is There a Cure for Narcissism?

The conventional wisdom generally precludes any effective treatment of narcissistic personality disorder. Narcissists almost never seek treatment for NPD, because, being unable to introspect, they never believe there is really anything wrong with them. The problem is the rest of the world, or bad luck or a spouse or parent.

Sometimes a narcissist will seek professional help for other psychological troubles. Depression and anxiety are common reasons they might seek help. It is almost unheard of that a narcissist begins a road of recovery from NPD as a result of such treatment efforts, however.

There is belief among some in psychology circles that treatment designed to help people with a different cluster B personality disorder might help narcissists, too. That's dialectical behavior therapy (DBT) and it's been shown to be beneficial to people who suffer with borderline personality disorder, once considered pretty much untreatable.

There is anecdotal evidence of a (very) small number of self-aware narcissists improving after long spans with concerted effort through treatment like DBT.

A key element of clinical narcissism is a lack of empathy and that shortcoming can be linked to an underdeveloped or damaged ventromedial prefrontal cortex. This is a physical defect that can be seen with some kinds of brain imaging and is generally not correctable.

There is new (bleeding edge) research emerging that suggests use of certain psychadelic drugs, namely psilocybin (more commonly known as magic mushrooms) may encourage growth of new neural pathways in the prefrontal cortex and enlarge one's capacity for empathy, but that research is in it's infancy at the time of publication of this book and should be taken with a grain of salt.

A danger victims of narcissistic abuse almost always face comes from hope — hope for the narcissistic object of their obsession to someday see the light and love them back. It's possible, like it's possible you'll become an overnight millionaire by hitting the winning numbers. It's not a realistic or healthy hope. It's a hope that will almost always lead to more misery.

Towards the bitter end, Tina said two things that laid it all out for me and I eventually realized that it's just this simple. She said, "You used to provide me with validation. You aren't doing that anymore." Validation is another way to look at narcissistic supply and questioning a narcissist's misdeeds is the opposite of validating.

After rejecting the very therapy that she'd suggested, she said, "I feel like you're trying to fix me. I don't want to be fixed."

Those two candid statement pretty much summed it all up!

Narcissistic personalities can't be healed, because they see nothing that needs curing. They like being the way they are.

For all practical intents and purposes, there is no cure for narcissism. There can be cures for the victims, but the first step toward healing is to remove yourself from the situation. Stay away from narcissists if at all possible. If dealing with them is unavoidable, do so dispassionately. Don't fall for their ploys to extract narcissistic supply. Be as a gray rock – dull, uninteresting and easily forgotten. Then, rediscover wonderful you and go on to live your best life!

This wide world is full of endless possibilities and there's absolutely no reason to let someone else's broken personality hold you back from being what you are meant to be.

About the Author

Dan McGrath is a survivor of narcissistic abuse and recovering codependent. He's now training to become a pilot and enjoying creative hobbies like painting and music production. He has extensive experience working in and around politics and government. He has served as executive director, president and communications director for non-profit organizations, a campaign manager for candidates, chairman of a ballot committee and a registered lobbyist. He has also launched several successful lawsuits against government entities and won cases in both the Minnesota and United States Supreme Courts. Dan has been featured in numerous national and local television and radio programs and newspapers. Learn more at DanMcGrath.net.

Other Books by Dan McGrath

*** Available at DanMcGrath.net, Amazon.com and other fine booksellers ***

MagiQuest

The Storm Tower

What Everyone Should Know About the Government

The Voter Fraud Manual

Crossword Therapy

Printed in Great Britain
by Amazon

72461719R00203